GAMBERO ROSSO
ROME

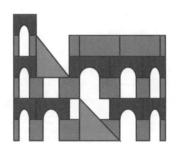

RESTAURANTS

TRATTORIAS

PIZZERIAS

WINE BARS

SNACKS

WINE SHOPS

GOURMET FOODS

HOME & TABLE

HOTELS

GAMBERO ROSSO
ROME

Chief Editors
Clara Barra, Stefano Bonilli, Giancarlo Perrotta

Editor
Cristina Tiliacos

Contributing Editors
Pina Acri, Alessandra Adiutori,
Elisabetta Adiutori, Annalisa Barbagli,
Francesco Baroni, Gianluca Bianchi,
Francesco Saverio Binetti,
Marco Bolasco, Dario Cappelloni,
Angelo Di Natale, Mara Nocilla, Marco Oreggia,
Stefano Petrecca, Giuseppe Tortora,
Valerio Varriale, Claudio Vecchietti

Cover and Illustrations
Moca

Translation
Jane Gruchy

Gambero Rosso Inc.
636 Broadway, Suite 1219
New York, NY 10012 - USA
Web site: www.gamberorosso.it
E-mail: gambero@gamberorosso.it
&
GAMBERO ROSSO EDITORE SRL
via Angelo Bargoni, 8 - 00153 Roma - Italy
tel. 06/58310125 - fax 06/58310170

Printed in Italy by
Tipografica La Piramide
Via Anton Maria Valsalva, .34 - Roma

CONTENTS

Welcome to Rome and the Gambero Rosso Guide to the city. We have worked hard to put together a picture of how the Italian capital prepared for the Jubilee Year. Most of Rome's hotels [and it was about time for some of them!] took advantage of the occasion to carry out restyling operations that have made them more inviting. One world-famous name alone will suffice to make our point: the legendary Grand Hotel, now the St. Regis Grand. We hope the entire sector will continue to make an effort to provide quality services worthy of the Eternal City. We have also gone through the restaurants with a fine-tooth comb and this sector, too, is in a state of ferment. New ones are opening and some of them are interesting, thanks to their hardworking young owners who are trying to offer quality at fair prices. Others are less appealing because their principal goals are numbers and profits. Then there are the historic addresses, the ones you can always count on [which is already saying quite a lot] and the trattorias, wine bars, pizzerias and ethnic restaurants. Finally there are the restaurants at the top of the range [price-wise too]: the ones for special occasions or when money is no object, substantially the same ones you always find at the head of the list in the guidebooks. But even excellent restaurants can have their stale moments. So there's something for everyone, except for those people who just want to eat authentic Roman cuisine. They are going to find it difficult, unfortunately, because there are really very few traditional places left, and it looks as though they are destined to diminish in number even further. We have suggested a lot of mouthwatering alternatives, however, to meet the reader's needs throughout the day, from that first breakfast *cappuccino e cornetto* through to the last drink at night. And for anyone who wants to make a little trip out of Rome we have also indicated a number of interesting possibilities further afield. We have charted this fascinating and appetite-whetting course from the point of view of the consumer, as always, to help visitors get their bearings in a metropolitan jungle where the unwary can easily fall victim to the unscrupulous. The tireless commitment of our whole editorial team has made this possible, so that anyone making use of the Guide can face Rome and the new century with a lighter heart. We're ready - now you can be too.

eating

at all hours

GAMBERO ROSSO FAVORITES

shopping

GAMBERO ROSSO FAVORITES

sleeping

**GAMBERO ROSSO
BEST VALUE AWARDS**

★★★ THE BEST THREE STAR HOTEL

RESTAURANTS

FORKS

The best eateries have a one, two or three forks symbol next to the name, according to the degree of excellence:

from 70 to 79/100   ❢

from 80 to 89/100   ❢❢

from 90 to 100/100   ❢❢❢

POINT SYSTEM

 ❢ **75**

- **Cucina 45**
- **Wine Cellar 15 • Service 7**
- **Ambience 8 • Bonus 0**

Scores are expressed as points out of a possible 100, awarded for cucina, wine cellar, service and ambience, with a maximum of 60 points for cucina, 20 for wine cellar, 10 for service and 10 for ambience. In some cases we award a bonus as a kind of pleasure index, to a maximum of 5 extra points.

TRATTORIAS, PIZZERIAS, WINE BARS AND EXOTIC RESTAURANTS

These are reviewed without applying the forks and points system.

VALUE FOR MONEY

OVER-PRICED

REASONABLY PRICED

EXTRA GOOD VALUE

These symbols take all aspects of the eatery concerned into consideration.

DETAILS

- **Closed:** indicates both days off during the week where applicable and annual holidays. NB: *in August* may mean only 10 days, not the whole month, so best to ring and enquire. Food stores are often closed on Thursday afternoons and other shops on Monday mornings.
- **Seats:** indicates maximum seating capacity inside.
- **L.** indicates the cost of an average meal [entrée, first course, main course and dessert]; wine *not* included.

🗎   Credit cards accepted

AE   American Express

POS   Bancomat

CSi   Visa

DC   Diners Club

Visa   Visa

℗   parking

🚗   garage

❋   air conditioning

🌲   outdoor tables

♿   wheelchair access

♿   wheelchair access if assisted

WARNING

Information regarding opening hours, days off, holiday periods, credit cards accepted and telephone numbers are provided by the management of the firms concerned. Gambero Rosso is not responsible for any eventual changes. Where not otherwise indicated, the opening hours and weekly days off for food stores are those established by Council regulations [see above]. Telephone numbers given are those in operation on 31 August, 1999.

HOTELS

KEYS

Hotels have either one, two, three or no keys next to the name, according to the degree of comfort:

No Key
BASIC COMFORTS

COMFORTABLE

VERY COMFORTABLE

🔑🔑🔑
EXTREMELY COMFORTABLE

★
★★
★★★
★★★★
★★★★★

The number of stars indicates the category assigned by Italian government regulations.

DETAILS

📞   800017703
     toll-free number

🛏   cost of single room

🛏   cost of double room

☕   breakfast

❋   air conditioning

📺   TV in room

🍷   minibar

🛎   room service

↕   elevator

🏊   swimming pool

🏃   sports facilities

🐕   small pets allowed

♿   conference room

🍽   restaurant

♿   wheelchair access

[1]   no. of rooms for disabled clients

♥   special charm

GAMBERO ROSSO BEST VALUE AWARDS

These are reserved for outstanding firms in all sections of the Guide: **Restaurants/Trattorias:** that offer particularly good value for money. **Speciality Foods:** stores distinguished by particularly polite service as well as high quality products. **Hotels:** where prices are particularly favourable in relation to overall quality.

Restaurants:
Gambero Rosso
Best Value Award

Trattorias:
Gambero Rosso
Best Value Award

At All Hours, Shopping, Drinking: A Gambero Rosso Favorite

Hotels:
Gambero Rosso
Best Value Award

The Best 3-Star Hotels

eating

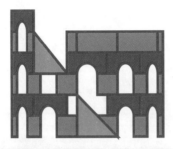

RESTAURANTS
TRATTORIAS
PIZZERIAS
ETHNIC RESTAURANTS
WINE BARS

IL 1°LI

CENTRO STORICO - NAVONA
via dei Soldati, 22
☎ 06/68135112

 70

- **Cucina 42**
- **Wine Cellar 13** • **Service 8**
- **Ambience 7** • **Bonus 0**

- **Closed:** Mondays [open evenings only]; annual holidays vary
- **Seats:** 80
- **L.** 55,000 w/o wine
  📇 all 🅟

Restaurant. Photography lovers will appreciate the beautiful prints lining the walls of the various dining rooms, big and small, that make up the "1°li" [pronounced Primoli]. Affable maître-owner Massimiliano Marcucci and his courteous staff put clients immediately at their ease. The wine list, though small, is well-suited to the menu and the wines are reasonably priced. The cuisine betrays a youthful hand – certainly in spirit and probably in terms of the cook's chronological age, too. The *pizzelle alla 1li* [small deep-fried pizzas stuffed with shrimps or cheese, artichoke and *carpaccio* mousse], are excellent and unusual. The *risotto alla Primoli* with smoked provola cheese and Prosecco wine is also very good, and so are the ravioli with eggplant, tomato and cheese. The thinly sliced

beef *tagliata* with artichokes is excellent, the fried vegetables in tempura delicate and delicious. A wide range of desserts and pizzas, too, if you prefer something lighter.

AL 34

CENTRO STORICO - SPAGNA
via Mario de' Fiori, 34
☎ 06/6795091

 67

- **Cucina 40**
- **Wine Cellar 12** • **Service 7**
- **Ambience 7** • **Bonus 1**

- **Closed:** Mondays; Aug 1-31
- **Seats:** 60
- **L.** 55,000 w/o wine
  📇 all ✳ 🌿 ♿

Restaurant. This restaurant's strong point is its position - in the heart of the centre's most exclusive shopping district. It's a little on the noisy side when full and the tables are a bit too close together, but the service is efficient – staff are obviously used to the pace. The very well-organised menu is divided into three sections [Roman, seafood and *di terra* – literally food from the land: bonus points]. Linguine all'astice [with lobster]; spaghetti with clams; a quite good version of *melanzane alla parmigiana* [eggplant baked with mozzarella, parmigiano and tomato sauce]; Messinese-style *involtini di pescespada* [swordfish roulades], and grilled fillet steak. Desserts of the day to finish off with - crème caramel and sorbets. The wine list needs expanding, but you'll find some good labels.

ACCHIAPPAFANTASMI

CENTRO STORICO
CAMPO DE' FIORI
via dei Cappellari, 66
☎ 06/6873462

- **Closed:** Tuesdays [never in summer]; open evenings only; annual holidays vary [open in August]
- **Seats:** 70
- **L.** 35,000 w/o wine
  📇 CSi, DC, POS, Visa
  ✳ 🌿 ♿

Pizzeria. This pizzeria stands out from the others because it offers not only rather good traditional pizzas but also quite a lot of interesting, delicious alternatives with a strong Calabrian influence [the owner comes from Calabria]. Eggplant parmigiana [baked with mozzarella, parmigiano and tomato sauce]; potato gâteau; baked mozzarella, anchovy and arugula rolls; cured meats; olives; mushrooms in olive oil; cheeses; spicy neonata [tiny fish]. Good desserts, a small wine list and a choice of beers. Efficient, courteous service.

AGATA E ROMEO

ESQUILINO
via C. Alberto, 45
☎ 06/4466115

 80

- **Cucina 46**
- **Wine Cellar 18** • **Service 7**
- **Ambience 8** • **Bonus 1**

- **Closed:** Sundays; annual holidays vary
- **Seats:** 40
- **L.** 130,000 w/o wine
  📇 all 🅟 ✳ ♿

Restaurant. More attractive and comfortable ever, this restaurant continues to be

something of a touchstone for quality here in Rome, and further afield too. The tables are large and attractively laid, the ambient temperature is perfect and this makes Agata Parisella's cooking even more enjoyable. She manages to marry tradition with a spirit of enquiry, though sometimes the results are not entirely successful. Our most recent samplings were: eggplant timbales with arugula sauce; a *pecorino di fossa* [sheep's milk cheese aged underground] flan with fig and honey sauce - maybe a little too rich; spinach-green *lasagnetta* with scorpion fish ragù garnished with tomato cubes [very good]; *raviolini* stuffed with eggplant in a goat's milk cheese sauce - a bit too much of a good thing; followed by meat dishes: squab leg and breast with vegetable *millefoglie;* lamb carré with country-style mustard and mint, and a not very convincing version of *baccalà in guazzetto* [poached with grapes, pinenuts and herbs]. For dessert, apart from Agata's legendary *millefoglie* [not to be missed], an iced cherry soufflé served with a delicious hot cherry sauce. The wine list is even

EATING

bigger and more varied than before, offering a number of rare and particularly interesting vintages, though a wine-tasting menu wasn't available on our last visit. Courteous service, but sometimes a bit slow.

AGUSTARELLO
TESTACCIO
via G. Branca, 100
☎ 06/5746585

- **Closed:** Sundays; Aug 7-Sept 7
- **Seats:** 40
- **L.** 45,000 w/o wine
🕭 no ❷ ♣

Trattoria. A very old family-run restaurant characterised by simple unpretentious surroundings and total fidelity to the Roman tradition. Here you can enjoy specialities impossible to find elsewhere, like *stufato* [stew] with celery, or *animelle* [pancreas and sweetbreads] and veal shank with mushrooms - two truly delicious, perfectly-executed dishes. Among the other treats on the menu, there's an excellent version of *tonnarelli cacio e pepe* [with pecorino cheese and black pepper]; *pajata* [milk-filled veal intestines]; *involtini* [roulades] braised in celery, and *cicoria ripassata* [boiled chicory stir-fried with garlic and chili]. Portions are

generous but never too heavy. Agustarello's son Alessandro officiates in the dining room and will recommend a good bottle of wine to go with your meal.

ALBERTO CIARLA
TRASTEVERE
p.zza S. Cosimato, 40
☎ 06/5818668

  79
- **Cucina 46**
- **Wine Cellar 16** • **Service 8**
- **Ambience 8** • **Bonus 1**

- **Closed:** never
- **Seats:** 80
- **L.** 100,000 w/o wine
🕭 all ✳ ♣ ⛄

Restaurant. This seafood restaurant always offers very high quality cuisine, making it one of the city's classics. The owner is one of the local restaurant scene's best-known personalities - always politely but constructively argumentative. The mixed antipasti - raw, cooked, smoked and marinated fish together, are delicious; the fisherman's style pasta and bean soup is good, and the monumental spaghetti with shellfish is exceptionally tasty. Main courses include herb-scented *spigola* [sea bass], and *mazzancolle al coccio* [terrine of king prawns], not to mention the fabulously crisp seafood fry. To finish off, chocolate profiteroles, pinenut and pastry-cream torte, and other excellent desserts. The wine list is of an equally high standard, even though our readers have complained of a few omissions. Truly excellent

service, especially from the impeccable maitre. A bonus for the owner's *simpatia*.

ALFREDO A VIA GABI
APPIO
via Gabi, 36
☎ 06/77206792

- **Closed:** Tuesdays; Aug 1-31
- **Seats:** 65
- **L.** 45,000 w/o wine
🕭 no ❷ ✳ ⛄

Trattoria. The Mancinelli family has the reins of this trattoria well in hand. It's one of the few good ones in this neighbourhood and despite the occasional lapse you always eat rather well here. From the wide-ranging menu we can recommend the pasta and bean soup with shellfish; spaghetti Sicilian-style or with swordfish; *rigatoni* with *pajata* [milk-filled veal intestines]; anchovy and artichoke timbales; *baccalà alla pizzaiola* [dried salt cod poached with tomatoes and herbs]; tripe *alla romana* and *coda alla vaccinara* [oxtail braised with celery]. Desserts include a rather good crème caramel. The wine list is limited to a few regional labels.

L'ANGOLO DIVINO
CENTRO STORICO
CAMPO DE' FIORI
via dei Balestrari, 12
☎ 06/6864413

- **Closed:** Monday evenings; in August
- **Seats:** 35
- **L.** 35,000 w/o wine
🕭 all ❷ ✳

Wine Bar. In little more than four years, L'Angolo Divino has won itself a well-earned place in the hearts of Roman winelovers, and the reasons are soon clear: pleasant surroundings, a youthful atmosphere and an excellent selection of wines to suit all pockets, including some interesting choices - also available by the glass. You can have either a simple *aperitivo* with an appetiser or one of the dishes of the day [various soups, savoury pies, smoked fish, mixed salads, cheeses and high quality cured meats served with delicious trimmings]. Plenty of gourmet desserts.

ANTICO ARCO
GIANICOLO
p.le Aurelio, 7
☎ 06/5815274

 80
- **Cucina 46**
- **Wine Cellar 16** • **Service 8**
- **Ambience 8** • **Bonus 2**

- **Closed:** Sundays [open evenings only; Sundays at lunchtime only]; Aug 15
- **Seats:** 80
- **L.** 70,000 w/o wine
🕭 all ❷ ✳

Restaurant. Its continuing success confirms Patrizia, Domenico and Maurizio's winning formula all down the line: the restaurant is comfortable without being pretentious, the atmosphere is friendly and courteous, the service attentive, the bill more than reasonable, the wine list well put together at honest prices and the cuisine always satisfying. What more could one ask? Well.. sometimes the occasional dish doesn't quite make you jump for joy, but it is all so pleasant… The menu boasts various tried and true standards [for example, spaghetti with cacio cheese, black pepper and zucchini flowers; risotto with Castelmagno cheese, and soft-centred chocolate cake], as well as seasonal novelties. Terrines of truffled egg yolks and asparagus tips topped with a filo pastry crust; eggplant *caponata* with basil mousse, and smoked sword fish with cream of avocado and fresh garlic, as well as *tagliolini* with squab breast and summer truffles; spicy rice with creamed green peppers and anchovy fillets, and *tagliatelle* with guinea fowl ragù and tomato purée seasoned with rosemary. Meat-only main courses: lamb carrè with stewed figs; zucchini and mint *millefoglie* [puff pastry slices]; veal cutlets with pear, and slices of duck breast served with orange chutney and sesame seeds. For a

perfect finish: hot *sfogliata* pastries with custard, and ricotta cheese towers topped with chocolate shavings and orange sauce.

ANTICO BOTTARO
CENTRO STORICO - POPOLO
passeggiata di Ripetta, 15
☎ 06/3236763

 ❙❚ **74**
• **Cucina 44**
• **Wine Cellar 13** • **Service 8**
• **Ambience 8** • **Bonus 1**

• **Closed:** Mondays; in August
• **Seats:** 100
• **L.** 65,000 w/o wine
🖃 all ♦ ✳ ⬥

Restaurant. Our many visits to this pleasant restaurant have slightly tempered our initial enthusiasm, although it must be stressed that the raw materials used are excellent and you do eat well here. All the same, the more elaborate dishes sometimes don't entirely satisfy. Mediterranean cuisine with a strong Neapolitan influence: buffalo mozzarella; octopus carpaccio; French bean soufflé with cheese sauce; *linguine* with cherry tomatoes and capers; *tagliatelle* in mushroom sauce; sautéed mixed seafood; veal *piccatine* in Amalfi lemon sauce; eggplant *caponata;* potatoes and onions cooked with fresh oregano. Typical desserts from the Campania region to finish off with. The wine list complements the menu well; the service is attentive and courteous.

ARANCIA BLU
via dei Latini, 65
☎ 06/4454105

• **Closed:** never [open evenings only]
• **Seats:** 90
• **L.** 40,000 w/o wine
🖃 no ♦ ⬥ ⬥

Trattoria. This is technically a "vegetarian club", but if that calls to mind a somewhat spartan if not downright funereal menu, you're wrong: this is real cuisine. A few dark wood tables, simple but tasteful furnishings, bottles of wine everywhere - this little place is always full. Pesto, humus and tabbouleh salads; ravioli filled with potatoes and mint or chickpeas and walnuts in a parmigiano and rosemary sauce; *orecchiette* with eggplant; parsley-flavored *troffiette* with sweet peppers, olives and capers; vegetarian meatballs in spicy tomato sauce sprinkled with coriander; eggplant baked in rich, flaky *pasta brisée.* Desserts of the same high standard as the rest of the menu, and a well-designed wine list. The evening draws to a pleasurable close sipping excellent liqueurs and coffee.

ARMANDO AL PANTHEON
CENTRO STORICO PANTHEON
salita de' Crescenzi, 31
☎ 06/68803034

• **Closed:** Aug 1-31
• **Seats:** 40
• **L.** 45,000 w/o wine
🖃 all ✳

Trattoria. Its felicitous location in the heart of the historic centre and excellent management by the Gargioli brothers are not this trattoria's only positive qualities – a cordial welcome and pleasant atmosphere render it even more agreeable. The cucina offers traditional Roman dishes: *spaghetti cacio e pepe* [with grated pecorino and pepper], *all'arrabbiata* [in spicy tomato sauce], *all'amatriciana* [with *guanciale*, tomato, chili and *pecorino romano* cheese]; *alla carbonara* [with egg, *guanciale* and black pepper]; *farro* [an ancient cereal] soup, then on to *saltimbocca alla romana* [braised veal, ham and sage]; tripe; steaks; chicken in white wine; roast potatoes; beans and onions. Homemade desserts - very good indeed - to finish off with. A small wine list; attentive and courteous service.

ASINOCOTTO
TRASTEVERE
via dei Vascellari, 48
☎ 06/5898985

 ❙❚ **75**
• **Cucina 44**
• **Wine Cellar 14** • **Service 7**
• **Ambience 7** • **Bonus 3**

• **Closed:** Mondays [open evenings only]; in August
• **Seats:** 35
• **L.** 50,000 w/o wine
🖃 AE, CSi, Visa ⬥

Restaurant. You really eat well in this gourmet haven created by young chef, Giovanni Brenna, and his troupe of youthful *appassionati* in a neighborhood notoriously seething with tourist traps. We started with sea bass and red chicory marinated in thyme, and prawns *in carpione* [fried, then marinated in herbs and vinegar] - not bad at all, and proceeded with vegetable soup served with a barley and basil soufflé, and fresh wholemeal pasta with lamb ragù and pecorino cheese - all exquisite, harmonious dishes. As main courses, swordfish with capers and shallots, and finely sliced beef drizzled with balsamic vinegar. Desserts are ordered from a separate menu which amongst other things suggests what to drink with them. Coffee, tea and tisanes are offered by the house [bonus]. We chose the chocolate and pistacchio terrine, and a slice of strawberry Bavarian cream: excellent, nothing to criticise here either. The wine list is particularly well-designed and not banal [bonus]; the service is fast, though sometimes a little unfriendly. Laudable prices [and here comes the third bonus]. A special mention for the wine bar downstairs, open from 5pm till midnight, where you can take a break for an *aperitivo*, a little cheese-tasting, a dessert or just a good bottle of wine.

ATM SUSHI BAR
TRASTEVERE
via della Penitenza, 7
☎ 06/68307053

- **Closed:** Mondays [open evenings only]; in August
- **Seats:** 50
- **L.** 45,000 w/o wine
  AE, CSi, Visa

Japanese. This charming restaurant-with-atmosphere has recently opened its doors onto one of the little streets that come off Via della Lungara in Trastevere; inside it's a single large techno/neo-modern space with soft lighting, minimalist furnishings and a counter on the left where fast-moving cooks prepare the raw fish dishes. Getting down to the menu: sushi – naturally, sashimi, chirashi, as well as California rolls, tempura and other classic Japanese specialities, accompanied by green tea, Japanese beer or wine by the glass.
All rather good and at moderate prices. Courteous service and good music at the right volume.

AUGUSTO
TRASTEVERE
p.zza de' Renzi, 15
☎ 06/5803798

- **Closed:** annual holidays vary
- **Seats:** 50
- **L.** 30,000 w/o wine
  no 🅿 ♣

Trattoria. A relaxed, friendly atmosphere, paper napkins and plastic glasses, always crowded by the most varied cross-section of humanity: this epitome of the authentic Trastevere trattoria is run by the Silvestri family - *sor* Augusto, his wife Leda and their young son Sandro. They offer dishes that are *romanissimi* and well and truly tried-and-tested: *rigatoni all'amatriciana; stracciatella* [clear broth with egg and parmigiano]; *pasta e ceci;* pasta and lentil soup; *bollito* [boiled meat]; *brasato* [braised meat]; roast chicken with potatoes; *salsicce in umido* [fresh sausages poached with tomato]; various tasty side dishes made with vegetables in season; and homemade tarts, all washed down with a carafe of honest Genzano wine.

LA BELLE EPOQUE
TRIESTE
via Ajaccio, 11
☎ 06/8553721

- **Closed:** Sundays [open evenings only]; in August
- **Seats:** 170
- **L.** 30,000 w/o wine
  POS 🅿 ✳

Pizzeria. The quality of the pizzas served in this cosy, comfortable pizzeria is guaranteed - it belongs to the Neapolitan pizzamakers' association. But that's not the only string to its bow: they also serve excellent buffalo mozzarella with *focaccia* or *fritti* [fried snacks]; several fish dishes, including sautéed clams, *rigatoni con le cozze* [with mussels]; spaghetti with lobster, or classic fried fish; pizzas [also available as takeaways]; traditional *calzoni* [pizza turnovers], and melted *scamorza* cheese. Delicious regional desserts from Campania provide a perfect finish. A small wine list; courteous service.

BOCCONDIVINO
CENTRO STORICO
CAMPO MARZIO
p.zza di Campo Marzio, 6
☎ 06/68308626

 73
- **Cucina** 43
- **Wine Cellar** 14 • **Service** 7
- **Ambience** 8 • **Bonus** 1

- **Closed:** Mondays; annual holidays vary
- **Seats:** 60
- **L.** 70,000 w/o wine
  AE, CSi, Visa ✳ ♣ ♿

Restaurant. Going through the front door of this restaurant can be quite an emotional experience – it's so old and so very beautiful. The walls inside are hung with works by famous painters, but without any ostentation; a divan runs all the way along the walls of the two dining rooms, decorated in pale hues, where two ancient columns are discreetly enhanced by lighting that is modern without being stark. But let's not get carried away - time to talk about food. Entrées include *vongole* [clams] sautéed in first-press olive oil; fried squash blossoms, and hand-sliced Norcia prosciutto. First courses: *gnocchi* with tomato and basil; *stringarelli ai moscardini* [with baby curled octopus]; then *spigola* [sea bass] baked in salt crust and baked veal shank. Classic desserts: crème brulée, zuppa inglese [trifle] and sorbets. There's a well thought-out wine list, with a rather good selection of Italian reds and whites.

DAL BOLOGNESE

CENTRO STORICO - POPOLO
p.zza del Popolo, 1/2
☎ 06/3611426

  73

- Cucina 42
- Wine Cellar 14 • Service 8
- Ambience 8 • Bonus 1

- **Closed:** Mondays; in August
- **Seats:** 130
- **L.** 75,000 w/o wine
  🖽 all ✳ ♣ ⅃

Restaurant. The facade on the piazza

is really worth a bonus. The rest is fairly standard stuff: a restaurant of the classical variety with comfortable dining rooms and an ample menu that hasn't changed in years. We chose the house chicken-liver paté and smoked salmon, followed by a good *vitello tonnato* [veal with tuna and mayonnaise sauce]. The pasta courses were less than perfect, in particular the *maccheroncini* au gratin and *tagliolini* with prosciutto. Main courses include the usual trolley of boiled meats; cutlets cooked Bolognese-style and *fritto misto* [mixed fried meats] – also Bolognese-style. For dessert, excellent gelato-filled fruit and vanilla ice cream. A good wine list; courteous service – efficient without being intrusive.

LA BOTTEGA DEL VINO DI ANACLETO BLEVE

CENTRO STORICO - GHETTO
via S. Maria del Pianto, 9/11
☎ 06/6865970

- **Closed:** Sundays; open lunchtime only except Wed, Thur and Fri; in August
- **Seats:** 50
- **L.** 40,000 w/o wine
  🖽 all ✳

Wine Bar. After years of begging and pleading, you can finally eat as well as drink in the evenings at this wonderful place - an authentic treasure trove of delights - and you'd do well to book in advance if you want a table. The setting

is tasteful and inviting and Anacleto and Tina rank among the truly great tireless professionals. You can sample the products of the best artisans in the country, carefully selected by the patron, and the most difficult part is choosing between the truffled mortadella; delicious *lardo;* splendid mozzarella and *burrata* cheeses; goose breast; *baccalà carpaccio;* cold roulades [our favourite is the tuna]; excellent salads; meatloaf, and hot vegetable timbales. Excellent homemade cakes or puddings for dessert before finishing off with a selection of tiny biscuits, chocolates and pastries that will drive you crazy. As for drinks, this is one of the best-stocked wine bars in Rome.

AL BRIC

CENTRO STORICO
CAMPO DE' FIORI
via del Pellegrino, 51
☎ 06/6879533

 75

- Cucina 42
- Wine Cellar 17 • Service 7
- Ambience 7 • Bonus 2

- **Closed:** Mondays [open evenings only]; in January and August
- **Seats:** 75
- **L.** 60,000 w/o wine
  🖽 all ✳ ⅃

Restaurant. You can't buy wine by the glass here anymore, but wine-lovers need not dismay – there's now a sizeable offering of half-bottles [bonus points] and a

magnificent weighty tome dominating the entrance to consult, listing every one of the wines available in Roberto Marchetti's restaurant. Pleasant and comfortable, it offers dishes based on first-class raw materials [another bonus], like baked foie gras with Muscat and *renette* [tangy apples]; grilled polenta with Arnad *lardo* [cured pork fat]; homemade *pappardelle* with lamb ragù; *mezzi bucatini* with cacio cheese and black pepper; pockets of veal filled with brie cheese and Sicilian broccoli; and a good charcoal-grilled steak. To finish off, a little cheese-tasting or a dessert accompanied by a suitable wine.

IL BRILLO PARLANTE

CENTRO STORICO - POPOLO
via della Fontanella, 12
☎ 06/3243334

- **Closed:** Sundays at lunchtime; in August
- **Seats:** 100
- **L.** 40,000 w/o wine
  🖽 all ✳ ♣

Wine Bar. This attractive wine bar is always incredibly crowded and rather noisy, with a counter at the entrance and a labyrinthine series of rooms downstairs. *Aperitivi* upstairs and food below: a bit of everything, though nothing really

EATING

startling. Cured meats, cheeses and artisanal specialities; ravioli filled with melted *gorgonzola* cheese; slices of Danish beef with cherry tomatoes and arugula; pizzas cooked in a wood-fired oven including some with unusual toppings like spinach and Stilton cheese, or potatoes and *guanciale* [cured pork jowl]. For dessert, cakes of the day and chocolate mousse. There's a wide range of wines and a fair selection of beers. Reservations essential.

IL BUCHETTO
FLAMINIO
via Flaminia, 119
☎ 06/3201707

- **Closed:** Sunday lunchtime, Tuesday evening; in August
- **Seats:** 60
- **L.** 20,000 w/o wine
🎨 no ✳ ♿

Pizzeria. The setting is simple and casual but the food is very good, and above all the prices are practically unbeatable. The pizzas are Roman style – thank goodness! – well seasoned, perfectly cooked, thin and crunchy – with traditional toppings and in normal or maxi formats. You can also try the *calzoni* [pizza turnovers]; their legendary *bruschetta* with *ciriola* [tiny eels]

– impossible to find anywhere else; various *crostini; focaccia primavera* [with spring vegetables and cubes of tomato] or with prosciutto. For a perfect finish: a *ventaglio* - puff pastry fans filled with *crema pasticciera* [baker's custard]. Given all these wonders, you obviously have to queue fairly often, but the system of little numbers available outside and the speedy service [extremely courteous, despite it all] mean the wait is not too hard to bear.

CAFFÈ DELLE ARTI
PARIOLI
via A. Gramsci, 73
☎ 06/32651236

  70
- Cucina 41
- Wine Cellar 12 • Service 8
- Ambience 8 • Bonus 1

- **Closed:** Monday evenings
- **Seats:** 130
- **L.** 60,000 w/o wine
🎨 all 🅿 ♣

Restaurant. Located inside the Galleria d'Arte Moderna, this restaurant has beautiful dining rooms and a splendid summer terrace overlooking the peaceful greenery of Valle Giulia [bonus!]. The live music provided by an excellent pianist/singer and the very courteous service would make it an ideal restaurant were it not for the slightly stereotyped menu and the

occasional disappointing dish. We tried an acceptable *risotto* with shrimps and *speck* [smoked ham] together with a decidedly unconvincing *farfalle* with squid; a passable lobster salad, and an under-done grilled swordfish. The wine list could stand improvement. On a positive note, both the food and wine bills are very reasonable. Given the place and its potential, it could all be done a great deal better.

AL CALLARELLO
AVENTINO
via Salvator Rosa, 8
☎ 06/5747575

- **Closed:** Sundays; annual holidays vary
- **Seats:** 50
- **L.** 50,000 w/o wine
🎨 CSi, Visa 🅿 ✳ ♣

Trattoria. This is an attractive place with a pleasant outdoor dining area in summer, offering classical cuisine centred mainly on fish dishes, from *linguine* with reef fish to spaghetti with clams; the inevitable sauté; octopus salad; mixed fried fish, and grilled squid. They also do some meat dishes, like sliced beef *tagliata*. The desserts are simple but good. The wine list is limited, and the service can be a little ragged, as is often

the case in this kind of trattoria, especially when they're very busy. If you prefer something cheaper, they also do pizzas in the evening.

LA CAMPANA
CENTRO STORICO - NAVONA
v.lo della Campana, 18
☎ 06/6867820

- Cucina 40
- Wine Cellar 13 • Service 7
- Ambience 7 • Bonus 1

- **Closed:** Mondays; in August
- **Seats:** 120
- **L.** 55,000 w/o wine
🎨 all ✳

Restaurant. They say this is one of the oldest restaurants in the city, certainly it's always the same, for better or for worse - the setting is comfortable and the service is entrusted to efficient, experienced staff. Even the cuisine seems to be caught in a time warp: smoked swordfish and squash blossoms as antipastos; then *rigatoni all'amatriciana, tagliolini* with fresh anchovies, and lasagna - fairly heavy dishes but very tasty. We had *ossobuco* [veal shanks braised with wine and herbs] with purée; fried *cervello* [brains] and artichokes, and roast lamb for our main courses. For dessert, *crema* gelato with hot berry sauce. The wine list is adequate for the menu.

EATING

CAMPONESCHI

CENTRO STORICO
CAMPO DE' FIORI
p.zza Farnese, 50
☎ 06/6874927

 73

- Cucina 43
- Wine Cellar 13 • Service 8
- Ambience 8 • Bonus 1

- **Closed:** Sundays [open evenings only]; in August
- **Seats:** 70
- **L.** 120,000 w/o wine
📷 all 🅿 ✱ ♣

Restaurant. Situated in one of the word's most extraordinary piazzas, the service is fast and efficient, and the regular clientele [politicians, actors, singers, beautiful women] are the kind of people who tend to provoke startled nudges from less famous diners. The restaurant is very pleasant inside too, and booking is essential, despite the high prices. It's a pity the menu suffers from that ancient vice - the idea that if it looks good that's good enough because after all clients can't tell the difference. The last time we went even some of the old Roman classics left a lot to desire: insipid tripe and an unexciting poached *baccalà.* The fried zucchini flowers and artichokes were better, while the bean, seafood and pasta soup was boring, and the *spaghetti cacio e pepe* was overdone. At the same time, the sea bass in salt crust was excellent [and huge], but the boiled lobster with rice pilaf [warmly recommended by the owner] was absolutely forgettable. As for the choice of wines, clients are "guided" in the direction of those produced by the firm's vineyards. There's a good choice of desserts from the trolley. A bonus for the set design.

CANDIDO

PRATI - ANGELICO
v.le Angelico, 275/277
☎ 06/37517704

- **Closed:** Tuesdays; in August
- **Seats:** 80
- **L.** 25,000 w/o wine
📷 all ✱ ♣ ♿

Pizzeria. Candido's is renowned for its pizzas cooked in a wood-fired oven, but also for its affordable prices. Young people and families are certainly not indifferent to either of these points and they crowd out this rustic pizzeria. For starters, a very good *fritto misto* with *supplì* [riceballs with mozzarella centres], *olive ascolane* [deep-fried stuffed olives] and croquettes. To follow, apart from the traditional pizzas [*margherita, napoletana, capricciosa,* and so on] they also do *crostini* and you could try the pizza Candido, plain with mozzarella, arugula, *bresaola* [cured beef] and fresh tomato. The service is efficient and polite.

LA CASETTA DEI GIRASOLI

CORSO FRANCIA
c.so Francia, 205
☎ 06/3296204

 67

- Cucina 40
- Wine Cellar 12 • Service 7
- Ambience 7 • Bonus 1

- **Closed:** Mondays [open evenings only except Sundays]; annual holidays · vary
- **Seats:** 50
- **L.** 70,000 w/o wine
📷 AE, CSi, Visa 🅿 ♣

Restaurant. You can see the taste and care with which it's all been put together the moment you walk through the door. Once inside you will be served and looked after with courteous efficiency, even when it's full and busy. The menu is more extensive than the wine list, which is not entirely satisfying: it needs a few serious labels and not just the fashionable ones. The sea bass *carpaccio* is excellent, and so is the prosciutto with buffalo mozzarella. We tried the *pennette* with a pesto made of arugula, cherry tomatoes, mussels and clams, and the risotto with asparagus [one of several on the menu] - a fraction over-cooked and too creamy, then the fillet of beef which had just the right amount of sauce and the *saltimbocca di spigola* [sautéd sea bass braised with sage and ham]. The desserts were better – tarte tatin and *torta caprese* [chocolate almond cake]. A bonus for the care and hospitality. It's open after the theatre if you book in advance.

AL CEPPO

PARIOLI
via Panama, 2/a
☎ 06/8419696

 78

- Cucina 45
- Wine Cellar 17 • Service 7
- Ambience 8 • Bonus 1

- **Closed:** Mondays; Aug 10-22
- **Seats:** 100
- **L.** 80,000 w/o wine
📷 all 🅿 ✱ ♣ ♿

Restaurant. Still something of a touchstone for quality on the rather difficult Roman restaurant scene, they offer an interesting, wide-ranging menu: *baccalà* with leek fondue and crispy artichokes; *trippa di coda di rospo* [angler fish tripe]; *prosciutto di montagna* with truffled *crostini,* then pasta and broccoli in *brodo di arzilla* [skate broth]; spaghetti with cuttlefish and chard, and risotto with smoked provola cheese and asparagus – all very good. Main courses include veal roulades with radicchio, parmigiano and a spinach flan; fillets of *triglia* [red mullet] crumbed with rosemary-flavoured bread and served with stuffed tomatoes; leg of lamb with olives and fried cheese. The desserts were good too. There's an excellent wine list, and we awarded a bonus for their monthly 'best labels' selection. The

EATING

service can slow down when they're busy.

DA CESARE
PRATI - CAVOUR
via Crescenzio, 13
☎ 06/6861227

 72

- Cucina 43
- Wine Cellar 13 • Service 7
- Ambience 7 • Bonus 2

- **Closed:** Sunday evenings and Mondays; Aug 1-31, Easter and Christmas
- **Seats:** 150
- **L.** 65,000 w/o wine
☐ all ✳ ♣ ㅎ

Restaurant. This comfortable place has been a reliable address for many years here in the Prati neighbourhood. It caters for all tastes with a wide range of classical dishes based on the use of first-class ingredients [bonus]: fresh fish, certified *chianina* beef, mushrooms, truffles and game in season, and pizzas cooked in a wood-fired oven, including a particularly good one topped with truffles, and an excellent plain *bianca* with mushrooms and tiny stuffed scamorza cheeses. We tried the seafood salad; swordfish *carpaccio;* boiled octopus; the house *fettuccine alla Cesare; farro* [an ancient cereal] with beans; an exquisite *coda di rospo in guazzetto* [poached anglerfish]; and a good *frittura di paranza* [mixed fried fish 'straight off the boats']. The desserts are good too. The wine list also offers a number of wines by the glass [another bonus]. Efficient, time-tested service.

CHARLY'S SAUCIERE
COLOSSEO
via S. Giovanni in Laterano, 270
☎ 06/70495666

 71

- Cucina 41
- Wine Cellar 13 • Service 8
- Ambience 7 • Bonus 2

- **Closed:** Sundays; open evenings only Mondays and Saturdays; in August
- **Seats:** 40
- **L.** 60,000 w/o wine
☐ all ✳ ㅎ

Restaurant. Karl Zyka has held the reins of this attractive, unostentatious restaurant firmly in his hands for many years now, practising his own very personal brand of French cuisine with great professionalism. The dishes are always much the same: homemade pâtès; mushroom-filled vol-au-vent pastries; onion soup; *fondue Bourguignonne;* escargots; beef tartare; rösti potatoes; a good selection of cheeses; gelato with hot chocolate sauce, and crêpe suzettes. The wine list is not huge but more than adequate for the menu. We've confirmed our double bonus for the consistently high quality and the particularly polite service.

CHECCHINO DAL 1887
TESTACCIO
via di Monte Testaccio, 30
☎ 06/5746318

 78

- Cucina 45
- Wine Cellar 17 • Service 8
- Ambience 8 • Bonus 0

- **Closed:** Sundays and Mondays; in August and at Christmas
- **Seats:** 95
- **L.** 75,000 w/o wine
☐ all ❷ ✳ ♣ ㅎ

Restaurant. The Mariani family has won itself a leading place on the Roman restaurant scene over the years and their restaurant continues to be one of the city's best. The knowledge and practice of traditional Roman cooking and enology are a point of honour with energetic Signora Nina, and with Elio and Francesco, the valiant sommeliers who run the dining room with great professionalism. The dishes have stayed unchanged over the years and that's exactly why it's so famous: *testina di vitello* [calf's head]; *zampetti di maiale* [pigs' trotters]; *rigatoni* with oxtail sauce; *bucatini alla gricia* [with *guanciale*, black pepper and grated pecorino cheese]; *coratella* [lamb organ meats] with artichokes; lamb *alla cacciatora* [hunter-style]; *pajata* [milk-filled veal intestines] and roasted *animelle* [pancreas and sweetbreads]. Everything is cooked to perfection using first-class ingredients. Cheeses paired with suitable wines and excellent homemade desserts, including a good version of ricotta torta, to finish off with. Their unique wine cellar is well worth a visit though the wine list is less varied than in the past. A final note: at these prices a tasting menu or at least a business lunch menu wouldn't be a bad idea.

CHECCO ER CARETTIERE
TRASTEVERE
via Benedetta, 10
☎ 06/5817018

 70

- Cucina 42
- Wine Cellar 13 • Service 7
- Ambience 7 • Bonus 1

- **Closed:** Sunday evenings
- **Seats:** 150
- **L.** 65,000 w/o wine
☐ all ❷ ✳ ♣

Restaurant. This is a family affair in the true sense of the word – when restaurant lore is in the blood and culinary wisdom has been handed down from generation to generation. You can see it in the 'Teutonic' efficiency with which Stefania Porcelli, daughter of the late, lamented Pippo, one of Rome's great hosts, runs the dining room, and in the care that has obviously gone into selecting the ingredients. It's what makes it so utterly reliable in a dicey area like Trastevere, notoriously seething with recently slung-together tourists traps. The setting is pleasantly rustic with a delightful summer outdoor dining area. The menu is classical, and next to typical Roman dishes you'll also find rather good fish main courses. So: *carciofi alla romana* [artichokes stuffed with garlic, parsley, and Roman mint]; spaghetti *alla carrettiera* - with tomatoes, mushrooms and tuna; *tagliolini* with scampi; mixed fried meat, fish and vegetables; baked turbot with potatoes; bream in wine white; *involtini alla romana* [Roman-style roulades], and *coda alla vaccinara* [oxtail braised in celery broth]. Good desserts, and a rather good wine list.

IL CHICCO D'UVA

CENTRO STORICO
PANTHEON
c.so Rinascimento, 70
☎ *06/6867983*

 70

- Cucina 40
- Wine Cellar 14 • Service 7
- Ambience 7 • Bonus 2

- **Closed:** Sundays [open evenings only]; annual holidays vary
- **Seats:** 50
- **L.** 65,000 w/o wine
🗆 all ✳ ♠ ♿

Restaurant. A nice place with a big counter at the entrance and two small comfortable dining rooms off to the left and right. The welcome is genuinely warm, and efficient young dining room staff go out of their way to put clients at

their ease [bonus]. Yummy tidbits while you consult the menu and the excellent wine list, full of well-chosen foreign labels as well as Italian wines, and recommendations as to what to drink - by the glass - with the desserts [another bonus]. The menu offers attractive-sounding but a bit too modish dishes that can lack personality when you actually sample them. Lemon-scented sea bass *carpaccio;* eggplant and parmigiana *sformatini* [timbales]; *farfalle* with shrimp, cherry tomatoes and pecorino cheese; risotto with *taleggio* cheese and orange [not very well cooked]; fillets of sea bass with porcini mushrooms and grapes [good fresh ingredients, but the sauce rather overwhelms the poor fish]; fillet steak with three kinds of pepper. Desserts include an absolutely delicious three-chocolate tart, and a *semifreddo* [soft frozen mousse] served with a strawberry and port wine sauce. Given the positive qualities we're sure any teething troubles will soon be overcome.

IL CIAK

TRASTEVERE
v.lo del Cinque, 21
☎ *06/5894774*

 70

- Cucina 42
- Wine Cellar 13 • Service 7
- Ambience 7 • Bonus 1

- **Closed:** Mondays [open evenings only]; annual holidays end July-early Aug
- **Seats:** 70
- **L.** 45,000 w/o wine
🗆 all ♠

Restaurant. This little Tuscan enclave with its rustic setting, chequered tableclothes, straw-bottomed seats and wooden tables has the pleasant atmosphere of a typical Tuscan trattoria, which tends to incline you to relax and enjoy your meal. Their meals are very good and, obviously, typically Tuscan: *pappardelle* with duck or wild boar sauce; *ribollita* [twice-cooked vegetable soup]; *farro* [an ancient cereal] with mushrooms; many different kinds of charcoal grilled meat including an excellent thick *fiorentina* T-bone; lamb brochettes and *spuntature* [pork spare ribs]; pork *fegatelli nella rete* [liver], and squab. Average desserts, and efficient service. The wine cellar contains mostly Tuscan labels, though the house Chianti available by the carafe is pretty good. Tables are set up outside in the characteristic *vicolo* in summer. Best to book.

CICCIA BOMBA

CENTRO STORICO
PIAZZA NAVONA
via del Governo Vecchio, 76
☎ *06/68802108*

- **Closed:** Wednesdays; in August
- **Seats:** 100
- **L.** 45,000 w/o wine
🗆 all ✳ ♠ ♿

Trattoria. Tastefully decorated with a pleasant cordial atmosphere and the kind of menu that keeps everybody happy. Depending on the day you'll find homemade *gnocchi* [Thursdays]; bean, mussel and octopus soup [Fridays]; *fettuccine allo scoglio* [with seafood]; *tonnarelli* with cacio cheese and pepper; as well as good grilled Argentinian meat, and fresh fish practically every day. Tasty pizzas issue forth from the wood-fired oven [only in the evenings, though], in both normal and giant-sized versions. Homemade desserts include tarts, crème brulée and *tiramisù*. The wine cellar offers a number of good bottles to go with it all. Efficient, courteous service.

TROIANI [FORMERLY IL CONVIVIO]

CENTRO STORICO - NAVONA
v.lo dei Soldati, 31
☎ *06/68805950*

 79

- Cucina 46
- Wine Cellar 17 • Service 8
- Ambience 8 • Bonus 0

- **Closed:** Sundays; annual holidays vary
- **Seats:** 50
- **L.** 130,000 w/o wine
🗆 all ℗ ✳ ♿

Restaurant. We haven't visited the Troiani brothers at their new address yet. The cooking betrayed a certain air of crisis on our

EATING

last visits to their old location, a pinch of disharmony in the combinations of ingredients and a certain repetitiveness. As entrées, we tried the foie gras-stuffed smoked duck breast served with pears and dried fruit [a bit too strongly flavoured] and shrimp salad with basmati rice and arugula sauce [not exciting]; followed by pasta *stracci* with a quail, foie gras and orange ragù [really good], and spaghetti with cacio cheese, pepper and *pecorino di fossa* [sheep's milk cheese aged underground] - a tiny bit overcooked. As main courses: lobster with potatoes, sweet peppers and Roman caciotta cheese [excellent]; and pan-fried *baccalà* [a bit gluey] with sultanas, pine nuts and buffalo mozzarella. For dessert we chose the usual [but always welcome] zabaglione *semifreddo* [soft frozen mousse] sprinkled with balsamic vinegar from Modena, hot fruit compotes, and a ricotta turnover with dried-grape wine ice cream and chocolate sauce. There's a substantial, well-designed wine list, with the praiseworthy inclusion of half-bottles, and a tasting menu at L.100,000.

ALLA CORTE DEL VINO
CENTRO STORICO
CAMPO DE' FIORI
via Monte della Farina, 43
☎ 06/68307568

• **Closed:** Mondays; annual holidays vary
• **Seats:** 50
• **L.** 30,000 w/o wine
CSi, Visa

Wine Bar. The basic idea seems to be that of offering representative products, given the objective impossibility of ever stocking or even providing an exhaustive analytical guide to everything. Or so it seemed to us when we tried to determine the criterion applied by the Reynaud brothers to their wine-tasting menu and the dishes designed to accompany the wines. In other words, when you look at the wine list, and especially the *mescita* wines [available by the glass], you're struck by a certain gift for synthesis: it's exhaustive without stunning you by its sheer size. Appetising dishes of cheeses and mixed cured meats ranging from peppery fresh Calabrian *'nduja* sausage to *mocetta* from Val d'Aosta; *culatello* [prized cured ham]; cured goose meats; Valtellina *bitto;* caciocavallo cheese aged in barrels; goat's milk cheeses and *formaggio di fossa* aged underground, are all served in an unostentatious setting where wood

predominates, together with salads, *focaccia,* savoury pies, a few hot dishes and one or two desserts. More than 200 wine and spirits labels line their shelves.

COURT DELICATI
AVENTINO
v.le Aventino, 41
☎ 06/5746108

• **Closed:** Mondays
• **Seats:** 60
• **L.** 20,000 w/o wine
no

Chinese. Don't forget to book if you don't want to go hungry, because admirers of this restaurant are legion, both Italians and foreigners [it's only a stone's throw away from the FAO headquarters]. Apart from all the well-known Chinese specialities they also serve Malay, Indonesian and Thai dishes like nasi goreng, shrimps with rice noodles, chicken satay and a visually stunning Thai fish soup. Classic jasmine tea, a few wines or Chinese beer to drink.

IL COVO
MONTI
via del Boschetto, 91
☎ 06/4815871

 69

• Cucina 42
• Wine Cellar 12 • Service 7
• Ambience 7 • Bonus 1

• **Closed:** Mondays [open evenings only]; annual holidays vary
• **Seats:** 60
• **L.** 50,000 w/o wine
AE, CSi, Visa ✳ ♣

Restaurant. A place to suit all tastes and pockets located right in the centre of

Rome. The pizzeria section serves *focaccia, bruschetta* [the one with olives is very tasty], and obviously pizza with various toppings. The kitchen offers a variety of meat and fish dishes according to how the chef's fancy takes him. *Bavette ai moscardini* [pasta with baby curled octopus]; *rigatoni alla Norma* [with tomato, eggplant, ricotta and basil]; *tagliolini alla polpa di riccio* [with sea urchins] - the house speciality; Sicilian-style swordfish; chateaubriand; sea bass baked in salt crust; *panna cotta* [silky milk custard] and chocolate mousse. The choice of wines could be a little broader but you'll find some good ones to have with your dinner. A bonus for the welcoming atmosphere.

CUL DE SAC
CENTRO STORICO - NAVONA
p.zza Pasquino, 73
☎ 06/68801094

• **Closed:** Monday lunchtimes; annual holidays vary [open in August]
• **Seats:** 60
• **L.** 30,000 w/o wine
CSi, POS, Visa
✳ ♣

Wine Bar. This year we found one or two small innovations [venison with polenta, and *coda alla vaccinara* – braised oxtail] in what has always been a high quality and very interesting menu, ranging from a good Valtellina soup *ai pizzocheri* [a classic], to lasagna, homemade paté and a vast selection of cheeses, cured meats and salami, as well as a few particularly delicious and unusual dishes like snails *alla bourguignonne;* tongue in green sauce, and chickpea timbales. Desserts include zabaglione gelato, the mandatory *Incredible coppetta,* and pine resin pudding. The monumental wine list merits a special mention, as it offers some very good wines at truly "incredible" prices.

DANTE TABERNA DE' GRACCHI
PRATI - CAVOUR
via dei Gracchi, 266/268
☎ 06/3213126

  73

• Cucina 43
• Wine Cellar 14 • Service 7
• Ambience 7 • Bonus 2

• **Closed:** Sundays and Monday lunchtime; Easter; Aug 10-20
• **Seats:** 160
• **L.** 65,000 w/o wine
▨ all ℗ ✻ ఈ

Restaurant. This restaurant is always a safe bet, for all tastes and ages. The setting is reassuring and comfortable, the service courteous and efficient, and the wine list is quite good [and getting better].
Praiseworthy, in a word, especially as it's always very busy but the quality never fails: the scampi *carpaccio* is a good example - it's rare to find one so fresh. The fried antipasti are excellent: tasty croquettes and *supplì* with unusual flavours. We chose spaghetti with clams and grilled fillet of beef to put the restaurant to the test, and it passed with flying colours. The *spigola* [sea bass] baked in salt crust is good, and so are the *bavette dei Gracchi* and the pasta in skate broth. Classic, well-made desserts: *millefoglie* [layered flaky pastry and custard]; crème caramel, and marzipan pastries. A bonus for the consistently high standard and reasonable prices.

DI PIETRO
OSTIENSE
p.zza di Porta San Paolo, 6/7a
☎ 06/5780252

• **Closed:** Tuesdays; annual holidays vary
• **Seats:** 80
• **L.** 30,000 w/o wine
▨ CSi, Visa ℗ ✻ ♣ ఈ

Pizzeria. This big rosticceria-pizzeria-trattoria located right in front of the pyramid is open till late, and always crowded by the most varied clientele. The wood-fired oven makes good thin, crunchy pizzas - both the classics and some more original versions [the one with *speck* and the one with anchovies and zucchini flowers
are delicious]; then there's a choice of first courses, traditional and otherwise [the fish dishes are particularly good] and their very satisfying salads served in bowls made out of pizza dough. Draught beer and a few good labels to go with it. Polite and very efficient service.

DITIRAMBO
CENTRO STORICO
CAMPO DE' FIORI
p.zza della Cancelleria, 74
☎ 06/6871626

• **Closed:** Monday lunchtime; in August
• **Seats:** 58
• **L.** 45,000 w/o wine
▨ all ✻ ♣ ఈ

Trattoria. Dining here is always pleasant, and not just because of the friendly hospitality, the polite service and the atmosphere, but also because the food is never boring or predictable. *Malfatti* with squash blossoms; cardamom-flavoured *tortelli* with mint; steamed fillets of bream with stewed vegetables *al Vermentino* [white wine]; grilled squid; mixed boiled meats in green sauce; as well as salads and vegetarian dishes. The desserts are good, too, and all homemade: cheese cake, various cakes like the ones with ricotta cheese or chocolate, and typical Emilian and Val d'Aosta tortes. A special mention for the high quality of the ingredients, especially the olive oil, and for the fact
that the pasta and bread are always homemade. There's also a wine list with very reasonable mark-ups. Always book.

IL DITO E LA LUNA
SAN LORENZO
via dei Sabelli, 51
☎ 06/4940726

 71

• Cucina 42
• Wine Cellar 15 • Service 7
• Ambience 6 • Bonus 1

• **Closed:** Sundays [open evenings only]; in August
• **Seats:** 90
• **L.** 55,000 w/o wine
▨ no ఈ

Restaurant. We never get tired of saying how irritating it is to not be able to pay bills above a certain figure with a credit card, but we've given this place a bonus all the same, because they often organise very interesting wine-tasting evenings with excellent wines. The food is always good: rabbit salad with plum sauce and balsamic vinegar; *vermicelli* with broccoli, cherry tomatoes and king prawns; *farfalle* with sweet peppers and salted ricotta sauce; fillet of grouper in black sauce; lamb cutlets served with a fondue. Don't miss the Sicilian *cannolo* [rich flaky pastry tubes filled with custard and candied fruit] for dessert. There's a well-designed wine list with reasonable mark-ups.

EATING

DITTA MARCELLO TESTA 1895

PINCIANO
via Tirso, 30
☎ 06/85300692

 73

- Cucina 41
- Wine Cellar 14 • Service 8
- Ambience 9 • Bonus 1

- **Closed:** Sunday evenings
- **Seats:** 65
- **L.** 60,000 w/o wine
🗐 all ✷ ♠

Restaurant. Until last summer, the name Ditta Marcello Testa 1895 was synonymous with a modish, multi-faceted operation: coffee bar, *tavola calda*, tea rooms and a bar with a DJ in the evenings, open until late into the night. Then came the transformation: substantial capital investments, massive renovations in the kitchen, extensions to the dining rooms and it has now re-opened as a restaurant and wine bar. It's splendid – decorated like a tremendously tasteful bourgeois salon with spacious, beautifully-laid tables set well apart from each other. The menu is varied and designed to cater for all needs, although it still seems to have a few teething problems: chicken galantine served with hot rolled *crostoni* [slices of buttered bread] filled with goat's milk cheese and fresh *pancetta; maccheroncini* with vegetables and buffalo scamorza cheese; ricotta and spinach-stuffed ravioli with fresh tomato and basil; leg of lamb baked with juniper berries; *stoccafisso* [dried cod] and chickpea casserole. The menu also suggests the best wine to drink with each dessert. The wine list, already good before the changes, is being continually extended. Sunday brunch; live music on Friday evenings.

LA DOLCE VITA SAPORI E SAPERE

OSTIENSE
l.re di Pietra Papa, 51
☎ 06/5579865

 68

- Cucina 41
- Wine Cellar 13 • Service 7
- Ambience 7 • Bonus 0

- **Closed:** Mondays [open evenings only]; Aug 16-31
- **Seats:** 100
- **L.** 65,000 w/o wine
🗐 all ❶ ✷ ♠ ♿

Restaurant. A restaurant with a classical ambience and a pleasant outdoor dining area offering equally classical cuisine that seems to lack a bit of originality or spirit of innovation. The wide-ranging menu offers meat and fish dishes and pizzeria fare. We chose *linguine* with scampi and squid; sautéd clams, and grilled scampi and squid - all satisfactory; the desserts were rather unexciting, though, and not of quite the same standard as the other dishes. The wine list offers a reasonable assortment of national labels, and the service is courteous and fairly efficient, even when the restaurant is at its busiest.

I DUE LADRONI

CENTRO STORICO
CAMPO MARZIO
p.zza Nicosia, 24
☎ 06/6896299

 72

- Cucina 43
- Wine Cellar 14 • Service 7
- Ambience 7 • Bonus 1

- **Closed:** Saturday lunchtime and Sundays; Aug 1-31
- **Seats:** 100
- **L.** 65,000 w/o wine
🗐 all ✷ ♠

Restaurant. This place is always full and dining at their outdoor tables in summer is very pleasurable. The setting is classical, pleasant and attractive and the service is entrusted to capable and courteous staff. The menu is consistently satisfying and designed to suit all tastes, ranging from smoked fish to prawn and avocado salad; spaghetti with *bottarga di muggine* [dried mullet roe]; *rigatoni alla Norma* [with tomatoes, eggplant, ricotta ad basil]; roast beef baked in salt crust; lobster *alla catalana; moscardini* [baby curled octopus] with cherry tomatoes; and eggplant and mozzarella terrines. For dessert, a good version of crème caramel and chocolate *torta caprese*. The well-designed wine list also offers half-bottles [bonus]. After-theatre dining if you book.

DUKE'S

PARIOLI
v.le Parioli, 200
☎ 06/80662455

 73

- Cucina 43
- Wine Cellar 13 • Service 8
- Ambience 8 • Bonus 1

- **Closed:** Saturdays [open evenings only]
- **Seats:** 100
- **L.** 55,000 w/o wine
🗐 all ♠ ♿

Restaurant. This happy new entry on the Roman restaurant scene offers a modern, airy space with "American" decor and an outdoor dining area reminiscent of a tourist village [a beautiful one, though!]. The service is attentive and extremely courteous: we were able to eat late [bookings are taken for two shifts, but it fills up easily, given its popularity - especially with young people] and we were presented with an unusual wine list: American whites and reds, Italian spumanti and dessert wines. The menu is along the same lines: salads, shellfish and meat. At least the Red Salad is Mediterranean, with excellent tomatoes; and the "Duke's appetizers" convinced us everything was fine after all. We tried an excellent rib-eye steak which was better than the fillet steak in red sauce, though it was good too, and so were the desserts - chocolate cake and cheesecake [of course]. All in all – very good and we predict a rosy future; with a bonus for the wine, also available by the glass.

L'EAU VIVE
CENTRO STORICO
PANTHEON
via Monterone, 85
☎ 06/68801095

 73

- **Cucina 42**
- **Wine Cellar 14 • Service 7**
- **Ambience 7 • Bonus 3**

- **Closed:** Sundays; Aug 1-31
- **Seats:** 170
- **L.** 50,000 w/o wine
🛏 all ❷ ✳

Restaurant. Yes, it's true, a lot of this restaurant's notoriety is due to its air of sanctity. It's run by an order of nuns with branches all over the world and its profits are entirely invested in good works [bonus]. But one of their good works can be enjoyed by anyone who comes here and samples their varied menu. Designed to suit all pockets [bonus] it offers mainly French cuisine with a few agreeble international digressions. We actually found the food very interesting: country-style paté; egg, spinach, and salmon tart; prosciutto crepes; onion soup; Alsatian quiche; fillet steak with a sauce of cognac and green

peppers; lobster; cod with creamed caviar; chocolate mousse and creme caramel - to name only a few. All their dishes are very well presented. The wine list, mostly French, is particularly well thought-out and includes half-bottles [another bonus]. So, if you do it out of real affection and not just curiosity, come at Christmas - there'll be carols sung in the languages of faraway countries with a few bongos and a guitar or two to touch the hardest heart.

EDY
CENTRO STORICO - POPOLO
v.lo del Babuino, 4
☎ 06/36001738

- **Closed:** Sundays; in August
- **Seats:** 45
- **L.** 40,000 w/o wine
🛏 all ⚓

Trattoria. If you're looking for evidence of the contrasts in this city, Edy's is it. Right in the centre, just a stone's throw away from the most exclusive shopping district, where wealthy tourists stroll and buy, and a lot of other people glue their noses to the shop windows, it's a good place to come and enjoy simple, tasty dishes. The menu is equally divided between traditional Roman dishes and fish. Try the *fettuccine* with artichokes; spaghetti with shellfish *al cartoccio* [baked in parchment]; *abbacchio alla cacciatora* [hunter-style spring lamb]; thinly-sliced beef *tagliata,* or baked

fish and potatoes. There's a respectable house wine and quite a few good bottles available to drink with it.

ELEONORA D'ARBOREA
PINCIANO
c.so Trieste, 23
☎ 06/44250943

 70

- **Cucina 42**
- **Wine Cellar 13 • Service 7**
- **Ambience 7 • Bonus 1**

- **Closed:** Mondays; Aug 15-31
- **Seats:** 80
- **L.** 65,000 w/o wine
🛏 all ✳ ⚓ ♿

Restaurant. Run by Sardinians, this is a friendly place with a good fish menu. If you choose their particularly rich and scrumptious *antipasto misto,* you may well not be able to eat more than a first course. At any rate, try the oysters; sea bass *carpaccio;* marinated salmon; classic spaghetti with *bottarga* [dried fish roe] and rich *linguine* with lobster and you won't be disappointed. Their main courses include a fragrant mixed fried fish; lobster *alla catalana,* and other fish depending on what's available at the markets. For dessert, we chose Sardinian biscuits and *seadas* [deep-fried honey-glazed ravioli filled with cheese] with a glass of homemade liqueur, though the house desserts are

rather good too. The wine list is well-suited to the menu; courteous and efficient service.

ENOTECA CAPRANICA
CENTRO STORICO
PANTHEON
p.zza Capranica, 99
☎ 06/69940992

 74

- **Cucina 43**
- **Wine Cellar 14 • Service 8**
- **Ambience 8 • Bonus 1**

- **Closed:** Sundays; in August
- **Seats:** 90
- **L.** 115,000 w/o wine
🛏 all ✳ ♿

Restaurant. Mario Rispoli took this restaurant over after running the dining room for several years, and things seem to work better now - most of the various flaws we noticed on previous visits appear to have been eliminated. The menu has stayed substantially the same, but the dishes seem better balanced. Lobster salad with squash blossom sauce; smoked *cernia* [grouper], salmon and swordfish; salmon *tortelloni* with king prawn ragù; spaghetti with scampi and *bottarga di muggine* [dried mullet roe]; herb-scented saddle of rabbit with vegetables; fillets of turbot baked in a rosemary-flavoured potato crust. An interesting selection of cheeses or a house dessert from a separate menu to

EATING

finish off with. The wine list is in the throes of reorganisation but already quite good. The service is always professional and attentive, and the ambience is very pleasant. A bonus for the non-smokers' dining room.

ENOTECA CORSI
CENTRO STORICO
ARGENTINA
via del Gesù, 87/88
☎ *06/6790821*

- **Closed:** Sundays; [open only at lunchtime]; Aug 1-31
- **Seats:** 110
- **L.** 30,000 w/o wine
⌨ all

Trattoria. Located right in the centre of Rome, this trattoria with a wine shop attached is always crowded. You soon realise why: affordable prices, super-traditional cuisine, and efficient service. The menu of the day is written up on a blackboard: *pasta e ceci* [chickpea and pasta soup]; pasta with potatoes; *penne all'arrabbiata;* spaghetti *all'amatriciana;* tripe cooked Roman-style; chicken with sweet peppers; *polpettone* [meatloaf]; poached *baccalà;* classic *saltimbocca alla romana* and many others. House wine or a good, very reasonably-priced label from the wine shop to drink.

DA ENRICO E BRUNO
PIAZZA BOLOGNA
via Michele di Lando, 28/36
☎ *06/44237738*

- **Closed:** Wednesdays; in August
- **Seats:** 135
- **L.** 35,000 w/o wine
⌨ all ♣ ♿

Trattoria. Bruno and Enrico, the owners, have managed to turn this place into one of the most reliable good eats in the neighbourhood. You'll be overwhelmed by their *simpatia,* cordiality and evident desire to be of help in every way. Nor is it commercial calculation on their part – they really are like that, as you realise when you see the other staff taking care of guests in the same attentive way. The menu offers a wide variety of dishes: there's a good pizza section [Roman-style thin-crust pizzas], as well as tasty *bruschetta,* and classics like spaghetti *alle vongole* [with clams] or the fish *trittico* [three different kinds together] all well-executed and served in generous portions. The wine list could be more imaginative.

EST! EST!! EST!!!
TERMINI
via Genova, 32
☎ *06/4881107*

- **Closed:** Mondays; [open evenings only]; in August
- **Seats:** 120
- **L.** 25,000 w/o wine
⌨ CSi, POS, Visa
🅿 ♣

Pizzeria. When you start talking about pizza, Italians tend to divide into two ferociously hostile camps [as in many other areas of national life] – the *pizza bassa* lovers [Roman-style with thin-crust pastry] on one side and the champions of *pizza alta* [Neapolitan-style: thicker, with a puffy ring border] on the other. This historic pizzeria with its lived-in looking decor, in the same premises since 1905 and better known as "the pizzeria on Via Genova", serves excellent pizza and they actually offer both *alta* and *bassa,* thus keeping both schools of thought happy. The *calzoni* [pizza turnovers], *crostini* [try the *crostino alla cardinale*] and the excellent *baccalà* fillets are worth trying. Beer and a few bottles of wine to drink.

DA ETTORE
TRIESTE
c.so Trieste, 129
☎ *06/8554323*

- **Closed:** Mondays; in August
- **Seats:** 40
- **L.** 35,000 w/o wine
⌨ all ♣ ♿

Trattoria. It must be in the genes: no matter where you go you always find natives of Amatrice running eateries of one kind or another. In a way this curious fact serves as a guarantee – you'll rarely be disappointed, particularly if you're clear about what you're looking for.

This trattoria, run by the *simpatico* Enrico, is the classic unpretentious family affair. The kitchen offers home-cooking: grilled vegetables, marinated anchovies and that's about it for antipastos. Then [naturally] *bucatini all'amatriciana;* homemade *agnolotti* and *gnocchi* with meat sauce; rice with fresh peas or vegetables served warm, not too hot; meatballs; veal roulades; *ossobuco* [veal shank braised with wine and herbs] and sometimes fish. Homemade desserts: crème caramel, hazelnut or sour cherry tart, and delicious hot apple pie served with vanilla ice cream. The wine list is a fraction limited; the service is not white-glove but always courteous and efficient.

FAURO
PARIOLI
via R. Fauro, 44
☎ *06/8083301*

- **Closed:** Sundays; annual holidays vary
- **Seats:** 50
- **L.** 50,000 w/o wine
⌨ all 🅿 ✳ ♣ ♿

Trattoria. It's hard to find another place in Rome that serves fish of the same consistently high standard at such reasonable prices. Franco Zambelli is an honest restaurateur with a passion for his work, and his culinary offerings are never disappointing, whether it's roast octopus seasoned with marinated herbs; *aguglie in saôr* [needlefish]; rich spaghetti with shellfish; the totally plain but impeccable spaghetti with fresh tomatoes and basil; *spigola* [sea bass] with shellfish and myrtle; or swordfish steaks cooked Mediterranean-style. There's an intelligently-planned wine list designed to provide quality products at good prices.

'A FENESTELLA
FLAMINIO
p.le Flaminio, 22
☎ 06/3225050

- **Closed:** Sundays; annual holidays vary
- **Seats:** 100
- **L.** 30,000 w/o wine
🗐 all ✳ ♣

Pizzeria. Despite our aversion for the whole series of places of this kind that keep opening around the city, this one run by Pippo Sanfilippo rises head and shoulders above the herd because it serves a very good pizza - the Neapolitan variety, with a nice big crunchy border. Everything else - fries, zucchini or eggplant *parmigiana*, salads - is fairly standard stuff. The desserts are

typically Campanian: chocolate *torta caprese*; rum babàs, *torta ischitana* [Ischian-style] made with spongecake, *limoncello* liqueur and ricotta cheese. Polite service from the earnest young staff.

FERRARA
TRASTEVERE
via del Moro, 1/a
☎ 06/5803769

 74

- **Cucina** 42
- **Wine Cellar** 17 • **Service** 7
- **Ambience** 7 • **Bonus** 1

- **Closed:** Tuesdays [Sundays in summer]; open evenings only except Sunday
- **Seats:** 45
- **L.** 50,000 w/o wine
🗐 all ♣ ♿

Restaurant. In this very attractive place in the heart of Trastevere, you can choose between classic selections of cheeses and cured meats [all of the highest quality], terrines, and dishes of the day, assisted by courteous, professional staff. We started with an ultralight chickpea and prawn purée followed by a tasty *lasagnetta* with zucchini and buffalo mozzarella, then the duck and king prawn *spiedino* [brochette] as a main course - a very interesting combination - with a fresh melon Bavarian cream to finish off with. All the dishes were very well-executed. Among the others offered in rotation : *orecchiette* with zucchini and ginger-scented king prawns; warm rabbit salad with couscous in spicy sauce; potato pie and *baccalà* with plum

tomatoes. And the wine list? One of the most wide-ranging and comprehensive in the city, it comes complete with the labels and all the information you need to make your choice.

AL FORNO DELLA SOFFITTA
NOMENTANO
via dei Villini, 1/e
☎ 06/4404642
PINCIANO
via Piave, 62
☎ 06/42011164

- **Closed:** Sundays; [open evenings only]; in August
- **Seats:** 90
- **L.** 30,000 w/o wine
🗐 CSì, Visa

Pizzeria. People come to both these pizzerias, the original in the Nomentano neighbourhood and its offspring in Via Piave, to eat certified Neapolitan-style pizzas, served on wooden plates that vary in size according to the number of people eating together. We warmly recommend the *margherita;* the pizza with mozzarella and squash blossoms; the *fumé* [smoked provola cheese and *speck*]; and the D'Annunzio [provola, onion and chilis]. They also offer buffalo mozzarella and classic fried foods. For a perfect finish: rum babàs, *pastiera* [rich ricotta and candied fruit pie], lemon-flavoured profiteroles and delicious, flaky *sfogliatella* pastries.

FORTUNATO AL PANTHEON
CENTRO STORICO PANTHEON
via del Pantheon, 55
☎ 06/6792788

 70

- **Cucina** 42
- **Wine Cellar** 13 • **Service** 7
- **Ambience** 7 • **Bonus** 1

- **Closed:** Sundays; Aug 15-31
- **Seats:** 130
- **L.** 65,000 w/o wine
🗐 all ✳ ♣

Restaurant. Frequented by the usual crowd of journalists, politicians and businessmen, Fortunato Baldassari's restaurant is reliable and super-classical with a rather good menu that never changes. The ingredients are first class and, even more important, they're expertly handled. You can try spaghetti with clams; *gnocchi* with gorgonzola cheese; *fettuccine* with porcini mushrooms; baked turbot and potatoes, or a well-cooked fillet steak, assisted by the efficient, experienced staff. The desserts are very traditional too; the wine list is well-suited to the menu.

LA GALLINA BIANCA
TERMINI
via A. Rosmini, 5
☎ 06/4743777

- **Closed:** annual holidays vary
- **Seats:** 100
- **L.** 25,000 w/o wine
🗐 AE, CSì, Visa 🅿 ✳ ♣ ♿

EATING

Pizzeria. This spacious, informal and rather noisy pizzeria is mostly patronised by young people. You can eat various kinds of pizza - the *luna piena* [full moon], for example, with ricotta, mozzarella, parmigiano, prosciutto cotto and tomato - as well as *fritti* [fried foods]; *bruschetta;* grilled meat and vegetables; first courses, including an interesting *orecchiette* with clams and broccoletti, and good desserts, which you can enjoy with a glass of sweet wine.

GAUDÌ
PARIOLI
via R. Giovannelli, 8/12
☎ *06/8845451*

- **Closed:** Saturday and Sunday lunchtime; Easter, Christmas and New Year's Eve
- **Seats:** 160
- **L.** 30,000 w/o wine
  📖 all 🅿 ✳ ♣

Pizzeria. This spacious place is always full, and in summer people are prepared to wait a long time for a table on its marvellous terrace. The menu offers mainly various kinds of Neapolitan-style pizza, the ones with the thick puffy border: the house speciality is the Battipaglia with buffalo mozzarella and cherry tomatoes. They also

do *calzoni* [pizza turnovers]; *fritti* [various fried foods]; charcoal grilled meats; salads, and Neapolitan desserts to finish off with. We feel obliged to note, however, that over time [and probably because of its very success] the food has become a bit standardised and in some cases the quality is not exactly staggering. The service is entrusted to a group of well-intentioned youngsters who occasionally [alas] miss a beat.

GEORGE'S
PINCIANO
via Marche, 7
☎ *06/42084575*

 75

- Cucina 42 • Wine Cellar 16 • Service 8
- Ambience 9 • Bonus 0

- **Closed:** Sundays; Aug 1-31
- **Seats:** 80
- **L.** 115,000 w/o wine
  📖 all 🅿 ✳ ♣

Restaurant. Very beautiful indeed, and reassuring, with its own special brand of ageless charm, George's offers professional hospitality and courteous service. There's also a very good wine list, with just about acceptable mark-ups. The dishes are as unchanging as the ambience, very pleasant if you want to dive into the *dolce vita* atmosphere of the Sixties. We sampled a modest salmon with a good salad, *astice* [lobster] and foie gras as antipastos; followed by *mazzancolle* [king prawns] and [hot!] rice pilaf spiced with curry; a good *tagliolini* with porcini

mushrooms, and quite a good orange duck. Having rejected their remarkable soufflé because of the wait involved, we chose an almond parfait and a crème brulée for dessert. Something a little more stimulating would be nice though, especially from the kitchen, which seems just a fraction tired.

GIACOMELLI
TRIONFALE
via E. Faà di Bruno, 25
☎ *06/3725910*

- **Closed:** Mondays; in August, at Christmas
- **Seats:** 100
- **L.** 25,000 w/o wine
  📖 no 🅿 ♣ ♿

Pizzeria. A neighbourhood pizza place that's been here forever, where they serve pizzas in three different sizes on metal plates. The Margherita is still our favourite, but the Mostro [*monster*], the house speciality, is good, too. They also offer the classic repertoire of *fritti* [fried food of various kinds], *crostini, bruschetta* and a few homemade desserts. Fast service.

DA GIANNI
PRATI - MAZZINI
via G. Avezzana, 11
☎ *06/3217268*

- **Closed:** Saturday evenings and Sundays; in August
- **Seats:** 30
- **L.** 25,000 w/o wine
  📖 no 🅿 ♣

Trattoria. Better-known as the Bettoletta or Cacio & Pepe, this very straightforward place is always full, especially of young clients, because it offers generous portions of *casereccia* [family-style] dishes at genuinely low prices. First courses are their strong point, including an outstanding *tonnarelli cacio e pepe* [with pecorino cheese and black pepper], and pasta with *pesto*. There are also various side dishes, and meatloaf or fried fresh anchovies among the main courses. A few homemade desserts and coffee served *al vetro* [in tiny glasses] to finish off. The tables out on the footpath are very pleasant. Best to book.

GINO
CENTRO STORICO
CAMPO MARZIO
v.lo Rosini, 4
☎ *06/6873434*

- **Closed:** Sundays; Aug 1-31
- **Seats:** 50
- **L.** 35,000 w/o wine
  📖 no ♿

Trattoria. Signor Gino and his son Fabrizio run this cheerful rustic place where you really do breathe the atmosphere of times gone by. The dishes haven't changed in years but they're

EATING

very good: homemade *tonnarelli alla ciociara* [with meat sauce, butter and parmigiano] or *all'amatriciana;* rabbit cooked in white wine; spring lamb *alla cacciatora* [hunter-style]; Savoy cabbage roulades and, best of all, a glorious homemade *tiramisù*. The wine list is meagre – a carafe of the house Morellino is a better bet.

Good Good
APPIO
via Latina, 103
☎ 06/7800855

- **Closed:** Mondays [open evenings only]; annual holidays vary
- **Seats:** 130
- **L.** 20,000 w/o wine
🖰 AE, CSi, Visa 🅿 ✳

Pizzeria. Yes, the food is everything the name claims and it's worth pointing out just how much care has gone into creating this very successful neighbourhood pizza parlour. The place itself is luminous and attractive, the service is extremely polite, and the pizzas are well made using carefully-chosen ingredients. Don't forget to stop at the inviting-looking buffet, piled high with delicious little things – all perfectly fresh. Homemade desserts, a few good wine labels and all the beer you can drink. Don't forget to book.

Le Grotte
CENTRO STORICO · SPAGNA
via della Vite, 37
☎ 06/6784117

 70
- Cucina 42
- Wine Cellar 12 • Service 7
- Ambience 7 • Bonus 2

- **Closed:** Mondays; in August
- **Seats:** 180
- **L.** 45,000 w/o wine
🖰 all ✳ ♠

Restaurant. Dining at this *centralissimo* restaurant is even better if you sit at one of the tables they put outside in the summer and become part of the explosion of pleasure the sun sets vibrating through the city. The menu is very wide-ranging [bonus]: *focaccia* with arugola and cherry tomatoes; spaghetti with clams; risotto *alla pescatora* [fisherman-style], or black with cuttlefish ink; sea bass *all'acqua pazza* [cooked in tomato-based court bouillon]; baked turbot with potatoes and porcini mushrooms; a good fillet steak and classic pizzas that are also available at lunchtime [unusual]. Extremely polite service [bonus] and a wine list that could be more extensive.

Il Guru
MONTI
via Cimarra, 4/6
☎ 06/4744110

- **Closed:** never [open evenings only]
- **Seats:** 70
- **L.** 40,000 w/o wine
🖰 all 🅿 ✳ ♿

Indian. You'll be struck by the very tasteful decor the

moment you enter this exotic restaurant. It offers courteous hospitality, efficient service and cooking of a very high standard and Thomas, the polite, *simpatico* owner, will guide you through the labyrinths of Indian cuisine and steer you away from dangerously hot dishes if necessary. All this makes it one of the best Asian restaurants in the city. There are a number of tasting menus, while the main menu proposes specialities like tandoori and curries, a great many vegetarian dishes, traditional desserts and gelati, Indian and other beers, and a few wine labels.

'Gusto
CENTRO STORICO · CORSO
p.zza Augusto Imperatore, 9
☎ 06/3226273

 76
- Cucina 43
- Wine Cellar 16 • Service 8
- Ambience 8 • Bonus 1

- **Closed:** Mondays
- **Seats:** 700
- **L.** 75,000 w/o wine
🖰 all ✳ ♠ ♿

Restaurant. No doubt about it: the 'Gusto inauguration was the event of 1998 and not just for Romans, and since May of that year it's enjoyed an uninterrupted success with the public. Certainly, it's been hard making a place as big as this work [the complex contains a wine shop, library, wine bar and pizzeria as well as the restaurant] and it went through a difficult period at the beginning. However everything now

seems to be sorted out and the overall quality is consistently high, thanks to the work of Dario Laurenzi and his hard-working young team. The restaurant menu is original and intriguing: eggplant and chickpea strudel in a goat's milk cheese and sesame seed sauce; veal liver served with a red onion and foie gras flan; *farro* [an ancient grain] soup with smoked duck and artichokes; *tagliolini* with king prawns, asparagus and star anise; tempura-fried vegetables and king prawns; and salted lamb *carré* baked in a crust of porcini mushrooms served with a potato timbale. The couscous and wok-cooked dishes are well worth trying. Desserts include a good cheesecake with bilberry sauce, and sour cherry pie with lemon custard. The wine list, still growing, offers more than 800 wines. Booking a must.

Hamasei
CENTRO STORICO · SPAGNA
via della Mercede, 35/36
☎ 06/6792134

- **Closed:** Mondays
- **Seats:** 115
- **L.** 70,000 w/o wine
🖰 all ✳ ♿

Japanese. The Hamasei [it means Beautiful Beach],

located right in the centre of the city, is one of Rome's most reliable Japanese restaurants. They offer special lunch menus starting at L.18,000, but in the evening the menu is à la carte and the prices go up. Dishes range from classic raw fish sushi and sashimi to sukiyaki, vegetable or fish tempura, soups and various kinds of noodles. Try a *teppanyaky,* an assortment of meat, fish and vegetables that clients cook themselves on a hotplate and season with soy sauce. The sushi bar is ideal for a fast lunch.

HARRY'S BAR
PINCIANO
via Vittorio Veneto, 150
☎ *06/484643*

- Cucina 45
- Wine Cellar 15 • Service 9
- Ambience 9 • Bonus 2

- **Closed:** Sundays; Aug 15; Dec 25-26; Jan 1
- **Seats:** 40
- **L.** 115,000 w/o wine
🖻 all 🅿 ✳ 🌲

Restaurant. A restaurant with tone, more than a cut above almost all the other restaurants in Rome. It opens in the morning and closes late at night, and you can come just for a coffee, tea or aperitivo [bonus]. Warm and comfortable inside, and very pleasant outside on the veranda, it offers extremely

professional service, directed in a masterly manner by Paolo Baggini who also superintends the kitchen. Particularly good dishes include the lobster salad with valerian and zucchini in paprika sauce; the 'cahors' salad [celery, carrots, duck breast, truffles, and *pecorino* cheese in a vinaigrette dressing]; *farfalle* with zucchini, scrambled egg and bacon; risotto with king prawns and *radicchio* [red chicory] cooked in Barbera wine. Main courses: a delicious Voronoff fillet with a mustard and Armagnac dressing - a classic but always delicious; and turbot with capers. For dessert, peach mousse in Moscato wine sauce; chocolate terrines with coconut cream, and hot apple *sfogliata* pastries in vanilla sauce. There's an excellent wine list, with very fair mark-ups. A bonus for the wide range of services offered, and for the fact that it's open till late all year round.

HASEKURA
MONTI
via dei Serpenti, 27
☎ *06/483648*

- **Closed:** Sundays; Aug 1-31
- **Seats:** 42
- **L.** 55,000 w/o wine
🖻 all 🅿 ✳

Japanese. Ito Kimji, the chef, offers all the traditional culinary specialities with precisely the combination of

courtesy, care, style, energy, choreography and atmosphere they require. It all adds up to that little something extra when you compare the Hasekura with the other Japanese restaurants in Rome. Excellent soups [*soba*] with buckwheat noodles, sushi, sashimi, tempura and sukiyaki, as well as excellent steaks with Japanese sauces and *shabu shabu* – a sort of meat fondue served with cold buckwheat noodles. Tea, beer and saké to drink. Prices are rather high but there are various special menus that enable you to limit the expense.

HIMALAYA PALACE
MONTEVERDE NUOVO
c.ne Gianicolense, 277
☎ *06/5826001*

- **Closed:** Monday lunchtime
- **Seats:** 70
- **L.** 30,000 w/o wine
🖻 all 🅿 ✳ 🌲

Indian. If you've never tried Indian cuisine and think it's time you did, or if you're familiar with some dishes but would like to extend your repertoire, pay a visit to this rather good Indian restaurant. Efficiently and courteously run, it offers classical *tandoori* dishes cooked in the traditional tandoor oven. Take advantage of one of the tasting menus [vegetarian and non]

which offer a good selection of the most typical dishes. Various beverages, including an excellent *lassi* made from yoghurt; fruit-flavoured versions are also available.

IPANEMA
MONTI
via dei Capocci, 26
☎ *06/4824758*

 72

- Cucina 43
- Wine Cellar 13 • Service 7
- Ambience 7 • Bonus 2

- **Closed:** Sundays; [open evenings only]; Aug 10-31
- **Seats:** 60
- **L.** 70,000 w/o wine
🖻 all 🅿 ✳ 🕭

Restaurant. Try their huge *plateau royal,* an enormous platter of raw seafood including various shellfish, scampi, grouper and salmon - or you could just start with oysters. You may have gathered that we're about to recommend the perfect port of call for fish-lovers, the charming and attractive Ipanema.The first courses are varied and delicious and they'll advise you as to the best kind of pasta to eat with each condiment. The main courses are also good: *orata* [a kind of bream] and *spigola* [sea bass] either baked in salt crust, grilled or *all'acqua pazza* [cooked in a tomato-based court bouillon]; scampi, and shellfish cooked in various ways. The lobster *alla catalana* is the best of dish of all. There aren't many desserts, but those they have are good and rigorously handmade. The wine list is well-planned and the mark-ups are reasonable.

JASMINE
PINCIANO
via Sicilia, 47
☎ 06/42884983

- **Closed:** Tuesdays
- **Seats:** 120
- **L.** 35,000 w/o wine
🍽 all ✳

Chinese. A clue as to the quality of this restaurant comes from the number of tourists who flock here – they're all Asian. So if they like it, we said to ourselves, this must be a potential field of serious enquiry. We have to admit we also enjoy finding ourselves among clients who don't all have the same faces you see every day in Trastevere or on the Via Salaria. This modern Chinese restaurant offers quality cuisine at slightly higher than average prices. The menu offers an interesting choice of dishes, including a delicate abalone and black mushroom soup; prawns with *guoba* [toasted rice]; and grilled tofu with oyster sauce. If you order in advance you can try more elaborate dishes like Mongolian stew and Peking duck.

JEFF BLYNN'S
PARIOLI
v.le Parioli, 103/c
☎ 06/8070444

 75

- **Cucina 44**
- **Wine Cellar 14 • Service 8**
- **Ambience 8 • Bonus 1**

- **Closed:** Mondays; Sundays in summer; Christmas period
- **Seats:** 80
- **L.** 90,000 w/o wine
🍽 all ✳ ♣

Restaurant. Beautiful - this restaurant really is beautiful, and the outdoor eating area is a perfect oasis. Their most recent innovation is a sushi bar, and the Sunday brunch [you have to book] is just as good as last year [bonus]. The well-organised and efficient service is entrusted to a group of very young staff. The menu is extensive and the dishes are made with first-class ingredients [if you look closely you'll find bread costs L.5,000 per 100 grams!]. Entrèes include buffalo mozzarella; oysters; caviar; smoked fish; fried *moscardini* [baby curled octopus], and seafood salad. The first courses are not particularly exciting, whether it's the *tagliolini* with prawns, swordfish and zucchini, or the classic spaghetti with clams, but as main courses they do rather good grilled king prawns and boiled lobster, and some really succulent hamburgers. For dessert, cheesecake, 'American-style' chocolate cake and apple pie. The wine list has a number of foreign labels, but a wider choice of

Italian wines and vintages wouldn't hurt.

LEITNER
CENTRO STORICO
CAMPO MARZIO
via Uffici del Vicario, 31
☎ 06/69924022

 75

- **Cucina 42**
- **Wine Cellar 15 • Service 8**
- **Ambience 8 • Bonus 2**

- **Closed:** Sundays; annual holidays vary
- **Seats:** 120
- **L.** 95,000 w/o wine
🍽 CSi, Visa ✳ ♿

Restaurant. Risen phoenix-like from the ashes of the Porcao, this classically elegant restaurant has splendid marble inlay floors, boiserie woodwork everywhere and beautifully laid tables. The formal, efficient service is performed by youthful uniformed staff. Most of the dishes on the menu are inspired by the northern Italian tradition, Venetian in particular: puff pastry *sfogliatina* filled with shellfish, asparagus and stuffed squash blossoms; goat's-milk cheese terrines with sweet peppers, black olives and basil; spinach-green *maltagliati* with fresh sausage, peas and rosemary; ravioli stuffed with *scorfano* [scorpion fish] in cuttlefish ink with scallops and vegetables; lobster with *animelle* [pancreas and sweetbreads] and *cannellini* beans on a bed of spinach; and a rather over-glazed goose leg stuffed with foie gras and black truffles Desserts: hot apple *sfogliatina* pastries

with cinnamon sauce, and dark chocolate mousse with vanilla sauce. King size portions, and a well-chosen wine list with high-quality labels. A bonus for the business lunch menu and another for the chance to pause a while at their very beautiful bar.

LA LOCANDA
QUARTIERE AFRICANO
via Massaciuccoli, 26
☎ 06/86207499

 74

- **Cucina 44**
- **Wine Cellar 13 • Service 8**
- **Ambience 6 • Bonus 3**

- **Closed:** Mondays; annual holidays vary
- **Seats:** 65
- **L.** 45,000 w/o wine
🍽 all 🅿 ♣ ♿

Restaurant. No, we haven't gone crazy and yes, we did give a Gambero Rosso Best Value Award to this modest-looking but, in our opinion, rather special restaurant. We did it as a tribute to someone who consistently offers genuine *cucina* based on high-quality ingredients at very reasonable prices, without a lot of backing capital and despite a limited clientele; who sticks to his guns and rolls out the excellent *tagliolini*, *lasagna* and *fettuccine* himself, buys the small but excellent selection of fresh fish, makes his own *mostarda* dressing for the cheeses, prepares the desserts, presents a wine list containing several little-known but quite remarkable bottles and serves them with uncommon grace and courtesy. Reason enough, surely? And here are the dishes we tried: zucchini and shrimp timbales; cod *carpaccio* with marinated fresh anchovies; spinach-green lasagna; *tagliolini* with truffles; *mazzancolle* [king prawns] cooked in white wine; *spigola all'acqua pazza* [sea bass poached in tomato-based court bouillon]; seared beef with porcini mushrooms. The desserts are good, too: hot apple *pasticcio* [turnover]; bitter-chocolate cake with whipped cream; chocolate mousse with *zabaglione*. They also do pizzas in the evenings.

LUNA PIENA
TESTACCIO
via Luca della Robbia, 15/17
☎ 06/5750279

  70

• Cucina 42 • Wine Cellar 12 • Service 7 • Ambience 7 • Bonus 2

• **Closed:** Wednesdays; June 23-July 22
• **Seats:** 40
• **L.** 35,000 w/o wine
🕭 all ♣ ᦒ

Restaurant. This classic restaurant is one of those places you can come back

to again and again, where you eat well at very reasonable prices. Not that the cuisine is extraordinary, by any means, but it's always more than satisfactory. They offer tasty flavoursome dishes, starting with *spuntature* [pork spare ribs] and classic *rigatoni* with *pajata*. Main courses include fish [depending on what's best at the markets], *coda alla vaccinara* [oxtail braised in celery broth]; thick sliced beef *tagliata* seasoned with herbs, and grilled swordfish steaks. Well-made desserts, a choice of wines well-suited to the menu; courteous and efficient service.

MACCHERONI
CENTRO STORICO
CAMPO MARZIO
p.zza delle Coppelle, 44
☎ 06/68307895

• **Closed:** Sundays; annual holidays vary
• **Seats:** 120
• **L.** 45,000 w/o wine
🕭 all ✳ ♣ ᦒ

Trattoria. Consistently high quality food is hard to come by in Rome and unfortunately this trattoria doesn't disprove the rule. A pity, because the place is attractive, the tables out on the little piazzetta are very pleasant and the hospitality is cordial. However, the quality of the service and consequently the cuisine drops off seriously at peak hour. If you time it right you can try some good dishes:

mozzarella; prosciutto; *maccheroni alla gricia* [with black pepper and grated pecorino] or *all'amatriciana;* spaghetti with *vongole veraci* [carpet-bed clams] or cherry tomatoes and basil; steaks; rib fillets; veal roulades; chicken *alla cacciatora* [hunter-style], and *carpaccio*. Among the desserts: creme brulée, chocolate mousse and *panna cotta* [silky milk custard]. A small wine list.

MAMMA SANTA
TRIESTE
via Malta, 14
☎ 06/8551324

• **Closed:** Saturday lunchtime and Mondays; in August
• **Seats:** 70
• **L.** 45,000 w/o wine
🕭 AE, CSi, Visa ♣ ᦒ

Trattoria. Mamma Santa's is a rustic and hospitable family affair in one of the city's most beautiful quarters where the Marinelli's, husband and wife, have been offering authentic family-style cooking for a number of years now. Many of the clients are habitués. Entrées include wild boar salami, tomato and mozzarella *spiedini* [brochettes], and grilled vegetables; then: spaghetti with tomato or *all'amatriciana;* gnocchi with fresh basil kneaded into the dough; spinach-green cheese-filled *ravioloni* with sauce; brochettes of veal roulades, red chicory, porcini mushrooms and

prosciutto; *stufatino* [stew] with potatoes; grilled steaks, and tomato *parmigiana* [baked with parmigiano and mozzarella]. Homemade desserts: the best are the peach and orange *semifreddo* [soft frozen mousse] and the wild-berry cake. There's also a small wine list. Friendly, attentive service.

MARCELLO
SAN LORENZO
via dei Campani, 12
☎ 06/4463311

• **Closed:** Saturdays and Sundays; [open evenings only]; Aug 1-31
• **Seats:** 70
• **L.** 35,000 w/o wine
🕭 no Ⓟ ✳

Trattoria. Noisy, informal and a bit chaotic, this is the place to come if you want to experience an authentic neighbourhood trattoria where workers in overalls eat side-by-side with young students from the nearby university, artists from the local 'loft' community and a lot of other odd, normal, *simpatico* types. The menu is fairly extensive but the best bets are the classics like *bucatini* with cacio cheese and black pepper or *alla gricia; amatriciana;* the excellent soups of the day; *spezzatino alla cacciatora* [hunter-style stew]; the traditional *bollito alla picchiapò* [boiled meat in sauce] and roast *pajata* [milk-filled veal intestines] - all very good. The side dishes are classics too, like the tasty *cicoria ripassata* [boiled chicory quick-fried with garlic and chili]. The wine list is surprisingly good.

LA MAREMMA

PARIOLI
v.le Parioli, 93/c
☎ *06/8086002*
PINCIANO
via Alessandria, 119/d
☎ *06/8554002*

• **Closed:** Mondays; in August
• **Seats:** 160
• **L.** 30,000 w/o wine
🗀 CSi, Visa 🅿 ✳ 🌲 ♿

Pizzeria. Both eateries have the same menu and similar decor and both feed hordes of starving people. Pizzas are available in both the Roman version with thin crunchy pastry, and the Neapolitan – thicker, with a puffy ring border. The rest of the menu is the classic repertoire of *fritti* [fried foods of various kinds]; *calzoni* [pizza turnovers]; gigantic *bruschetta,* and first courses, plus a few typically Tuscan dishes. Desserts of the same order. Efficient service – so as not to keep the queuing masses waiting too long.

MASOLINO

FLAMINIO
via Masolino da Panicale, 2
☎ *06/3208366*

 72

• **Cucina** 43
• **Wine Cellar** 13 • **Service** 7
• **Ambience** 7 • **Bonus** 2

• **Closed:** Sundays; [open evenings only]; Aug 1-31
• **Seats:** 30
• **L.** 40,000 w/o wine
🗀 all 🅿 ✳ ♿ ♿

Restaurant. This small, well-run restaurant continues to be a very good place to eat. You can either opt for the tasting menu, or choose from among the dishes of the day written up on the blackboard in their simple, cosy dining room. The cuisine is light and tasty, based on carefully - and often quite creatively - prepared first-class fresh ingredients. We started with a delicious vegetable and provola cheese strudel; followed by exquisite ravioli filled with *gallinella di mare* [a kind of scorpion fish]; *tagliolini pollorcini* with chicken and porcini mushrooms; scrumptious squid with salmon mousse; and delectable veal, zucchini and *grana* cheese roulades. Homemade desserts include white chocolate mousse or eggplant *bavarese* [Bavarian cream] with dark chocolate. A bonus for the pleasant family atmosphere and another for the courtesy.

MATRICIANELLA

CENTRO STORICO
CAMPO MARZIO
via del Leone, 4
☎ *06/6832100*

 72

• **Cucina** 42
• **Wine Cellar** 14 • **Service** 7
• **Ambience** 7 • **Bonus** 2

• **Closed:** Sundays; annual holidays vary
• **Seats:** 60
• **L.** 50,000 w/o wine
🗀 all 🌲

Restaurant. Right in the centre, in the heart of the shopping district, this pleasant restaurant has two small, attractive dining rooms furnished in rustic style and a lovely outdoor dining area. We've given bonuses for the wine by the glass and the reasonable bill. It offers good solid cuisine with well-defined flavours, but not too rich. Try their *bucatini* or *rigatoni all'amatriciana,* speciality of the house, or the *fettuccine* with chicory and porcini mushrooms; good homemade *gnocchi* with tomato and basil, or rice scented with fresh aromatic herbs. Main courses include grilled fillet steak; eggplant *parmigiana* [baked with parmigiano and mozzarella]; fried lamb cutlets and brains; *animelle* [pancreas and sweetbreads] with artichokes. The menu also offers some very rich salads and all the traditional Roman dishes - starting with *pajata* [milk-filled veal intestine] and *coda alla vaccinara* [braised oxtail]. We expected a little more of the

desserts: crème caramel, strawberry *bavarese* and *tiramisù.* The wine list is full of interesting labels, including some from overseas.

IL MATRICIANO

PRATI - COLA DI RIENZO
via dei Gracchi, 55
☎ *06/3212327*

- 🔼 + 🍴 **70**

• **Cucina** 42
• **Wine Cellar** 14 • **Service** 7
• **Ambience** 7 • **Bonus** 0

• **Closed:** Saturdays in summer; Wednesdays in winter; in August; New Year's Eve
• **Seats:** 140
• **L.** 55,000 w/o wine
🗀 all ✳ 🌲

Restaurant. This is one of those restaurants where you often run into cinema or showbiz personalities and it's always the same, for better or for worse. The service is efficient without too much standing on ceremony: getting one's hands on the [quite good] wine list requires considerable persistence and they tend not to show even the menu. The dishes never change either: buffalo mozzarella or mixed fried broccoletti, squash blossoms and *supplì* [deep-fried riceballs with melted mozzarella hearts] as entrées, then their famous *bucatini* or *rigatoni all'amatriciana; tagliolini alla gricia* [with guanciale, grated pecorino and black pepper] and *fettucine* with porcini mushrooms; followed by fillets of beef, high quality fish and other classic dishes as main courses. Desserts of the same order.

LA MEDITERRANÉE
PARIOLI
*via R. Fauro, 7
[ang. via Castellini]*
☎ 06/80663694

 76

• **Cucina 44**
• **Wine Cellar 14** • **Service 8**
• **Ambience 8** • **Bonus 2**

• **Closed:** Sundays; annual holidays vary
• **Seats:** 56
• **L.** 75,000 w/o wine
🗂 all

Restaurant. Our initial enthusiam for this elegant restaurant has waned a little. There's an expert maître, and the service is extremely courteous and professional when the proprietor is present - when she's not there can be a few problems. On our last visit we sampled the lobster and black truffle salad, and the sardines and clams scented with Sicilian herbs, followed by *linguine* with shellfish, olives and sun-dried cherry tomatoes, and a delicious saffron-scented seafood soup served with *crostini* and garlic sauce. The grilled bream fillet with couscous and vegetables is delicious, and the fillets of lamb baked in pastry crust with spicy sauce betray a light and expert hand. For dessert, tarte tatin with vanilla icecream, and crème brulée with pistacchio nuts. On other occasions, however, the food was not quite up to the same standard. A bonus for the elegance and the extreme courtesy as well as the passion displayed by father and sons – neophytes still, but very skilled.

IL MELARANCIO
CENTRO STORICO - POPOLO
via del Vantaggio, 43
☎ 06/3219382

 69

• **Cucina 42**
• **Wine Cellar 12** • **Service 7**
• **Ambience 7** • **Bonus 1**

• **Closed:** never
• **Seats:** 60
• **L.** 50,000 w/o wine
🗂 no ✻ 🌲

Restaurant. In a *centralissimo* location, this restaurant offers simple, tasty cuisine in a pleasant, relaxing setting. It's frequented by a devoted clientele which gives it a rather special atmosphere: you can see that people recognise each other and feel comfortable here. Add the advantages of it being open seven days a week, with a kitchen that closes late, and polite, attentive service, *et voilà*... you realise that it has quite a lot going for it. Among the first courses: *bombolotti* with a light, well-made amatriciana sauce or tomato and basil; *fettuccine* with eggplant and zucchini, and the inky black cuttlefish *risotto* that everyone orders - and rightly so. Then baked *abbacchio* [spring lamb]; veal *involtini* with eggplant or *radicchio* [red-leafed chicory] and the Melarancio roast [with smoked provola cheese and potatoes]. The homemade desserts are good too. A few sure-bet labels to drink.

MIRÒ
CENTRO STORICO - NAVONA
via dei Banchi Nuovi, 8
☎ 06/68808527

 70

• **Cucina 43**
• **Wine Cellar 12** • **Service 7**
• **Ambience 7** • **Bonus 1**

• **Closed:** Tuesdays; annual holidays vary
• **Seats:** 100
• **L.** 45,000 w/o wine
🗂 all ✻ 🕭

Restaurant. You wouldn't think so from the outside but this restaurant is quite big, with a series of small pleasant rustic dining rooms that the particularly warm and polite hospitality offered by the owners [bonus] makes even more attractive. The menu draws inspiration from the Calabrian and Mediterranean traditions, offering a wide choice of tasty dishes. We started with marinated anchovies; spicy mussel *pepata;* potato timbales; roulades and eggplant *parmigiana* [baked with tomato, parmigiano and mozzarella]; Calabrian cured meats and *sottoli* [vegetables preserved in oil]; followed by tasty first courses including *gnocchetti alla 'nduja* [with peppery fresh sausage]; *pappardelle* with swordfish, and spaghetti *allo scoglio* [with seafood]. As main courses, fresh Calabrian sausage; brochettes, and fish in particular, stuffed squid and swordfish roulades. For dessert, rum babàs with limoncello liquor; Sicilian *cassata* and *cannoli* [rich, flaky pastry tubes filled with pastry cream and candied fruit] and Calabrian ice cream. The wine list is small and lacks good vintages and producers. Pizzas are available in the evenings.

MONSERRATO
CENTRO STORICO
CAMPO DE' FIORI
via Monserrato, 96
☎ 06/6873386

 71

• **Cucina 43**
• **Wine Cellar 12** • **Service 7**
• **Ambience 7** • **Bonus 2**

• **Closed:** Mondays; in August; at Christmas
• **Seats:** 50
• **L.** 50,000 w/o wine
🗂 all 🌲 🕭

Restaurant. Visitors are often warned that the centre of Rome is lined with tourist traps for the hungry and unwary and in part it's true, though the situation is improving. All the more reason to point out restaurants like this one which serve consistently high quality cuisine [and to reconfirm last year's bonus]. The meat dishes are good and the fish even better. As entrées, swordfish *carpaccio;* cuttlefish salad or sautéd clams and mussels. Homemade pastas to follow: *bigoli* with shrimps and asparagus tips; *gnocchi* with clams; *fettuccine allo scoglio* [with seafood] and excellent *bombolotti* with lobster. Main courses include baked turbot and potatoes; *mazzancolle* [king prawns] cooked in wine; various grilled or roast fish like sea bass and bream, and a good fillet steak. Homemade desserts. A reasonably-priced wine list; courteous, attentive service, and a splendid outdoor dining area in the summer.

MONTE CARUSO
ESQUILINO
via Farini, 12
☎ 06/483549

 74

* Cucina 44
* Wine Cellar 14 • Service 8
* Ambience 7 • Bonus 1

• **Closed:** Sundays and Monday lunchtime; Aug 1-31
• **Seats:** 40
• **L.** 65,000 w/o wine
🍴 all **ⓟ ✳**

Restaurant. This restaurant has always been one of *the* places to come for Lucanian cooking and offers a wide selection of dishes,

classics and otherwise, in pleasant, elegant but unpretentious surroundings. Next to the more 'normal' first courses like *vermicelli* with cacio cheese and pepper, you'll find regional specialities like *orecchiette* [little pasta ears] in *ragù* sauce, *cataurogni,* and *ciabatte favolose.* Main courses include zucchini stuffed with mozzarella; and Lucanian specialities with fanciful names like *pezze pazze, giù-giù* and *sette veleni.* The homemade bread is excellent and don't, whatever you do, miss the profiteroles. The sauce-drenched gelatos, and the *stregone* with Strega liquor are good, too. A bonus for the two tasting menus, the *dell'amicizia* [friendship] at L.65,000 and the *gran menu degustazione* at L.75,000. Attentive service, and a wine list of appropriate range and quality.

LA MONTECARLO
CENTRO STORICO - NAVONA
vicolo Savelli, 12
☎ 06/6861877

• **Closed:** Aug 1-15
• **Seats:** 100
• **L.** 20,000 w/o wine
🍴 no **✳ ♣ ♿**

Pizzeria. With its tables lining the street ouside in summer, this pizzeria is like a lively anthill, where the cheerful, laughing diners already seated seem happily oblivious to the groups of hopefuls standing around waiting their turn. The service is

fast and friendly but the queueing that the Montecarlo's obvious popularity makes inevitable can be a bit wearing, and it's much the same story in winter. When you finally get your table you remember why you bothered – their pizzas are excellent and very low-priced. Apart from pizzas, they also do excellent mixed *bruschetta, supplì,* a few fried dishes and roast vegetables.

MONTI
ESQUILINO
via di S. Vito, 13
☎ 06/4466573

  71

* Cucina 42
* Wine Cellar 13 • Service 7
* Ambience 7 • Bonus 2

• **Closed:** Tuesdays; Aug 1-31, Christmas and Easter
• **Seats:** 50
• **L.** 50,000 w/o wine
🍴 all **ⓟ ✳**

Restaurant. Brothers Enrico and Sandro offer good, reasonably-priced food in comfortable surroundings at this classically family-run restaurant [Mamma Franca is in the kitchen]. The menu is equally divided between dishes from Lazio and dishes from Le Marche, all very tasty and served in generous portions. Fried olives and *ciauscolo* [typical *marchigiana* sausage] as antipasti, and don't miss the *tortelli* [vegetable and ricotta-filled ravioli] tossed in egg yolk and white Acqualagna truffles, in season; or the *tagliatelle* with porcini mushrooms, and *minestra al sacco.* Other

appetising dishes include fried brains and artichokes; spring lamb cutlets; beef shank cooked in red wine, and roast *baccalà* [dried salt cod]. The desserts are very tasty and there's a good, though not enormous, wine list.

LA MORA
NEMORENSE
p.zza Crati, 13
☎ 06/86206613

• **Closed:** Tuesdays; annual holidays vary
• **Seats:** 60
• **L.** 25,000 w/o wine
🍴 all **✳ ♣**

Pizzeria. La Mora offers the same consistently high quality, reasonable prices and efficient service as when last we came. Good pizzas, especially the Tuscan *ciaccino* [focaccia stuffed with provola cheese and *lonzino* – cured pork] but also the ones topped with onions; chicory and sausage, or *gorgonzola* cheese and eggplant. They also serve supplì and various fried foods as well as good fillet steaks and truly delicious *fagioli all'uccelletto* [beans cooked in tomato, sage and garlic]. Very satisfactory desserts to finish off with: pastry cream and pinenut cake; strawberry cake; apple cake; crème caramel, and *panna* cotta [silky milk custard].

MYOSOTIS

CENTRO STORICO
CAMPO MARZIO
v.lo della Vaccarella, 3/5
☎ 06/6865554

 ❚ **73**

- Cucina 43
- Wine Cellar 15 • Service 7
- Ambience 7 • Bonus 1

- **Closed:** Sundays; in August
- **Seats:** 90
- **L.** 60,000 w/o wine
▨ all ✳ ᵶ

Restaurant. Two years on it's hard to say whether opening the second Myosotis was a wise move or not - neither of them seem to be in very good shape at the moment. This one, in the centre, suffers somewhat from the coldness of the setting and the rather slack service, not to mention the excessive cordialty of the owner which can verge on downright intrusiveness. As far as the cooking is concerned, we definitely prefer the meat dishes, made with first class ingredients. On our last visit we tried the creamed chickpea and porcini mushroom soup; gnocchi *al Morellino di Scansano* [a Tuscan wine]; a splendid thick *fiorentina* T-bone steak; veal *animelle* [pancreas and sweetbreads] and *rognoncini* [kidneys]; and finished off with lemon sorbet and

wild strawberries. The wine list is still a good one and the reasonable mark-ups warrant a bonus.

DA NATALINO E FIGLI

TRASTEVERE
c.ne Gianicolense, 2
☎ 06/5812020

- **Closed:** Wednesdays; Sept 20-30
- **Seats:** 100
- **L.** 25,000 w/o wine
▨ all ℗ ✳ ♣

Pizzeria. If you're looking for a good Roman-style thin crust pizza cooked in a wood-fired oven, Natalino's pizzeria is one to bear in mind. Directly opposite Termini Station, it's an unassuming place but always reliable. Apart from pizzas, they also offer the classic repertiore of *focaccia, bruschetta, supplì, crochette* and *calzoni;* a choice of first courses [like fisherman-style spaghetti *alla pescatora* baked in parchment], as well as meat and fish dishes. Fast, courteous service. Beer and a few rather good bottles of wine to drink.

LA NINFA DE L'HOTEL MAJESTIC

PINCIANO
via Vittorio Veneto, 54
☎ 06/42010693

 ❚ **73**

- Cucina 42
- Wine Cellar 12 • Service 8
- Ambience 8 • Bonus 3

- **Closed:** never
- **Seats:** 50
- **L.** 60,000 w/o wine
▨ all ℗ ✳

Restaurant. Beautiful. Elegant. Comfortable. Come

here any time between 11 in the morning and 1am, after the theatre – it's always a good idea, because you'll be greeted and served with polite professionalism, you can drink a good wine from a small but well-chosen wine list, well-suited to the menu, and you can relax quietly in maximum comfort even though the tone is deliberately simple [they use tablemats instead of tablecloths, but they're beautiful tablemats!] A lean but appealing menu - interesting salads, sandwiches and hamburgers; a choice of first courses - we sampled a very good spaghettini with shrimps tossed in cuttlefish ink, and an impeccable *amatriciana;* and light, appetizing main courses like the perfectly cooked salmon, and steak with sweet peppers [idem]. The desserts are of an equally high standard: *tarte tatin* with vanilla gelato, Sacher torte, and fruit tart [the latter not exceptional]. We've awarded a big bonus for the fact that it's open 7 days a week, 365 days a year, with the opening hours noted above.

NINO

CENTRO STORICO - SPAGNA
via Borgognona, 11
☎ 06/6795676

 ❚ **73**

- Cucina 43
- Wine Cellar 14 • Service 7
- Ambience 7 • Bonus 2

- **Closed:** Sundays; Aug 1-31
- **Seats:** 90
- **L.** 65,000 w/o wine
▨ all ✳ ᵶ

Restaurant. One of the centre's most reliable restaurants, in the heart of the shopping district, it's decorated in plain, classical dark wood and the service is efficient and courteous. The menu offers a number of tried and true specialities: with black truffles; bean soup; rib eye fillet *all'arrabbiata;* grilled *hascé di filetto* [chopped fillet steak], but also a few interesting alternatives like zucchini timbales or risotto with squash blossoms. Desserts include apple and pinenut cake, and the traditional *castagnaccio* [a soft pastry made of chestnut flour, pinenuts and sultanas]. The wine list complements the food well.

DA OIO A CASA MIA

TESTACCIO
via N. Galvani, 43/45
☎ 06/5782680

- **Closed:** Sundays; annual holidays vary
- **Seats:** 65
- **L.** 45,000 w/o wine
▨ all ℗ ♣ ᵶ

Trattoria. Though it's one of the most recently opened of its kind, this trattoria has rapidly become one of the most successful, so booking is a must. It serves mostly traditional Roman dishes. For appetisers, *nervetti* [strips of cartilage], tongue and beans; then *rigatoni* with *pajata* [milk-filled veal intestines]; *minestra di arzilla* [skate soup]; *tagliolini cacio e pepe* [with pecorino cheese and black pepper]; excellent pan-fried *animelle* [pancreas and sweetbreads]; baked spring lamb, and classic tripe. The desserts are a bit banal but not bad, the best is a very good version of crème caramel. House wine and not much more to wash it all down.

Oliphant

CENTRO STORICO
PANTHEON
via delle Coppelle, 31
☎ *06/6861416*

- **Closed:** Saturday and Sunday lunchtime in summer; Aug 5, Dec 25
- **Seats:** 130
- **L.** 40,000 w/o wine

AE, CSi, Visa ✻ ♿

Mexican and North American. We always enjoy coming to this place with its Yankee atmosphere and its wooden tables and benches, TV, jukebox and background music. There's always a huge variety of cocktails, a lot of American beers and good Tex Mex cuisine: spicy chicken wings in *gorgonzola* cheese and BBQ sauce; hot corncobs dripping melted butter; hot dogs; a variety of burgers like the "Lonestar" [225 grams of meat seasoned with BBQ sauce]; tacos [you can fill them yourself]; fajitas; nachos; quesadilla; spare ribs; fried chicken guacamole; wild-berry cheese cake, chocolate pudding with ice cream and hot chocolate. Two praiseworthy children's menus. Fast, polite service.

L'Ortica

CORSO FRANCIA
via Flaminia Vecchia, 573
☎ *06/3338709*

79

- Cucina 47
- Wine Cellar 14 • Service 8
- Ambience 8 • Bonus 2

- **Closed:** open evenings only except Sundays; in August
- **Seats:** 50
- **L.** 90,000 w/o wine

all Ⓟ ♿

Restaurant. Vittorio Virno really loves this restaurant of his and now he has further expanded it and added a new menu called "L'Ortica per due", especially for young [well, more or less] couples at very reasonable prices [bonus]. Classic scrumptious starters: buffalo mozzarella; vegetable *cianfotta* [ragout]; pizza with escarole; deep-fried *pizzelle;* then *linguine rosecarielle* [well-browned and crispy] with Gaeta olives, capers and sweet peppers; *stroncatura;* an anchovy-flavored mixture of different broken-up pastas; octopus *arreganato* [flavoured with fresh origano] but also tasty meat dishes like *granatine dopo il mare* [tiny basil and mozzarella-filled meatballs] served with a green tomato salad; lamb with *papacelle* [sweet peppers]; and for dessert, an excellent *torta caprese* [chocolate and almond cake]; *pasticciotto* made with short pastry, custard and sour cherries; choux pastries, and rum babàs. The wine list no longer offers only Campanian wines; the service is always efficient and courteous. Another bonus for the passion, the setting and the attention devoted to the clients. You won't regret the expense.

Osteria ai Mercati

OSTIENSE
p.zza del Gazometro, 1
☎ *06/5743091*

- **Closed:** Saturday lunchtime; annual holidays vary
- **Seats:** 40
- **L.** 40,000 w/o wine

all ✻

Trattoria. You go down a few steps to enter this little place where the welcome is warm and the service polite. There are two dining rooms, and the tables are comfortable, if a bit close together. The menu offers meat and fish dishes, mostly satisfactory except for some heavy-handed seasoning here and there. For starters, various kinds of *bruschetta* or smoked salmon with arugula; then spaghetti with tomatoes or clams; *rigatoni* with *pajata* [milk-filled veal intestines]; *culurgiones* [big Sardinian ravioli]; *cecamariti* [corkscrew-shaped pasta], or soups - the *sirena* with pasta and fish is not at all bad. Main courses: squid or king prawn brochettes; various kinds of *scaloppine; rognone* [kidneys] with mushrooms; fillets of pork with porcini mushrooms and chestnuts, or lavish salads. Homemade desserts to finish off; a minimal wine list.

Osteria Antichi Sapori da Leo

BOCCEA
via Aurelia, 366
☎ *06/6627014*

- **Closed:** Sundays; in August
- **Seats:** 30
- **L.** 25,000 w/o wine

no ✻ ♿

Trattoria. A smallish rustic dining room, pleasant family-style hospitality and *cucina casereccia* [home cooking] at very reasonable prices are the salient characteristics of this Osteria near Piazza Irnerio. They offer a L.15,000 lunch menu and two evening tasting menus at L.20,000 and L.25,000 all included. *Bruschetta* with tomato or *ricotta forte* [ripened soft cheese]; *caponata* [eggplant, onion, tomato, anchovies, olives and pinenuts];

Sardinian *gnocchetti* with smoked provola cheese and zucchini; *farfalle* with arugula pesto; *rigatoni all'amatriciana;* fried meatballs with tomato cubes; eggplant roulades; turkey and potato stew; *tiramisù* and crème brulée. House wine and a few Apulian labels to drink, and coffee served *al vetro* [in tiny glasses] to finish off with. Best to book in the evenings.

OSTERIA DEL VELODROMO VECCHIO

TUSCOLANO
via Genzano, 139
☎ 06/7886793

- **Closed:** Sundays; Dec 23-Jan 2
- **Seats:** 36
- **L.** 40,000 w/o wine
CSi, Visa 🅿 ♣ ♿

Trattoria. We're very pleased with ourselves for having discovered this unpretentious trattoria that offers high quality food in a particularly pleasant context. Alessandra in the dining room with her politeness and her gentle smile will help you order dishes prepared by Matteo, her capable consort. The menu varies with the seasons and the markets, so we're mentioning the pasta with potatoes; *bucatini all'amatriciana;* country-style *involtini,* and coda

alla vaccinara [braised oxtail] just to whet your curiosity. On the appointed days [Tuesdays and Fridays] they also have fresh fish. Don't miss the homemade desserts, always a welcome surprise, and there's also an intelligently planned wine list, offering very good value for money. What more can we say? If only there were more places like this...

OSTERIA DELL'ANGELO

TRIONFALE
via G. Bettolo, 24
☎ 06/3729470

- **Closed:** Sundays; open evenings only except Tues and Fri; in August, at Christmas
- **Seats:** 52
- **L.** 35,000 w/o wine
no ♣ ♿

Trattoria. Two noisy dining rooms with wooden tables and paper napkins where traditional Roman dishes with a few seasonal variations are served. The service is not exactly white-glove, and the host's rather brusque welcome can be a little off-putting but the atmosphere is as pleasant as it's informal. Depending on the day you'll find *rigatoni all'amatriciana;* their legendary *tonnarelli cacio e pepe;* skate and broccoli *minestra* [soup]; *gnocchi;* and *spezzatino alla picchiapò* or meat stew without a lot of meat, but the *scarpetta* at the end - soaking up what's left of the sauce with

a piece of bread - is a real pleasure. They also do *baccalà;* wonderful-smelling tripe; and *coda alla vaccinara* [braised oxtail]. Wine or aniseed-flavoured *ciambelline* [ring-shaped biscuits] with sweet dessert wine to finish off with. There's a fixed-price, all-included menu in the evenings, but not at lunchtime. Booking essential.

OSTERIA DELL'INGEGNO

CENTRO STORICO
CAMPO MARZIO
p.zza di Pietra, 45
☎ 06/6780662

 70

- **Cucina 41**
- **Wine Cellar 13** • **Service 7**
- **Ambience 7** • **Bonus 2**

- **Closed:** Sundays; in August
- **Seats:** 50
- **L.** 50,000 w/o wine
all ✳ ♣ ♿

Restaurant. This restaurant has an enviable position in one of Rome's prettiest piazzas, now a pedestrians-only zone. The interior is a delight, too, from the big counter at the entrance to the little tables. Very crowded, especially at lunchtime because of the various high-powered offices located nearby, the Osteria offers an intriguing menu though with rather uneven results. Apart from the salads, there's a good cured horsemeat *bresaola* served with pear and arugula; fresh salmon marinated in citrus fruit and ginger; *pasta incasciata* Sicilian-style with eggplant; *farfalle* with zucchini,

squash blossoms and buffalo mozzarella; rabbit stewed in white wine and olives, and bream fillets poached in tomatoes, capers and fresh herbs. A bonus for the wine available by the glass; the wine list itself is rather good. Polite and attentive service.

OSTRICHE A COLAZIONE

TRASTEVERE
via dei Vascellari, 21
☎ 06/5898896

 74

- **Cucina 44**
- **Wine Cellar 13** • **Service 8**
- **Ambience 8** • **Bonus 1**

- **Closed:** Sundays and Mondays; [open evenings only]; Aug 1-31
- **Seats:** 40
- **L.** 100,000 w/o wine
AE, CSi, Visa 🅿 ✳ ♣ ♿

Restaurant. We think this pleasant, tranquil and rather elegant place deserves greater success. The welcome is particularly polite and the service is attentive and professional. The cuisine, based exclusively on first-class fish, is light, balanced and rather good - apart from an occasional lapse with cooking times. As appetisers, we sampled the marinated grouper with orange; swordfish with thyme and vinegar; cod with tartare sauce; raw scampi and marinated anchovies. They also do good shellfish and hot sautès. We proceeded with *penne* and sardines; classic spaghetti with clams; seabass baked in salt crust; shrimps poached in Verduzzo wine, and lobsters with cheese and lettuce. From among the few desserts offered we opted for an unexciting chocolate cake and a *millefoglie* filled with wild berries. The wine list could be improved.

PAPÀ BACCUS
PINCIANO
via Toscana, 36
☎ *06/42742808*

 78

- **Cucina 46**
- **Wine Cellar 15 • Service 8**
- **Ambience 7 • Bonus 2**

- **Closed:** Saturday lunchtime and Sundays; Aug 10-20; Dec 24-Jan 7
- **Seats:** 60
- **L.** 65,000 w/o wine
🛇 all 🅿 ✳ ♣

Restaurant. This restaurant continues to be one of the best for traditional Tuscan fare, with particularly good meat dishes [bonus], though anyone wanting to eat first-class fresh fish in the centre of Rome can rest assured they'll find it here, prepared in highly original ways. We tried three memorable fish dishes: the *zuppetta Calafuria* [a fish soup], the octopus *soppressata* [cured

sausage], and a splendid turbot with potatoes. However, if you want to sample some more typical Tuscan cooking, try their authentic *fiorentina di carne chianina* [thick premium rare steak]; splendid cured meats and *crostini*; *acquacotta* [egg and vegetable soup]; *ribollita* [Tuscan cabbage and bread soup]; excellent homemade pastas and so on down to the traditional *cantuccini* biscuits to dip into sweet Vin Santo wine. Fast, polite, professional service as befits their numerous business clientele; a few outdoor tables in summer and a dining room reserved for non-smokers [another bonus]. Excellent desserts served from a trolley and a good wine list with various national and foreign labels at reasonable prices.

AL PARADISO
CENTRO STORICO
ARGENTINA
via Monterone, 14/b
☎ *06/68801687*

- **Closed:** never
- **Seats:** 110
- **L.** 30,000 w/o wine
🛇 all ✳ ♣

Chinese. Better than average Chinese cuisine, with a particularly good Peking duck, one of the specialities of the house, served with all sorts of crepes, vegetables and sauces, and for once you don't have to order it in advance. Other interesting dishes include frogs' legs and king prawns in *jiao yan* [salt and pepper] or ginger

sauce. Polite, efficient service overseen by the owner.

PARIS
TRASTEVERE
p.zza S. Calisto, 7/a
☎ *06/5815378*

 75

- **Cucina 44**
- **Wine Cellar 16 • Service 7**
- **Ambience 7 • Bonus 1**

- **Closed:** Sunday evenings and Mondays; in August
- **Seats:** 90
- **L.** 65,000 w/o wine
🛇 all ✳ ♣ 👤

Restaurant. This restaurant in Trastevere, one of Rome's most characteristic old quarters, run by husband-and-wife Dario and Iole Cappellanti, has a long-standing reputation of being a good place to sample simple, traditional Roman dishes, as well as fish. They offer very good versions of homemade *bresaola* [lean cured beef]; *gran fritto* [mixed fried meat, fish and vegetables], which can be a bit on the heavy side; *pasta e ceci* [chickpea and pasta soup]; *tagliolini* with scampi and squash blossoms; tasty pan-fried *pajatina* [milk-filled veal intestines]; *coda alla vaccinara* [oxtail braised with celery] as well as baked fish of the day. The dessert department could be improved and sometimes the service is a trifle

slow, but there's a good wine list that enables diners to pair dishes with suitable wines.

PAULINE BORGHESE DE L'HOTEL PARCO DEI PRINCIPI
PARIOLI
via G. B. Pergolesi, 2
☎ *06/854421*

 75

- **Cucina 43**
- **Wine Cellar 14 • Service 9**
- **Ambience 8 • Bonus 1**

- **Closed:** never
- **Seats:** 60
- **L.** 115,000 w/o wine
🛇 all 🅿 ✳ 👤

Restaurant. Immersed in greenery, this elegant restaurant at the Hotel Parco dei Principi opposite the Villa Borghese gardens has recently been given a new lease of life by excellent chef Roberto Antonelli. The menu offers light, skilfully executed dishes with a strong Mediterranean influence, often based on unusual combinations of ingredients. There are two menus: the Roman Menu [L.95,000] and the Tasting Menu [L.120,000]: duck terrine with green apple salad; petals of veal in Castelmagno cheese and acacia honey with a white turnip salad; *tonnarelli* in skate and coriander sauce; *cavatelli* with asparagus tips, zucchini and shrimp; stuffed squid served with a mint-flavoured mixed legume couscous; mustard seed-sprinkled lamb carré served with potato *millefoglie* and sun-dried tomatoes. For dessert, basil-scented lemon terrine with wild berry sorbet, and bitter chocolate *sfoglia* [rich flaky pastries] with a banana and rum mousse. The wine list is not yet of quite the same standard as the food; the service is attentive and impeccable. Sunday brunch [bonus].

LA PENNA D'OCA

CENTRO STORICO - POPOLO
via della Penna, 53
☎ 06/3202898

 72

- Cucina 42
- Wine Cellar 14 • Service 7
- Ambience 7 • Bonus 2

- **Closed:** Sundays; in August
- **Seats:** 35
- **L.** 65,000 w/o wine
  ⬛ all ✳ ♣ ♿

Restaurant. Taken over little more than a year ago by Francesco Tola, who has considerable experience gained in some of Rome's most prestigious eateries, this attractive restaurant right in the centre of the city is a decidedly interesting place. The service and hospitality both merit bonuses, and so does the very pleasant outdoor dining area. The wine list is ample and well-designed,

and also offers half-bottles and dessert wines by the glass, while the food menu offers rather good meat and fish dishes. We sampled the *triglia* [red mullet] marinated in thyme and rosemary; shellfish timbale with zucchini, red onions and marjoram; brown rice with celery and *bottarga di muggine* [dried mullet roe]; Portofino spaghetti with clams, mussels, squid and vegetables [not entirely convincing]; Neapolitan-style baby octopus in white wine, and very good grilled lamb cutlets. For dessert, an eyecatching vanilla soufflé with hot chocolate and vanilla sauce, and Neapolitan rum babàs with hot pastry cream, rum and sour cherries.

LA PENTOLA D'ORO

TRIONFALE
via Rodi, 16
☎ 06/39743393

 71

- Cucina 43
- Wine Cellar 12 • Service 7
- Ambience 7 • Bonus 2

- **Closed:** Sundays and Mondays; Aug 1-31
- **Seats:** 34
- **L.** 55,000 w/o wine
  ⬛ CSi, Visa ℗ ✳ ♿

Restaurant. Selvaggia Rispoli offers seafood cuisine with a strong Neapolitan influence, including succulent sautéd clams and mussels; marinated swordfish; tasty seafood salads with octopus, and squid *alla luciana* [cooked with tomato, garlic and chili]. The house speciality is the absolutely wonderful *tonnarelli*

all'imperiale with mussels, clams, shrimps, king prawns, mantis prawns, scampi and fresh tomatoes. Alternatively, *penne* with shrimps and mussels; shellfish poached with tomato and herbs, and other fish of the day cooked to order. Homemade desserts. The wine cellar contains mostly wines from the Campania region. Cordial, family-style service; booking a must.

PEPE VERDE

TRIESTE
v.le Gorizia, 38
☎ 06/85301181

- **Closed:** Mondays; [open evenings only]; in December
- **Seats:** 120
- **L.** 25,000 w/o wine
  ⬛ all ℗ ✳ ♿

Pizzeria. Pizzas are definitely the main attraction, but this spacious, pleasant place also offers other possibilities, starting with tasty fried antipastos and good first course dishes. Then there's the classic repertoire of *bruschetta,* salads and various traditional pizzas [also take-away] like the Amalfi [with buffalo mozzarella, cherry tomatoes and arugula], the Rapallo [mozzarella, red chicory, creamy Stracchino cheese and mushrooms] and many others, among them the

house speciality, pizza Pepe Verde. Well-made desserts; the service is fast and always polite.

LA PERGOLA DE L'HOTEL ROME CAVALIERI HILTON

BALDUINA
via A. Cadlolo, 101
☎ 06/35091

⬛ 📶 ▨▨▨ **90**

- Cucina 49
- Wine Cellar 19 • Service 9
- Ambience 9 • Bonus 4

- **Closed:** Sundays and Mondays; [open evenings only]; Jan 1-31
- **Seats:** 60
- **L.** 170,000 w/o wine
  ⬛ all ℗ ✳ ♣ ♿

Restaurant. This is the second year in a row that we have awarded the Pergola our highest rating. The restaurant seems to have gone through a period of adjustment which could explain why some of our recent visits have not been entirely satisfactory. On one occasion, after magnificent medallions of fried grouper; marinated mussels; anchovies, cherry tomatoes and salmon paté, a very nearly over-cooked spaghetti with scorpion fish, zucchini and sweet peppers appeared. On another visit we waited twenty minutes for our coffee which eventually arrived minus the sugar and warmer-lid. Certainly, since Heinz Beck is a great chef passionately devoted to his work, authentic marvels of exquisitely balanced flavours and technique like the turbot baked in salt crust on a bed of cherry tomatoes, or the stupendous salmon and wild rice patties served with vinaigrette-drizzled oysters and greens will also appear on your table. Beck's cuisine is based on the use of exceptionally fresh first class ingredients, which allow him to prepare wonderful dishes like *garganelli* with mushrooms, quail and asparagus; finely-sliced tuna on a bed of tomato and basil; shellfish and lobster consommé; veal medallions served on potato rösti with sweet pepper quenelles. On the other hand, you could order the squab baked in filo pastry and be disappointed, but it could just be a bad day or the uncertain hand of an assistant. The La Pergola coffee mousse, the tiny biscuits and pastries and the after-dinner chocolates are exceptionally good. The wine list is one of the best and most ambitious in Italy; the service ranges from perfection [almost always] to inattention [rare]. The restaurant also boasts one of the most breath-taking panoramas to be found in Rome. Tasting menus at L.160,000 and L.180,000.

40

IL PERISTILIO
PRATI - MAZZINI
via Col di Lana, 6/b
☎ 06/32649022

 74

- Cucina 43
- Wine Cellar 14 • Service 8
- Ambience 8 • Bonus 1

- **Closed:** Mondays; Aug 1-31
- **Seats:** 250
- **L.** 75,000 w/o wine
🖾 all ✳

Restaurant. Everything about this restaurant breathes serene reassurance. You won't find flights of fancy or a tendency to run risks, but sometimes a clear sense of direction is important and here you have it. Comfortable and relaxing, with extremely courteous service and beautifully - laid tables, it's the ideal place for a business dinner or an anniversary celebration, but also for a romantic tryst. Antipasti include lobster salad with string beans and tomatoes; raw meat and ricotta roulades. We followed them with *bavette* with scampi and zucchini, and saffron-scented risotto with lobster, mozzarella and tomato; then turbot with artichokes, fillet steak cooked in herbs, and duck breast. For dessert, *tiramisù* and Grand Marnier *semifreddo* [soft frozen mousse]. The wine list is more than satisfactory. A bonus for the courtesy and the atmosphere.

PI.GRI. DI RODI
TRIONFALE
via Rodi, 18/a
☎ 06/39726743

- **Closed:** in August
- **Seats:** 170
- **L.** 30,000 w/o wine
🖾 all ❷ ✳ ♿

Pizzeria. While you're waiting for the pizza... as it says on the menu, you can sample their excellent hand-sliced *prosciutto crudo* and buffalo mozzarella, then the mixed fries - mostly *crocchette* and *olive ascolane* [deep-fried stuffed olives]. On, then, to all you can eat of every conceivable kind of pizza, from the classics to the *Principessa* [tomato, mozzarella, asparagus and artichokes] or the *Indiavolata* [melted scamorza cheese, fresh sausage, *gorgonzola* and sweet peppers]. For those who prefer more, shall we say, significant and substantial dishes they also offer excellent grilled meat [*fiorentina* T-bones, fillet steak, sirloin, spring lamb], first course dishes and classic desserts. The wine list offers a limited choice but at reasonable prices.

PIPERNO
CENTRO STORICO - GHETTO
Monte de' Cenci, 9
☎ 06/68806629

 70

- Cucina 42
- Wine Cellar 13 • Service 7
- Ambience 8 • Bonus 0

- **Closed:** Sunday evenings and Mondays; Aug 1-31; main public holidays
- **Seats:** 100
- **L.** 85,000 w/o wine
🖾 all ✳ ⛾ ♿

Restaurant. This restaurant enjoys a solid reputation despite the fact that the menu as a whole seems to have gone a little flat. The house specialities are always the same: whole fried artichokes *alla giudia;* fillets of *baccalà;* squash blossoms stuffed with mozzarella and anchovies; the classic *carbonara; gnocchi al ragù* and *pasta e ceci.* Main courses include tripe, *coda* [oxtail] and *abbacchio* [spring lamb] but also some rather good fish dishes. The dessert speciality is called "grandpa's balls" [*palle del nonno*] – made of ricotta cheese. The wine list could benefit from a little attention; the service is efficient.

PIZZA CIRO
CENTRO STORICO - SPAGNA
via della Mercede, 43/45
☎ 06/6786015

- **Closed:** never
- **Seats:** 150
- **L.** 30,000 w/o wine
🖾 all ✳ ♿

Pizzeria. Located right in the centre of the city, with several dining rooms, this pizzeria is unusual because it's open right through the day and all year round. Their pizzas are the Neapolitan variety, with thick crusts and high puffy borders, like the Coscienza topped with mushrooms, mozzarella, peas and salami, or the eight-flavoured Otto Gusti: tomato, mozzarella, mushrooms, cheese, *prosciutto,* baby artichokes and shellfish. They also do *calzoni* [pizza turnovers], *pizzicotti* [a kind of *panino* made with pizza pastry], various kinds of fries, first courses, charcoal grilled meats and several salads. Neapolitan desserts and gelati to finish off.

PizzaRé

CENTRO STORICO - POPOLO
via di Ripetta, 14
☎ *06/3211468*
PRATI - MAZZINI
via Oslavia, 39
☎ *06/3721173*

- **Closed:** in August
- **Seats:** 70
- **L.** 25,000 w/o wine
🖃 all ✽ ⅁

Pizzeria. One of the best Neapolitan-style pizzas in the city, and it's worth the inevitable queuing [especially in the evening] to get a table. The only real problem is choosing between them all, but we'd argue for the undeniable merits of their traditional *calzone* [filled with tomato, mozzarella and *prosciutto cotto*] and the classic pizza Margherita. Try the *frittura mista* [deep-fried bites of meat, fish and vegetables], it's well worth it, especially if you get there early; otherwise one of the rich

salads, *pagnottielli* [pizza sandwiches] or meat dishes. Neapolitan desserts to finish off with. Their branch in Prati is not as good as the original in Via di Ripetta.

Dar Poeta

TRASTEVERE
vicolo del Bologna, 45
☎ *06/5880516*

- **Closed:** Mondays; [open evenings only];
- **Seats:** 70
- **L.** 20,000 w/o wine
🖃 AE, CSi, Visa ✽

Pizzeria. Located in the heart of Trastevere, the ambience is relaxed and *simpatico* and the expertly made pizzas are available in both the thin-crust Roman *bassa* style and the Neapolitan *alta* version with thick high borders. Numerous varieties: Campagnola, Salmone, Bodrilla... as well as *bruschetta, calzoni* and so on. The desserts are also good [don't miss out on the one with ricotta and Nutella].

Poldo e Margherita

FLAMINIO
via G. Sacconi, 53
☎ *06/3220218*

- **Closed:** Monday evenings, Sat and Sun lunchtimes; in August
- **Seats:** 100
- **L.** 30,000 w/o wine
🖃 CSi, Visa ✽ ♣

Pizzeria. High quality food and courteous service place this pleasant neighbourhood pizzeria a cut or two above the rest. The wide-ranging menu

offers classics like *bruschetta* and *fritti* [fried foods], smorgasbord salads and a variety of hamburgers: chicken, turkey, beef, pork and the Poldo special. They also serve pizzas - of course - both *pizze alte,* with thick, puffy pastry borders [for a minimum of two people] and the thin-crust *pizze basse,* and there's an *Angolo della leggerezza* [Lightweights' Corner] where you can find soy-flour pizzas, grilled meat and desserts made with fructose. This time we tried the plain *pizza bianca* with vegetables of the day; pizza with buffalo mozzarella and cherry tomatoes and, being rather sweet of tooth, the delicious *valigetta* [little suitcase] packed with Nutella, [a chocolate and hazelnut butter] – absolutely not to be missed. They also offer a small selection of beers and wines.

Al Ponte della Ranocchia

APPIO
c.ne Appia, 29
☎ *06/7856712*

- **Closed:** Sundays; annual holidays vary
- **Seats:** 40
- **L.** 45,000 w/o wine
🖃 all ❷ ♣

Trattoria. A useful address to have in this neighbourhood [and in general] - you can eat and drink well at reasonable prices in a relaxed atmosphere, though the service is not always as good as

everything else. They offer typically Roman fare as well as some equally good but more original dishes. For starters: *guanciale* [cured pork jowl] with vinegar; smoked horsemeat; cabbage, pear and cheese salad drizzled in balsamic vinegar; then a rather good version of pasta with broccoli in stingray broth; ravioli stuffed with *baccalà,* porcini mushrooms and fennel in anchovy sauce; *pennette capriccio del sud* [with sun-dried tomatoes, olives and provola cheese]. To follow, very good cuttlefish with artichokes and an interesting quail in ginger-scented grape sauce. For a perfect finish: creamed almond cake, pear with vanilla sauce and pistacchio mousse in caramel sauce.

Il Quadrifoglio

MONTI
via del Boschetto, 19
☎ *06/4826096*

🍴 **70**

- **Cucina** 43
- **Wine Cellar** 13 • **Service** 7
- **Ambience** 7 • **Bonus** 0

- **Closed:** Sundays; [open evenings only]; Aug 1-31
- **Seats:** 40
- **L.** 70,000 w/o wine
🖃 all ❷ ✽

Restaurant. Decidedly cuisine from Campania with Mediterranean horizons and all the region's salient characteristics – generosity,

EATING

imagination and versatility, as well as elegance and love of beauty [personified in this case by the hospitable Signora Annamaria]. The restaurant is attractively decorated and the cooking extremely tasty; the antipasti are excellent, among them Neapolitan *pizzella* [small deep-fried pizzas], crusty buffalo mozzarella pies and *calzoni* filled with escarole. First courses include *penne alla scarpariello, cavatelli alla sorrentina* and pasta *alla genovese*. To follow, Posillipo-style baby octopus and fish roulades garnished with wild fennel and potato gâteau. Inviting-looking desserts like the traditional *pastiera* [rich ricotta, wheat berry and candied fruit pie], *torta caprese* [chocolate almond cake] with Chantilly cream and *semifreddo* with Strega liqueur. The wine cellar stocks mainly Campanian wines.

QUI SE MAGNA OSTERIA DA VALERIA
CASILINO
via del Pigneto, 307/a [ang. via A. Zuccagni Orlandini]
☎ *06/274803*

- **Closed:** Sundays; in August
- **Seats:** 35
- **L.** 30,000 w/o wine
- no ♣

EATING

42

Trattoria. Rustic wooden tables, two enormous fridges bursting with bottles, a huge plastic wine cask they fill the carafes from, paper napkins, plastic glasses: you really breathe the atmosphere of bygone days here. Simple, honest *casereccia* cooking like grandma used to make it - prosciutto and various cured meats, or *olive ascolane* [deep-fried stuffed olives] for starters; then spaghetti, *fettuccine* or *bombolotti* with either tomato and basil, *ragù, amatriciana, carbonara, pajata* [milk-filled veal intestines] or clams, depending on the day. They also serve *gnocchi* on Thursdays in winter. Main courses include beans with *cotiche* [pork skin]; *ossobuco* with peas; stew; tripe; meat roulades; *pajata* casserole, and meatballs as well as a few fish dishes on Fridays. Dessert of the day and a few bottles of wine.

RAIS
PINCIANO
via Collina, 56
☎ *06/42818303*

  70

- Cucina 42
- Wine Cellar 12 • Service 7
- Ambience 7 • Bonus 2

- **Closed:** Sundays; annual holidays vary
- **Seats:** 50
- **L.** 75,000 w/o wine
- CSi, Visa ✳

Restaurant. The Rais is a welcoming and rather attractive restaurant offering mainly fish dishes, including wonderful

shellfish which arrive fresh each day from the owners' fish farm at nearby Sabaudia. The menu is varied with some genuinely original dishes, though the outcomes of their more experimental efforts are still a bit up-and-down. For example, the warm seafood salad with clams, cuttlefish and zucchinis was good, whereas the lobster salad with potatoes was a tiny bit over-cooked. The mussels, potato and marjoram soup was interesting and tasty but the combination of tagliolini with *bottarga* [dried fish roe] and fava beans was rather less successful. We followed them with a good mixed seafood and vegetable fry, another slightly over-cooked boiled lobster and a truly delicious fish couscous. To finish off: puddings dessert, including an excellent green apple sorbet. A small wine list. A well-deserved double bonus for the fast-service lunchtime menus from L.19 – 35,000 and the after-theatre dining.

IL REGNO DI NAPOLI
PINCIANO
via Romagna, 20
☎ *06/4745025*

- **Closed:** Saturday and Sunday lunchtime; in August
- **Seats:** 60
- **L.** 30,000 w/o wine
- AE, CSi, POS, Visa
- **P** ✳ ♿

Pizzeria. A Neapolitan pizzeria in the heart of Rome whose name proudly asserts its claim to being a kind of cultural enclave on foreign territory - the Kingdom of Naples. The setting is exceptionally pleasant and attractive, the service is polite and efficient and the menu obviously reflects the Neapolitan gastronomic tradition. For starters, a buffet of appetizing antipasti: *caprese* – mozzarella, fresh tomato and basil; eggplant *parmigiana; cianfotta* [vegetable ragout] and others, as well as croquettes, including the traditional *arancini* [rice, peas and innards]. Then various kinds of pizza – among them *pizza lasagna;* plain *pizza bianca* with *cicoli* [tasty scraps of pork] and provola cheese, or sausages and *friarelli* [broccoletti]; the Pizza Regno di Napoli [ricotta, *treccia di Sorrento* mozzarella and tomato], and the *campagnola* [country cousin] with vegetables; as well as eggplant turnovers, *calzoni* and salads. Desserts include *torta caprese* [chocolate almond cake], lemon-flavoured profiteroles and wildberry tart.

AL REGNO DI RE FERDINANDO II

TESTACCIO
via di Monte Testaccio, 39
☎ 06/5783725

 68

- Cucina 41
- Wine Cellar 13 • Service 7
- Ambience 7 • Bonus 0

- **Closed:** Sundays
- **Seats:** 100
- **L.** 50,000 w/o wine
🛇 all 🅿 ✳ ♣

Restaurant. Typically Neapolitan dishes served in a rustic, casual setting: for starters the traditional delicious delicacies or *sfizi* – deep-fried *pizzelle*, potato croquettes, fried polenta cubes and *arancini* [rice, innards and pea croquettes]; then *linguine* with lobster or baby squid, *sartù* [rice, meat, egg and mushroom timbales] and *pennette alla scarpariello* to follow. Main courses include *polpetti alla luciana* [octopus cooked with tomato, garlic and chili], fried *paranza* [seafood 'fresh off the boats'] and buffalo mozzarella *in pizzaiola* [poached in tomato and herbs]. A wide selection of desserts, including gelati, sorbets, *pastiera* [ricotta, wheat berry and candied fruit pie, once an Easter treat only] and rum babàs. The menu also offers a reasonable range of pizzas. Professional service; the wine list offers mainly wines from the Campania region.

RELAIS LA PISCINE

PARIOLI
via Mangili, 6
☎ 06/3216126

 76

- Cucina 45
- Wine Cellar 14 • Service 8
- Ambience 8 • Bonus 1

- **Closed:** never
- **Seats:** 60
- **L.** 120,000 w/o wine
🛇 all 🅿 ✳ ♣

Restaurant. The cuisine is still problematical - enormous potential, expertly chosen ingredients and imaginative combinations, but some of the dishes are disappointing. One could reasonably expect a larger and better thought-out wine list and a less banal selection of breads. We started with the warm lobster salad with fried artichokes [cold, unfortunately] and grilled king prawns with parmigiano and basmati rice, followed by creamed pumpkin with freshwater shrimp, and wholemeal *gnocchi* and *pennette* with vegetables and *formaggio di fossa* [rare cheese aged underground]; a convincing chicken Supreme; lobster with asparagus and morel mushrooms; a good baked *orata* [bream] in lemon sauce with olives and sun-dried cherry tomatoes; and a warm salmon *carpaccio* with basil and cherry tomatoes, which could have been better. The trolley dessert are anonymous, in stark contrast to the high standard of those on the menu, which have to be ordered in advance: crisp *sfogliatella* pastries filled with creamed pistacchio and exotic fruit; pink grapefruit *semifreddo* [soft frozen mousse] with almond-flavoured meringues; hot chocolate biscuits with mint sauce.

RELAIS LE JARDIN DE L'HOTEL LORD BYRON

PARIOLI
via G. de Notaris, 5
☎ 06/3220404

 73

- Cucina 43
- Wine Cellar 14 • Service 8
- Ambience 8 • Bonus 0

- **Closed:** Sundays; in August
- **Seats:** 60
- **L.** 140,000 w/o wine
🛇 all 🅿 ✳

Restaurant. Every year we come to this beautiful restaurant hoping to find that they've carried out the improvements which would finally make it a gastronomic destination worth a special mention. But no, once again we can only recount an experience that left us totally unmoved - except for the moment when we were presented with the bill, as always far higher than warranted by the quality of the food. We started with cold onion mousse served with tiny sheep's milk cheeses melted in hot squash blossom sauce, and king prawns sizzled in raspberry-scented vinegar with grilled tomatoes, crisped onions and coriander; followed by *trofiette* in a sauce of ripened ricotta, cherry tomato, corn and black olives sprinkled with fresh oregano; and melon and yoghurt soup with *capesante* [scallops] in tartare sauce. We proceeded with pea and anchovy-stuffed red mullet fillets on a bed of green beans doused in goat cheese sauce, and medallions of roast lamb on a bed of fried sweet peppers with crisped onions. For dessert we chose the honey-glazed apple strudel with vanilla sauce and poppy seeds. All the dishes were made with excellent ingredients but often were simply far too elaborate. The wine list is too small and the mark-ups are absurd. Professional but not impeccable service.

REMO

TESTACCIO
p.zza S. Maria Liberatrice, 44
☎ 06/5746270

- **Closed:** Sundays; [open evenings only]; Aug 1-31; Christmas
- **Seats:** 150
- **L.** 20,000 w/o wine
🛇 no ♣

Pizzeria. You'll have to queue to get into this pizzeria, but try to think of it as part of the local colour. While you're in line you'll get to meet all the very various specimens of humanity, local and otherwise, who come here to eat – kids, students, noisy revellers, serious-faced intellectuals, beautiful women - because Remo's is the most famous pizza parlor in the Testaccio neighbourhood. The pizzas are the typically Roman thin-crust *bassa* variety [naturally]. Before the pizzas, try their *supplì* and tasty fried *baccalà* and zucchini flowers. The service is maybe a bit too speedy and the dining room tables more suited to a bistrot than the natural expansion of the human form produced by a good pizza.

RIPA 12

TRASTEVERE
via S. Francesco a Ripa, 12
☎ 06/5809093

 69

- **Cucina** 42
- **Wine Cellar** 12 • **Service** 7
- **Ambience** 7 • **Bonus** 1

- **Closed:** Sundays; in August
- **Seats:** 55
- **L.** 60,000 w/o wine
🍴 all ✳ ♣ ♿

Restaurant. This classical, comfortable restaurant offers rather good food and hospitality characterised by the kind of measured cordiality we always find very pleasant. As for the cuisine, we still prefer the fish dishes which vary according to what's available and

best at the markets: raw marinated *spigola* [sea bass]; grilled anchovies; *tagliolini* with lobster; the *classicissimi* spaghetti with clams; and a good sea bass baked in salt crust. The wine list, a bit small and banal, could be improved. Worthy of mention [bonus] is the very useful arrangement they have with a local garage which enables you to hand your car over and eat in peace without having to worry about parking fines.

ROKKO

CENTRO STORICO - TRITONE
via Rasella, 138
☎ 06/4881214

- **Closed:** Sundays; end Aug-beg Sept; Dec 24-26
- **Seats:** 60
- **L.** 60,000 w/o wine
🍴 all ✳

Japanese. Discreet tones characterise the orderly ambience of this traditionally-styled Japanese restaurant. The menu offers a wide variety of classic dishes: sushi [evenings only] and sashimi, soba and udon [noodles in consommé], sukiyaki, yakitori [chicken brochettes], tempura, and tofu in vegetable consommé. They offer a choice of lunch menus starting at L.35,000. Efficient service.

ROMAN GARDEN LOUNGE DE L'HOTEL D'INGHILTERRA

CENTRO STORICO - SPAGNA
via Bocca di Leone, 14
☎ 06/69981500

 72

- **Cucina** 43
- **Wine Cellar** 14 • **Service** 7
- **Ambience** 8 • **Bonus** 0

- **Closed:** never
- **Seats:** 40
- **L.** 130,000 w/o wine
🍴 all ✳

Restaurant. Two long years of renovations are finally over and at last we were able to visit this restaurant with it looking and offering its best. The dining room is very cosy but the tables are really rather too small – the plates barely fit on. We expected something more of the table decor, too, especially the glasses and the wine service. The menu offers light dishes - a fraction too light, in the sense that even though obviously the work of an expert hand we noticed a certain lack of flavour and intensity. As appetizers, we chose steamed king prawns and artichoke timbales flavoured with Roman mint, and a vegetable terrine with ricotta, eggplant and tomatoes. To follow, spinach-green *fettuccine* with tomatoes and shellfish; red ravioli with fava beans, scallions and lamb sauce; medallions of *rana pescatrice* [anglerfish] with eggplant and squash blossoms; *dentice* [sea bream] with artichokes and tomatoes. From the dessert menu we chose a good cherry *semifreddo* with yoghurt sauce and a

chocolate tart with ricotta ice cream. A well-assorted wine list, with a number of excellent labels [although a few more vintages would be desirable].

LA ROSETTA

CENTRO STORICO PANTHEON
via della Rosetta, 9
☎ 06/6861002

 83

- **Cucina** 49
- **Wine Cellar** 16 • **Service** 8
- **Ambience** 8 • **Bonus** 2

- **Closed:** Sundays; in August
- **Seats:** 50
- **L.** 170,000 w/o wine
🍴 all ✳ ♣

Restaurant. One of those places where you know exactly what you'll find, which in this case is another way of saying it's one of the best restaurants in Rome and the entire Lazio region. High prices, it's true, but the quality is absolute, the ingredients irrephensible and Massimo Riccioli interprets them in masterly fashion. You could begin your meal with shellfish, either raw [unforgettable!] or marinated, like the dish we chose - the extraordinarily fresh shrimp, grapefruit and raspberry salad. But the lobster, shrimp, tomato, onion and basil salad is wonderful too, and the splendid *gran misto di crostacei* [mixed shellfish] is a real triumph of flavours.

EATING

The first courses were exquisite: *strozzapreti* with clams, shrimps and chard; *pennette* with sardines, wild fennel, pinenuts, sultanas and juniper berries; *linguine* with lobster garnished with cherry tomatoes. As main courses we chose baby cuttlefish in ink with sautéd fennel; coriander-flavoured red king prawns with string beans, and fried *moscardini* [curled baby octopus] with mint. The chocolate cake, hot pear cake with chocolate sauce, and apple cake desserts provided a perfect finish. A wide-ranging, well-planned wine list, and impeccable service. As for the setting, comfortable and attractive though it is, the tables are a little too close together. In compensation, the acoustics are much improved after the recent renovations [bonus].

SABATINI IN TRASTEVERE

TRASTEVERE
p.zza S. Maria in Trastevere, 13
☎ 06/5812026

 73

- **Cucina 43**
- **Wine Cellar 14** • **Service 7**
- **Ambience 8** • **Bonus 1**

- **Closed:** Aug 10-20
- **Seats:** 60
- **L.** 100,000 w/o wine
🗄 all ✻ ♣ 占

Restaurant. Sabatini in Trastevere is an institution, in fact it

bears the same relation to the marvellous piazza with its splendid Romanesque church as the cobbled paving stones, the *palazzi* and the fountain – it's hard to imagine the piazza without it. [A bonus for the outdoor tables]. The menu offers mainly seafood – good, well-executed dishes made with high quality ingredients: a rich seafood antipasto, followed by *linguine* Sabatini with mussels, clams, *scampi* and cherry tomatoes or spaghetti with *vongole veraci* [carpet-bed clams] cooked in white wine. Then plain grilled fish: [bream], *spigola* [sea bass] and *dentice* [sea bream], all very fresh and served with a delicious citrus and parsley dressing prepared at the table by the waiter. A few simple desserts, friendly service and a well-structured wine list. We learnt as we went to press that Sabatini's is about to open a second venue at 18, Vicolo Santa Maria in Trastevere, right next door to the historic original.

SAN TEODORO

PALATINO
via dei Fienili, 50
☎ 06/6780933

 72

- **Cucina 43**
- **Wine Cellar 14** • **Service 7**
- **Ambience 7** • **Bonus 1**

- **Closed:** in February
- **Seats:** 75
- **L.** 65,000 w/o wine
🗄 all 🅟 ♣ 占

Restaurant. Have you ever tried to find one of those

gorgeous little places with outdoor tables in the centre of Rome where you can eat decently, and failed miserably? Well, at San Teodoro's, only a few steps away from the Roman Forum, you can actually eat very well. The hospitality is as good as it comes and the outdoor dining area is one of those magical spaces that put you at peace with the world. The ample wine list is full of excellent labels and the service is friendly and professional. The menu offers a wide range of dishes including *carciofo alla giudia* [whole fried artichokes]; an excellent sea bass *carpaccio;* spaghetti with scampi tails, squash blossoms and pecorino *di fossa* [aged underground]; puff pastry *sfoglie* filled with prawns and oregano. Main courses are either fish, like the *sampietro* [John Dory] in a nest of potatoes, or meat, like the *campanello* [rump steak] cooked in nutmeg. Desserts include outstanding gelato-filled fruit jellies, and figs with vanilla gelato drizzled in Grand Marnier and hot chocolate. A defect? Prices have gone up and the service charge is high, but it's still no more expensive than a lot of other banal *centro storico* trattorias.

SANGALLO

CENTRO STORICO
CAMPO MARZIO
v.lo della Vaccarella, 11/a
☎ 06/6865549

 75

- **Cucina 45**
- **Wine Cellar 13** • **Service 8**
- **Ambience 8** • **Bonus 1**

- **Closed:** Sundays; [open evenings only]; in August
- **Seats:** 40
- **L.** 90,000 w/o wine
🗄 all ✻ 占

Restaurant. The changing of the guard in the kitchen [Emanuela Bellucci has gone back to Nettuno where she has re-opened the restaurant of the same name] hasn't caused any massive upheavals in this attractive place in the heart of the old city centre. In fact the clever young chef who has taken her place has so far prevented her being too sadly missed. The cuisine is perhaps simpler than it was in the past and all dishes feature excellent fresh fish brought in daily from the Roman coast. Huge plates of raw scampi and king prawns; steamed shellfish; truffled *carpaccio* made with the fish of the day; *tonnarelli* with clams and *bottarga* [dried fish roe]; sea bass ravioli with shellfish; fried *paranza* [fish 'fresh off the boats'] with vegetables; and truffled fillets of *dentice* [sea bream] were the dishes we sampled on our last visit – all very good, and so were the desserts. The wine list, though not enormous, has been very carefully designed. Professional, attentive service.

IL SANPIETRINO

CENTRO STORICO
ARGENTINA
p.zza Costaguti, 15
☎ *06/68806471*

 74

- Cucina 43
- Wine Cellar 13 • Service 8
- Ambience 8 • Bonus 2

- **Closed:** Sundays; [open evenings only]; Jan 1-8, Aug 10-31
- **Seats:** 56
- **L.** 65,000 w/o wine
  🛋 all 🅿 ✲ ⮜

Restaurant. This attractive, welcoming place is situated in the heart of the Jewish Ghetto, one of the most characteristic quarters of the city and offers good cuisine with a number of interesting novelties. We warmly recommend the turbot, salmon and spinach rolled roast; anchovy *parmigiana; tagliolini* with cuttlefish and Roman broccoli; scampi and artichoke risotto; veal, *guanciale* [cured pork jowl] and provola cheese turnovers, and the sea bass baked in salt crust. The desserts are truly delicious, like the dome-shaped chocolate *zuccotto*

pudding doused in hazelnut cream, to name just one. The wine list concentrates on regional labels but also offers some good national wines. After-theatre dining if you book in advance.

LE SANS SOUCI

PINCIANO
via Sicilia, 24
☎ *06/4821814*

 87

- Cucina 49
- Wine Cellar 16 • Service 10
- Ambience 10 • Bonus 2

- **Closed:** Mondays; [open evenings only]; in August
- **Seats:** 80
- **L.** 175,000 w/o wine
  🛋 all 🅿 ✲

Restaurant. We just have to say it - this place is an absolute dream. Walking in here is like walking into a fairytale, and when you leave it's a bit of a shock to re-enter the real world. It's a *casa*, a home, but if everyone had homes like this we'd all be kings and queens. The effect derives from the extravagant taste with which the interior is decorated and the fact that practically every material known to man has been used: wood, silver, fabric, iron, bronze, steel, ceramics, leather - look closely and you'll see the extraordinary care that has gone into every single detail. The service is flawless, from the parking facilities [they take care of everything] to the manager, barman, maitre, sommelier - all the perfect dining room staff. It probably has no equal anywhere in the Italy; and the

wine list offers exquisitely served memorable bottles. The cuisine: in the course of various visits over the past year we've been able to verify the expertise of chef Patrice Guillet and his team: fish tartare in mixed herb emulsion; truffled foie gras terrine; shrimp *millefoglie* scented with the aromas of the Amalfi coast; marinated duck breast with coriander; cheese soufflé, *onde* [waves] of egg pasta with scampi; risotto with garden vegetables; Normandy lamb carré with thyme; lobster and *animelle* fricassé with truffles; sea bass and shrimps seasoned with finely-chopped herbs *al cartoccio* [baked in parchment]; followed by another magnificent soufflé, either chocolate or vanilla, or else with crêpes flambées prepared at the table, tarte tatin, chocolate or lemon *bavarese* [Bavarian cream] or one of the many other original, international, delicious dishes. A bonus for the rare pleasure of the perfectly executed music.

SAWASDEE

PIAZZA BOLOGNA
v.le XXI Aprile, 13/c
☎ *06/8611036*

- **Closed:** Saturday lunchtime and Sundays
- **Seats:** 30
- **L.** 30,000 w/o wine
  🛋 all ✲ ⮜

Thai. This is undoubtedly the more authentic of Rome's two Thai restaurants, insofar as their Thai chef makes no concessions to other Oriental traditions. It's true that the setting is less appealing and the tables are very simply laid, but the essentials are all there. Try the fish, chicken or beef patties; pork, beef or chicken brochettes; fried meat roulades; rice with mushrooms and bamboo shoots; soy-flour noodles with meat and vegetables; soup with stuffed cucumbers or spicy shrimps; fried beef in oyster sauce; sweet and sour pork; red curried chicken with.bamboo shoots. Traditional Singha beer to go with it all, and very reasonable prices. Best to book.

LE SCALETTE DA EZIO

TRIESTE
via Chiana, 89
☎ *06/8411714*

 77

- Cucina 47
- Wine Cellar 15 • Service 7
- Ambience 7 • Bonus 1

- **Closed:** Saturday lunchtime and Sundays; Aug 1-31, Easter and Christmas
- **Seats:** 180
- **L.** 100,000 w/o wine
  🛋 all 🅿 ✲

Restaurant. They know all about fish here and you'll find aquariums in full view at the entrance,

EATING

comfortable tables, a pleasant ambience and efficient, discreet and courteous service. But it's the primary ingredient that holds centre stage and the hosts understand it better than most. Shrimps; scampi; clams; oysters; sea bass; various kinds of bream; *scorfani* [scorpion fish]; lobster and any other marine creature that comes to mind – they have them all, fresh and very good. We recommend the Gran Gala antipasto; shellfish; spaghetti with *cozze* [mussels]; *tagliolini* with *bottarga* [dried fish roe] and squash blossoms; *bombolotti* with lobster; *arzilla in guazzetto* [skate casserole]; sea bream with Vernaccia wine and olives; and sea bass baked in salt crust - we've tried and enjoyed them all. To put it in a nutshell: it's worth spending a little more [and not a lot more, given the quality] for a memorable meal. They also offer excellent homemade desserts, beautifully choreographed compositions of fruit and a very good selection of spirits. The Sardinian *dolcetti* bear witness to the origins of the hosts. A well-deserved bonus for the extreme politeness and the passion with which it has all been done.

SEMIDIVINO
PINCIANO
via Alessandria, 230
☎ 06/44250795

- **Closed:** Saturday lunchtime and Sundays; Aug 1-31
- **Seats:** 28
- **L.** 35,000 w/o wine
▣ all 🅿 ✳

Wine Bar. Opened more than ten years ago by Iranian host Fashid Nourai, the Semidivino is a good address for wine lovers, even though at this point the choicc of wincs could be a little wider, especially those available by the glass. Comfortable surroundings and a pleasant atmosphere, where you can always find good quality smoked fish, mixed salads, fish and meat *carpaccio* and a range of cured meats and cheeses. Hot dishes of the day - at least one soup and a pasta - are also available. Delicious dessert puddings complete the offering.

DA SERGIO
CENTRO STORICO
CAMPO DE' FIORI
v.lo delle Grotte, 27
☎ 06/6864293

- **Closed:** Sundays; in August
- **Seats:** 70
- **L.** 35,000 w/o wine
▣ no ♣ ♿

Trattoria. This rustic trattoria attracts throngs of devotees who spread out into the shady *vicoletto* in summer. A family affair on the classic pattern, it serves simple market-fresh dishes that have all the savour of genuine family fare. You'll almost always find *carbonara, amatriciana, penne all'arrabbiata* and *gnocchi* as well as rather good grilled meats or lamb *scottadito* [grilled finger-burner chops], *involtini* [roulades], steaks, *lombate* [chops] and side dishes.

LO SGOBBONE
FLAMINIO
via dei Podesti, 8/10
☎ 06/3232994

- **Closed:** Sundays; in August
- **Seats:** 70
- **L.** 35,000 w/o wine
▣ CSi, Visa 🅿 ♣

Trattoria. They say you shouldn't change a winning formula, and fortunately this trattoria hasn't. Famous for many years now for its wide selection of excellent, tasty pastas served in generous helpings: with *vongole veraci* [carpet-bed clams], or shrimps and arugula; *amatriciana;* cold *orecchiette* with eggplant and tomato; *gnocchi al gorgonzola* and an infinity of other dishes, including an excellent *pasta e fagioli* [bean and pasta soup] and *pasta e ceci* [chickpea and pasta soup]. They also offer *bruschetta;* squid *alla luciana* [cooked in tomato, garlic and white wine]; baked veal; *cotoletta primavera* [cutlets with vegetables]; stuffed zucchini and even a few good desserts – the sour cherry tart is the best. The house wine is not bad either. Fast, polite service.

SHANGRI LÀ CORSETTI
EUR
v.le Algeria, 141
☎ 06/5916441

- Cucina 42
- Wine Cellar 14 • Service 7
- Ambience 7 • Bonus 2

- **Closed:** in August
- **Seats:** 200
- **L.** 65,000 w/o wine
▣ all 🅿 ✳ ♣

Restaurant. The menu offers well-cooked, well-presented classical dishes, both Italian and international, that are never banal or boring. After a cordial welcome you're led into a spacious dining room with a large outdoor eating area where you'll be assisted by polite, attentive staff. Appetizers include mixed smoked fish and fresh mixed fish *carpaccio*. To follow *trofie mare-monti* [seafood and mushrooms], a mild version of *penne all'arrabbiata;* a good spaghetti *alle vongole* [with clams]; baked turbot and potatoes; grilled scampi or *straccetti* [miniscule squid] with tomatoes and arugula. Desserts include chocolate mousse, fruit, gelati and sorbets. There's a well-structured wine list which also offers half-bottles.

SICILIAINBOCCA

PRATI

via E. Faà di Bruno, 26

☎ 06/37358400

 70

- Cucina 43
- Wine Cellar 12 • Service 7
- Ambience 7 • Bonus 1

- **Closed:** Sundays; in August
- **Seats:** 30
- **L.** 55,000 w/o wine

🗟 POS ♣ ♿

Restaurant. One of the newer restaurants around town, and its cuisine, reasonable prices [bonus] and the pleasure of the whole experience place it a cut or two above the others. The service is courteous and efficient, almost a fraction too fast; the wine list offers only a few Sicilian labels. From the ample menu we chose boiled octopus sprinkled with olive oil and lemon, and the Sicilian *sfizi* [delicious nibbles] of the day - *caponata;* sun-dried tomatoes; chili-flavoured cheese; stuffed olives and eggplant roulades as appetizers; followed by *lumachine di Aci Trezza* [pasta snails] with fava beans, wild fennel and pecorino cheese [a bit insipid, to be honest]; and an excellent spaghetti with clams, mussels, and shrimps. Our main courses - *spiedino di Aci Trezza* [a scampi, shrimp, squid and swordish brochette], and steamed swordfish were very

good, and so were the desserts: almond *semifreddo* [soft frozen mousse] served with hot chocolate sauce, and lemon cream bignès [choux pastries].

IL SIMPOSIO

PRATI - CAVOUR

p.zza Cavour, 16

☎ 06/3211502

 77

- Cucina 46
- Wine Cellar 14 • Service 8
- Ambience 7 • Bonus 2

- **Closed:** Saturday lunchtime and Sundays; Aug 1-31
- **Seats:** 55
- **L.** 70,000 w/o wine

🗟 all 🅿 ✳ ♿

Restaurant. The Simposio seems to have finally shifted into high gear thanks to the tireless efforts of Arcangelo Dandini and his youthful but talented staff. After a rather uncertain period, this restaurant seems to have come into its own again and now offers an even more interesting menu than before. The dishes are expertly executed and never banal. We've made several visits over the past year, so the dishes we are mentioning here are only a few of the many we sampled: *coratella* [lamb organ meats] mousse with shrimps and *carciofi alla romana* [artichokes stuffed with garlic, parsley and Roman mint]; spinach-stuffed pears in cheese sauce; cold green tomato soup with baby cuttlefish and Roman ricotta; creamed chickpeas with duck sausage

and *baccalà; baccalà al cartoccio* [baked in parchment] with shellfish and roast potatoes; *tagliata* [thick slices] of beef seasoned with herbs. Well-made, well-presented desserts, from the fresh *bavarese* [Bavarian cream] made with pear, basil and grappa to the chocolate mousse with dried fruit and rum sauce. The wine list is not yet as good as it could be.

SOGO ASAHI

CENTRO STORICO - SPAGNA

via di Propaganda Fide, 22

☎ 06/6786093

- **Closed:** Sundays
- **Seats:** 120
- **L.** 90,000 w/o wine

🗟 all ✳ ♿

Japanese. The sakura with its traditional Japanese tatami mats is undeniably charming. As everyone knows by now, atmosphere and ritual are an integral part of Japanese gastronomy. Situated not far from the Spanish Steps, this restaurant is divided into several different dining areas, among them the sushi bar, the teppanyaki room and the sakura. The menu offers all the classic Japanese specialities, including sushi, sashimi and tempura. They also have a tasting menu which works out more economical at lunch time, but more costly in the evening, and on Saturday

evenings there's a sushi buffet [half-price for children]. Polished, courteous service. Booking essential.

SORA LELLA

CENTRO STORICO - GHETTO

via di Ponte Quattro Capi, 16

☎ 06/6861601

 76

- Cucina 44
- Wine Cellar 16 • Service 7
- Ambience 8 • Bonus 1

- **Closed:** Sundays; Aug 1-31
- **Seats:** 45
- **L.** 70,000 w/o wine

🗟 all ✳

Restaurant. The Trabalza family has long displayed a praiseworthy commitment to keeping this small, always-crowded restaurant among the best of its kind. Situated on beautiful Tiberina Island in the middle of the Tiber just near Trastevere, it offers typically Roman cuisine, so you can try pasta and broccoli in skate broth; *gnocchi all'amatriciana;* rigatoni with *pajata* [milk-filled veal intestines]; *coda alla vaccinara* [oxtail braised with celery]; *abbacchio brodettato* [lamb cooked in egg sauce] - the house specialty; *animelle* [pancreas and sweetbreads]; cuttlefish with artichokes; *baccalà in guazzetto* [dried cod poached with tomato, onion, sultanas and pine nuts]. The small

EATING

selection of cheeses and the rather good desserts deserve a special mention, and both can be enjoyed with a glass of suitably matched wine. The wine cellar boasts a wide range of labels though the mark-ups are a bit high. The service is courteous and efficient, if occasionally a trifle brusque.

SORA MARGHERITA
CENTRO STORICO - GHETTO
p.zza delle Cinque Scole, 30
☎ 06/6864002

- **Closed:** Saturdays and Sundays, [open lunchtime only]; Aug 1-31
- **Seats:** 36
- **L.** 25,000 w/o wine
🕾 no 🅿 ✳

Trattoria. Still no sign outside and the same simple formica-topped tables - nothing ever seems to change at Margherita Tomassini's little trattoria. Family-style meals with generous servings of the best-known traditional Roman dishes: *pasta e ceci* [chickpea and pasta soup]; thick vegetable *minestrone;* excellent *fettuccine cacio e pepe* [with pecorino cheese and black pepper]; *gnocchi* [on Thursdays]; *baccalà;* meatballs; whole-fried *carciofi alla giudia* [in season]; anchovies with curly

endive. House wine, and ricotta or jam tart to finish off.

T-BONE STATION
CENTRO STORICO - TRITONE
via F. Crispi, 29
☎ 06/6787650
CORSO FRANCIA
via Flaminia Vecchia, 525
☎ 06/3333297

- **Closed:** never
- **Seats:** 60
- **L.** 35,000 w/o wine
🕾 all ✳

Mexican - North American. The news item of the year is that T-Bone Station has opened another outlet. The decor is practically identical to that of the "mother house" but in a more modern, almost futuristic, key. It's quite unnecessary to add, of course, that the new T-Bone is already a wild success and packed, mostly with young people, until far into the night. The menu is also the same: fried onions, *bruschetta,* lavish salads but first and foremost the legendary T-bone steak itself [the house specialty, naturally] as well as baked potatoes, fried chicken, steaks and various kinds of hamburgers. Don't miss the typically American hyper-caloric desserts. The centre city T-Bone has a convenient arrangement with a car park not far away.

TAVERNA ANGELICA
VATICANO
p.zza delle Vaschette, 14/a
☎ 06/6874514

 73

- **Cucina 43**
- **Wine Cellar 14** • **Service 7**
- **Ambience 7** • **Bonus 2**

- **Closed:** Monday lunchtime and Sundays; in August; at Christmas
- **Seats:** 20
- **L.** 65,000 w/o wine
🕾 AE, CSi, POS, Visa
🅿 ✳ 🕭

Restaurant. Massimo and Daniela's little restaurant is truly delightful – intimate, romantic, and candlelit in the evenings which makes the atmosphere even more enchanting [bonus]. Massimo takes care of the service in the dining room and helps guests chose their wines from the very good wine list, while Daniela presides in the kitchen producing the most delicious, imaginative dishes: lobster-filled *conchiglioni* [pasta shells]; chicken salad; spaghetti with *bottarga* [dried fish roe] and string beans; stuffed leg of rabbit; duck breast drizzled in balsamic vinegar. The chocolate crepe with *gelato* for dessert is a must. All in all, one of the best restaurants in the area - keep it in mind and don't forget to book, as it only seats twenty people.

IL TEMPIO DI ISIDE
ESQUILINO
via P. Verri, 11
☎ 06/7004741

 70

- **Cucina 42**
- **Wine Cellar 12** • **Service 7**
- **Ambience 7** • **Bonus 2**

- **Closed:** Saturday lunchtime and Sundays; annual holidays vary
- **Seats:** 60
- **L.** 50,000 w/o wine
🕾 all ✳ 🌲 🕭

Restaurant. "Young" management in every sense of the word - the present owners are a group of dedicated youngsters for whom food is a passion, and they took over only last June. The ample menu centres on fish, simply and expertly prepared. We started with an abundant mixed seafood antipasto: salmon *carpaccio;* peppered mussels; grilled *straccetti* [miniscule squid]; fried squash blossoms stuffed with shrimps; seaweed fritters [which could have been a little lighter]; boiled *neonata* [tiny fish]; an exquisite *coccio al forno* [a crust-topped fish soup terrine]. Next, *maltagliati* with clams and porcini mushrooms; *tagliolini* with dried fish roe; grilled squid, and sea bass cooked in Vernaccia wine. To finish off: a delicious soft-centred chocolate *tortino.* The wine list is minimal, but a bonus for the particularly polite service and another for the very reasonable prices.

La Terrazza de l'Hotel Eden

PINCIANO
via Ludovisi, 49
☎ 06/47812752

 72

- Cucina 42
- Wine Cellar 14 • Service 8
- Ambience 8 • Bonus 0

- **Closed:** never
- **Seats:** 60
- **L.** 180,000 w/o wine
🗃 all Ⓟ ✳ ♿

Restaurant. It may happen [as it did to us] that when you ring to book you discover it's not up to you to decide the hour: you're told 7.30 or 10pm – take it or leave it. But that's not the only inexplicable thing about this place, though the panoramic view over the Eternal City alone would make the visit worthwhile. The complimentary appetizers included a stone-cold fritter; the bread [of various kinds] was stale; the staff cleared tables right under our noses while yelling instructions at each other and, worst of all, the dishes we ordered [not exactly cheap] were not much consolation. For starters, duck-liver terrine with caramelized peaches and figs [good], and a truffle-sprinkled scallop salad served with roast potatoes and candied tomatoes,

followed by *tagliolini* tossed with saffron stigmas; [diminutive] king prawns served with very thick-skinned tomatoes and basil; *gnocchi* filled with ricotta and spinach served with fresh tomato and mint. We proceeded with strip bass baked in parchment with string beans, black olives and coriander, and roast capon with crisp-fried vegetables and sesame seeds – both reasonably good. For dessert, lemon cream and cherries, and chocolate almond cake, each paired with an appropriate dessert wine. The wine list is limited and pricey.

Thien Kim

CENTRO STORICO
CAMPO DE' FIORI
via Giulia, 201
☎ 06/68307832

- **Closed:** Sundays; [open evenings only]; in August
- **Seats:** 40
- **L.** 40,000 w/o wine
🗃 AE, CSi, Visa ✳

Vietnamese. At a time when a lot of ethnic restaurants, and Oriental restaurants in particular, are beginning to get a little tired, this small eatery a few metres away from Campo de' Fiori remains a good place to dine. The decor is plain and straightforward [no glitzy bits-and-bobs] and the service is always courteous and helpful. The dishes are the same ones they've served for

years now – antipasto alla Thien Kim; various kinds of soup; fried king prawns in hot sauce; ginger-spiced shrimps; squid in pineapple sauce; celery with mushrooms, and sesame-sprinkled spinach, to name just a few. But what's pleasantly surprising is how different their versions of these dishes are from those served up elsewhere – lighter, stronger-flavoured and never over-cooked. There's a small but carefully-chosen selection of wine and quality beers that go well with the food. Booking essential.

La Torricella

TESTACCIO
via E. Torricelli, 2/12
☎ 06/5746311

- **Closed:** Mondays
- **Seats:** 130
- **L.** 35,000 w/o wine
🗃 AE, CSi, Visa Ⓟ ✳ ♣ ♿

Trattoria. The old favourites: *rigatoni all'amatriciana* or *alla carbonara* and spaghetti *alle vongole* [with clams], all served in generous helpings. As you will gather, the *cucina* here is simple, straightforward and generous - like Testaccio itself, one of Rome's oldest working-class neighbourhoods. For starters, excellent hand-carved prosciutto followed by first courses all just as good as the

ones mentioned above; then *pajata* casserole, chicory *ripassata* [boiled then lightly fried with garlic and peppers]; prize Tuscan *chianina* steak and, when they have it, roast fresh fish. Alternatively they do good, thin, crunchy pizzas. Two other strong points – they're open all year round and have outdoor tables in the summer. A little more politeness on the part of the staff wouldn't hurt, though.

Dal Toscano

PRATI - ANGELICO
via Germanico, 58
☎ 06/39723373

 69

- Cucina 43
- Wine Cellar 12 • Service 6
- Ambience 7 • Bonus 1

- **Closed:** Mondays; Aug 10-30; Dec 24-Jan 2
- **Seats:** 150
- **L.** 55,000 w/o wine
🗃 CSi, DC, POS, Visa
Ⓟ ✳ ♣

Restaurant. People who come here regularly know what to expect – some of the best meat available in Rome, some of the slackest service and a pretty noisy dining room. But… that's the way it is. Fillet steak, *fiorentine* [thick, premium, rare steaks], entrecôtes, and the kind of sirloin that brings tears to the eyes of serious carnivores. Add excellent hand-carved prosciutto and homemade

EATING

bread; *fagioli al fiasco* [slow-cooked beans], mixed fried meat [not a light dish]; Tuscan-style *pappardelle* and, if you've still got room, the house dessert drenched in hot chocolate. One or two good reds if you look hard, but otherwise not much in the way of wine.

TRAM TRAM
SAN LORENZO
via dei Reti, 46
☎ 06/490416

- **Closed:** Mondays; in August
- **Seats:** 50
- **L.** 45,000 w/o wine
⛭ all 🅿 ✳ ♣

Trattoria. Beautiful, charming and very good at what they do, the Di Vittorio sisters and their mother run one of the most successful and *simpatica* trattorias in San Lorenzo. A wide-ranging menu, an interesting wine list [with very reasonable mark-ups], a certain amount of noise and affordable prices are the ingredients of its continuing good fortune. Vegetable lasagna; *cavatelli* with swordfish; *fettuccine* with porcini mushrooms; grilled lamb *pajata* [milk-filled veal intestines]; baked *rombo* [turbot] with potatoes; golden-fried anchovies - all very satisfactory. Homemade dessert puddings to finish off. Booking a must.

TRAMONTI E MUFFATI
TUSCOLANO
via Santa Maria Ausiliatrice, 105
☎ 06/7801342

- **Closed:** Mondays; annual holidays vary
- **Seats:** 24
- **L.** 35,000 w/o wine
⛭ no 🅿

Wine Bar. Do the old things better and keep experimenting with the new is the philosophy that lies behind the recent addition of gastronomic treats to the repertoire of this little place, run by brother-and-sister Marco and Laura Berardi in the Appio Tuscolano quarter and dedicated to the art of good drinking. You'll enjoy the hot vol-au-vent pastries; platters of cured meats or Italian and French cheeses, ranging from Zibello *culatello* [prize cured ham] to a tasty Guilmi *ventricina* [soft, smoky, peppery salami] and an exquisite baked sheep's milk ricotta; stuffed polenta; white truffle fondue; mixed salads and various other delicacies paired with good wines by the glass. They also offer desserts, biscuits, tortes, puddings like the dark chocolate, hazelnut or chestnut mousse – all prepared by Laura.

TRATTORIA CADORNA DAL 1947
PINCIANO
via R. Cadorna, 12
☎ 06/4827061

- **Closed:** Sundays; in August
- **Seats:** 60
- **L.** 45,000 w/o wine
⛭ all 🅿 ♣ ♿

Trattoria. The cooking here is genuine *casalinga* [family-style] of the really enjoyable kind. Everything is made while you wait [so you can wait quite a while] and butter and cream are banned from their menu. Don't miss their rich, delicious *antipasto alla Cadorna* [bread fritters, grilled veal meatballs, soft creamy *burrata* cheese, buffalo mozzarella, eggplant with vegetables, and *bruschetta*]. To follow, *farro* [an ancient cereal] soup, spaghetti with buffalo mozzarella and cherry tomatoes, *saltimbocca alla romana,* grilled squid, jam tart and crème caramel. Courteous and efficient service.

AI TRE SCALINI
COLOSSEO
via dei SS. Quattro, 30
☎ 06/7096309

 75

- **Cucina 44**
- **Wine Cellar 14 • Service 8**
- **Ambience 7 • Bonus 2**

- **Closed:** Sundays; annual holidays vary
- **Seats:** 22
- **L.** 65,000 w/o wine
⛭ all ✳ ♣

Restaurant. Skilled sommelier and passionate gastronome Angelo Bettazzi Annarumi

has taken over and completely renovated this restaurant, and he's turned it into a delightful place, cosy and comfortable, where he offers interesting tasty cuisine to a limited number of guests. The menu offers both fish and meat dishes. As appetisers we chose the artichoke *millefoglie* [actually more like a filo pastry turnover] with borlotti beans and a cheese fondue, and glazed marinated anchovies with sweet and sour onions, both good. First courses: saffron-tinted *gnocchetti* with squid and artichokes, nettle-flavoured *tacconelle* with river shrimp and cherry tomatoes. The main courses were good, too: curried king prawns with endive braised in juniper berries, and duck casserole [a tiny bit over-cooked] with scallions drizzled in balsamic vinegar and a spicy chicory timbale. For dessert we chose their mixed platter [not for weightwatchers]: strawberry-filled pastries with crème chantilly, a three-chocolate pyramid doused with sweet Malvasia wine, and red currant blancmange in mint sauce; and an excellent hot chocolate *gianduia* soufflé with crispy wafers and vanilla ice cream. There's a well-designed, interesting wine list with some prices a little high. A bonus for the special lunch menu at L.32,000 and for the particularly attentive service.

TRIMANI IL WINE BAR
TERMINI
via Cernaia, 37/b
☎ *06/4469630*

- **Closed:** Sundays; in August
- **Seats:** 80
- **L.** 40,000 w/o wine
🗂 all 🅿 ✳ ♣ ♿

Wine Bar. Trimani's is an institution, as Roman winelovers know. The whole family is involved in this enological "mission" and their wine bar has become a favourite haunt of enophiles as well as a venue for wine-tasting events and very interesting courses. But you also eat well here in tasteful surroundings without it costing an arm and a leg. You'll always find mixed cured meats, cheeses and various kinds of smoked fish [the Scottish salmon is absolutely wonderful], as well as creamed celery and carrots; polenta served with herb-scented veal and *pancetta* roulades; vegetable pilaf timbales; an excellent fillet of beef [in both normal and magnum versions]; pork

shank in red wine sauce, and potato torte. The desserts are good, too. The choice of wine, needless to say, is more than satisfactory in terms of both quality and price.

TULLIO
CENTRO STORICO - TRITONE
via S. Nicola da Tolentino, 26
☎ *06/4745560*

 73

- **Cucina 43**
- **Wine Cellar 15 • Service 7**
- **Ambience 7 • Bonus 1**

- **Closed:** Sundays; annual holidays vary
- **Seats:** 100
- **L.** 60,000 w/o wine
🗂 all 🅿 ✳

Restaurant. Rome is not a cosmopolitan city but fortunately it has always been subject to regional influences and always will be. Tullio's is a little piece of Tuscany transported holus-bolus to the capital, offering the best of the Tuscan culinary tradition just a stone's throw away from Piazza Barberini [but don't be put off by the idea of hellish centre city traffic, it's in a very quiet little street]. The perpetual crowd of clients testifies to the high quality of the cuisine, though the numbers have no negative effects on the service - always courteous and professional. Regional specialities are expertly prepared here using first-class ingredients [try the excellent *fiorentina* T-bone, for example]. Classic *crostini;* cured meats;

carpaccio; beef tartare, and various fried meats and vegetables as appetisers; then *pappardelle;* bean or vegetable soup; charcoal-grilled meat with the celebrated *fiorentina* at the head of the list; grilled lamb chops *a scottadito* [finger-burners]; *ossobuco* [veal shank braised in wine and herbs]; sirloin, or exceptionally fresh fish - grilled or cooked in various ways. Good traditional desserts. A well-planned wine list with several very prestigious labels.

UNO E BINO
SAN LORENZO
via degli Equi, 58
☎ *06/4460702*

 74

- **Cucina 43**
- **Wine Cellar 14 • Service 7**
- **Ambience 7 • Bonus 3**

- **Closed:** Mondays; [open evenings only]; in August
- **Seats:** 36
- **L.** 50,000 w/o wine
🗂 CSi, DC, Visa ✳ ♿

Restaurant. Giampaolo and Gloria, aided by Andrea in their kitchen and the extremely polite young dining room staff, have made this delightful, exquisitely-decorated bistro one of the most dependable eateries in the city [bonus]. Recent innovations include the introduction of chocolate-tasting and a very good cheese trolley. The rest of the menu is pretty appealing, too, and the dishes when they actually appear are generally more than satisfactory.

Brussels sprouts and feta cheese flan; hake and lettuce timbale; *tortelli* filled with sweet peppers and king prawns in tomato sauce; *strozzapreti* pasta with asparagus, fava beans and peas; sea bass and eggplant roulades served on a bed of creamed sage and scallions; loin of rabbit with diced roast peppers and a *cannellini* bean timbale. For dessert we chose a mint-flavoured melon *bavarese* [Bavarian cream] in peach sauce, and baked crème caramel. The wine list is as remarkable as ever, both for its range and the originality of the choices [second bonus]. Along with everything else Giampaolo also organises courses for winelovers [another bonus].

VECCHIA LOCANDA
CENTRO STORICO ARGENTINA
v.lo Sinibaldi, 2
☎ *06/68802831*

 72

- **Cucina 42**
- **Wine Cellar 14 • Service 7**
- **Ambience 7 • Bonus 2**

- **Closed:** Sundays; Dec 23-Jan 20
- **Seats:** 40
- **L.** 55,000 w/o wine
🗂 all ✳ ♣

Restaurant. This restaurant is in an excellent central location, and offers fare that, if not exactly stunning, is always of a high

EATING

standard [bonus]. In summer the little tables set outside in the tranquil *vicolo* create a truly delightful atmosphere. The menu is the kind to suit all tastes, with meat and fish dishes like spaghetti *alle vongole; tonnarelli* and artichokes; *fusilli* with broccoletti and fresh sausage; *saltimbocca alla romana; tagliata* [thin slices of beef] dressed in various different ways, and grilled salmon steaks. *Torta* of the day and a good version of crème caramel to finish off. An adequate wine list; polite service.

VECCHIA ROMA

CENTRO STORICO - GHETTO
p.zza Campitelli, 18
☎ 06/6864604

  72

• Cucina 42
• Wine Cellar 14 • Service 7
• Ambience 8 • Bonus 1

• **Closed:** Wednesdays; Aug 13-31
• **Seats:** 70
• **L.** 90,000 w/o wine
AE, DC 🅿 ✳ ♣ ♿

Restaurant. If you happen to find your attention wandering from your meal to the stunning beauty of this charming, secluded little piazza, don't let it worry you - the Vecchia Roma owes a great deal of its fame to its superb location, even more wonderful in summer when you can dine outside, though the interior is tasteful

and attractive, too. The cuisine is not of the unforgettable variety, perhaps a fraction too classical though it acquits itself honourably within the canons. The ample, wide-ranging menu offers anchovy and potato timbales; risotto with *straccetti* [miniscule squid] cooked in white wine; *lombrichelli* with squid, olives and capers; bean and *moscardini* [baby curled octopus] soup; sea bass with shellfish; turbot with potatoes; liver and vegetables in sweet and sour sauce; sliced beef au gratin with *taleggio* cheese; and spring lamb with *cacio* cheese and egg. A very good wine list.

LA VERANDA DE L'HOTEL COLUMBUS

VATICANO
b.go di Santo Spirito, 33
☎ 06/6872973

 73

• Cucina 42
• Wine Cellar 14 • Service 8
• Ambience 8 • Bonus 1

• **Closed:** never
• **Seats:** 60
• **L.** 80,000 w/o wine
all 🅿 ✳ ♣ ♿

Restaurant. The enormously charming Veranda with its soft lighting and discreet music looks out onto the gardens of the austere Palazzo della Rovere, and in summer you dine caressed by gentle breezes. After complimentary hors d'oeuvres you order from a bilingual [Italian/English] menu offering meat and fish dishes as well as a number of variations on traditional Roman

specialities: *baccalà,* sweet peppers and caper salad; anchovy and ricotta timbale; spinach-green *tonnarelli* in seafood sauce baked in parchment with chickpeas; pockets of sea bass stuffed with buffalo mozzarella and ginger; duck medallions with celery and mustard seed. Desserts include chocolate tart served with a citrus compote, and *millefoglie* pastries with peaches. The assortment of cheeses – at least on the evening we dined there – was not of the standard the tone of the restaurant leads one to expect. The dishes are well made, the service is professional and attentive [maybe even a little too attentive]; the wine list is sufficiently ample with acceptable prices. A bonus for the fact that they never close.

LA VERANDA DE L'HOTEL MAJESTIC

PINCIANO
via Vittorio Veneto, 50
☎ 06/486841

 78

• Cucina 46
• Wine Cellar 14 • Service 8
• Ambience 8 • Bonus 2

• **Closed:** Sundays; Aug 10-21
• **Seats:** 100
• **L.** 115,000 w/o wine
all 🅿 ✳ ♣ ♿

Restaurant. This is now one of the best hotel restaurants in Rome, performing well in all the categories we take into consideration when judging an eatery [though the wine list contains a

few too-high prices]. The dining room is very beautiful, and the service is excellent - unusually courteous and professional. From the kitchen: beef *carpaccio* with celery, truffles and *formaggio di fossa* [rare cheese, aged underground]; steamed lobster tail with almonds and lightly seared spinach; *fusoli* with marinated wild boar; squash, chestnut and sage fritters; crust-topped lentil, duck and truffle soup. To follow, fillets of hake with ginger-flavoured red chicory; loin of lamb with broccoli, potatoes and a beetroot emulsion. All good or very good dishes, with a noteworthy finale – mandarin *Delizia* with hot tangerine sauce and the *gran piatto* of chocolate. A bonus for the hot breads, and the attention to detail with which the elegance of the whole has been achieved.

VINAMORE

CENTRO STORICO
PIAZZA NAVONA
via Monte Giordano, 63
☎ 06/68300159

• **Closed:** Monday lunchtime; in August
• **Seats:** 40
• **L.** 25,000 w/o wine
no

Wine Bar. In the pleasantly relaxing

atmosphere of this simply-furnished but comfortable wine bar, Francesco Zegretti offers a good selection of Italian labels, a few foreign wines, a *mescita* service [wine by the glass], an assortment of cured meats and quality cheeses, and simple tasty dishes like salads, *carpaccio,* and *focaccia.* Don't miss the baked potatoes with various fillings - the house speciality. The dessert selection could be wider. They also organise regular wine-tasting courses for neophytes [phone for information].

VINERIA IL CHIANTI
CENTRO STORICO - TRITONE
via del Lavatore, 81
☎ 06/6787550

• **Closed:** Sundays; in August
• **Seats:** 60
• **L.** 40,000 w/o wine
🗫 all 🏷 🌲

Wine Bar. A most attractive place where the hospitality is particularly courteous; you eat at wooden tables in a cheerful and rather noisy atmosphere. The selections of cured meats and cheeses are always good, and so are the Tuscan *crostini* and various *carpaccio,* salads, a few tasty first courses [like the *fettuccine al Chianti*], and pizzas, and to finish off -

dolcetti – tiny biscuits and pastries. The wine list concentrates principally on Tuscan labels. A very pleasant place to stay late over a good glass of wine, especially at the weekends.

LA VOLPE ROSSA
ESQUILINO
via Alfieri, 4
☎ 06/70453517

• **Closed:** Sundays; [open evenings only July 1-Aug 31]; annual holidays vary
• **Seats:** 45
• **L.** 35,000 w/o wine
🗫 CSi, Visa 🏷

Trattoria. At last something good in this neighbourhood: spotless, simply-furnished with a host who passionately loves his work and offers unpretentious homey fare based on the use of first class ingredients. The cuisine is fully within the Mediterranean tradition - lots of vegetables, aromas and fish on the traditional days [Tuesdays and Fridays]. For starters: *panzanella* [tomato and bread salad]; marinated anchovies, and a Campanian antipasto [buffalo mozzarella, arugula and cherry tomatoes]. Then, *lasagna mediterraneo* with vegetables, *spaghetti cacio e pepe,* and *macheroncini* with zucchini flowers. Main courses include rabbit seasoned with rosemary, duck breast drizzled in balsamic vinegar and a very tasty

zucchini *parmigiana.* The dessert section needs work - when we visited it offered only a homemade *zuppa inglese* [trifle]. A few carefully-chosen labels make up the wine list. If you choose a fish dish the price goes up by L.5,000.

OUTSIDE ROME

ACUTO [FROSINONE]
77 KM FROM ROME

LE COLLINE CIOCIARE
via Prenestina, 27
☎ 0775/56049

• **Cucina** 49
• **Wine Cellar** 16 • **Service** 8
• **Ambience** 8 • **Bonus** 2

• **Closed:** Mondays and Tuesday lunchtime; annual holidays vary
• **Seats:** 22
• **L.** 100,000 w/o wine
🗫 all 🅿 ✳ 🏷 🌲

Restaurant. A warm but professional welcome, simple elegant surroundings, relaxing background music, beautifully-laid tables – and a totally convincing *cucina.* With a tasting menu of our own devising [bonus] we began with excellent pork-barded trout scented with *mentuccia* [Roman mint] in fennel sauce; wild asparagus soup with hot ricotta; quail and artichoke salad with herb-scented barley. Then we swaddled ourselves [metaphorically speaking] in soft, delicate chickpea *tortelli* in rosemary sauce, and *animelle* ragù and succumbed to the intense savour of *frascatelli* with cauliflower, herrings and pecorino. The baked leg of goat basted with

mentuccia and orange-rind was equally delicious. Special praise for the cheeses paired with exquisite compotes of green tomatoes and squash from the trolley. An excellent dessert finale with *cannoli* [rich flaky pastry tubes] filled with creamed ricotta and dried kumquats, and strawberries with crème chantilly-filled *millefoglie* pastries, as well as their legendary soft-centred chocolate *tortino.* The choice of wines [they finally have a wine list] reveals a grand passion, despite one or two ingenuous inclusions.

ALBANO LAZIALE [ROME]
24 KM FROM ROME

ANTICA ABAZIA
via S. Filippo Neri, 19
☎ 06/9323187

• **Cucina** 42
• **Wine Cellar** 12 • **Service** 7
• **Ambience** 7 • **Bonus** 2

• **Closed:** Mondays
• **Seats:** 80
• **L.** 45,000 w/o wine
🗫 all 🅿 🌲

Restaurant. This truly delightful little place with its cosy indoor dining rooms and pleasant outdoor tables in summer is run by Annalisa and Massimo Vinciguerra, youthful brother-and-sister team and impassioned food lovers. Apart from the pizzas [available in the thin, crunchy Roman version with various toppings], the

EATING

menu offers interesting dishes presented with grace and care; *fettuccine* with porcini mushrooms; *bucatini all'amatriciana;* *ravioli* stuffed with zucchini flowers; spring lamb *romanesco;* high quality buffalo mozzarella and excellent *tagliata,* thick slices of truffle-sprinkled beef. Don't deny yourself the desserts, beautiful to look at and very good, prepared personally by Annarita. A very extensive but well-designed wine list with reasonable mark-ups.

ANGUILLARA SABAZIA [ROME]

32 KM FROM ROME

CHALET DEL LAGO
v.le Reginaldo Belloni [lungolago]
☎ 06/99607053

 73

• **Cucina 43**
• **Wine Cellar 12** • **Service 8**
• **Ambience 8** • **Bonus 2**

• **Closed:** Sunday evenings and Thursdays; Feb 1-15
• **Seats:** 70
• **L.** 60,000 w/o wine
🍽 all **℗** ♣

Restaurant. This little place, right on the edge of the lake, offers a fantastic panorama [bonus]. Its foreign owners have given the dining room their own special touch of quiet *eleganza* and added a dash of originality to the menu. We started

with truffled liver patè; salmon trout terrine; smoked salmon with salad; *crostini* and fillets of lake fish marinated in a spicy sauce - all good. Then, *cannelloni* stuffed with squash and gorgonzola cheese; a barley and porcini mushroom broth; and *malfatti* with broccoletti. As main courses we chose the chicken breast stuffed with asparagus and the three-fillets of lake fish, with different sauces for each fish. Delicious desserts, among them an outstanding orange and chocolate cake served with hot chocolate sauce. A small but well-chosen wine list. They also organise interesting cooking courses [bonus].

APRILIA [LATINA]

44 KM FROM ROME

IL FOCARILE
via Pontina km 46, 500
☎ 06/9282549

 78

• **Cucina 44**
• **Wine Cellar 17** • **Service 8**
• **Ambience 8** • **Bonus 1**

• **Closed:** Sunday evenings and Mondays; in August; at Christmas
• **Seats:** 60
• **L.** 80,000 w/o wine
🍽 all **℗** ✳

Restaurant. Every time we come to visit the Lunghi brothers we can't help but think with admiration of the effort they've had to make here in an area that's not a particularly easy or happy one for restaurateurs. However, for the last couple of years our

visits have been a bit disappointing and we feel obliged to acknowledge that the restaurant is in something of a lull - hoping it's a transitory phenomenon. The service is still unfailingly polite, the hospitality pleasant as always and the prices on the attractive and well-furnished wine list [bonus] are still extremely reasonable. However, to relate one of our recent experiences: as appetizers we tried the cold marinated swordfish [a bit too marinated], octopus salad [not the most tender] and tuna *ventresca* [the softer, richer belly flesh] fishballs.The hot dishes were better, the shrimp croquettes with basil best of all. The first courses were good, *tagliolini* with *gialloni* mushrooms and cuttlefish; *sfogliatina* pastries with basil-scented scallops, and *sedanini* with swordfish and eggplant. As main courses we chose a tasty scampi with zucchini flowers; turbot au gratin served with baby cuttlefish and zucchini cooked in wine [the wine flavour was too strong], and the rich *gran fritto Italia* [fried zucchini, squash flowers, mushrooms, ricotta, lamb, etc.] which was quite good. The *piccola pasticceria* [tiny

biscuits and pastries] and desserts were scrumptious, especially the *cassata* doused in raspberry purée and the *semifreddo al torroncino* [soft frozen mousses with honey and toasted nuts] with hot chocolate sauce.

BRACCIANO [ROME]

39 KM FROM ROME

PICCOLA TRATTORIA
via G. Tamburri, 7
☎ 06/99804536

• **Closed:** Tuesdays; Aug 1-31
• **Seats:** 36
• **L.** 35,000 w/o wine
🍽 no **℗** ✳

Trattoria. Fresh fish from Lake Bracciano and local game are the principal specialities Silvio Morbidelli offers his clients with great courtesy and cordiality. The menu is interesting and well-executed, with home-produced ingredients as its strong point. For appetisers, we sampled *bruschetta, schiacciata* [focaccia] with truffles, and other delicious morsels. As first courses, spaghetti with clams and mussels, *gnocchetti* with porcini mushrooms, *mezze maniche* with perch and arugula. For our main courses we chose roast bass, fish croquettes, and whole boned *coregone* [lake salmon]; but they also offer meat and, in winter, game dishes. Simple, tasty homemade desserts and carefully-chosen wines.

VINO E CAMINO
via delle Cantine, 11
☎ 06/99803433

- **Closed:** Mondays; [open evenings only except weekends in summer]; annual holidays vary
- **Seats:** 40
- **L.** 35,000 w/o wine
🍴 all ♣

Wine Bar.
Something new is in the air at this wine bar run by Massimo Baroni [in the dining room] and his sister Cristina [in the kitchen]. In fact they're due to move into more spacious surroundings at 11 Piazza Mazzini – just below the Castle, and their opening hours will probably be extended. The atmosphere and hospitality will stay the same, and so will the menu wich offers appetising snacks and light meals including selections of cheeses; various cured meats; meat and smoked fish *carpaccio;* duck or quail terrines; artisan-made *porchetta* [herb-roasted pork] and salads. Equally tasty desserts and a good selection of wines, also available by the glass.

L'ANGOLO D'ABRUZZO
p.zza A. Moro, 8
☎ 0863/997429

 🍴 **82**

- Cucina 46
- Wine Cellar 18 • Service 7
- Ambience 7 • Bonus 4

- **Closed:** Mondays; July 1-15
- **Seats:** 80
- **L.** 70,000 w/o wine
🍴 all ℗

Restaurant. This restaurant just keeps getting better. It's always been one of the best in Rome [actually it's in Abruzzo, but it doesn't take long to get there – no longer than you often spend caught in the traffic travelling from one part of Rome to another]. Owner Lanfranco Centofanti is special: because of the way he searches out authentic regional recipes and first-class, authentic ingredients [mushrooms and truffles are the main ones, but the meats, vegetables and rare cheeses are equally good]; because of his passionate and knowledgable love of wine [the wine list has been further improved and is now one of the best in Italy]; but above all because of his relationship to his clients, who are all delighted not just by what they eat and drink but also with the way they're made to feel while they're here. No one ever wants to go home. We'll just briefly mention the *ovoli* and *porcini* mushroom salad; *bruschetta* topped with black truffles; risotto with *porcini* mushrooms; *fettuccine* with white truffles; fillets of beef or lamb *agliu cutturu* [slow-cooked in terracotta casserole]; roasted *porcini* mushrooms; and the memorable desserts. Our best wishes to Lanfranco and the whole family, especially those very bright youngsters.

AL CAMINETTO
via degli Alpini, 95
☎ 0863/995105

 🍴 **74**

- Cucina 42
- Wine Cellar 16 • Service 7
- Ambience 7 • Bonus 2

- **Closed:** Mondays; in July
- **Seats:** 160
- **L.** 50,000 w/o wine
🍴 all ♿ ♣

Restaurant. This very large place with its pleasant outdoor dining area is well worth a visit as it manages to successfully combine large scale with high quality food. Concetta Centofanti [sister of Lanfranco of the *Angolo d'Abruzzo*] and Fernando Anzini, passionate sommelier, are responsable for selecting the ingredients, so the menu offers a great deal of grilled meat, porcini mushrooms and truffles, but also good fresh trout and river prawns [delectable with the *tagliolini*]. Courteous service and a notable assortment of wines are further reason for warmly recommending this restaurant [you can also visit their wine cellar]. The desserts are homemade, too, and include a remarkable pineapple and custard *semifreddo* [soft frozen mousse]. Pizzas available in the evenings.

ANTICO RISTORANTE PAGNANELLI DAL 1882
via A. Gramsci, 4
☎ 06/9360004

 🍴 **71**

- Cucina 40
- Wine Cellar 15 • Service 7
- Ambience 7 • Bonus 2

- **Closed:** Tuesdays
- **Seats:** 300
- **L.** 65,000 w/o wine
🍴 all ℗ ♣

Restaurant. Traditional local cuisine based, when you get down to it, on the relationship between a strip of water and a patch of land. The view across the lake is charming enough to reconcile one to the world [bonus], and the restaurant offers cosy dining rooms with fireplaces and a garden. Smoked *sgombro* [mackerel] with orange and *radicchio* [red chicory]; *dindo speck* [turkey 'bacon'] with buffalo mozzarella, and cured game meats as appetisers. For first courses, lentil and shellfish soup; *fettuccine alla papalina* [Pontiffstyle – Castel Gandolfo is the Pope's summer residence]; *orto bosco* [farm and forest] with mixed mushrooms and eggplant. Main courses include lake trout, wild boar with apple sauce, and stuffed squid. Chestnut mousse, classic *tiramisù* and gelati for dessert. Polite and attentive service. Last, but certainly not least, you must visit their extraordinary underground wine cellar [another bonus], which contains a truly excellent selection of Italian and foreign wines and is divided into various niches where you can sit and enjoy a little wine-tasting.

CIVITA CASTELLANA [VITERBO]

79 KM FROM ROMA

L'ALTRA BOTTIGLIA
via delle Palme, 18
☎ 0761/517403

 84

- Cucina 47
- Wine Cellar 19 • Service 8
- Ambience 8 • Bonus 2

- **Closed:** Wednesdays [open evenings only except Sundays and public holidays]; Aug 1-31
- **Seats:** 28
- **L.** 120,000 w/o wine
- 🗐 all 🅿 ✳

Restaurant. As dedicated winelovers we were sorely tempted to fill the whole review singing the praises of this

delightful restaurant's most extraordinary wine cellar - probably the best in the whole of central and southern Italy after Florence's Enoteca Pinchiorri. But the most pleasant surprise on our last visit here was rediscovering the pleasures of serious dining, which obliges us to describe in detail some of the delicious delicacies we were offered by Ermanno Romano, our very kind host, prepared with incomparable skill by his wife Sandra. After the simple but appetising complimentary entrée of *crostino* with sweet peppers, we had an extremely tasty pig trotter salad; sliced foie gras served on a bed of creamed borlotti beans sprinkled with balsamic vinegar; a soup of Castelluccio lentils and *lardo* [cured pork fat]; exquisite *tagliolini* with broccoletti sauce, and foie gras topped with parmigiano shavings. Nor were the main courses disappointing: the pork carré was delicious even though its bed of orange-scented potato purée wasn't entirely convincing and the casseroled duck with onions and cinnamon was simply exquisite. For dessert we chose orange and ricotta cream and coffeecake. To round out the picture, they also serve excellent *piccola pasticceria* [tiny cakes and biscuits] and offer three tasting menus from L.90,000 to L.120,000 [bonus]. The wine mark-ups

are so reasonable they deserve another bonus.

FIANO ROMANO [ROME]

36 KM FROM ROME

HOSTARIA L'OCA GIULIVA
via Cavour, 6
☎ 0765/389134

78

- Cucina 47
- Wine Cellar 14 • Service 8
- Ambience 7 • Bonus 2

- **Closed:** Sun evenings and Mon; [open evenings only except Sat and public holidays]; Aug 1-31; Dec 24-Jan 1
- **Seats:** 20
- **L.** 100,000 w/o wine
- 🗐 all 🅿 ✳

Restaurant. The passion and dedication displayed by Valerio Zaccarelli in the dining room and Emanuela, his wife, in the kitchen deserve praise. Their pretty restaurant - only a few minutes by car from Rome - is a pleasant oasis for gourmets offering a good wine list, an excellent selection of spirits and harmonious, original dishes based on very carefully selected ingredients [bonus]. When we dined there last spring, after an appetising complimentary entrée we sampled rolled roast of rabbit stuffed with foie gras and braised red onions served with fresh rhubarb and cardamom; crisp-fried *animelle* [pancreas and sweetbreads] with a potato mousse scented with lime

and star anise; ravioli stuffed with zucchini *parmigiana* and smoked provola cheese; splendid fettuccine with fresh porcini mushrooms tossed in goose and white wine sauce; an excellent *faraona* [guinea fowl] parfait with curry sauce and apple; slices of foie gras with crisp-fried spinach and candied tomatoes; delicious squab fillet with *speck* and plum sauce or baked with foie gras in a pastry crust. The desserts were good and beautiful to look at: dark chocolate tart with citrus sauce; *zabaglione* gelato doused in 10-year-old Vecchio Samperi Marsala wine; and *millefoglie* pastries with apple and apricot mousse. Another bonus for the pasta, the fragrant breads and the *piccola pasticceria* [tiny biscuits and pastries] - all homemade.

FIUGGI [FROSINONE]

82 KM FROM ROME

LA TORRE AL CENTRO STORICO
p.zza Trento e Trieste, 18
☎ 0775/515382

80

- Cucina 46
- Wine Cellar 16 • Service 8
- Ambience 7 • Bonus 3

- **Closed:** Tuesdays; end of June; Nov 15-30
- **Seats:** 50
- **L.** 70,000 w/o wine
- 🗐 all 🅿 ✳ ⅙ ♣

Restaurant. Still undoubtedly one of the best in Lazio, Antonio and Maria Ciminelli's restaurant offers an extremely pleasant, attractive setting and very courteous, professional hospitality in the dining room where Antonio presides. Maria creates authentic masterpieces inspired by the local tradition: trout in a nest of potatoes topped with tasty sweet garlic sauce; crispy turnovers filled with Fiuggi *ricottina* drizzled with sweet scallion sauce; duck-filled *ravioli* in black Campoli truffle sauce with chives and fresh pecorino cheese; artichoke soup served with croutons and a light fondue. The main courses range from rack of lamb scented with Roman mint served with *carciofi alla romana* [artichokes stuffed with garlic and parsley] to delicious braised guinea fowl in a Cesanese del Piglio wine sauce served with a potato and zucchini timbale. The delectable desserts are prepared fresh for each guest: tiny Williams pear sponge cakes, and chestnut honey gelato in a pear and vanilla sauce. The wine list is remarkably well-designed. Excellent homemade breads. Tasting menu at L. 65,000.

BASTIANELLI AL MOLO
via Torre Clementina, 312
☎ 06/6505358

   73

• **Cucina 43**
• **Wine Cellar 13** • **Service 8**
• **Ambience 8** • **Bonus 1**

• **Closed:** Mondays; Jan 1-31
• **Seats:** 120
• **L.** 95,000 w/o wine
🖪 all 🅿 ♣

Restaurant. If you ever happen to find yourself at the Leonardo da Vinci airport ravenous with hunger, this restaurant could be the solution [after all, that's why they're here]. It offers courteous, professional service and five [!] tasting menus, from L. 60,000 to L. 90,000 [bonus]. But... we found the mixed hot and cold antipasto very disappointing on our last visit, and decidedly over-priced. As first courses, we sampled a quite good spaghetti with clams, a rather bland shrimp and asparagus risotto, and a very good *bavette* with lobster and cherry tomatoes. The main courses were satisfactory: steamed scampi; mixed fried seafood, and red king prawns [a bit on the small side, to be honest]. We finished off with the mixed dessert platter – hard to go wrong. We found the wine list considerably reduced in size and missing several essential labels – a pity.

FRESCOBALDI BOTTEGA DEL VINO
Aereoporto Leonardo da Vinci Voli Nazionali Molo A6
☎ 06/65958667

• **Closed:** never
• **Seats:** 20
• **L.** 15,000 w/o wine
🖪 AE, CSi, Visa 🅿 ✳

Wine Bar. The Bottega del Vino di Anacleto Bleve, one of the best wine bars in Rome, has now "landed" here at the domestic airport terminal together with the Marchesi de' Frescobaldi as part of a franchising operation which, for the moment, is the only one of its kind. The idea is undoubtedly a winner: excellent wines to buy or sample by the glass, and delicious snacks to nibble on while you wait for your flight: for example, stuffed Mongetto chili peppers in oil from Vignale Monferrato; truffled cheese from Alba; thick slices of artisan-made *mortadella;* or the legendary Falomi cured meats from Greve in Chianti made with Cinta Senese pork; *formaggio di fossa* [rare cheese, aged underground] made by Vittorio Beltrami in Cartoceto near Fano in Le Marche, also famous for his splendid extra vergine olive oil. To round it all off, chocolate *baci* [kisses] flavoured with Barbaresco or

---

Moscato wine, made by Bisco, the pastry-chef from Costigliole d'Asti. All the speciality foodstuffs are made by the most exclusive traditional crafts-producers in Italy. They also sell books and gadgets for winelovers.

ISOLA D'ORO
loc. Isola Sacra via della Scafa, 166
☎ 06/6584595

 71

• **Cucina 42**
• **Wine Cellar 14** • **Service 7**
• **Ambience 7** • **Bonus 1**

• **Closed:** Mondays; in September; at Christmas
• **Seats:** 120
• **L.** 60,000 w/o wine
🖪 all 🅿 ✳ 🚫 ♣

Restaurant. Fish cuisine - obviously - here by the sea, where most eateries use first-class fresh ingredients. But you won't always find the first-class dishes offered by this restaurant, prepared with that special touch and extra care that make all the difference. Appetisers include baby cuttlefish roulades; roasted anchovies; smoked swordfish *carpaccio;* sautéd clams and mussels. First courses: risotto *alla pescatora* [fisherman's-style]; spinach-green *tonnarelli* with arugula and shellfish; *gnocchetti*, squash

EATING

blossoms and shrimps; spaghetti with clams; risotto with creamed scampi. Main courses: *scorfano* [scorpion fish] with cherry tomatoes; [turbot] au gratin; *frittura di paranza* [fried fish 'fresh off the boats']; *coccio* [piper] with capers and olives; sea bream with potatoes and porcini mushrooms; red king prawns and asparagus and - but only if you order in advance - *zuppa di pesce* [mixed fish soup]. Puddings for dessert: *semifreddo* [soft frozen mousse] flavoured with Amaretto liqueur; *panna cotta* [silky milk custard] with a berry compote; lemon sorbet, and creamy chestnut Bavarian cream. A very well-structured wine list. If you prefer something other than fish they also have a spacious pizzeria area which serves good pizzas cooked in a wood-fired oven.

FRASCATI [ROME]

21 KM FROM ROME

CACCIANI

via A. Diaz, 13
☎ 06/9420378

 ¶ **74**
• **Cucina 44**
• **Wine Cellar 14** • **Service 7**
• **Ambience 7** • **Bonus 2**

• **Closed:** Mondays; in January and August
• **Seats:** 200
• **L.** 70,000 w/o wine
🖪 all 🅿 ✳ ♣

Restaurant. Cacciani's has become something of an institution, and not just for the local inhabitants. It's always full and often does banquets and receptions, and in summer you can eat outdoors on their extremely pleasant terrace [bonus]. Their culinary offerings are always satisfying but in our opinion the non-traditional dishes are less successful than the others. At any rate, the *crostino* with anchovies and buffalo milk *provatura* cheese; cured meats; *fettuccine* with chicken innards; *spaghetti* with pecorino cheese and black pepper; *minestra di cicerchie* [chickpea soup]; *pollo al mattone* [grilled chicken], and grilled spring lamb are good dishes. They also serve fish on the traditional days [Tuesdays and Fridays]. The rigorously homemade desserts are very good, especially their legendary *zuppa inglese* [trifle] and the pear and apple cake with custard. The wine list is well-suited to the menu but could range a little wider. The "theme evenings" organised throughout the year deserve a special mention [bonus].

ENOTECA FRASCATI

via A. Diaz, 42
☎ 06/9417449

• **Closed:** Sundays; [open evenings only]; Aug 1-31
• **Seats:** 130
• **L.** 40,000 w/o wine
🖪 AE, CSi, Visa 🅿 ✳

Wine Bar. This restaurant offers cuisine that is very sensitive to regional traditions but also able to look beyond them. In fact the continual positive transformations this wine bar has gone through are no doubt due to just that spirit of enquiry and fascination with the processes of change. Located in the heart of Frascati, the Enoteca has a wine cellar dug into the local *tufo* stone filled with hundreds of labels and offers a vast range of tasty dishes in a warm, welcoming and attractive setting. For appetisers: mixed smoked fish; a wide variety of *crostini* - with vegetables, *ciauscolo* [cured pork sausage], Colonnata *lardo* [cured pork fat] or ham patè; and smoked *lavarello* [lake fish] in Mediterranean sauce. To follow, *farro* [an ancient cereal] and lentil soup; *fettuccine* with tomatoes; *rigatoni* with *pajata* [milk-filled veal intestines]; *bucatini all'amatriciana*, and *penne* with eggplant and smoked ham. Main courses include *oca alla contadina* [goose cooked peasant-style]; beef with *radicchio* [red-leafed chicory]; grande

guignol entrecote; smoked mozzarella with basil; oxtail braised with celery, and tripe. There's a wide choice of cured meats and cheeses, among them a magnificent Stilton with bitter *corbezzolo* honey, and *caprino muffato* [blue goat's milk cheese]. The desserts are all homemade: jam tarts, *tiramisù*, marrons glacés served with whipped cream, ricotta mousse and vanilla *semifreddo* [soft frozen mousse] with sultanas.

ZARAZÀ

v.le Regina Margherita, 21
☎ 06/9422053

• **Closed:** Mondays; [Nov 1/Easter also Sunday evenings]; Aug 1-31
• **Seats:** 35
• **L.** 40,000 w/o wine
🖪 AE, CSi, Visa 🅿
♿ ♣

Trattoria. Not far from beautiful Piazza Vescovile, with a pleasant terrace, this trattoria alternates traditional fare with more original dishes that are not always entirely successful. After one of the delicious appetisers, try their chickpea soup; *mezze maniche alla carbonara; penne all'arrabbiata; gnocchi* [on Thursdays]; beans cooked with *cotiche* [pork skin]; grilled lamb chops *scottadito* [finger-burners]; *baccalà* [on Fridays] or tripe [Saturdays]. Tasty homemade desserts, and you'll find a few good bottles in the wine cellar to wash it all down with.

FREGENE [ROME]

31 KM FROM ROME

BAFFONE
loc. Maccarese
via della Muratella, 627
☎ *06/6678068*

- **Closed:** Fridays; in January and August
- **Seats:** 120
- **L.** 40,000 w/o wine
  no ⓟ

Trattoria. A forest of TV antennas are this trattoria's garrulous-looking substitute for a neon sign; you can see them from a long way off and use them as a guide. They're the host's rather endearing vice – he's strewn TV sets everywhere, almost as if he feels the need to build a bridge between this big place in the countryside between Rome Airport and the sea [not exactly an enchanting spot, we have to admit] and the world beyond. But he's remained an absolutely genuine and cordial character and the kitchen offers rigorously home-style cooking. People come here for the meat, which is sold by weight and

you choose it with him before it goes on the grill. Everything else is mere background to this central culinary focus – first courses of the day: *pennette, ravioli* and *fettuccine;* beans with onion; potatoes with rosemary, and spinach. *Tiramisù* and *panna cotta* [silky milk custard] for dessert and a good local bottled red to drink. Coffee served *al vetro* [in tiny glasses] and *limoncello* liqueur bring the evening to a plesant close.

IL DIAVOLETTO
loc. Maccarese
v.le delle Tamerici, 2/a
☎ *06/6678823*

- **Closed:** Wednesdays [never in summer]; Dec 20-30
- **Seats:** 50
- **L.** 50,000 w/o wine
  CSi, Visa ⓟ ✳ ♿ ♣

Trattoria. Every now and then a little devil - the eatery's namesake – seems to stick his fork into the works and something doesn't quite run smoothly, but with a name like that... On the other hand, given that you can eat fresh, well-cooked fish here prepared in simple traditional ways that exalt its natural flavour, at very reasonable prices – a certain amount of indulgence is in order. For starters:

marinated anchovies; *bruschetta* with clams, tomatoes or seafood; *linguine* with squash blossoms and king prawns; spaghetti with mussels and *friggitelli* [tiny green peppers]; *risotto alla pescatora* [fisherman's style]; sautéd clams and mussels; *orata Diavoletta* - baked bream and potatoes – and *frittura mista* [mixed fried fish]. To finish off: homemade desserts like peach or chocolate cake and gelati. The wine cellar is adequate.

SAN GIORGIO
loc. Maccarese
p.zza della Pace, 6
☎ *06/6678060*

 69

- Cucina 42 • Wine Cellar 13 • Service 7 • Ambience 6 • Bonus 1

- **Closed:** Wednesdays; Nov 1-30
- **Seats:** 120
- **L.** 60,000 w/o wine
  all ⓟ ♿ ♣

Restaurant. Strong, simple flavours characterise this seafood cuisine based on the use of only the freshest ingredients, which should be the norm for all purveyors of fish dishes but unfortunately is not always the case. So, hats off to this restaurant in the ancient *borgo* of Maccarese with its flowerpots filled with blossoms and aromatic herbs, and

its beautiful pergola. Fish *carpaccio* of various kinds; marinated baby scampi; *orecchiette* with clams and arugula; spaghetti with clams; *tagliolini* with baby scampi; seafood risotto; a good fried *paranza* [mixed fish 'fresh off the boats'], and baked or salt-crusted whole fish. Homemade desserts include apple cake, mousse or *bavarese* [Bavarian cream]. The wine list has been designed with further development in mind.

GENZANO [ROME]

28 KM FROM ROME

IL BOMBARDINO
via M. Moscato, 39
☎ *06/9362632*

73

- Cucina 42 • Wine Cellar 14 • Service 8 • Ambience 7 • Bonus 2

- **Closed:** Sunday evenings and Thursdays; annual holidays vary
- **Seats:** 45
- **L.** 60,000 w/o wine
  all ⓟ

Restaurant. The pleasant rustic setting, polite hospitality excellent wine list, various tasting menus, and the fact that you can order a snack rather than a full meal if you prefer - all these things remain the strong points of this restaurant [bonus]. The dishes we sampled were more than satisfactory: sheep's milk *ricottina* mousse with river

EATING

prawns and salmon trout; an excellent platter of mixed cured meats; tasty *bruschetta;* Carnaroli rice creamed with sheep's milk *ricottina;* squash blossoms with black truffles; duck breast garnished with onion rings pickled in balsamic vinegar and bay leaves, and a three-chocolate mousse.

GROTTAFERRATA [ROME]

20 KM FROM ROME

LA BRICIOLA
via G. D'Annunzio, 12
☎ 06/9459338

 ❙❙ **73**

- Cucina 44
- Wine Cellar 13 • Service 7
- Ambience 7 • Bonus 2

- **Closed:** Sunday evenings and Mondays; in August
- **Seats:** 35
- **L.** 55,000 w/o wine
📷 no ❷ ♿ ♣

Restaurant. Easy to find [just follow the directions for the Chiesa di San Nilo], Adriana Montellanico's restaurant has been synonymous with good cuisine for many years now. The atmosphere is very pleasant and the kind of rapport the hostess and her husband create with their clients only adds to the pleasure of the visit. One small complaint [sorry to insist] - they still don't accept credit cards, but we sampled with the usual pleasure their celebrated zucchini

alla velletrana [Velletri-style]; *vignarola* [artichokes, fava beans and peas]; ravioli stuffed with *baccalà;* chestnut and chickpea soup; *girelle* [baked pasta] with mushrooms; roast beef drizzled with balsamic vinegar, and truffled guinea fowl. Special merit points for the desserts, especially the famous *millefoglioline* [tiny puff pastry-and-custard slices] topped with crème chantilly – Adriana's own creation. Wine list of the appropriate standard.

IL TINELLO
via Domenichino, 9 [*via XX Settembre, 8*]
☎ 06/9458395

 ❙❙ **71**

- Cucina 43
- Wine Cellar 13 • Service 7
- Ambience 7 • Bonus 1

- **Closed:** Tuesdays
- **Seats:** 60
- **L.** 55,000 w/o wine
📷 no ❷

Restaurant. A tight operation, in the sense that all the elements work well together – something fairly rare around here [and not just here, to be honest]. Sometimes excellent food is served in dismal surroundings, attractive settings are not infrequently betrayed by poor cuisine, and mouth-watering menus have been known to lack the wine cellar they deserve. Not

here: the Tinello, in the centre of Grottaferrata, continues to be a very pleasant place, characterised by great courtesy in the dining room and good cuisine - obviously influenced by local traditions. Excellent squash blossoms and vegetables preserved in oil and good first courses: *farfalle,* artichokes and *guanciale* [cured pork jowl]; *fusilli all'amatriciana; pappardelle* with mushrooms. Excellent main courses, including tripe *alla romana;* casseroled squab; *animelle* [sweetbreads and pancreas] with artichokes, and spring lamb. The desserts are good: crepes with pastry cream, and *millefoglioline* [custard-filled puff pastry slices]. The wine cellar is adequate and evidently in the process of remedying previous omissions.

LABICO [ROME]

39 KM FROM ROME

ANTONELLO COLONNA
via Roma, 89
☎ 06/9510032

 ❙❙❙ **86**

- Cucina 48
- Wine Cellar 18 • Service 9
- Ambience 8 • Bonus 3

- **Closed:** Sunday evenings and Mondays; Aug 1-31
- **Seats:** 40
- **L.** 110,000 w/o wine
📷 all ❷ ✳♿

Restaurant.
Antonello Colonna is lively, intelligent, and *simpatico.*
He was practically born in the kitchen and has already accumulated a great deal of international experience. In his "kingdom" here in Labico he's put another bright idea into practice: in part of his beautiful wine cellar there's now a remarkable selection of cigars and it has become a kind of sanctuary and meeting place for smoke-fiends. In a word, high standards everywhere including, of course, the restaurant, with which we were already familiar, but now there's another novelty there, too - a well-choreographed and praiseworthy service designed to let the person eating see the person who prepared the dish. There are also more dining room staff to help put clients completely at their ease. The wine list? It's very good, extensive and well-organised, and you'll have no difficulty finding the right label. A few of their dishes: foie gras served with a quince and tomato compote; Savoy cabbage timbale with cured pork fat, sheep's milk cheese and truffles; sweetbread-stuffed *cappelli di prete* in kidney sauce [spectacular!];

raviolini stuffed with *baccalà*, tomato and marjoram; squab breast flavoured with fresh aromatic herbs; kid cutlets; chocolate cake with *gianduia* and coffee cream; tarte tatin. A big bonus for a restaurant worth visiting – again and again.

MARINO [ROME]

22 KM FROM ROME

CANTINA COLONNA
via G. Carissimi, 32
☎ *06/93660386*

- **Closed:**
  Wednesdays;
  [open evenings only except Saturdays and Sundays];
  Aug 1-31
- **Seats:** 52
- **L.** 45,000 w/o wine
  🗪 all 🅿 ✲

Trattoria. Thank goodness for this warm, attractive Cantina inside an ancient aristocratic *palazzo* - always a safe harbour for gastronomes, where Umberto Paolucci and Iole in the kitchen feed their clients tasty well-made meals. The abundant *antipasto misto* is always good, and to follow there are *gnocchi;* homemade pasta *alla carbonara, all'amatriciana, alle rigaglie di pollo* [with chicken innards] or with porcini mushrooms [in season]; then grilled lamb chops *scottadito* [finger-burners]; oxtail

braised with celery; chicken with sweet peppers; *spuntature* [pork spare ribs]; *baccalà alla pizzaiola* [dried salt cod poached in tomato, olives and herbs]. Good homemade desserts; mostly local wines.

MONTE PORZIO CATONE [ROME]

25 KM FROM ROME

I TINELLONI
via dei Tinelloni, 10
☎ *06/9447071*

- **Closed:**
  Wednesdays;
  annual holidays vary
- **Seats:** 70
- **L.** 40,000 w/o wine
  🗪 AE, CSi, Visa 🅿 ♣

Trattoria. The Pompei family have become an institution - reliable, discrete [like all solid institutions, they don't need to attract attention by doing anything outlandish] and secure. The guarantee they represent has been built up with years of patient work and rests on the robust shoulders of Signor Enzo [who'll welcome you and guide your choices] and in the skilled and capable hands of his wife Tina, in the kitchen. The cuisine is *casereccia* [home-style] in the best sense: real flavours, generous helpings and ingredients selected

with love and care. Trust them. Vegetables au gratin and *bruschetta; amatriciana; gnocchi*; broccoli and pasta in skate broth, and various *minestre* [soups] - the house speciality; then *coratella* with artichokes; goat's meat cooked in broth; rabbit; *saltimbocca alla romana;* spring lamb and other meat dishes. The homemade desserts are excellent, especially the tarts. A straightforward wine list.

MONTEROTONDO [ROME]

26 KM FROM ROME

SAN ROCCO
via U. Bassi, 21
☎ *06/90623277*

 72

- **Cucina 44**
- **Wine Cellar 12** • **Service 7**
- **Ambience 7** • **Bonus 2**

- **Closed:**
  Wednesdays [open evenings only except Sundays];
  in August
- **Seats:** 60
- **L.** 45,000 w/o wine
  🗪 POS ✲

Restaurant. Marco Milani, a young but already highly skilled chef with an enviable range of professional experiences to his credit, decided not so long ago to open his own restaurant with the help of valid partner Sandro Zeppilli. They took over one of the town's old *osteria*

and have turned it into a very pleasant place, likely to grow better but already rather good. The service is entrusted to attentive, capable young staff [bonus]; the wine list is limited for the time being, but pleasant surprises keep arriving. Original, well-made dishes issue forth from the kitchen, from steamed ricotta-stuffed squash blossoms to *panzanella* [tomato and bread salad] with swordfish *carpaccio,* and tasty mixed fried vegetables in batter. We followed them with a warm *farro* [an ancient cereal] soup with asparagus and quail eggs; *pennette* with dried fish roe, buffalo mozzarella and cherry tomatoes; basil-scented *sgombro* [mackerel] served with a white fava bean timbale; boned whole chicken stuffed with tomatoes and peppers; and duck eggs cooked *in acqua pazza* [a tomato-based court bouillon]. The desserts are of a very high order, too, whether it be the *millefoglie* [layered puff pastry and custard] with crème chantilly or the chocolate tart. The friendly service and reasonable prices deserve another bonus. They also offer pizzas.

NEPI [VITERBO]

35 Km from Rome

Casa Tuscia

p.zza E. Minio, 6
☎ 0761/555070

71

- Cucina 42
- Wine Cellar 13 • Service 7
- Ambience 7 • Bonus 2

- **Closed:** Mondays; [open evenings only]; annual holidays vary
- **Seats:** 35
- **L.** 40,000 w/o wine
CSi, Visa ✿ ❋ ♿

Restaurant. The setting is very stylish rustic - a large dining room with wooden beams, stone walls, terracotta paving and tasteful tables. The cuisine is interesting because it offers mostly reinterpretations of ancient recipes and other original dishes. The day's options are written up on a blackboard; the wine list reveals a great deal of care taken over the choices [bonus]. As appetizers we had trout baked in a potato crust and balsamic vinegar-drizzled Colonnata *lardo* [cured pork fat] with an onion flan. To follow, sea bass and pesto moussaka; *cavatelli* with ricotta and mint; a tripe and egg timbale, and rabbit *trionfo dell'estate* [Summer Triumph]; then walnut cake and *gualdrappa* [cream, ricotta and jellied fruit of the season] for dessert. The prices merit another bonus; booking is a must.

OLEVANO ROMANO [ROME]

56 Km from Rome

Sora Maria e Arcangelo

via Roma, 42
☎ 06/9564043

75

- Cucina 44
- Wine Cellar 15 • Service 7
- Ambience 7 • Bonus 2

- **Closed:** Monday evenings and Wednesdays; Feb 1-10; July 10-30
- **Seats:** 80
- **L.** 50,000 w/o wine
all ✿

Restaurant. People don't usually just wander in to Olevano Romano as it's rather out of the way, though this pretty town is definitely worth a visit. But if you are in the area don't miss the chance to dine at this pleasant, attractive restaurant. The cuisine is inspired by the regional tradition, intelligently reinterpreted; the portions are just right; the menu is truly extensive; the wine list knowledgeably designed - and all at very reasonable prices. For appetizers, excellent *crostini* with citrus-scented game toppings and tasty roulades of salty meat, mesclun, truffles and ricotta; then as first courses, *cannelloni* au gratin [the house speciality] and *maltagliati* in rabbit ragù with garden vegetables and

salted ricotta - both very good. To follow, grilled Angus rib fillets [cooked to perfection], herb-scented rabbit, and pocket of veal stuffed with pink-peppered prosciutto [probably the least convincing dish]. An astounding selection of perfectly-ripened French cheeses, a good choice of desserts and exquisite chocolates to accompany the coffee. The service is so very courteous you can forgive the occasional wait during their busier moments.

ORTE [VITERBO]

63 Km from Rome

Taverna Roberteschi

via V. Emanuele, 7
☎ 0761/402948

70

- Cucina 42
- Wine Cellar 12 • Service 7
- Ambience 7 • Bonus 2

- **Closed:** Mondays; annual holidays vary
- **Seats:** 40
- **L.** 40,000 w/o wine
AE, CSi, Visa ♣

Restaurant. You dine under the high vaulted ceiling of a rustically decorated dining room at this restaurant, inside a fifteenth-century *palazzo* only a few steps away from the Cathedral. Rosario, the Sicilian chef, prepares interesting dishes very different to the somewhat monotonous fare offered elsewhere in the area. After the

appetisers *-crostini* and sliced meats – come the *tagliolini* in cuttlefish ink with fish ragù; *tagliatelle* made from chestnut flour with porcini mushrooms, and plain *tagliatelle* served in either a horsemeat or river prawn ragù.
Then, red king prawns with a balsamic vinegar sauce; fried frogs' legs; grilled fillets of Argentinian beef; fillets of ostrich meat, and loin of deer or wild boar. Good homemade desserts; a small wine list.
A bonus for the particularly attentive service, the elasticity of the opening hours, and the presence of a tasting menu at L.28,000, all included. There's a pizza service in the evenings, and also a Sicilian menu that requires ordering in advance.

OSTIA [ROME]

28 Km from Rome

Le Bizze de il Tino

via dei Lucilii, 17/19
☎ 06/5622778

80

- Cucina 46
- Wine Cellar 15 • Service 8
- Ambience 8 • Bonus 3

- **Closed:** Sunday evening and Mondays [open evenings only except Sundays]; Jan 1-15; Aug 15-30
- **Seats:** 35
- **L.** 95,000 w/o wine
all ✿ ❋

EATING

Restaurant. The Salvatori brothers were very young when they first started out. They now run this excellent and very attractive little restaurant offering hospitiality and gastronomic pleasures of a very high order [and they're still very young]. The service is exceptionally courteous, and the wine list has decidedly improved in both range and quality since our last visit here. Their passion for good food and wine is evident from the menu: lobster tails served on a bed of squash blossoms stuffed with chives and grouper; *baccalà carpaccio* drizzled with balsamic vinegar; iced tomato soup served with chunks of seafood; lightly-grilled *totanetti* [a type of squid] with fresh herb-sprinkled beans; marinated medalliions of beef, and fresh *caprino* cheese with a spiced melon sorbet. All well-made dishes, and so are the desserts: coffee-flavoured *semifreddo* [soft frozen mousse]; almond blancmange with wild berries, and mint gelato in a dark chocolate crust. All in all, one of the best restaurants in the Rome area, well on its way to a glorious future. Bonus points for the

homemade breads and pastries, and the wine available by the glass – a praiseworthy option that's finally becoming more common, though still not widespread enough.

LA CAPANNINA
lungomare A. Vespucci, 156
☎ *06/56470143*

 71

- **Cucina 43**
- **Wine Cellar 13** • **Service 7**
- **Ambience 7** • **Bonus 1**

- **Closed:** Mondays [never in summer]; Nov 1-30
- **Seats:** 130
- **L.** 60,000 w/o wine
🖃 all 🅿 ⛄ ♨

Restaurant. Pasquale Lubrano is a serious professional and his restaurant adjoining the beach club of the same name, right on the sea [bonus], offers high quality fish cuisine based on the use of first-class ingredients. If you're lucky [or else check that they're available before you come] you'll find truly delicious raw oysters and shellfish. Otherwise, try his mixed fish *antipasto misto;* bean and pasta soup with mussels; *risotto alla pescatora* [fisherman's-style]; pasta and broccoli in skate broth; cuttlefish with artichokes, or baked *rombo* [turbot] and potatoes, and a tasty homemade

apricot tart to finish off with. There's a good, reasonably-priced wine list; the service is polite and efficient. Book in advance, especially in summer.

IL SEGRETO DI PULCINELLA
via R. Namaziano, 31
☎ *06/5672194*

- **Closed:** Mondays [never in summer]; in October
- **Seats:** 120
- **L.** 25,000 w/o wine
🖃 no 🅿 ✳ ♨

Pizzeria. Pulcinella's Secret [as this pizza parlour is called] is soon revealed: a triumphant array of more pizzas than you can count in every conceivable shape, colour and flavour. Neapolitan-style, with thick, puffy borders and curious, inviting names like Masaniello [with shellfish], Carrettiere [fresh sausage and Neapolitan broccoletti], Disco [a closed double pizza filled with ricotta, mozzarella and prosciutto crudo], and many others as well as the traditional varieties. They also do *calzoni* [pizza turnovers], including an interesting one filled with *ciccioli* [tasty pork pieces]; fried pizzas; first courses and a *fritto misto* of fried *zeppole* [traditional Neapolitan doughnuts],

mozzarella in carrozza [fried cheese sandwich], *arancini* [croquettes made of rice, peas and innards], and fried squash blossoms. For dessert: rum babà, *savarin* and *cannolini* filled with lemon pastry cream.

SPORTING BEACH
lungomare A. Vespucci, 8
☎ *06/56470256*

 70

- **Cucina 42**
- **Wine Cellar 12** • **Service 7**
- **Ambience 7** • **Bonus 2**

- **Closed:** never
- **Seats:** 100
- **L.** 60,000 w/o wine
🖃 all 🅿 ♨

Restaurant. This restaurant is inside the beach club of the same name, but if you find watching the graceful antics of muscular windsurfers and beach volleyball enthusiasts a bit tiring, you can focus your energies here on a less physically demanding but very satisfying national sport – dining. The menu offers traditional, mainly fish dishes to enjoy on the terrace or the veranda: delicate seafood salad; scampi cocktail; shrimps with artichokes, and other fresh fish dishes depending on what's available at the markets. First courses include *linguine alle canocchie* [a type of shrimp], spaghetti alle vongole [with clams] or *allo scoglio* [with mixed seafood]; *tonnarelli* with shrimps and zucchini flowers; *risotto alla pescatora* [fisherman's-style]; *fritto misto* [mixed fried seafood], and fish of the day prepared in the traditional ways. Homemade desserts. Attentive, polished service; the wine cellar could offer a wider choice.

ROCCA DI PAPA [ROME]

26 KM FROM ROME

LA FORESTA

via dei Laghi, km 12
☎ 06/94749167

  75

• **Cucina** 43
• **Wine Cellar** 15 • **Service** 7
• **Ambience** 8 • **Bonus** 2

• **Closed:** Tuesdays
• **Seats:** 800
• **L.** 55,000 w/o wine
all 🅿 ✳ ⅃ ♣

Restaurant. Dining at the Ferri family's restaurant is always a pleasurable experience, because of its beautiful location [especially in summer when eating outside in the peaceful green woods is a real delight], because the service is so efficient and courteous, and because their dishes are always very carefully prepared and presented, even when they're at their busiest. Give in to temptation and try their splendid selection of cured game and other meats as an appetiser; then the rice with *ovoli* mushrooms [in season]; *tagliatelle* with porcini mushrooms, and *pappardelle* with hare sauce. Main courses include baked squab; fillet steak - either grilled or *all'alpina* [with porcini mushrooms]; *famigliole* and *galletti* mushrooms poached in tomato sauce, and fried *sfocatelli* [wild mushrooms found under local oak trees]. For dessert, *zuppa inglese* [trifle], strawberry charlotte and *tiramisù*. An extensive wine list at very reasonable prices [bonus].

SAN CESAREO [ROME]

30 KM FROM ROME

OSTERIA DI SAN CESARIO

via F. Corridoni, 60 [l.go Villa di Giulio Cesare]
☎ 06/9587950

 75

• **Cucina** 45
• **Wine Cellar** 13 • **Service** 7
• **Ambience** 7 • **Bonus** 3

• **Closed:** Mondays; Aug 15
• **Seats:** 35
• **L.** 45,000 w/o wine
all 🅿 ⅃ ♣

Restaurant. In 1995, after nearly fifty years at the helm of the family butchery, Anna Dente [known to everyone as Sora Anna] decided to open a restaurant. She wanted to cook for visitors as well as friends, principally to make sure that the traditional local dishes wouldn't just gradually disappear. Just as well, or we might have lost one of the best culinary traditions in the whole Lazio region. Two small, rustic but comfortable dining rooms and a beautiful garden [Anna says the limited number of places guarantees the quality of the food]. Naturally-leavened, homemade bread made with stone-ground flour and genuine homegrown ingredients [among other things the Dente family also has their own fruit and vegetable farm]. Don't miss the *gnocchi a coda di soreca* [a kind of *tonnarelli*] with a memorable *amatriciana* sauce, or the *lane der pecoraro* [pasta made with soft wheat flour and water] in *baccalà* and pecorino sauce. Among the main courses, *coda alla vaccinara* [oxtail braised in celery]; *arista* [pork roast] and *tordi alla zagarolese* [spicy meat roulades]. Excellent desserts. The wine and spirits list has been very thoughtfully designed and there's also a separate coffee menu. Friendly, informal service; booking a must.

SEGNI [ROME]

58 KM FROM ROME

CASALE AMASONA

via Casilina, km 54
☎ 06/9770311

 70

• **Cucina** 43
• **Wine Cellar** 13 • **Service** 7
• **Ambience** 6 • **Bonus** 1

• **Closed:** Mondays; Aug 16-31
• **Seats:** 80
• **L.** 50,000 w/o wine
all 🅿 ✳ ⅃ ♣

Restaurant. Good quality at reasonable prices makes Giorgio Bicorni's restaurant one of Lazio's most reliable ports of call for fish dishes. Everything is simple and unpretentious here – the setting, the cordial, helpful service and the very good cooking [bonus]. Excellent, well-balanced appetisers: grilled eggplant with marinated anchovies; *seppia* [cuttlefish], cherry tomatoes and arugula; boiled salmon, avocado and *radicchio* [red-leafed chicory]. First courses include an excellent squash and shrimp risotto, and an exceptionally delicate *tagliolini seppie e nero* [with cuttlefish in black cuttlefish ink]. To follow, different kinds of fish [according to market availability] cooked in various different ways – we recommend the magnificent *frittura* [mixed fried fish]. A good sorbet and other desserts. The wine cellar [which keeps growing] is quite good and they also offer some fine spirits.

TIVOLI [ROME]

32 KM FROM ROME

ANTICA HOSTARIA DE' CARRETTIERI

via D. Giuliani, 55
☎ 0774/330159

 71

- Cucina 43
- Wine Cellar 13 • Service 7
- Ambience 7 • Bonus 1

- **Closed:** Wednesdays; annual holidays vary
- **Seats:** 35
- **L.** 45,000 w/o wine 🗠 all Ⓟ

Restaurant. The Dedoni sisters are bred-and-born Sardinians, and they evidently use the legendary wisdom of the islander to run this restaurant, which has won the affection and respect of both local food-lovers and those from further afield. Totally devoid of metropolitan pretensions and with that characteristically Sardinian reserve that nevertheless goes hand-in-hand with a capacity for warm hospitality, they offer simple but tasty cucina. *Rigatoni all'amatriciana; gnocch*i with spicy cream cheese sauce; mixed fried mushrooms, zucchini, artichokes, asparagus and cheese; herb-buttered fillet of beef, and roast beef spiced with three peppers. For dessert: Sardinian *seadas* [honey-glazed, deep-fried cheese-filled ravioli], coffee-flavoured gelato, and *consolazione della suocera* – [the mother-in-law's consolation!], made with spongecake, pastry cream, pine nuts and caramel. Our meal was exemplary and gives you an idea of the quality of their cooking. The wine list is a work-in-progress with solid foundations and reasonable prices. A bonus for the passion.

TREVIGNANO ROMANO [ROME]

44 KM FROM ROME

VILLA VALENTINA GIARDINO DELL'EDEN

via Settevene Palo km 9, 600
☎ 06/9997647

 71

- Cucina 43
- Wine Cellar 13 • Service 7
- Ambience 7 • Bonus 1

- **Closed:** Wednesdays; Nov 1-30
- **Seats:** 150
- **L.** 45,000 w/o wine 🗠 all Ⓟ ♿ ♣

Restaurant. On the shores of Lake Bracciano, this restaurant offers tasty, carefully prepared dishes in pleasant, rustic surroundings. The menu offers not only typical local dishes but also - unexpected pleasure - Argentinian specialities: after you've enjoyed the excellent plain *pizzelle* [small fried pizzas] offered by the house you could try the *empanadas* stuffed with meat and vegetables, and maybe follow them up with a good octopus salad, or spinach-green *tagliatelle* with grouper and shrimps. Main courses include crunchy fried squid and shrimps, an excellent roast *coregone* [lake salmon] with grilled eggplant, and an impeccable *asado* [grilled meat] with fried potatoes. Homemade desserts and exquisite *pecorino* served with honey-drizzled slices of pear. Courteous, attentive service and quite a good wine list.

VELLETRI [ROME]

38 KM FROM ROME

BENITO AL BOSCO

c.da Morice, 20
☎ 06/9641414

 77

- Cucina 45
- Wine Cellar 16 • Service 7
- Ambience 7 • Bonus 2

- **Closed:** Tuesdays
- **Seats:** 80
- **L.** 65,000 w/o wine 🗠 all Ⓟ ❋ ♣

Restaurant. The *bosco* is a real one, one of those dense Mediterranean mountainside woods that thin out abruptly into pasture land - vital sites for pagan culture in ancient times, where curious deities and tree spirits were venerated and ritual celebrations of the body were held - before the desire for sanctity put knickers on us all. Longtime restaurateur Benito offers guests a real feast - a pagan festival of the palate. But don't expect only earthy dishes; here the sea gods are worshipped too. Next to Velletrian specialities like artichokes *alla matticella,* or Brussels sprouts and *baccalà* soup, and Roman classics like *bucatini all'amatriciana;* spaghetti *cacio e pepe;* mixed fries *alla romana,* and grilled *animelle* - all very tasty - you'll find excellent fish dishes: lightly sautéd basil-scented shrimps; raw scampi with orange; home-smoked and marinated fish; rice with squash blossoms and shrimps; delicious *linguine* with shrimps, tomatoes and basil, and *fettuccine* with porcini mushrooms. The second courses are equally good: fried *paranza* [mixed fish 'fresh off the boats']; sea bream baked in salt crust with candied lemon; red mullet poached with herbs and tomato; sea bass *al cartoccio* [baked in parchment] with porcini mushrooms, as well as *tagliata* [thin slices of beef] drizzled with balsamic vinegar; spring lamb; suckling pig, and fillets of beef cooked in 101 different ways [or so they say]. Good desserts, and a well-stocked wine cellar of the same high standard as the food, with a wide selection of Italian and foreign labels and a few special treats.

at all hours

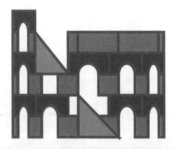

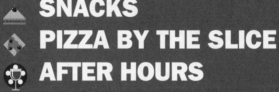

ACCADEMIA

TRASTEVERE
vicolo della Renella, 88/90
☎ 06/5896321
• **Closed:** August
• **Hours:** 6.30pm – 2am

Two big dining rooms and a huge terrace, always full of young, cheerfully noisy people. We recommend an expertly-mixed aperitivo at their well-stocked cocktail bar comfortably seated on a bar stool, or better still, a romantic supper looking out at the magnificent view of Rome's ancient rooftops.

ALDEBARAN

TESTACCIO
via Galvani, 54
☎ 06/5746013
• **Closed:** Sundays; August
• **Hours:** 10pm – 2.30am

The gigantic cocktail menu offering excellent, expertly-prepared and complicated delights continues to be the Aldebaran's strong point. In fact they also organise winter-time courses for aspiring cocktail-makers. In the summer the menu widens to include good *gelati* served at their outdoor tables.

ANTONINI

PRATI - MAZZINI
via Sabotino, 21/29
☎ 06/37517845
• **Closed:** never
• **Hours:** 7am – 9pm

Their savoury hors d'oeuvres and other marvellous morsels make it the favourite bar of aperitivo-lovers, but the sweet pastries are no less potent, with pastry-cream or chocolate-filled choux pastry *bigné* among the innumerable specialities

that force you back again and again. Cakes range from jam tarts and *semifreddo* [soft frozen mousse] to their legendary *bomba*, everything a sweet-toothed gourmet could possibly desire. They also do interesting savoury snacks at lunch-time.

AP - PIZZA ART

MONTEVERDE NUOVO
via Fonteiana, 63
☎ 06/5896646
• **Closed:** never
• **Hours:** 9am – 10.30pm

One of three pizzerias founded by champion pizzamakers Pietro and Annamaria with Massimiliano Moresi. Their pizzas obey all the Pizza Club canons: only naturally-leavened pastry dough, extra vergine olive oil and first class ingredients. Unlike the mother house, the pizza here is sold by the slice. They also do various fried foods and take-aways if you order in advance.

AP - PIZZA ART

PIAZZA BOLOGNA
via Pisa, 46
☎ 06/8611250
• **Closed:** never
• **Hours:** 10am – 10.30pm

The third and most recently-opened of the Pizza Art pizzerias, member of the Pizza Club and founded by Pietro and Annamaria with Massimiliano Moresi [see above]. Here, apart from his prize-winning pièce de résistance topped with champignon mushrooms, Parma prosciutto, arugula, and creamy walnuts with *stracchino* cheese, Massimiliano also makes a Margherita with buffalo mozzarella and cherry tomatoes, a pizza topped with roast artichokes, another with grilled eggplant and smoked buffalo mozzarella, and many more. Lots of fried foods: potato croquettes; traditional meat-flecked *supplì* riceballs as well as a shellfish version;

fillets of *baccalà;* chicken meatballs; *olive ascolane* [stuffed olives]; miniscule *calzoncini* [pizza turnovers]; and *zoccolette* [fried pizza dough] with Nutella.

AP - PIZZA ART

BOCCEA
via Monti di Creta, 9
☎ 06/66016768
• **Closed:** never
• **Hours:** 9am – 11pm

No-one can stop them now, and 1997 World Pizza Champions Annamaria and Pietro have tripled the size of their operation. They belong to the Pizza Club, an association whose members guarantee that their pizzas are made with first-class ingredients and naturally-leavened dough [and are therefore easily digestible]. Heaps of different kinds, all delicious, are on display in their trays. Novelties include pizza with asparagus, mozzarella and shrimps, to eat hot, and closed pizzas filled with arugula, mozzarella and *speck* [smoked ham], or grilled eggplant, mozzarella, and porcini mushrooms to eat cold. Various good fried snacks.

ARCIONI

NEMORENSE
p.zza Crati, 22/25
☎ 06/86206616
• **Closed:** Mondays
• **Hours:** 7am – 9.30pm

Wine shop, bar and delicatessen, Arcioni has now taken its rightful place in the charmed circle of Roman Breakfast Temples. Its winning cards include excellent coffee made with its own arabica blend roasted on the premises and served in delicate, beautiful porcelain cups, fragrant breakfast *lieviti*, outdoor tables and an excellent position. Arcidoni, a shop specialising in food and wine accessories, has just opened next door at 16/17 Piazza Crati.

ARTÙ

TRASTEVERE
l.go M. D. Fumasoni Biondi, 5
☎ *06/5880398*
• **Closed:** Mondays; August
• **Hours:** 5pm – 2am

Paolo Cappellanti has made his Artù known and much appreciated in just a few short years.
His latest innovation is the introduction of an aperitivo ritual, not a very widespread habit in Rome, with a wide choice of *tartine* [canapés] to nibble on during happy hour from 5pm to 9pm. Afterwards, if you want to stay on, you can choose from a series of appetizers including vinegar-drizzled baby anchovies, cured beef *bresaola* or swordfish *carpaccio*, or else move straight on to the first courses, like Valtellina *pizzoccheri* [a kind of tagliatelle] or polenta with porcini mushrooms, *spuntature* [pork spare ribs], or *formaggio fuso* [melted cheese]. Main courses include an excellent casseroled beef *stracotto*, veal meatballs, and very light, classic fried foods. Homemade desserts of a similarly high order: *tiramisù*, crème caramel and chocolate mousse.

BANDANA REPUBLIC

PINCIANO
via Alessandria, 44
☎ *06/44249751*
• **Closed:** August
• **Hours:** 12 – 3.30pm; 7pm – 2am

The Bandana follows a singular Tuscan-Irish gastronomic trajectory all its own: next to the Irish stew and beef braised in beer we found a new dish based on a choice of Tuscan *finocchiona* [fennel-flavoured *mortadella*], cured pork *ciauscolo*, wild boar sausage and spicy olives called Bandana Maremma. They also do *carpaccio*, fried or curried chicken, a dozen or so salads, various delicious *panini* and a small number of excellent desserts. We greatly appreciated the recent inauguration of a non-smokers' dining room.

LE GRAND BAR DEL ST. REGIS GRAND

TERMINI
via V. E. Orlando, 3
☎ *06/4709*
• **Closed:** never
• **Hours:** 8:30am - 1:30am

Its raised position above the vast lobby makes it an excellent site for all-day people-watching. The bar has been famous for generations, especially for the memorable cocktails prepared by its internationally renowned barmen. Light meals all day long.

BARBAGIANNI

PRATI - COLA DI RIENZO
via Boezio, 92/a
☎ *06/6874972*
• **Closed:** July 15 – Aug 31
• **Hours:** 8.30pm – 2am; Sundays 4.30pm – 2am

Still a small corner of paradise for boardgames-lovers, the Barbagianni now has more than 100 available for patrons. You'll also find classic Irish draught beers to accompany salads, sweet and savoury crepes or stuffed focaccia.

BEEFEATER

OSTIENSE
via G. Benzoni, 42/44
☎ *06/57300300*
• **Closed:** Moday evenings
• **Hours:** 11am – 2pm

The Beefeater offers a variety of excellent services to meet its clients needs throughout the day. If you're in a hurry you can choose from more than 30 *panini*, 12 *piadine* [focaccia] or 8 *crostoni* [meat on toast]. For more leisurely and substantial snacks they offer cold meat and fish dishes, steaks [Italian beef only], a dozen salads and a potato soufflé with egg called the Bull's Eye. 7 different kinds of beer are permanently on tap with another available on a monthly rotation basis, plus a number of good wine labels, and the tea room opens in the afternoon with a range of newspapers and magazines available for patrons. But the house's pride and joy are their single-malt whiskies, for which there'll soon be a special menu with all the necessary information about their origins, ages and characteristics.

IL BELLO E LE STREGHE

APPIO
via Cerveteri, 21a/b
☎ *06/70475299*
• **Closed:** Mondays; July 15 – Aug 30
• **Hours:** 7.30pm - 2am; Sundays 5pm – 2am

The varied menu offers numerous salads, Mexican specialities and hamburgers but we prefer the house speciality - irresistibly tempting baked potatoes-in-their-jackets with various fillings. Boardgame-lovers are well-catered for with more than 50 different games available and sometimes you can also have your cards read.

BLOB

PRATI - VIA COLA DI RIENZO
via degli Scipioni, 96
☎ *06/668356*
• **Closed:** Sundays;
   July 1 – Aug 31
• **Hours:** 9.30pm – 6am

This casual but extremely attractive, comfortable place has become an obbligatory stopping-off point for city night owls who come for the tropical cocktails, lovingly and skilfully prepared by Enrico Venafra, or to assuage sudden attacks of nocturnal hunger with the Blob – a mixed plate of cured meats and cheeses; the Goloso - smoked ham roulades stuffed with *gorgonzola*, arugula and walnuts; or a Greek *macedonia* [fruit salad] served with yoghurt, honey and walnuts. Happy hour from 9.30 till 10pm, and a Monday night special whereby clients chose a cocktail for the evening and stick with it at L.5,000 a shot. Very varied background music.

LE BON BOCK CAFÉ

MONTEVERDE NUOVO
c.ne Gianicolense, 249
☎ *06/5376806*
• **Closed:** Wednesdays;
   August
• **Hours:** : 12 – 3pm;
   5pm – 2am; Sundays and
   holidays 6pm – 2am

You'll find seven different draught beers to choose from here: five German, a Czech pilsner and another one chosen by Stefano, beer-lover and connoisseur, that changes each month and is exclusive to the café, plus an unbelievable number of single-malt whiskies

70

- more than 100. They also do a much-appreciated *panino on demand:* you choose the type of bread [classic rolls, pita bread or *crescia*, the traditional pizza from Gubbio in Umbria] and one of twenty fillings; as well as a number of light meals, including cured beef *bresaola*, swordfish *carpaccio*, and salmon trout. There's a tea room offering *piccola pasticceria* [tiny biscuits and pastries] open every afternoon. You can take a look at www.lebenbock.com

LA BOTTICELLA

CENTRO STORICO - NAVONA
via Tor Millina, 32
☎ *06/6861107*
• **Closed:** Mondays;
   annual holidays vary
• **Hours:** 8pm – 2am

Despite his youth, Giovanni runs the Botticella with the wisdom of a veteran and a passionate enthusiasm that drives him to sing the praises of a good glass of wine even to beer-drinking kids who'll probably never touch the stuff. The "something-for-everyone" formula continues to pay off for all concerned: habitués and tourists just passing through relax inside or at the outdoor tables with one of 4 different draught beers or 30 bottled varieties [or a good bottle of wine].

BOULEDOGUE

SAN LORENZO
via dei Volsci, 4
☎ *no*
• **Closed:** July 15 – Sept 1
• **Hours:** 5.30pm – 2am

Attention to detail and a commitment to quality are the hallmarks of this little pub run by a *simpatico* young couple you warm to the moment you set eyes on them. The evenings slip away over a pint of beer or a glass of single-malt to a background of garage music, rock or blues. A must-visit for lovers of Forties' and Fifties' objects.

BREK

CENTRO STORICO - ARGENTINA
l.go di Torre Argentina, 1
☎ *06/68210353*
• **Closed:** never
• **Hours:** coffee bar/pizzeria
   7am – 1am; restaurant
   11.30am – 3.30pm,
   7 – 11pm

There's a pizzeria and coffee bar on the ground floor where they serve an excellent coffee with a complimentary chocolate; the restaurant is upstairs, with several dining rooms and various "islands" devoted to drinks and breads, first courses, salads and vegetables, meat and fish, fruit and desserts. Everything is prepared with the freshest raw materials while you watch.

CAFÉ RENAULT

CENTRO STORICO - VIA NAZIONALE
via Nazionale, 183/b
☎ *06/47824452*
• **Closed:** never
• **Hours:** 7am – 2am;
   7am – 8pm in August

A late-night haunt of showbiz people, it offers huge spaces, modern decor and traditional coffee bar service with a wide choice of *cornetti* and *lieviti*, aperitivi and snacks, a hot self-service buffet, gelateria, and restaurant service in the evenings [best to book] specialising in fish dishes, shellfish in particular. Service is provided by a team of very polite young staff. e-mail: info @caferenault.com or have a look at www.caferenault.com

CAFFETTERIA NAZIONALE

TERMINI
via Nazionale, 26/27
☎ *06/48991716*
• **Closed:** Sundays;
   early Aug – beginning Sept
• **Hours:** 9am – 8pm

In among the wood, marble, boiserie wood-panelling and neo-antique mirrors you can enjoy an excellent coffee blend with normal-sized or tiny breakfast pastries. For midday snacks they offer *tartine* [canapés]; *rustici* and tiny *bottoncini* [big and small flaky pastry turnovers]; *panini* [rolls]; *tramezzini* [sandwiches] and *piadine* [flat bread] as well as classic Italian fast food dishes which you can either gobble standing up or dawdle over comfortably seated in the big dining rooms at the back or downstairs with one of the Italian or foreign newspapers available for clients.

GRAN CAFFÈ LA CAFFETTIERA

CENTRO STORICO - POPOLO
via Margutta, 61/a
☎ 06/3213344
• **Closed:** August
• **Hours:** 8.30am – 9pm
CENTRO STORICO - PANTHEON
p.zza di Pietra, 65
☎ 06/6798147
• **Closed:** Sundays in summer
• **Hours:** 7am – 9pm

Two Neapolitan enclaves in the heart of Rome where you can find an excellent *tazzulella* [very strong espresso] prepared in the traditional way. *Sfogliatella* and *pasticciotto* pastries for breakfast, as well as classic breakfast buns.
An excellent range of gateaux, timbales, rice *sartù* [meat, mozzarella, egg and mushroom timbale]; maccheroni fritters; pizza with escarole; Neapolitan *panini* with *ciccioli* [tasty scraps of pork]; *supplì* [meat-flecked riceballs] and *arancini* [innards, pea and rice croquettes] for lunch. Their splendid new premises in Via Margutta have an atmosphere all their own with elegant tables and divans lit from above by a skylight. Impeccable service. They're

also open for evening dining – best to book. Credit cards accepted.

CIAMPINI

CENTRO STORICO - CAMPO MARZIO
via della Fontanella di Borghese, 59
☎ 06/68135108
CENTRO STORICO - CAMPO MARZIO
p.zza San Lorenzo in Lucina, 29
☎ 06/6876606
• **Closed:** Sundays; August
• **Hours:** 9am – 8.30pm

The quality of its coffee bar services place the Ciampini head and shoulders above its confreres. It's also very central, in Piazza San Lorenzo in the heart of the Campo Marzio quarter, with outdoor tables under huge umbrellas - an irresistible invitation to watch the world go by in summertime, soothed by balmy breezes. Apart from the usual repertoire of good *gelati*, drinks, *tramezzini* and *panini*, it's just the place for a slow breakfast with their traditional or tiny bite-sized *cornetti*.

CIAMPINI AL CAFÉ DU JARDIN

CENTRO STORICO - SPAGNA
v.le Trinità dei Monti
☎ 06/6785678
• **Closed:** Wednesdays; early November – mid-March
• **Hours:** 8am – 7pm; 8am – 1am in summer

The perfect place to take the weight off your feet and indulge in a bit of what Romans call *dolce far niente* [doing sweet nothing] while gazing across the city's most beautiful rooftops from the shade of perfumed plants. Admirably run by Marco Ciampini, the café offers classic coffee bar and gelateria services as well as ready-to-eat hot dishes. The restaurant is particularly magical in the evening [best to book] and offers a wide range of hot

and cold dishes, including buffalo mozzarella and *bottarga* [dried fish roe]; fish-filled *raviolini* with eggplant and mussels, and fillet of beef baked in a pistachio-nut crust. They also have a rather good wine list.

CLAMUR

TESTACCIO
p.zza dell'Emporio, 1/2
☎ 06/5754532
• **Closed:** August
• **Hours:** 5pm – 2am

This pub is located just across the Tiber from the famous Porta Portese markets in Testaccio, one of Rome's oldest working-class neighbourhoods. Apart from the usual range of Irish beers, the Clamur also offers numerous *panini* and some interesting non-local dishes as well as pizzas and a few traditional first courses – all much appreciated by the late-night clientele. You can also pay to watch soccer games on video with enthusiastic supporters of the red-and-yellow Roma team.

DIFRONTE A...

CENTRO STORICO - SPAGNA
via della Croce, 38
☎ 06/6780355
• **Closed:** never
• **Hours:** 11am – 12.30am

Coffee bar, restaurant and pizzeria, this very big space [600 sq. m.] often hosts exhibitions and also provides a giant video screen for clients who don't want to miss their favourite TV programmes. The menu ranges from traditional Italian bar fare and quick lunches to candlelit suppers in the evenings [for which it's best to book]. High prices; outdoor tables.

DONEGAL

OSTIENSE
v.le Marco Polo, 47b
☎ *06/57284499*
• **Closed:** August
• **Hours:** 6pm – 2am

Irish, Irish – everything here is Irish, from the beer to the food with [Irish] stew, fish and cheese as well as hamburgers and hotdogs and a rather good choice of salads. Happy hour every day from 6pm to 9pm, while on Sundays you can watch Rome's Roma and Lazio soccer teams on pay TV.

DONEY

PINCIANO
via Veneto, 145
☎ *06/47082805*
• **Closed:** Mondays
• **Hours:** 8am – midnight

One of those places you can always confidently recommend because of the unfailing quality, professional service and the fact that it never closes. Excellent breakfasts with tasty *lieviti*, and an aromatic espresso or cappuccino served in finest porcelainware, as well as equally good aperitivi, long drinks, snacks, tea and pastries. They also offer fixed-price business lunches at L. 35,000 and a splendid and abundant Sunday brunch, from midday on, at L. 15 – 50,000 a head. Indoor and outdoor tables. Take home the house brand of scrumptious chocolates or biscuits.

DRUID'S DEN

MONTI
via S. Martino ai Monti, 28
☎ *06/4880258*
• **Closed:** never
• **Hours:** 7pm – 1am

The main ingredients of this pub's success are their generous pints of draught beer, the cheerful [often multi-lingual] socialising it engenders and the extraordinary warmth and friendliness of the staff, whose welcome makes you feel immediately at home.

DRUNKEN SHIP

CENTRO STORICO · CAMPO DE' FIORI
p.zza Campo de' Fiori, 20/21
☎ *06/68300535*
• **Closed:** Mondays
• **Hours:** 5pm – 2am

From the tables of the Drunken Ship you gaze around one of the most beautiful piazzas in the world, and from opening hour on you'll always find lots of people here enjoying it all and also taking advantage of happy hour [5-9pm]. Rivers of beer, tequila, vodka and rum as well as cocktails and American-style long drinks are the main things clients order. Rock music turned up as loud as it will go sets the mood at this pleasant [youthful] meeting place.

L'ENOTECA ANTICA DI VIA DELLA CROCE

CENTRO STORICO · SPAGNA
via della Croce, 76/b
☎ *06/6790896*
• **Closed:** annual holidays vary
• **Hours:** 11am – 1pm

One of the most beautiful wine shops in the city with old, old furniture, splendid original floors and shelves creaking with wine bottles, little tables at the back and a magnificent counter with bar stools for a quick snack. There's an attractive selection of wines by-the-glass written up on the blackboard [a pity they don't put the producer names and vintages, though]; plus various salads, *carpaccio*, cold dishes like the ubiquitous *caprese* [tomato,

mozzarella and basil]; first courses of the day; eggs prepared in several different ways, and even pizzas. Polite service which can fray around the edges a bit at peak-hour. High prices, but all major credit-cards accepted. Outdoor tables.

THE FIDDLER'S ELBOW

ESQUILINO
via dell'Olmata, 43
☎ *06/4872110*
• **Closed:** never
• **Hours:** 4.30pm – 1am

There are a lot of Irish pubs in Rome but this is practically the only one that can boast twenty years of honourable and uninterrupted service. The time-tested formula provides for a ritual after-work drink or beer [only a few snacks or chips at most to go with it], more drinks, leisurely conversation or trying your hand at one of the interminable games of darts.

FINNEGAN

COLOSSEO
via Leonina, 66/67
☎ *06/4747026*
• **Closed:** never
• **Hours:** 5pm – 1am
in winter;
11am – 1am
May - September

This is pretty much an Anglosaxon enclave: the staff are all rigorously mother-tongue English speakers [though the owners are real seventh generation-plus Romans], Sky TV is permanently on, interminable darts games are played and there's an authentic pool table out the back. Oceans of beer to drink, obviously, and a good choice of whiskies and various cocktails. Live music Friday and Saturday nights in winter.

FONCLEA

PRATI - CAVOUR
via Crescenzio, 82/a
☎ *06/6896302*
• **Closed:** Saturday and
  Sunday lunchtime
• **Hours:** 12am – 3pm;
  7pm – 2am

One of Rome's longest-running eateries with more than twenty years of successful activity behind it, the Fonclea's undeniable success has never tempted its owners to rest on their laurels, and year after year they've always managed to anticipate the needs and tastes of their vast and heterogenous clientele. Hence the opening of a non-smoking dining room and the introduction of two fixed-price buffet lunch menus: L. 12,000 for a plate of either mixed first courses [minestra, risotto, timbales, *cannelloni*, crepes and quick-serve pastas] or a selection of raw or cooked vegetable dishes; for L. 20,000 there's the choice of any one of all the dishes on the menu that day. The cocktail bar continues to offer excellent drinks. Live music every evening with preference given to vocalists.

FOUR GREEN FIELDS

TRIONFALE
via Morin, 38/42
☎ *06/3725091*
• **Closed:** never
• **Hours:** 7pm – 2am

The Four Green Fields is another pub that offers numerous Italian first course dishes like risotto and pasta or else a *tirolese* [würstel sausage, *pancetta*, sausage and sauerkraut] to go with the Irish beers. Live music from Wednesday through to Sunday nights, with

Wednesday dedicated to Irish music. All the championship matches played by Rome's Roma and Lazio football teams are available on pay TV.

FOUR XXXX PUB

TESTACCIO
via Galvani, 29/29a
☎ *06/5757296*
• **Closed:** August
• **Annual holidays :** August
• **Hours:** 7pm – 2am

Though it started off as just a pub, the Four XXXX has rapidly undergone a process of Latinisation, and we warmly recommend it to anyone who's enjoyed the summer "Fiesta" festival of which it is a sort of wintertime continuation. Latin cocktails, tequila, tequilera and draught beer accompany the whole classic Tex-Mex repertoire: tacos, paella, nachos and various kinds of chili bean dishes. Live trad jazz at weekends and discobar with a DJ Wednesdays and Thursdays.

FRONTONI DAL 1921

TRASTEVERE
v.le Trastevere, 52
☎ *06/5812436*
• **Closed:** never
• **Hours:** 10am – 1.30am

This historic bread shop specialises in Roman *pizza bianca* [plain, light and salty], which it churns out in truly astounding quantities, to have with the filling of your choice. They offer a total of 60 combinations, from figs and prosciutto to the *morettiana* [in honour of film director Nanni Moretti] with Nutella. Frontoni's also runs La Ristoreria at 145, Circonvallazione Gianicolense.

GREEN ROSE PUB

CENTRO STORICO - POPOLO
passeggiata di Ripetta, 33
☎ *06/3215548*
• **Closed:** Sundays; August
• **Hours:** 7.30am – 2am

You can happily start the day here with coffee and excellent homemade breakfast buns, but it's the lunchtime snacks that are really varied and interesting: 15 or more salads like the Green Rose [shrimps, arugula, tomatoes and mozzarella]; delicious *crostoni* [cheese on toast] named in curious homage to outlying Roman suburbs like the *Tufello* [mozzarella, tomato, oregano and parsley], or the *Tor Bella Monaca* [smoked scamorza cheese, porcini mushrooms, truffle sauce and parsley]; sweet or savoury crêpes, and a range of tasty desserts. Six kinds of very well-poured beer [mostly English], and live music twice a week, with preference given to Irish music.

GREGORY'S

CENTRO STORICO - SPAGNA
via Gregoriana, 54/a
☎ *06/6796386*
• **Closed:** Mondays; August
• **Hours:** 7pm – 3.30am

With its wood decor, draught beer and dartboards Gregory's looks like a typical Irish pub when you first walk inside, but you only have to go upstairs to find yourself in the totally different atmosphere of the quintessential jazz club. Omar and Viviana, the owners, have created a perfect environment for the musicians who come here for jam sessions [Wednesday nights] or regular concerts [from Thursday to Sunday]. An excellent cocktail bar and an equally good selection of more than 70 whisky labels. Irish stew, curried chicken or salads and various *panini* to eat.

HOP HOLE

MONTEVERDE NUOVO
c.ne Gianicolense,. 190/d
☎ *06/no*
• **Closed:** annual holidays
  vary
• **Hours:** 6pm – 12.30pm;
  Saturday and Sunday
  6pm – 1.30am

Most Roman pubs model themselves on the British or Irish versions, so it's not easy to find one that offers a good range of German beers. But in this little place you can sample five different varieties, all from the Munich area, very professionally poured and served: a classic lager, a weiss, a light 6° bock, a tasty, full-bodied red bock and a pleasant dark beer – toastier but very easy to drink. Wooden tables in simple, attractive surroundings and friendly, efficient service. A good selection of desserts [including an excellent strudel], tasty *panini*, *bruschetta* and salads, as well as cocktails and a few excellent Scotch labels. Reasonable prices.

 ## INDIAN FAST FOOD

ESQUILINO
via Mamiani, 11
☎ *06/4460792*
• **Closed:** Sundays; annual
  holidays vary
• **Hours:** 10am – 10pm

If you've actually been to India the *déjà vu* effect is guaranteed. In this tiny hole-in-the-wall in Rome's most multicultural quarter you can enjoy *samosa* and *chola*, *dhal* and *chapatis*, *pakora* and *nan*, chicken curry and birijani rice, various vegetable sauces and condiments, and typical Indian desserts - also available as takeaways.

Mainly beer to drink, with Indian Kobra beer in first place. A big TV in the background plays a ceaseless stream of Indian videomusic clips for the joy of patrons, mother-tongue or otherwise.

 ## ITALIA - PALMERINO AMICONE

PINCIANO
c.so d'Italia, 103
☎ *06/44249771*
• **Closed:** Sundays; August
• **Hours:** 9am – 9pm

The name Palmerino Amicone has been synonymous with good pizzas for more than ten years. They're made with a special blend of flours, including soy flour, and naturally leavened [for a minimum 24 hours]. New toppings include black Norcia truffles with prosciutto and mozzarella, the very popular pizza *alla carbonara* with the same ingredients as the famous Roman pasta: *guanciale* [cured pork jowl], egg, cream and *pecorino romano* cheese, and the Diavola, topped with hot salami, chili peppers and fresh tomato. Their pizza with salmon and shrimps finds a lot of takers in summer.

 ## BIRRERIA MARCONI

ESQUILINO
via di Santa Prassede, 9/c
☎ *06/486636*
• **Closed:** never
• **Hours:** 12pm – 1.30am

Good quality at reasonable prices goes hand in hand here with a healthy mixture of various culinary traditions that sets fish and chips and lamb chops side by side with goulash [served with sauerkraut and würstel sausage] and Irish breakfasts, as well as salads and desserts. A casual but decidedly welcoming atmosphere.

 ## MEDITERRANEO

TRASTEVERE
vicolo del Cinque, 15
☎ *06/5803630*
• **Closed:** Tuesdays; August
• **Hours:** 9pm – 3am;
  5pm – 3am Saturdays
  and Sundays

Youthful Roberto is actually something of an old seadog who has chalked up valuable professional experience in bars all over the world. His passions and predilections are all reflected in the menu which offers more than 200 cocktails with names like Sea Breeze, Kamikaze, Cape Coder - mostly of Anglo-Hispanic inspiration, but there are some more personal and original ones like his legendary Mezzo Litre. The tea room [Saturdays and Sundays in winter] and the live music on Friday and Saturday nights are very popular.

 ## NADIA E DAVIDE

VIMINALE
via Milano, 33
☎ *06/4882842*
• **Closed:** Sundays;
  2-3 days around Aug 15
• **Hours:** 7.30am – 9.30pm

The two *pizzaioli* whose names are on the sign prepare classic pizzas [with tomato or tomato and mozzarella; potatoes; or mushrooms], thick soft *foggiana* pizzas and several other more imaginative varieties laid out invitingly in trays. Among their most recent creations: pizza with salmon, arugula and fresh cheese, and pizza with fresh porcini mushrooms and truffles. Apart from the traditional stuffed pizzas, they also do ones filled with creamy *stracchino* cheese, arugula and cooked ham;

squash blossoms, cherry tomatoes and buffalo mozzarella or *gorgonzola*, cherry tomatoes and cooked ham.

L'Oasi
della Birra

TESTACCIO
p.zza Testaccio, 41
☎ 06/5746122
• **Closed:** Sundays
  in summer; August
• **Hours:** 7.30pm – 1am
TESTACCIO
via A. Vespucci, 42
☎ 06/5757894
• **Closed:** Sundays
  in summer; August
• **Hours:** 8pm – 1am

More innovations at Mario Palombi's wine shop and delicatessen in Testaccio. Recent extensions have increased its seating capacity [there are tables upstairs now in the beautiful, elegant wine shop] and the range of gastronomic delights has broadened, with several new dishes like stuffed duck leg or wild boar in Barolo wine to enjoy with literally hundreds of beers of every kind [beer-lovers from all over Italy stock up here], from the most important traditional Scottish labels to artisan-made Belgian varieties. They also offer a remarkable selection of cheeses and cured meats, including more than 40 different types of cheese from all over the world, 36 varieties of cured meat and 10 different kinds of *lardo* [cured pork fat].
There is also a well-stocked [and continually evolving] wine list. The pub in Via Vespucci offers a selection of bottled beers on a rotating system, delicious hot dishes and some interesting draught beers.

Ombre Rosse

TRASTEVERE
p.zza Sant'Egidio, 12
☎ 06/5884155
• **Closed:** Sunday mornings
• **Hours:** 7.30am – 2am

One of the most pleasurable things you can do for yourself is embark on the kind of gentle shipwreck of normal concerns that happens when you stop for a while at one of Ombre Rosse's outdoor tables. Time seems suspended as you slowly leaf through the daily paper munching on delicious snacks offered by the house with their many drinks and aperitivi. Apart from very good draught beer, they also keep a couple of dozen good wine labels and numerous bottles of excellent single-malt whisky.

Orusdir Pub

CENTRO STORICO - CAMPO DE' FIORI
via dei Cappellari, 130
☎ no
• **Closed:** Sundays; August
• **Hours:** 8pm – 2am

Small but very cosy, the Orusdir Pub is a good place to snatch a little peaceful relaxation. Don't miss the *piatto Orusdir* that combines deer, goat and wild boar salami with cured pork *ciauscolo* sausage from Le Marche, the owners' birthplace; their *panini, piadine* and *bruschetta* are good, too. Scottish beer on tap and a rather good choice of grappas.

Paladini

CENTRO STORICO - NAVONA
via del Governo Vecchio, 29
☎ 06/6861237
• **Closed:** Thursday afternoons;
  Saturday afternoons in
  summer; Aug 15-31
• **Hours:** 8am – 7pm

A bakery and grocery store since 1914, Paladini's has always been a good place for a quick lunch. The numerous clientele, mostly young, crowd the entrance from midday onwards, queueing for the classic Roman *pizza bianca* cooked in a wood-fired oven and filled as you watch with cured meats, cheeses, *sottoaceti* [pickles], tomatoes, beans or prosciutto and figs.

Palombini

EUR
p.le Adenauer, 12
☎ 06/5911701
• **Closed:** August
• **Hours:** 7am – midnight;
  open till 1am Saturdays
  and before public holidays

To Romans the name Palombini immediately conjures up visions of a mega coffee bar bursting with gastronomic delights: various kinds of coffee with *cornetti* for a truly delicious breakfast; a buffet of ready-to-eat delicacies; cakes and pastries; gelati, and from late morning on, a self-service smorgasboard of hot and cold dishes – all first-class. They also stock rare and wonderful confectionery. It's in a marvellous position, in a tranquil building next to the Palazzo della Civiltà del Lavoro, unworried by the generally noisy Eur quarter traffic, with beautiful outdoor tables.

Il Piccolo

CENTRO STORICO - NAVONA
via del Governo Vecchio, 74
☎ 06/68801746
• **Closed:** never
• **Hours:** 12 – 3pm;
  4.30pm – 3am

Small by name and small by nature, the ambience of this delightful and very tastefully decorated little place is very

AT ALL HOURS

French and its walls are completely lined with bottles of excellent Italian and foreign wine. At midday the menu includes two or three hot dishes, roasts, various salads [also fish] and desserts, always varied and based on what's best at the markets and in season. In the afternoon and evenings, out come the carefully selected cured meats and cheeses, *carpaccio*, *torte rustiche* [savoury pies], desserts and other delicious treats to accompany the wines and spirits – all of them, every single one, available by the glass.

LE PIRAMIDI

CENTRO STORICO - CAMPO DE' FIORI
vicolo del Gallo, 11
☎ 06/6879061
• **Closed:** Mondays;
  23 Aug – 7 Sept
• **Hours:** 10.30am – 2am;
  4.30pm – 2am in August

A small, pristine place where friendly and *simpatici* Piera and Mimmo [Muhammed] serve light, tasty Middle Eastern dishes to eat on your feet until late at night. Couscous, falafel, shawerma, shish kebab, sishtaouk and desserts – all prepared while you wait and served with tasty sauces in abundant portions. They also do *supplì* [meat-flecked riceballs], and croquettes, including Sicilian *arancini*. Various rice dishes with appetising condiments at lunchtime. Very courteous service, very reasonable prices and takeaway service if you prefer.

RICCIOLI CAFÉ OYSTER WINE BAR

CENTRO STORICO - PANTHEON
p.zza delle Coppelle, 10/a
☎ 06/68210313
• **Closed:** Sundays; August
• **Hours:** 12pm – 2am

This cafè was opened by Massimo Riccioli, who runs the best fish restaurant in Rome [and not just in Rome]. A gathering place for food-lovers, this delightful place with its outdoor tables offers gastronomic pleasures to satisfy the most demanding gourmet. The various kinds of oysters, shellfish and seafood [shrimps, squid, scampi, etc], are all super fresh and the dishes are prepared while you wait. They also offer imaginative salads, with or without fish, stunning prosciutto and *culatello* [top-quality cured ham], cheeses, caviar, foie gras and other culinary specialities. Homemade cakes and desserts to finish off with and beer, cocktails, *frullati* [milkshakes] and the best Italian and foreign wines to drink. From 3pm till 7pm Yara, Massimo's wife, presides over the tearoom where you'll find special tea blends, biscuits and sweet pastries.

LA RISTORERIA FRONTONI DAL 1921

MONTEVERDE NUOVO
c.ne Gianicolense, 145
☎ 06/58209090
• **Closed:** Monday mornings
• **Hours:** 11.30am – 3pm;
  7pm – midnight

Run by brothers Claudio and Giuseppe Frontoni, scions of the famous dynasty of Roman bakers, you'll find their speciality, *pizza bianca romana* [plain, light and salty] to eat with fillings of all kinds and combinations, from *prosciutto crudo* to Nutella, as well as more than sixty different brands of beer from all over the world.

RIVE GAUCHE 2

SAN LORENZO
via dei Sabelli, 43
☎ 06/4456722
• **Closed:** never
• **Hours:** 8pm – 2am;
  Sundays 6pm – 2am

The spirit of its founders has never been betrayed - Rive Gauche 2 continues to offer an excellent selection of beverages by the glass [the wines and spirits are particularly good] at prices so reasonable it can be embarrassing.

ROCK CASTLE

CENTRO STORICO - GHETTO
via Beatrice Cenci, 8
☎ 06/68807999
• **Closed:** August
• **Hours:** 8pm – 2am

Entering here is like descending into the dungeons of a mediaeval castle, except that the atmosphere is anything but grim and sinister – music, cheerful chatter and oceans of beer set the tone.

LA ROCKA

APPIO
via Gallia, 93
☎ 06/7092021
• **Closed:** August
• **Hours:** 6pm – 2am

This little pub wins your heart from the first time you go down the stairs leading to its door. It serves classic Irish beers and a few cocktails, often to the notes of small jazz combos with a predilection for reworked versions of two all-time greats: Tom Waits and Fred Buscaglione.

ROSTICCERIA

TRIONFALE
via Famagosta, 18
☎ 06/39726744
• **Closed:** Mondays; August
• **Hours:** 11am – 11pm

Its menu is original and unusual for Rome, not standard *rosticceria* fare at all, ranging from eggplant croquettes to falafel and kebabs. They also do *ranette* [little frogs] – small delicious *panini* with various fillings like sweet peppers and mozzarella; roast meat and tomato; or buffalo mozzarella and smoked ham; salads at lunchtime; really good *supplì* [rice croquettes with mozzarella centres]; focaccia and *taschine* [little pockets] of pita bread with a choice of fillings. There's also pizza *al taglio* [by the slice] with many different toppings - zucchini flowers, eggplant *parmigiana* and the classic *Margherita* with tomato, mozzarella and oregano, with the traditional round takeaway version available in the evenings. They even have a few homemade desserts like tarts and cream cake. Very reasonable prices.

S.GT PEPPER'S PUB & MUSIC

TRIONFALE
via della Giuliana, 93/95
☎ *06/39741303*
• **Closed:** Sundays; August
• **Hours:** 12.30pm – 3.30pm; 7.30pm – 2am

Everything here, from the menu to the music, is the product of authentic passion and the desire to offer the best. We recommend it unreservedly for lunch: *crostini*, assorted *bruschetta*, hamburgers, hot dogs, grilled vegetables, grilled *scamorza* cheese, baked potatoes, and above all their maxi-salads like the Ajanta [shrimps, arugula, turkey, and red chicory with curry sauce]; the Waikiki [salad greens, turkey, carrot, pineapple and mustard]; or the Cheddar [cheddar cheese, pear and arugula]. For dessert, *panna cotta*, cheesecake with wild berries, and apple pie – all homemade. In summer you can eat outside but it's very

comfortable indoors, too. There's a piano and a guitar there for anyone who feels inclined and Beatlemaniacs are strongly advised to pay a visit – apart from the perfectly attuned ambience they're in for a special and very pleasant surprise.

SAXOPHONE

PRATI - COLA DI RIENZO
via Germanico, 26
☎ *06/39723039*
39723039
• **Closed:** Tuesdays; August
• **Hours:** 4.30pm – 2am

The Saxophone has recently added a series of new dishes to its menu: the Extralarge [giant Würstel sausage, *scamorza* cheese, hamburger meat, red chicory, mushrooms, sauerkraut and eggplant – all grilled]; the Tre Caravelle [three baked potatoes: one stuffed with *gorgonzola* cheese, one with brie and truffle sauce, and one with *fontina* cheese and cheddar sauce] and a number of specialities dedicated to jazz giants, like the Louis Armstrong – hamburger, *pancetta* [unsmoked bacon], and hot sauce on toast garnished with carrot, tomato, red chicory and onion. Five draught beers to enjoy with *panini* offered by the house during happy hour from 6pm till 8pm.

LA SCALA

TRASTEVERE
p.zza della Scala, 60
☎ *06/5803763*
• **Closed:** 2-3 days around Aug 15
• **Hours:** 7pm – 2am

La Scala has been one Rome's best-known and most popular night spots ever since it opened because an evening passed here is always pleasurable and often

memorable. The bubbly, music-filled atmosphere absorbs you the moment you enter the two upstairs lounges and the music is often live or hosted by a DJ. The cocktails and long drinks prepared by their expert barmen will satisfy even the most demanding palates. If you prefer something a little more tranquil, the downstairs dining room is an ideal place for a romantic candlelit supper.

SISINI

TRASTEVERE
via San Francesco a Ripa, 137
☎ *06/5897110*
• **Closed:** Sundays; August
• **Hours:** 9am – 10pm

All the classic pizzas as well as some original and delicious specialities like pizzas topped with creamed artichokes; mushrooms and four cheeses; zucchini flowers, anchovies and mozzarella; or arugula, shrimps and olives; and the thick soft *foggiana* with olives, chopped tomato and oregano. Spit-roasted chicken, *supplì* [fried riceballs]; potato or chicken croquettes, and Sicilian *arancini* [fried balls of rice, peas and innards].

TORNATORA

EUR - TORRINO
v.le della Grande Muraglia, 100
☎ *06/52248623-52207802*
• **Closed:** Mondays; annual holidays vary
• **Hours:** 6am – 9pm
BOCCEA
via Aurelia, 428
☎ *06/6622322*
• **Closed:** Sunday afternoons and Mondays; Aug 15-31
• **Hours:** 6am – 9pm; Sundays 6am – 2pm

OSTIENSE
via Oderisi da Gubbio, 27
☎ 06/5593658
• **Closed:** never
• **Hours:** 6am – 9pm

 The original in Via Oderisi da Gubbio has a good *tavola calda*, but the Tornatora on the corner of Circonvallazione Cornelia close to Piazza Irnerio is the best of the three. Its crowning glories are the excellent desserts and some of the most fragrant, appetising breakfast *lieviti* to be found in Rome – they really do melt in your mouth, from the *cornetti semplici* [plain croissants] to the sublime pastry cream-filled *cornetti alla crema*, jam-filled *cornetti alla marmellata*, *fagottini* turnovers, plaited *trecce* and *girelle* with sultanas, and irresistable *maritozzi* filled with whipped cream. Enjoy them at the counter sipping coffee or a cappuccino while you cast a wandering eye over delicious *tramezzini* and canapés and consider what to have for a lunchtime snack. Their pastries are excellent, from the tiny *mignon* choux to the cakes, each one better than the last.

 ## TRINITY COLLEGE

CENTRO STORICO - PANTHEON
via del Collegio Romano, 6
☎ 06/6786472
• **Closed:** lunchtime
  Saturdays and Sundays
• **Hours:** 8am – 4pm

An enchanting location, wide-ranging menu and international atmosphere especially in the evening: Trinity College is a coffee and breakfast bar in the morning, a snack lunchbar at midday,

serves tea and beer in the afternoon, and becomes a typical Roman pub where you can dine in the evening. Later on, various beverages, music and dancing for those who care to. The cost varies, from L.25,000 upwards.

 ## VANNI

PRATI - MAZZINI
via Col di Lana, 10
☎ 06/3223642
• **Closed:** never
• **Hours:** 7am – 12.30am

Always open, even in the heart of summer, Vanni's offers a complete range of high quality gourmet products. Under a single roof, there's a *pasticceria* [pastry shop] with breakfast or afternoon tea treats, in both traditional or tiny *mignon* sizes; tortes and *semifreddi* [soft frozen mousse]; a gelateria section [don't miss the *Vannini*: small delicious chocolate-covered ice cream balls]; a corner devoted to Californian frozen yoghurt; a bar counter serving classic aperitivi with *tartine* [canapès]; and a buffet with *tramezzini*, pizza, croquettes, toasted sandwiches and other savoury delights. There's also the Archipelago, a self-service area with various food islands and, in the evening, tasty pizzas cooked in a wood-fired oven or grilled fish and, last but not least, the more formal Peristilio restaurant on the floor above.

VOLPETTI PIÙ

TESTACCIO
via A. Volta, 8
☎ 06/5744306
• **Closed:** Sundays;
  Aug 10-25
• **Hours:** 9am - 3.30pm;
  6 -10pm

A few years ago the famous Volpetti's in Via Marmorata opened this *tavola calda* just around the corner from their delicatessen. Good pizzas and fried foods, meaning *supplì* [fried riceballs] and *crocchette*, as well as the classical *tavola calda* repertoire - baked pasta, roast chicken, and various side dishes. The quality is medium to high, like the prices.

 ## ZÌ FENIZIA

CENTRO STORICO - GHETTO
via S. Maria del Pianto, 64/65
☎ 06/6896976
• **Closed:** Friday afternoons and Saturdays;
  annual holidays vary
• **Hours:** 7am – 9pm

Cinzia and Michele make some of the best *pizza al taglio* [pizza by the slice] in Rome, here in the Jewish quarter. The pizzas are all made according to *kosher* norms and are light, thin and crunchy, topped with interesting combinations of quality ingredients. They serve the classics [cherry tomatoes and arugula, zucchini flowers, potato, mushrooms] as well as more original ones inspired by the Roman Jewish or Middle Eastern traditions, like those with anchovies and escarole, beef or chicken sausage, or stuffed with falafel and onion-and-mushroom *burecas*. There are also croquettes like the traditional *supplì* and *arancini*, hot dogs, chicken fillets, hamburgers and *shawerma* [spiced meat cut from a skewered rotating roast].

shopping

BREAD

AGOSTINI

PIAZZA BOLOGNA
via Catania, 58/60
☎ *06/44236798*
• **Closed:** Wednesday
afternoons;
Saturday afternoons
in summer

Agostini's has been an
excellent place
to go for daily bread and
bakery products for many
years – fragrant, crusty
casereccio; special
breads made with
wholemeal flour or *farro,* soy,
and durum wheat; herb-
flavoured breads; *maltagliati*
[little loaves made with a
mixture of bread
and pizza doughs];
spighe, pizza and pizzette,
breakfast buns, biscuits
and homestyle cakes.
They also stock some
good packaged products
like artisanal dried pastas
and Campofilone
maccheroncini.

ARNESE

TRASTEVERE
via del Moro, 15/16
via del Politeama, 29
☎ *06/5817265*
• **Closed:** always open
including Sundays

Apart from their
excellent breads
[traditional, wholemeal,
Terni and Genzano] they also
make biscuits, homestyle
pastries and a rich,
appetising array of trays
of the pizza *al taglio*
[to buy by the strip]
dear to the hearts of
traditional Trastevere pizza
lovers. Open straight through
until 9pm.

L'ARTE DELLA FARINA

TRIONFALE
via Candia, 61
☎ *06/39723899*
• **Closed:** Thursday
afternoons; Saturday
afternoons in summer

A vast display of bread and
other bakery products, where
next to the traditional
casereçcio, a number of
special breads with various
seasonings and flavours, and
the typical Lariano, Genzano
and Allumiere loaves, you'll
also find dried *grissini,*
freselle and *taralli,* vol-au-
vent pastries, crackers, plain
or stuffed egg pastas, a few
semifreddi, breakfast buns
and cakes. They'll also do
special orders: from tiny rolls
to extra-large bread formats.

COMPAGNIA DEL PANE

COLLI PORTUENSI
v.le Colli Portuensi, 515
☎ *06/65747412*
• **Closed:** Sundays

It's not easy to define shops
like this one, because they
sell so many different things.
Bread first of all, made the
traditional way, of every
shape, variety and size, from
pane casereccio to sesame
rolls, plus a wide range of
biscuits and pastries. Then
there's an above-average
cured meats and cheeses
section, a number of shelves
devoted to gourmet
specialities like homemade
pasta sauces, rice, and
artisanal dried pastas, and
best of all, a coffee bar with
a few tables where you can
relax and enjoy a fabulous
breakfast – the excellent
house coffee blend with
delicious *panzerotti,* deep-
fried custard-filled *bombe,*
plain or fancy *cornetti* - all
worthy of the most
sophisticated pastry shop.
They also do generously filled
panini at lunchtime. Open
straight through.

VENANZIO CONTI

CENTRO STORICO - CAMPO DE' FIORI
via dei Pettinari, 70/71
☎ *06/68801477*
• **Closed:** Saturday
afternoons

A vast choice of breads:
rosette [traditional hollow
flower-shaped buns], *panini*
all'olio [with olive oil in the
dough], *grissini* [breadsticks],
frustine, plain and tomato-
topped pizza, biscuits and a
few simple cakes.

ANTICO FORNO CORDELLA

CENTRO STORICO - GHETTO
p.zza Costaguti, 30/31
☎ *06/68803012*
• **Closed:** Sunday afternoons;
Saturday and Sunday
afternoons in summer

Located in the centre of the
Jewish quarter, between
Piazza Costaguti and Piazza
Cinque Scole, this is a very
traditional bakery, both in
appearance and the choice of
bread it offers [*rosette, filone*
and *pagnotta* loaves, plain
and tomato-topped pizza]. The
ossi - tasty, crunchy rolls - are
rather special.

FIOR DI FARINA

PRATI - MAZZINI
via de' Calboli, 38/40
☎ *06/3724367*
• **Closed:** Thursday
afternoons;
only Sundays in summer

A bakery that also sells
various groceries. Here you'll
find *pane casereccio,* pizza
and biscuits.

FORNO BIOLOGICO

CASILINO
via Casilina, 79/83
☎ *06/7029852*
• **Closed:** Saturday afternoons

One of the best bread shops in Rome, where only organic flour is used and all the bread is naturally leavened. You can choose between loaves made with wholemeal, soy, durum or buckwheat flour; bread with olives, sesame seeds or sultanas; and bread made from soft wheat-either plain or mixed with rice, millet, barley or oats. They also make biscuits, rusks, cakes and a *panfrutto* [bread with malt and dried fruit] with no added sugar. High prices.

FORNO DEI DESIDERI

PRATI - MAZZINI
via G. Avezzana, 33/37
☎ *06/3217350*
• **Closed:** Saturday
   afternoons

Here you'll find traditional bread next to wholemeal loaves, bread made from a variety of cereals, *panini all'olio* and a number of specialities. Inviting-looking pizzas and pizzette fight for space with *rustici* [savoury turnovers], savoury tortes, jam or ricotta tarts and lots of other sweet pastry options.

IL FORNO DI CAMPO DE' FIORI

CENTRO STORICO - CAMPO DE' FIORI
Campo de' Fiori, 22/22a
☎ *06/68806662*
• **Closed:** Sundays;
   also Saturday afternoons
   in summer

On the corner of one of Rome's best-loved piazzas, the Forno di Campo offers every conceivable kind of bread and bakery product: *rosette, frustine, filoni, panini* with olive oil or milk mixed into the dough, herb-scented breads, crusty *casereccio*, sesame-sprinkled Sicilian bread, pizza and homestyle cakes and pastries.

IL GIANFORNAIO

PONTE MILVIO
p.le di Ponte Milvio, 36
☎ *06/3333487*
• **Closed:** Sundays

The range of bread and bakery products offered here is truly vast: from traditional breads to savoury mini-croissants, vegetable turnovers, pizzette, *focaccine, panini al latte* flavoured with smoked ham, walnuts, sultanas, pine nuts, rosemary or cheese; *grissini,* wholemeal loaves, bread made from a variety of different cereals, special loaves [with olives, sesame, etc.] and typical Lariano bread. They also do excellent pizza *al taglio* [by the slice], rusks, biscuits and breakfast buns, and an interesting range of fresh pastas. You can order savoury *panettoni* for home entertaining and stunning gift baskets made out of bread, filled with coloured *panini.*

MOSCA

TRIONFALE
via Candia, 16
☎ *06/39742134*
• **Closed:** Thursday
   afternoons; Saturday
   afternoons in summer

Next to the *filone* and *pagnotta* loaves, pizza, biscuits and homestyle cakes you'll also find the very traditional *ciriole* rolls, a rarity these days, and *martufano,* a kind of *pane casereccio* with a dry, crunchy crust and a lot of holes inside left by air bubbles in the dough baked in the old brick oven that dates back to the early 1900's.

PALOMBI

PINCIANO
via Veneto, 114
☎ *06/4885817*
• **Closed:** Sundays;
   also Saturday afternoons
   in summer

This bakery boutique now has a little coffee bar, so you can have a good house blend espresso or cappuccino with something from their inviting-looking buffet of breakfast *lieviti* – various *cornetti* [croissants], *veneziani* [brioches], *napoletani* and apple turnovers before turning your attention to the fresh loaves [*casereccio,* herb-scented or made with special cereals and flavourings] or dried breads [*soffietti, taralli* and *grissinetti*]. They also offer pizza, cakes, jam tarts and fresh pastas.

PANELLA

ESQUILINO
l.go Leopardi, 4/10a
☎ *06/4872344*
• **Closed:** Thursday
   and Sunday afternoons;
   Saturday afternoons
   and Sundays in summer

Twenty years or so ago this used to be a classic *pasticceria* where you went on Sunday mornings for a tray of *bigné* or *granatine* [choux pastries] for Sunday lunch. Since then Panella has broadened its repertoire to include breads and bakery products of all kinds, ranging from traditional Roman varieties to bread and water sculptures and pizza with various toppings. They've also widened their range of sweet pastries [from the fruit *Martorana* to typical Middle Eastern delicacies] and added a homemade gelati and sorbet section, as well as a coffee bar counter with an attractive assortment of breakfast buns and lunchtime snacks. There's an interesting section devoted to packaged foodstuffs worthy of the best-stocked emporium: cereals and pulses, spices, baking ingredients, dried and candied fruits, organic foods, sauces, honey, jams and preserves, natural cosmetics, and a rather good choice of wines. They also do special week-long promotions dedicated to ancient Greece, Sicily and so on. Gourmet prices.

PASSI

TESTACCIO
via Mastro Giorgio, 87
☎ *06/5746563*
• **Closed:** Thursday
   afternoons; Saturday
   afternoons in summer

Locals come here for the wide variety of bread and bakery products: *pane casereccio* baked in a wood-fired oven, *filone, frustine, rosette,* plain and herb-scented *grissini,* Lariano bread, good pizza [plain, Genovese or with tomato topping], various biscuits [including tasty almond-flavoured *amaretti*] and homestyle cakes.

PIASTRA DAL 1895

COLOSSEO
via Labicana, 12/14
☎ *06/70495577*
• **Closed:** Saturday
   afternoons

There are a number of good reasons why it's worth paying a visit to this historic bakery, apart from the pizza, biscuits and homestyle cakes - the *Altamura* bread made with semolina from Apulia, the naturally-leavened Frascati *pane casereccio,* the typical breads of Emilia Romagna or Pesaro, the increasingly hard-to-find *ciriole* rolls or, on June 13, their special Saint Anthony's Day *panini,* made with the original baking moulds created by one of Piastra's ancestors.

GIOVANNI RIPOSATI

CENTRO STORICO - TRITONE
via delle Muratte, 8
☎ *06/6792866*
• **Closed:** Thursday
   afternoons;
   never in summer

This is the oldest bakery in Rome. It's been here on the corner of Piazza di Trevi and Vicolo del Forno since the 1700's, and it gave its name [Baker's Lane] to the little alley where, according to Roman legend, the Marchese del Grillo used to park his carriage to avoid being stoned and spat on by the population when he came to buy bread here. In the course of the centuries it's been expanded and transformed; next to the bread, homestyle cakes, biscuits, and pizza-by-the-slice they also offer a few gourmet foodstuffs, well-filled *panini* and fresh fruit, principally for the armies of passing tourists.

MARCO ROSCIOLI

CENTRO STORICO - CAMPO DE' FIORI
via dei Chiavari, 34
☎ *06/6864045*
• **Closed:** Sundays;
   also Saturday afternoons
   in summer

Pagnotte, filoni, pane casereccio, panini, rosette, grissini, freselle, vol-au-vent pastries, biscuits, homestyle cakes, sponge cakes, etc. Their speciality is plain, tomato or tomato-and-mozzarella topped pizza sold in slices, in two versions, either wafer-thin and crunchy, or thick and soft in the Apulian style.

PIETRO ROSCIOLI

ESQUILINO
via Buonarroti, 43/46
☎ *06/4467146*
• **Closed:** Thursday
   afternoons; Saturday
   afternoons in summer

They have to give out numbers to regulate the swarm of clients who come

here for their daily bread: normal or wholemeal, special varieties or loaves made with various different cereals like soy flour, but also for the dried *grissini* and *freselle,* biscuits and simple cakes, plain and tomato-topped pizza, fancy biscuits, croissants and many other treats.

OUTSIDE ROME

CERALLI

FRASCATI [ROME]
p.zza Bambocci, 15
☎ *06/9420439*
• **Closed:** Mondays;
   open Sunday mornings

Situated just behind the open market, the historic Ceralli bakery has been synonymous from time immemorial with bread and bakery products, from crusty *pane casereccio* to *pizza romana* [plain, light and salty], and traditional local cakes and biscuits fresh from their wood-fired oven.

MOLINARI

FRASCATI [ROME]
via Giuseppe Calasanzio, 8 ang. via Garibaldi
☎ *06/9420301*
• **Closed:** Thursday afternoons

Clients come here for the long, crunchy *francesini* [baguettes], the house speciality, and all the other excellent breads baked daily in their wood-fired oven, the pizza and the classic Castelli Romani cakes and biscuits - *ciambelle al vino, serpette al latte, pepetti,* and *torroncini.* At Christmas they make *pangialli* [dried fruit and honey loaf] and *panpepati* [dried fruit, honey and black pepper], at Easter *pizza cresciuta,* and all year round the *pupazza*

BREAD

frascatana [traditional three-breasted pastry doll].

SOGNATESORI

GROTTAFERRATA [ROME]
via delle Sorgenti, 12
☎ *06/9415226*
• **Closed:** Wednesday,
  Thursday and Sunday
  afternoons; Sunday
  afternoons in summer

From their wide range of very good bread and bakery products, a special mention for the excellent *pane casereccio* and the homestyle cakes and biscuits: tiny *cornetti* [croissants], tortes and tarts, ricotta-filled *sfogliatine* [puff pastry slices] and wine-flavoured *ciambelline al vino*.

BIAGI

LARIANO [ROME]
via Napoli, 7
☎ *06/9655362*
• **Closed:** Thursday
  afternoons

Here you can buy the celebrated Lariano bread made with traditional artisanal methods and baked in a wood-fired oven. The splendid, irregularly-shaped loaves with their delicious taste and aroma are made with stone-ground flour from the Carosi mill across the way and cooked in the fiery cavern out back.

CAROSI

LARIANO [ROME]
via Napoli, 6
☎ *06/9655744*
• **Closed:** Thursday
  afternoons;
  also Mondays in summer

This historic mill has been run by the Carosi family for more than a century. The

flour [cornflour, wholemeal with a few husks left in it, and the semi-refined wholemeal the famous Lariano bread is made from] is ground here between ancient millstones. Excellent quality and very reasonable prices.

MARRONI

MARINO [ROME]
borgo Garibaldi, 21
☎ *06/9385140*
• **Closed:** every afternoon
  except Thursday
  and Saturday

Good *pane casereccio* baked in a wood-fired oven and traditional Castelli Romani cakes and biscuits: *tozzetti, pepetti,* almond or chocolate-flavoured biscuits, *biscotti della sposa, amaretti, brutti e buoni* [ugly but good], plain or spicy *taralli*. During the grape harvest you'll find ring-shaped *ciambelline* made with grape must, and at Easter, salty *pizza sbattuta* and *pizza cresciuta*.

CAFES & BARS

BAR DEL GIANICOLO

MONTEVERDE VECCHIO
p.le Aurelio, 5
☎ *06/5806275*
• **Closed:** Mondays

Aficionados come here for a leisurely coffee, snack or drink in the small indoor salon or under the outdoor pergola in the sunny season. Parisian bistrot atmosphere.

BAR DEL PALAZZO DELLE ESPOSIZIONI

CENTRO STORICO - TRITONE
via Milano, 7
☎ *06/4828540*
• **Closed:** Tuesdays

This bar and restaurant is inside the Palazzo delle Esposizioni with a separate entrance off Via Milano. The interior is big, luminous and

beautifully organised. Fairly standard offerings in the coffee bar, but the self-service restaurant on the roof garden has a more interesting menu: rolls, focaccia and hot and cold dishes.

BATTELLA

TRIESTE
via Benaco, 13
☎ *06/8548636*
• **Closed:** Tuesdays

Bars that offer really delicious *cornetti* are few and far between. The Battella is one of them, with really outstanding *cornetti alla crema* [with baker's custard]. Since it was renovated a couple of years ago, however, its *lieviti* have dropped off just a fraction from a size point of view: too small to our mind to be sold at full price. Also on the menu: *maritozzi, veneziane, danesi, bombe, ciambelle* and savoury croissants. Pleasant outdoor cafe tables.

BAR BELLI

TRASTEVERE
p.zza Belli, 4
☎ *06/5815054*
• **Closed:** never

Fifties' décor and good *cornetti*, espressos and cappuccinos – the coffee has arabica beans in the mix. Have an *espresso* with tiny biscuits or pastries then take home packets of sweets and specially blended coffee.

CAFFÈ GRECO

CENTRO STORICO - SPAGNA
via Condotti, 86
☎ *06/6785474*
• **Closed:** Sundays

The Caffè Greco, in the same premises on Via dei Condotti

since 1760, is celebrating the new century with a change of ownership. The new management plans to completely revamp both the menu [everything from breakfast croissants and pastries through ready-to-eat lunch dishes, snacks and coffee] and the whole operation. We wish them every success – this glorious cafe whose unique late-18th century interiors have sheltered generations of famous international artists and literati deserves a menu worthy of all that beauty and history.

BAR PASTICCERIA CARLINI

TESTACCIO
via G. Branca, 52
☎ *06/5742100*
• **Closed:** Wednesdays

A small selection of classic *dolci*, from tarts to tea biscuits, plus plain or custard/chocolate/jam-filled *cornetti*, deep-fried *bombe* and *ciambelle*. The country-style sandwiches are good.

CARLO & CARLO

PRATI - COLA DI RIENZO
via Fabio Massimo, 16
☎ *06/3243250*
• **Closed:** Sundays

A small bar and tobacconist with above-average food: breakfast *cornetti* [full-size or mini], *focacce* [in summer the ones with figs and prosciutto are particularly good] and deliciously-filled *panini*. Efficient service.

IL CIGNO

PARIOLI
v.le Parioli, 16
☎ *06/8082348*
• **Closed:** never

Literally besieged in the mornings, mainly for its rich and variegated buffet of *cornetti* and breakfast pastries spread out all along the counter. A couple of dozen different varieties in all: wholemeal and soy flour *cornetti* ; traditional *cornetti* with baker's custard, jam, honey, marron glacé, ricotta, marzipan, Nutella or apple fillings; Danish pastries; *veneziane*; *bombe* and *ciambelle*. The savoury snacks are not bad, either. A well-stocked pastry section and professional service.

CLEMENTI

SAN GIOVANNI
via Gallia, 152
☎ *06/70496575*
• **Closed:** Mondays

Bar, coffee shop, a traditional pastry-shop counter and an old-style *cremeria* [milkbar] with a vast assortment of goodies. Tasty breakfast pastries: *maritozzi* with sultanas, *lumachine*, *fazzoletti*, plain or fancy *cornetti*, and ciambelle. Good-quality *tavola calda* dishes and savouries at lunchtime and genuine homemade gelati at very reasonable prices. Outdoor tables.

DOLCE VITA

CENTRO STORICO - NAVONA
p.zza Navona, 70/a
☎ *06/68806221*
• **Closed:** never

This bar is in a marvellous position in one of the world's most beautiful piazzas. Any opportunity is worth snatching to sit at one of their outdoor tables and gaze at Borromini's church and Bernini's Fountain of the Four Rivers: from that first morning coffee to the last drink at night.

LE DUE FONTANE

FLAMINIO
p.zza Perin del Vaga, 13
☎ *06/3214105*
• **Closed:** Sunday and Saturday afternoons

This little bar offers all kinds of good things: fragrant cornetti with various fillings in the mornings; hot ready-to-eat tavola calda dishes and homemade savouries at lunchtime; biscuits, *ciambelloni* [ring-shaped cakes] and tarts. Homemade gelati in summer.

DUE G BAR

NEMORENSE
p.zza Verbano, 17/19
☎ *06/8548245*
• **Closed:** Wednesdays

Very close to the Villa Ada gardens, Due G is a good place to bear in mind for breakfast. They offer a variety of tasty breakfast buns, from *cornetti*, plain or with various fillings, to variously-flavoured *fagottini* [turnovers], as well as savoury midday snacks, *aperitivi* and sweet pastries.

CAFFÈ FIUME

PINCIANO
via Salaria, 55/57
☎ *06/8549062*
• **Closed:** Sundays

Good breakfast *cornetti* in a vaguely Art Nouveau setting, with a lavish lunchtime buffet of ready-to-eat culinary delights later on, to enjoy either standing at the counter or sitting down in the inside dining room. It turns into a tea room in the afternoon with associated treats and ritual.

IL MARITOZZARO

PORTUENSE
via E. Rolli, 50
☎ *06/5810781*
• **Closed:** Sunday afternoons and Wednesdays

The setting is not the most inviting but here you'll find

the most delicious *maritozzi* buns, split down the middle and overflowing with fresh whipped cream, laid out on huge trays. Open from 2am till 8pm, it doesn't close at all on Fridays and Saturdays.

MEETING PLACE

PIAZZA BOLOGNA
p.zza Bologna, 1a/d
☎ 06/44237704
• **Closed:** never

Lots of good *lieviti* [breakfast buns] for breakfast to go with an arabica blend espresso or cappuccino. *Tavola calda* service and a rich buffet of ready-to-eat gastronomic treats: *tramezzini* [triangular sandwiches], *panini* [rolls], well-filled *pizza romana* [plain light and salty] and *piadine* [flat unleavened *focaccia*]. Chocolates, candy, pastries and other confectionery on sale, plus a tobacconist's counter open till late.

BAR PICCOLINO

CENTRO STORICO - NAVONA
via del Teatro Valle, 54/a
☎ 06/6872279
• **Closed:** Sundays

Tiny by name and tiny by nature: in a remarkably small space there's a counter with a coffee machine, a display case for the *panini*, stuffed pizzas and sandwiches, a little table and a single chair, with a few more tables outside opposite the Teatro Valle shaded by big umbrellas in summer. Come for the hazelnut-flavoured coffee, the house speciality, original and delicious.

CAFFÈ POERIO

MONTEVERDE VECCHIO
via A. Poerio, 10/a
☎ 06/5816005
• **Closed:** Sundays

The fact that it's located in the heart of the hip Monteverde Vecchio quarter with outdoor tables in summer is no doubt reason enough to recommend the Poerio, but they also offer excellent brands of confectionary and chocolates, a good house coffee blend and above-average breakfast buns.

RIV

APPIO
via Taranto, 122
☎ 06/70302652
• **Closed:** Sundays

Riv is short for *rivendita*, which means retail outlet - in this case for bar products, tobacco and now classical music CD's, and the peculiarity of this unusual bar run by two partners both named Roberto is the wonderful classical music always playing in the background. A small selection of *panini* and tramezzini to eat at the tables or perched on barstools.

ROSATI

CENTRO STORICO - POPOLO
p.zza del Popolo, 5
☎ 06/3225859
• **Closed:** never

This historic cafe [established in 1922] has preserved the original Art Nouveau mirrors, furnishings and *boiserie* wood-work. The coffee, drinks, snacks and *pasticceria* [sweet pastries and biscuits] are better than average, their plain breakfast *cornetti* are as good as those from a pastry shop, and the cakes on display at the back are delicious. Very pleasant outdoor tables on the piazza, shaded by big umbrellas in the summer. A la carte menu at lunchtime.

SACCHETTI

TRASTEVERE
p.zza S. Cosimato, 61/62
☎ 06/5815374
• **Closed:** Mondays

Their sweet pastries and *granatine* [zabaglione-filled choux pastries], bite-sized *mignon*, tortes and biscuits are all made in their own bakery out the back, and so are the *cornetti* served at the coffee bar. Tasty *rustici* [savoury turnovers] with prosciutto, cheese and vegetables or anchovy-and-tomato fillings and rather good gelati. Outdoor tables on one of the Trastevere quarter's most popular piazzas.

SANT'EUSTACHIO

CENTRO STORICO - PANTHEON
p.zza Sant'Eustachio, 82
☎ 06/6861309
• **Closed:** Mondays

The principal attraction at this bar has stayed the same since 1938, the year it was founded, [even though it's now under new management]: their arabica coffee blend and variations on the theme – including the *gran caffè speciale* [a sort of double-dose espresso with sugar, their own invention], parfaits, granitas with whipped cream, Irish coffee, and packets of the house blend to take home. The superlative espresso is sugared by the barman: if you don't like it very, very sweet, order a *caffè amaro* and sugar it yourself.

SOTO BAR

VATICANO
b.go Pio, 170/173
☎ 06/6865539
• **Closed:** Mondays

This bar adjoins the Scialanga family's restaurant and *tavola calda*, and it's something of an institution for the inhabitants of the Borgo Pio quarter, who come principally for the breakfasts and the desserts. Espressos and cappuccinos made with an excellent house blend accompany *lieviti* [breakfast buns], *cornetti* [croissants], and various *pasta sfoglia* [puff pastries]. Try the wholemeal ones filled with pineapple or fresh apricots, or the organic flour and honey version, and don't miss their crisp *sfogliatelle* filled with chocolate and ricotta. Open from 7am till 11pm.

TEICHNER

CENTRO STORICO - CAMPO MARZIO
p.zza San Lorenzo in Lucina, 17
☎ *06/6871683*
• **Closed:** Sundays

One of Rome's most famous bars because of its classic espresso - a robust, vigorous drop made with the house blend toasted on the premises. The morning buffet of *lieviti* [breakfast buns] gives way at midday to a spread of *tramezzini, panini* and a number of cold dishes you can eat at the outdoor tables in the piazza. The delicatessen of the same name is next door.

VEZIO

CENTRO STORICO - GHETTO
via de' Delfini, 23
☎ *06/6786036*
• **Closed:** Sundays

Everything is concentrated into a few square metres here, including the bar counter. People come for a cup of coffee and not much else. Yet Vezio's, or Caffè Bla Bla as it's also called, in a tranquil corner of the old Jewish Ghetto, has a devoted clientele. The atmosphere and the wooden bench invite you to sit down and rest for a while, and the slogans,

posters and photos of the historic leaders of international socialism papering the walls make it into a kind of club open to anyone who shares its philosophy.

OUTSIDE ROME

BAR DEGLI SPECCHI

FRASCATI [ROME]
via Cesare Battisti, 3
☎ *06/9420293*
• **Closed:** giovedì pomeriggio

People come here for the excellent espresso [there's arabica in the blend], the traditional *pupazza frascatana* [a pastry shaped like a doll with three breasts], and its famous distorting mirrors.

BAR MODERNO

GROTTAFERRATA [ROME]
c.so del Popolo, 11
☎ *06/9458214*
• **Closed:** Mondays

Everything offered at the Moderno is quality, whether it's the espresso, the house aperitivi, or their desserts and savoury snacks. Pastries and cakes are the house speciality: *cornetti* baked on the premises in the morning, classic cakes like the *Saint-Honoré* [a ring of caramel-glazed custard-filled pastry puffs], or the chilled sponge, fruit and custard *Charlotte*, and local speciality desserts.

CHEESE

ANTICA CACIARA TRASTEVERINA

TRASTEVERE
via S. Francesco a Ripa, 140/a-b
☎ *06/5812815*
• **Closed:** Sundays

A fine selection of cheeses made from cow and sheep's milk next to better-known,

more commercial foodstuffs. Courteous service.

AURIEMMA

PRATI - COLA DI RIENZO
via Barletta, 25
☎ *06/3721903*
• **Closed:** Sundays
BOCCEA
via Aurelia, 382/b
☎ *06/6624998*
• **Closed:** Sundays

Various milk products and cheeses produced by the dairy of the same name at Aurianova, in the province of Caserta: mozzarella in various shapes and sizes, including the braided *treccia*; buffalo ricotta; pear-shaped *scamorza*; mild, strong or smoked *caciotta*; plain and smoked *caciocavallo*. There are also *bocconcini alla panna* [tiny mozzarellas stuffed with cream], *burrata* [ultra-creamy soft cheese], as well as *sfoglia* pastries and *cornetti* made from dough flavoured with smoked *scamorza*, both with various fillings. Reasonable prices, and it's open straight through from 9am till 8pm. Goods arrive fresh each day.

AVENATI

VIMINALE
via Milano, 44
☎ *06/4882681*
• **Closed:** Sundays

Once just a little *bottega di latticini* selling Southern milk products, Avenati's has broadened its range over the years but not lost its vocation for cheeses: buffalo mozzarella; *burrata* and *nodino* from Puglia; smoked *provola*; Sicilian *caciocavallo* [firm, slightly salty stretched-curd cheese] with pistachio nuts; pecorino from Pienza; *formaggio di fossa* [rare cheese aged underground];

tiny Piedmontese *tomino* as well as French *crottin* and *chevrotin*, and butter from Normandy. Everything else has a strong Southern flavour: from spicy Avellino sausages to Neapolitan *cafone*, country-style bread baked in a wood-fired oven. Doesn't close for lunch.

LA BARONIA

PARIOLI
via V. Locchi, 21
☎ *06/8072903*
• **Closed:** Sundays
QUARTIERE AFRICANO
via Scirè, 24
☎ *06/8605504*
• **Closed:** Sundays
MONTEVERDE NUOVO
via Fonteiana, 31
☎ *06/5811602*
• **Closed:** Saturday afternoons
PRATI - COLA DI RIENZO
via Varrone, 2/c
☎ *06/6833113*
• **Closed:** Sundays
OSTIA [ROME]
v.le Cardinal Ginnasi, 24
☎ *06/5621325*
• **Closed:** Sundays

Fresh cheeses and dairy products arrive daily at the La Baronia outlets in Rome from their dairy in Vitulazio in the province of Caserta – an area famous for its buffalo mozzarella. *Treccia* [mozzarella braids] and other mozzarella cheeses of various shapes and sizes; delicious buffalo ricotta; pear-shaped *scamorza*; mild, strong and smoked *caciotta*; stuffed *scamorza* and ring-shaped *ciambella*; plain and smoked *caciocavallo*, made with plain cow's milk or a mixture of cow and buffalo milk.
Don't miss the traditional scrumptious Campanian desserts available in winter at their Parioli shop.

BRUNELLI

PRIMA PORTA
via della Stazione di Prima Porta, 20
☎ *06/33610144*
• **Closed:** Saturdays and Sundays; opening hours 8am – 4pm

The retail outlet here on site at the Brunelli dairy sells real *pecorino romano* cheese [made from the milk of the Sopravissana herds that graze in the Roman countryside], sheep's milk ricotta, fresh and ripened *caciotta*.

FANTASIE DI LATTE

NEMORENSE
via Nemorense, 76
☎ *06/86213453*
• **Closed:** Sundays

It looks as though Romans can no longer survive without buffalo mozzarella. This is one of several retail outlets that provides fresh daily supplies from San Nicola la Strada in the province of Caserta. You'll also find dairy products from Andria: cow's milk ricotta and mouth-watering sheep's milk ricotta, *nodino* with cream or stuffed in various ways, delicious *burrata*, and *treccia* [mozzarella braids]. Their prices are not exactly low but freshness and quality are guaranteed. Orders can be placed by phone.

LA MAZZONARA

ESQUILINO
via Merulana, 76/a
☎ *06/70453464*
• **Closed:** never

This is the retail outlet for the Fichele Dairy in Cancello Arnone [Caserta]. Fresh buffalo mozzarella in various shapes and sizes arrives daily [including mozzarellas weighing 10 kilos if you order in advance]; *ricotta*; many different cheeses including Sardinian *pecorino*; herb-

flavoured *giuncata*; smoked and plain *scamorza*; excellent homestyle *casereccio* bread; *freselle* and *tarallucci* biscuits, and sausages, too, in winter. Best to ring before you go as the opening hours can be somewhat erratic.

CASA DEI LATTICINI MICOCCI

PINCIANO
via Collina, 14
☎ *06/4741784*
• **Closed:** Thursday afternoons; Saturday afternoons in summer

One of the first shops to specialize in dairy products, Micocci's sells medium quality cheeses and other milk products from all over Europe. You'll find everything from huge wheels of *grana padana* to little Piedmontese *tomini*, English Stilton and French brie and Roquefort.

COOP. AGRICOLA STELLA

MONTEVERDE NUOVO
via Donna Olimpia, 11/a
☎ *no*
• **Closed:** Saturday afternoons
SALARIA
via Garigliano, 68
☎ *06/8542681*
• **Closed:** Saturday afternoons

These are the retail outlets of the Stella Cooperative in Amaseno [in the province of Frosinone] whose buffalo herds produce good hand-made mozzarella [from 30 grams to 3 kilos in size], plain or smoked; *trecce* and *treccine* [big and small mozzarella braids]; fresh or ripened buffalo *rosine* [somewhere between a goat's milk *caprino* and a soft *cacioricotta*] and buffalo ricotta [available in the afternoons].

CHEESE

Mini Caseificio Costanzo

GENZANO [ROME]
via Colabona, 34
☎ *06/9364040*
• **Closed:** Sunday afternoons and Mondays
GROTTAFERRATA [ROME]
loc. Squarciarelli
via delle Sorgenti, 77
☎ *06/9459491*
• **Closed:** Sunday afternoons and Mondays

These are the twin Castelli Romani retail outlets of the Costanzo mini-dairy in Lusciano [Caserta]. On their pristine premises you'll find unbeatable buffalo cheeses: delicious mozzarella in various shapes and sizes [giant, normal and little egg-shaped *ovoline*], either plain or stuffed with fresh cream; ricotta; smoked *provola*; and if you order in advance *burrata* [soft cheese with added cream]; braided mozzarella *treccia* and *pizza* [thin sheets of stretched curd cheese to fill, roll and slice before serving]. Also available: *caciocavallo*, plain and smoked baby *scamorzina* made from cow's milk. Fresh arrivals daily at 6.30pm.

CHOCOLATE

La Bottega del Cioccolato

COLOSSEO
via Leonina, 82
☎ *06/4821473*
• **Closed:** Saturdays and Sundays

Entering this shop-cum-artisan's workshop is, not surprisingly, like walking into a giant chocolate box. The master chocolate-maker is Maurizio Proietti, son of Marcello Proietti, the owner of Moriondo & Gariglio [see below]. They come from the same school: their chocolates are made using traditional methods and only the best Brazilian cocoa according to recipes tried and tested in the paternal kitchens. Maurizio's innovations: fifty or more different varieties of chocolates including white ones, the superbitter "80%" and delicious soft-centres, are smaller and not quite as sweet as his father's.

Giuliani

PRATI - COLA DI RIENZO
via Paolo Emilio, 67/67a
☎ *06/3243548*
• **Closed:** Sundays

The place to come for marrons glacès since 1949 – in all its possible variations: whole, eleborately reworked, with baker's custard or preserved in syrup. Also chocolates, pralines, jellied fruit and fruit fashioned from marzipan.

Moriondo & Gariglio

CENTRO STORICO - PANTHEON
via del Piè di Marmo, 21/22
☎ *06/6990856*
• **Closed:** Sundays; also Saturday afternoons July 1-31

A chocolate jeweller's shop - both in appearance [it's like a casket full of jewels inside] and prices. The name harks back to the great Northern Italian chocolate-making traditions, brought to Rome in 1886 by the Turinese pastry chefs Moriondo and Gariglio. Marcello Proietti, the owner, was formerly the star pupil of a Piedmontese master. Now his son Attilio presides in the workshop as bearer of the family tradition: the best cocoa [from South America], artisanal production methods and classical recipes like the "Parisien" invented in the Twenties. All in all, 80 different varieties of chocolates, pralines, dark chocolate, toffee and jellied fruit.

Puyricard

CENTRO STORICO - SPAGNA
via delle Carrozze, 26
☎ *06/69202191*
• **Closed:** Sundays

This soberly elegant shop is the first branch of the French Provençal chocolate house to open in Italy. More than 92 different types of chocolates, all handmade using highest quality cocoa and other equally irreprehensible raw materials, and all worth trying, especially the ones filled with chocolate mousse, fresh cream or orange marinated in Grand Marnier. Classic candied orange and lemon slices [also chocolate-covered], candied almonds and hazelnuts, candied violets, fruit jellies, sweets, white and dark nut chocolate, and splendid French-made marrons glacès which won the international championships. The *calissons* – delicious tiny pastries made of almond paste with candied orange and lemon – are the most original item. Also, classic chocolate bars [including the 100% bitter cocoa version – no sugar] and flakes of almond, white and dark chocolate available for home cooking. Gorgeous gift packs and very pretty containers for the chocolates. Extremely polite and polished service.

COFFEE ROASTING HOUSES

Antico Caffè del Brasile

COLOSSEO
via dei Serpenti, 23
☎ *06/4882319*
• **Closed:** Sundays

They still roast coffee in a wood-fired oven at this very old shop where jute sacks and arcane machinery are just visible behind the counter displaying the various blends: *famiglia, risparmio* [economical], *gemme do Brasil* and *caffè del papa* [John Paul II used to buy it when he was a student in Rome]. There's a coffee bar for espresso-tasting.

GIOVANNI DE SANCTIS

TRIESTE
via Tagliamento, 88
☎ 06/8552287
• **Closed:** Thursday afternoons; Saturday afternoons in summer

 You can count the number of historic *torrefazione* [coffee roasting houses] on the fingers of one hand. The De Sanctis shop, formerly the Postiglione [opened in 1924], is one of them. Nothing has changed here since the early 1900's – the beautiful dark wood decor, roasting machines, tins of sweets, even the original enamel labels are all still intact. This coffee-fiends' paradise is the place to come for prize blends like Ethiopian Limu Harrar, Costarica or the best Brazilian Santos, packed for clients under the watchful eyes of the incurably courteous De Sanctis family – Giovanni, Maria and their son Roberto. High quality is also the salient characteristic of their selection of biscuits, sweets and chocolates.

MISTER COFFEE

FLAMINIO
via Fracassini, 22 e 30
☎ 06/3207850
• **Closed:** Sundays; also Saturday afternoons in summer

This coffee house offers a carefully-chosen selection of quality products: sweets, chocolates, biscuits, honeys and jams, tisanes, teas, natural foodstuffs and gourmet specialities. Apart from the house coffee blends roasted on their own premises you'll also find Estasi, Bar, Sprint, Aroma, Caracolito from Santo Domingo, Costa Rica, Guatamalan Maragogype, decaf and American blends. There's a display window filled with savoury specialities including artisanal dried pastas.

SCIASCIA DAL 1922

PRATI - COLA DI RIENZO
via Fabio Massimo, 80/a
☎ 06/3211580
• **Closed:** Sundays

This coffee-roasting house was opened by the Sciascia family in 1922 and has been run by them ever since. Anna and Adolfo Sciascia import the raw coffee from Africa and South America, then roast it themselves. Next to the various coffee blends [100% arabica, decaf, lighter or stronger blends to suit varying tastes and uses] you'll also find fresh toasted *orzo* [for a barley-based drink] various sweets and dietary products. Open straight through.

TAZZA D'ORO

CENTRO STORICO - PANTHEON
via degli Orfani, 84
☎ 06/6792768
• **Closed:** Sundays

In this historic coffee bar and roasting house with its vaguely Forties atmosphere and occasional piece of colonial memorabilia you can taste and buy Tazza D'Oro coffee, the one that has the exotic girl sowing coffee beans as its logo. The house blends are all arabica, various varieties from the specially favoured countries – Jamaican Blue Mountain [the rarest and most expensive], Maragogype from Nicaragua [lighter with less caffeine] as well as a mixed arabica blend [Regina del

Caffè], decaf and American roast. There are classic espressos [if you don't want yours sugared tell the barman so straight away], sumptuous cappuccinos and authentic coffee granitas to have at the counter or at one of the tables inside in the Casa del Caffè. In the afternoons you can watch the beans being roasted while you sip your coffee.

DELICATESSENS

ANDREOLI

CENTRO STORICO - CAMPO DE' FIORI
via del Pellegrino, 116
☎ 06/68802121
• **Closed:** Thursday afternoons; Saturday afternoons in summer

People flock to this classic delicatessen for the sheep's milk *caciotta* and *ricotta* cheeses produced by the family firm, and for the typical Lazio cured meats prepared on the premises: fresh sausages, *lonza* [spicy cured pork shoulder]; rolls of *pancetta* [un-smoked bacon]; *guanciale* [cured pork jowl]; *coppa* and prosciutto.

APISTICA ROMANA

PRATI - CAVOUR
via Ulpiano, 55/57
☎ 06/6868004
• **Closed:** Saturday afternoons

Honey and honey products of all kinds assembled by biologist Domenico Nicastro, from *millefiore* [a thousand flowers] honey to the single-blossom varieties, propolis and royal jelly. They also offer jams, bakery products and honey-flavoured liqueurs, cosmetics, dietary supplements and herbal products.

BRAGADIN DI ANTONIO PACIOTTI

TRIONFALE
via M. Bragadin, 53
☎ *06/39733646*
• **Closed:** Sundays

A huge assortment of cured meats and cheeses, including typical regional products and specialities, from tasty *salama da sugo* [salami cured in wine and spices] in winter to aged *parmigiano reggiano*. Open straight through from 7am till 8.30pm.

CAMBI

CENTRO STORICO - CORSO
via del Leoncino, 30
☎ *06/6878081*
• **Closed:** Thursday afternoons

Signor Domenico Cambi's *salsamenteria* has been a touchstone for quality and reliability in the area for many years. Next to speciality foodstuffs, a small wine section and a good selection of artisan-made dried pastas, there's a beautiful display of excellent cured meats and cheeses, buffalo mozzarella [plain and smoked], various ready-to-eat gourmet dishes and also a bakery section offering Altamura bread, good *pane casereccio* [thick, crusty home-style bread] and pizza.

LA CANTINA DEL SUD

VATICANO
borgo Pio, 40
☎ *06/68214185*
• **Closed:** Monday mornings

Guido Turato, born in Rome but of Calabrian origin, is the proprietor of this shop near the Vatican which specializes in typical gourmet foodstuffs from Calabria. Masses of chili peppers: whole chilis, chili powder, stuffed chili or chili roulades, creamed chili, chili jam and even chili syrup! The same with tomatoes: red and green tomato pâté, tomatoes in oil, creamed with tuna, or transformed into delicious sauces. Jams and marmalades made with citron, bergamot and elderberry, as well as *caciocavallo* and *butirri* cheeses; fresh mixed goat and sheep's milk cheese; smoked ricotta; *soppressata* [cured pork sausage]; peppery, *'nduja* and other fresh sausages; *capocollo steccato* [cured pork shoulder]; traditional pastas [*paccheri, filei, spigazzuoli*]; liquorice; *frese, taralli* and other biscuits; liqueurs; condiments; Sila mushroom pâté; wild *sponza* artichokes and *talli* [caper sprouts] in oil. Special Sila gift baskets.

CASTRONI

PRATI - COLA DI RIENZO
via Ottaviano, 55
☎ *06/39723279*
• **Closed:** Sundays

A rich assortment of *lieviti* [breakfast buns] and coffee prepared with the excellent house blend, plus a wide selection of various speciality foodstuffs, from confectionery, chocolates and international gourmet treats like French mustard, to English Marmite and Australian Vegemite.

CASTRONI

PRATI - COLA DI RIENZO
via Cola di Rienzo, 196
☎ *06/6874383*
• **Closed:** Sundays

Here you'll find the largest assortment of international gourmet specialities in Rome, with the basic ingredients of famous recipes organised according to their country of origin. There's also a vast assortment of rice, legumes, spices, aromatic herbs, dried fruit, honey, sauces, condiments, pâté, jams, tea, confectionery, cakes and chocolates. Excellent house coffee blends to buy or sample at the bar.

CASTRONI

FLAMINIO
via Flaminia, 28/32
☎ *06/3611029*
• **Closed:** Sundays

Exotic foodstuffs, herbal teas, spices, sauces and jams and, at the appointed times, Italian and foreign Christmas cakes and pastries, and Easter eggs of all kinds. An excellent coffee blend to buy or enjoy at the bar.

CIANI

MONTEVERDE NUOVO
via di Donna Olimpia, 74/76
☎ *06/5346659*
• **Closed:** Thursday afternoons; Saturday afternoons in summer

A wide choice of breads, pizza and other bakery products [the original business of the Ciani family], as well as cured meats, cheeses, fresh pasta, some ready-to-serve gourmet dishes and speciality foodstuffs.

LA CORTE

CENTRO STORICO - PANTHEON
via della Gatta, 1
☎ *06/6783842*
• **Closed:** Saturday afternoons

Selected smoked fish from specialised firms: salmon, sturgeon, trout, eel, tuna, swordfish; as well as Italian caviar, smoked fish pâté, and frozen foods including vegetables, fish and shellfish, berries, meat, *olive ascolane* [deep-fried stuffed olives], ravioli and other stuffed pastas, fillets of *baccalà*.

DANESI

PRATI - MAZZINI
via G. Ferrari, 43/45
☎ 06/3720858
• **Closed:** Thursday afternoons; Saturday afternoons in summer

This most un-metropolitan shop has fulfilled the exacting requirements of its wealthy clientele here in the Prati quarter for more than seventy years. Customers come to this very family-style supermarket for the Danesi coffee blends toasted on the premises and the international gourmet specialities, wide selection of pastries and desserts, beers, wine, champagne and spirits, or just to do the daily shopping.

DE CAROLIS

PRATI - MAZZINI
via Sabotino, 28
☎ 06/3724050
• **Closed:** Sundays

One of the best addresses in the neghbourhood for many years now selling typical cured meats and cheeses, including several artisan-made specialities: camembert and *taleggio* made from raw milk; cured goose and game meats; kosher cured meats; Prague ham; genuine *guanciale* [cured pork jowl]; *zamponi* [pig's trotters] and *cotechino* [cured pork sausage] before Christmas. Among the vast range of speciality foods available: first-class smoked salmon; lentils from Castelluccio in Umbria; *pizzoccheri* [a pasta similar to tagliatelle] from Valtellina in Lombardy; sauces

and condiments. Fresh cuts of pork meat, fresh pasta and a few gourmet dishes like fish or rice salad, roast beef, etc. Professional service; hefty prices. Open all day.

F.LLI FABBI

CENTRO STORICO - SPAGNA
via della Croce, 27/28
☎ 06/6790612
• **Closed:** Thursday afternoons; Saturday afternoons in summer

One of the few surviving city centre *salsamenteria* – the others have gone to make way for *jeanserie* and other clothes shops. A delicious range of cured meats and cheese with particularly good fresh cheeses and other dairy products. Typical *centro storico* prices.

FOCACCI

CENTRO STORICO - SPAGNA
via della Croce, 43
☎ 06/6791228
• **Closed:** Tuesday afternoons; Saturday afternoons in summer

Another of the very few *salsamenteria* to survive in the tourist heart of the city, it offers quite a good selection of cheeses and cured meats.

FOCACCI

PRATI - CAVOUR
via Marianna Dionigi, 27
☎ 06/3210525
• **Closed:** Thursday afternoons; Saturday afternoons in summer

Owned by relatives of the *salumieri* of the same name in Via della Croce, its strong points are the fresh cuts of pork and pork products from Visso in Le Marche, birthplace of the owners.

FRANCHI

PRATI - COLA DI RIENZO
via Cola di Rienzo, 200/204
☎ 06/6874651
• **Closed:** Sundays

One of the best food-stops in town: a combination of *alimentari* [grocery store], *rosticceria* [roast meat takeaway] and *tavola calda* [ready-to-eat hot and cold dishes]. There's no culinary itch you can't scratch here: magnificent cured meats and cheeses; delicious Italian and foreign specialities like truffles, caviar, smoked salmon, *bottarga* [dried fish roe], delectable preserves. Unforgettable *supplì al telefono* [riceballs] with melted cheese hearts, croquettes, including traditional *arancini* [rice, peas and innards], and other deep-fried fish and vegetable delights pour ceaselessly from the kitchen. The kitchen fires where skewered chickens slowly roast are always burning. At lunchtime there's a lavish buffet, with steaming first courses and seafood and meat dishes. Open all day. Pricey.

CARLO GARGANI

PINCIANO
via Lombardia, 15
☎ 06/4740865
• **Closed:** Sundays

Not far away from Via Veneto, Gargani's offers Italian specialities, foreign delicacies and ready-to-serve dishes of the house. Next to typical cheeses and cured meats like Zibello *culatello* [top-grade cured ham]; little *tomini* and goat's milk *caprino* cheeses from Piedmont; raw milk camembert and English cheddar, wines and spirits, you'll find a range of ready-to-serve dishes, from pastry-crusted roast meats to whole fish in aspic. Open all day.

Ruggero Gargani

PARIOLI
v.le Parioli, 36 b
☎ *06/8078264*
• **Closed:** Sundays

Here you can find cured meats and cheeses, Italian and foreign speciality foods like camembert made with raw milk, gourmet delicacies, homestyle cakes, fresh pasta, and ready-to-serve dishes. Among their bakery products, there's an excellent naturally-leavened *pane casereccio* [homestyle bread].

Innocenzi

TRASTEVERE
p.zza San Cosimato, 66
☎ *06/5812725*
• **Closed:** Thursday afternoons; Saturday afternoons in summer

The appearance of this grocery store and the goods it offers hark back to bygone times. Part of the space inside is taken up by huge sacks of legumes and cereals from all over the world. The shelves are filled with all the necessary ingredients for baking cakes, making desserts or preparing exotic dishes, as well as herbal teas, spices, tea and coffee, dried and candied fruit, organic foodstuffs, dietary supplements and a small selection of artisan-made products. Courteous service.

Korean Market

ESQUILINO
via Cavour, 84/86
☎ *06/4885060*
• **Closed:** Sunday mornings

This supermarket is filled with exotic products, mainly Korean - packaged foods, tins and glass jars of preserves and numerous frozen foods [ravioli, sweet and savoury *gnocchi,* oysters and fish dishes].

Kosher Delight di Ouazana

MARCONI
via S. Gherardi, 18
☎ *06/5565231*
• **Closed:** Saturdays

Alberto Ouazana sells fresh *kosher* beef and Piedmontese veal as well as dried meats, *bresaola* and beef salami of his own production, cheeses, wine and various preserved foods. Open straight through on Thursdays.

Mandara

TRIONFALE
via Leone IV, 62
☎ *06/39732502*
• **Closed:** Sundays

 This very attractive retail outlet was opened recently by one of the most famous producers of buffalo mozzarella in Mondragone [Caserta]. Needless to say, the fresh mozzarella that arrives daily from the dairy has pride of place, but you can choose from among another 350 types of Italian and foreign cheese including *formajo embriago, reblochon, pecorino di fossa* [rare cheese, aged underground], *scimudin, burrata* [a cream-enriched soft cheese] and many others, depending on the season. They also have an extremely well-stocked cured-meats section with a number of special treats: Colonnata *lardo* [cured pork fat]; cured buffalo meat; sheep and goat's meat salami; smoked Angus beef; ostrich ham; fillet of bison; cured donkey meat; goose breast, and innumerable other delectable delicacies you can sample in a *panino* at lunchtime. Mandara's also offers a small selection of quality wines and grappas. Extremely polite service.

Marchetti Specialità Abruzzesi

TRIESTE
via Tagliamento, 72/74
☎ *06/8417636*
• **Closed:** Thursday afternoons; Saturday afternoons in summer

An excellent delicatessen that specializes in products from the Abruzzo region - Poggio Cancelli cured meats and excellent cheeses made with naturally-treated milk curd: mozzarella; fresh *giuncata* on Fridays; little *provolette*; smooth, firm *caciocavallo* from Rivinsodoli, Sulmona and Castel di Sangro; sheep's milk *pecorino* from Pizzoli and Atri, as well as preserves and organic honey from Carsoli, regional wines and oils. They also offer ready-to-serve gourmet dishes.

La Peonia Cose di Sardegna

CENTRO STORICO - SPAGNA
via delle Carrozze, 85
☎ *06/6788432*
• **Closed:** Monday mornings

This shop is located in one of the city's most exclusive streets and it has risen to the occasion - the decor is pure boutique and so are the prices. On their shelves or in beautiful wicker baskets you'll find lots of Sardinian specialities: grey mullet or tuna *bottarga* [dried fish roe] of their own production; myrtle liqueur; spindletree or cardoon honey; typical preserves like cardoon and artichokes in oil; *pecorino* and *fiore sardo* cheeses; cured meats; traditional biscuits and pastries; cosmetics made with honey, and various artisanal products. There's another phone number: 0360/812476.

PUNTURI

PINCIANO
via Flavia, 48/50
☎ *06/4818225*
• **Closed:** Sundays

Change is in the air at Punturi's - the cured meats, cheeses and gourmet specialities have been moved into the historic bakery [it dates back to 1918] and can now be found on display opposite the bread counter with its innumerable bakery products: loaves of home-style *pane casereccio*; thin, crunchy *grissini;* biscuits, and fresh pastas like *tortellini;* the *lievito* counter with its breakfast buns, and another counter selling pizza by the slice. You'll also find bread from Lariano and Altamura. Open straight through.

RE CAVIALE
ERCOLI DAL 1928

PRATI - MAZZINI
via Montello, 26
☎ *06/3720243*
• **Closed:** Tuesday
   afternoons;
   Sundays only in summer

 Ercoli will be 70 this year, and he's celebrating the event the best way a veteran like him can, by expanding the business. Last year he created a new company, Re Caviale, which imports and sells fresh Iranian caviar, supervising the entire process from selection and packaging of the product on site in Iran, to its distribution in Italy to restaurants, shops and individual clients. There are six varieties, differing in colour, size and flavour: Sevruga, Asetra, Beluga, Silver Grey, Royal Black and Imperial Gold. In September he'll also begin importing foie gras directly from France. Italian and foreign cheeses

are available too, from an excellent *pecorino* from the Lazio Maremma district to a number of French delicacies, as well as gourmet cured meats, including Prague ham and spicy cured Zibello *culatello* ham; conserves, wines and a few ready-to-serve roast meats. They also organise regular themed tasting evenings.
Open straight through from 7am till 9pm.

RETTAROLI

AVENTINO
via Annia Faustina, 14
☎ *06/5740892*
• **Closed:** Saturday
   afternoons

Warehouse and retail outlet of the Rettaroli pasta-making company, whose factory in Abruzzo produces dried pasta made with the finest semolina in twenty or so classic formats. Its nationwide distribution network centres on the capital and the Lazio region.

RICCI

CASSIA
via Bragaglia, 23
☎ *06/30889404*
• **Closed:** Thursday
   afternoons;
   Sundays only in summer
VIGNA CLARA
l.go di Vigna Stelluti, 9
☎ *06/3293257*
• **Closed:** Thursday
   afternoons;
   Sundays only in summer

A wide selection of cured meats, cheeses and gourmet delicacies plus a lavish buffet of ready-to-serve dishes, especially in the Vigna Clara store.

RICERCATEZZE

PARIOLI
via Chelini, 17/21
☎ *06/8078569*
• **Closed:** Monday mornings;
   Saturday afternoons in July

A few years ago this was just a high quality grocery store, but Ricercatezze now specialises in gourmet gifts, offering conserves, jams, vegetables in oil, exquisite sweets by the *etto* [100 grams] or packed in rustically elegant wicker baskets, chocolates in beautiful burrwood boxes, bottles of spirits, decorative silver objects and so on. Open straight through in winter.

IL SALUMIERE
DI GIUSEPPE CIAVATTA

CENTRO STORICO - TRITONE
via del Lavatore, 31
☎ *06/6792935*
• **Closed:** Thursday
   afternoons; Saturday
   afternoons in summer

Good wines, artisan-made dried pastas, first-press olive oil, conserves, delicacies like truffles and mullet *bottarga* [dried roe], an interesting selection of cured meats [from tasty *prosciutto di montagna* to Colonnata *lardo* - cured pork fat] but above all cheeses, including regional specialities made from Alpine *malga* milk or raw milk: a creamy three-milk *robiola*; *maccagnetta*; *bruss*; fresh cheeses from Fagagna, Vezzena and Bettelmatt; *pecorino* wrapped in walnut leaves, as well as some foreign dairy delights like French chèvres and raw-milk cheeses.

ZENO SANTI

MONTEVERDE VECCHIO
via G. Carini, 27
☎ *06/5800500*
• **Closed:** Thursday
   afternoons; Saturday
   afternoons in summer

A good neighbourhood *salsamenteria* offering a varied selection of quality cured meats and cheeses: extra-aged *parmigiano reggiano; ciauscolo* [cured pork sausage from le Marche]; mozzarella and other fresh cheeses from Basilicata; *burrata* [a cream-enriched soft cheese] from Puglia, fresh wild boar sausages and so on.

SAPORI GENUINI MEDITERRANEI

EUR
v.le degli Astri, 46
☎ *06/52205151*
• **Closed:** Thursday afternoons; Saturday afternoons in summer

This shop sells typically Southern foods: dried pasta from Puglia; olive oil, fresh sausages and conserves from Basilicata; Calabrian *soppressata* [cured pork sausage] and *'nduja* [peppery fresh sausage]. They also offer bakery products [bread, focaccia, *spighette* rolls shaped like grains of wheat, and various sweet pastries], wines and liqueurs.

SELLI INTERNATIONAL FOOD STORE

ESQUILINO
via dello Statuto, 28
☎ *06/4745777*
• **Closed:** Wednesday afternoons; Saturday afternoons in summer

The Selli family offers a wide selection of all the typical *drogheria* products: the basic ingredients of Oriental cuisine, Italian and foreign rice, sweet and savoury foreign gourmet specialities; also natural foods, artisan-made dried pastas, grappa and quality sweets, mushrooms, truffles, and the best brands of oil, conserves and jams.

TEICHNER

CENTRO STORICO - CAMPO MARZIO
via San Lorenzo in Lucina, 17
☎ *06/6871449*
• **Closed:** Sundays; also Saturday afternoons in winter

Next door to their celebrated bar, Teichner's boutique of gastronomic delights offers rare and special things at prices appropriate to its reputation and location. Taking them as they come: mullet bottarga [dried fish roe]; sheep's milk pecorino di fossa [aged underground] and pecorino cheese from Pienza; Spanish *jamon* and hand-made goat's-milk cheese from La Mancha; truffles; first-class tuna; wine-cured Zibello culatello ham; fresh wild boar sausages; traditional balsamic vinegar from Modena; Hungarian salami; finest-brand sauces and jams; fresh pasta, and a few interesting wines.

LA TRADIZIONE DI BELLI E FANTUCCI

TRIONFALE
via Cipro, 8/e
☎ *06/39720349*
• **Closed:** Thursday afternoons;
Sundays only in summer

Renzo Fantucci and Valentino Belli run one of the best delicatessens in Rome where you'll find a rich and inviting array of dairy products including a number of specialities made from Alpine or raw milk, as well as cheeses they have personally selected on site and then had aged inside natural grottoes in Umbria's Val Nerina: little Piedmontese *tome*, Montasio, Monte Veronese and Vezzana cheeses; goat's-milk gorgonzola; *taleggio* made with raw milk; and so on, as well as the house specialities: *caciocavallo* aged in wooden barrels with mountain herbs, and *pecorino* wrapped in walnut leaves. The cured meats section is equally interesting and comprehensive: *lardo* [cured pork fat from Arnad and Colonnata]; Zibello

culatello; Varzi salami; fillets of beef in Barolo wine; cured beef *bresaola* from Valtellina, and excellent salami specially aged in cellars. To complete their range, a wine shop corner with a well-thought out selection of beers; fresh pastas; selected breads; speciality foods like *bottarga* and first-press olive oil, as well as several ready-to-serve gourmet dishes. Professional, courteous service.

EMILIO VOLPETTI

TESTACCIO
via Marmorata, 47
☎ *06/5742352*
• **Closed:** Tuesday afternoons; Sundays June through September

Pioneers in the Roman delicatessen business, the Volpetti's in Via Marmorata was the first to offer personally selected speciality foodstuffs on site and educate Roman palates to appreciate them, blazing a trail for future generations of gastronomes. They continue to offer high quality selections of cured meats, cheeses and gourmet delicacies, as well as organising regular tasting evenings to promote their products. Prices correspondingly high.

GINO VOLPETTI

COLLI PORTUENSI
v.le G. Sirtori, 15/19
☎ *06/55265258*
• **Closed:** Thursday afternoons; Saturday afternoons in summer

A relative of the more famous Volpetti's in Via Marmorata, Gino Volpetti offers a varied assortment of quality cured meats, cheeses, breads and preserved food products.

DELICATESSENS

VOLPETTI ALLA SCROFA

CENTRO STORICO - CAMPO MARZIO
via della Scrofa, 31/32
☎ *06/6861940*
• **Closed:** Sundays;
  the *salsamenteria*
  also Tuesday afternoons

One of the centre's most famous *gastronomia,* with a wide selection of cheeses and cured meats, gourmet delicacies [sauces, caviar, dried fish roe, salmon, mushrooms, truffles] and an interesting cooked foods section offering traditional fried foods, various vegetable and side dishes, baked pasta, *gnocchi* [on Thursdays], roast chicken or hot, spicy chicken *alla diavola*, fish dishes and a few desserts. You can either eat standing at the counter or in the little dining rooms downstairs. Open straight through.

OUTSIDE ROME

UMBERTO ZOFFOLI

MARINO [ROME]
via Roma, 53
☎ *06/9387055*
• **Closed:** Thursday
  and Sunday afternoons

 People come to this little shop full of good things, run by Umberto and Mirella Zoffoli, for the artisan-made dried pastas, home-cured prosciutto, the *pancetta* delicately smoked with juniper leaves and aromatic herbs and aged for 2 years, *parmigiano reggiano stravecchio* [aged for three years] and real *pecorino romano* cheese, legumes to buy by the kilo, and fresh farm butter. But they come above all for Signora Zoffoli's jams and cakes made with first-class fresh ingredients and packaged with her own

Dolcetti di Mirella label: wine-flavoured *ciambelle al mosto* [ring-shaped biscuits], traditional Marino *amaretti* or black pepper and honey-flavoured *tozzetti* biscuits, *pangiallo* and *panpepato* [rich dried fruit loaves] at Christmas; salty *pizza cresciuta* or cheese-flavoured *pizza* cakes at Easter; jam tarts; *ciambelloni* [ring-shaped cakes]; *brutti ma buoni* biscuits and splendid sponge-cakes. The other reason people come are the owners themselves: they'll chat with you like old friends about their most recent innovations or if you happen to be a vintage car enthusiast, about the latest rally.

FORNO MORELLI

OSTIA [ROME]
via delle Zattere, 7
☎ *06/5694760*
• **Closed:** afternoons
OSTIA [ROME]
via Capo Passero, 42
☎ *06/5695903*
• **Closed:** afternoons

Together with bread baked in a wood-fired oven, *pizza bianca romana* [plain, light and salty] and other bakery products, the Morelli's offer gourmet fare, particularly in their Via Capo Passero shop: cured meats and cheeses from all over Italy, sauces and preserves, hand-made dried pastas and other gastronomic delights.

LA FAMILIARE

ROCCA DI PAPA [ROME]
via Frascati, 270
☎ *06/9497789*
• **Closed:** Thursday
  and Sunday afternoons

Go through the garden leading to Massimo Davata's shop and you'll find cured meats and cheeses from all

over Italy, some stored at ideal temperatures in an old grotto, and a corner devoted to fruit and vegetables. Courteous service.

FRESH & CURED MEATS

ANNIBALE

CENTRO STORICO - POPOLO
via di Ripetta, 236/237
☎ *06/3612269*
• **Closed:** Thursday
  afternoons;
  open till 4pm Mon-Wed,
  till 7.30pm Fri and Sat.

The shop dates back to the beginning of the 1900's and has kept all the original furniture and fittings: the old ceramic tiles, shiny brass scales and hooks for hanging the sides of beef. Enchanting flower arrangements glow among the pork roasts and the fillets. Annibale Mastroddi, a true artist, selects the various cuts, oversees the preparation with impeccable skill and conducts his butchery like a perfect host – a smile and a word for everyone. It would be worth the visit for all this alone but you'll also find fabulous *fiorentine* [thick premium steaks]; ultra-fresh *frattaglie* [entrails] – including untreated tripe - and an excellent veal *pajata* [at the beginning of the week]; rabbits and free-range chickens; traditionally-made sausages; perfect cuts for casseroles or roasts; ready-to-cook marinades and crumbed cutlets prepared in the workshop out the back. A wide choice of Christmas *bollito* cuts [for boiling] as well as hens, capons, tongue and *testina* [calf or lamb's head] are available in the festive season. Annibale is assisted by excellent staff.

La Bottega della Carne

PRATI - MAZZINI
via G. Avezzana, 17
☎ *06/3217917*
• **Closed:** Saturday
afternoons

Robert Dionisi's Bottega keeps expanding. It started out as a butchery with a workshop area for preparing the various cuts of meat, now it specialises increasingly in ready-to-cook or pre-cooked items, and not just meat. Next to classic cuts and specialities executed with flair and expertise [roasts; pastry-crusted fillets; meatballs; rolled roasts; meat sandwiches; saddle of veal and creamed truffles; delicious pâtés shaped like ducks or piglets] he now offers a number of fish specialities [grilled sweet peppers stuffed with tuna; sea bass in aspic; cuttlefish with peas; salmon pie; salmon and tuna pâté], and vegetable preparations, with a variety of stuffed vegetables including rice-filled tomatoes. Open straight through.

Sandro Bufacchi

APPIO
c.ne Appia, 38
☎ *06/7810289*
• **Closed:** Thursday
afternoons, Saturday
afternoons in summer.

Sandro Bufacchi is an expert butcher who offers finest quality cuts of meat prepared in strictly supervised conditions. Inside his display counter you'll find cuts of Mantuan veal from animals raised in natural conditions; rabbits from Le Marche; lamb from the Roman or Abruzzo countryside; Cinta Senese pork; Danish beef and, especially just before Christmas, free-range chickens from Ascoli Piceno

and Livorno; hens; ducks; guinea fowl, and some game. There are also ready-to-cook dishes prepared as you watch or you can order boned stuffed whole chickens in advance.

C.A.C.S.
Antica Norcineria

CENTRO STORICO - CAMPO MARZIO
via della Scrofa, 100
☎ *06/68801074*
• **Closed:** Thursday
afternoons, Saturday
afternoons in summer.

One of the last traditional pork butcheries, as both the appearance of the shop and the quality of the meat make clear. A magnificent, flavoursome mountain ham dominates the scene, waiting to be sliced by hand, but there's also *mortadella* from Campotosto or Bologna; *ciauscolo* [cured pork sausage] from Le Marche; *salame schiacciato* from L'Aquila; *speck* [smoked ham] and Felino salami. A big counter displays all the fresh cuts of pork. Open straight through.

F.lli Carilli

CENTRO STORICO - ARGENTINA
via Torre Argentina, 11/12
☎ *06/68803789*
• **Closed:** Thursday
afternoons

This is the place to come for excellent hand-carved mountain prosciutto; fresh cuts of pork; ready-to-cook Umbrian-style *fegatelli* [pieces of pork liver wrapped in caul fat] prepared with sultanas and pine nuts; and cured meats of their own production. But you may be tempted by even more interesting delicacies: tasty salted anchovies; marinated *baccalà* [dried salt cod] and chickpeas [on Thursdays and Fridays]; excellent Sardinian and Tuscan *pecorino* cheese; artisan-made dried pastas;

fabulous buffalo mozzarella [every other day] and, especially just before Christmas, eel and marinated anchovy-like *lattarini*, stupendous smoked herrings and *tortelli* stuffed with pumpkin. Flexible opening hours.

De Angelis

PINCIANO
via Flavia, 74/76
☎ *06/4824676*
• **Closed:** Thursday
afternoons; Saturday
afternoons in summer.

 This street has a high concentration of excellent gourmet shops, and De Angelis is one of the best. Its historic premises date back to 1927, and renovations carried out a few years ago haven't disfigured its appearance - the old pale marble has been preserved and the new counters blend in with the original decor. You'll find excellent cuts of meat here: real Danish beef; Dutch veal; pré-salé lamb; ostrich meat; French *barberie* duck; game [order a week in advance]; chickens and capons from Bresse in France. They also offer a vast range of ready-to-cook specialities according to the season or festivity, expertly prepared on the premises; in December mainly various kinds of fowl with Christmas stuffing – veal, chestnuts, tangy rennet apples, brandy and sultanas. Professional courteous service.

Luciana De Filippi

AURELIO
via Gregorio VII, 300/302
☎ *06/630694*
• **Closed:** Thursday
afternoons, Satuday
afternoons in summer.

Luciana De Filippi and her husband Graziano Mangani

were both born to the trade and are now veteran practitioners. They sell good traditional cuts of meat and an attractive range of ready-to-cook preparations. Stuffed vegetables and pockets of meat; roasts; and meat loaves, as well as ready-to-serve dishes like roast beef, tripe and chicken salad. Open from seven o'clock in the morning.

ANGELO FEROCI

PRATI - CAVOUR
via Muzio Clementi, 15
☎ *06/3222163*
• **Closed:** Thursday afternon; Thurs and Sat afternoons from June 1-Sept 1.

The same management as the better-known Feroci in Via della Maddelena with the same wholesale sources of Danish beef and Dutch veal. This shop, run by two brothers, scions of the famous dynasty of butchers, also sells poultry, pork meats, lamb, rabbits and game.

ANGELO FEROCI

CENTRO STORICO - PANTHEON
via della Maddalena, 15
☎ *06/68307030*
• **Closed:** Thurs afternoon; open mornings only in August

Feroci was one of the first butcheries to open in Rome and has been famous for its excellent cuts of beef for many years. They sell Danish beef, one of the best on the market, and Dutch veal. If you order a few hours in advance they can also supply poultry, pork, spring lamb and game. The original marble decor and a certain aura of austerity characteristic of old-fashioned butcher's shops have been maintained.

SERGIO GIGLIANI

AVENTINO
via A. Palladio, 4
☎ *06/5750823*
• **Closed:** Saturday afternoons

In this little butcher's shop on delightful Piazza Bernini, you'll find good beef and pork, lamb, rabbit and poultry, including excellent capons, un-treated tripe and one or two ready-to-cook preparations.

F.LLI GIOVANNELLI

PARIOLI
via Antonelli, 37/a
☎ *06/8072153*
• **Closed:** Thursday afternoons; Saturday afternoons in summer

Giovanelli's is a solid, reliable butchery offering Danish beef; free-range chickens from Livorno; homegrown Italian lamb; pork from Abruzzo; fresh *interiora* [various innards]; ready-to-cook preparations and so on. The very helpful staff offer "keys in hand" service, like singeing off the last of the chickens' feathers while you watch or giving you a parting gift of fresh herbs chosen to match the type of meat and cooking method you've chosen.

GRANIERI

CENTRO STORICO - GHETTO
via dei Delfini, 30
☎ *06/6781016*
• **Closed:** every afternoon except Friday

People come here for the excellent beef steaks [from traditional farms in Le Marche] but also for the free-range chickens [Wednesdays], spring lamb, various cuts of pork, and handmade sausages. Open straight through till 3.30pm except on Fridays, when it closes at 7.30pm. A stone's throw away from Piazza Margana.

LA NORCINERIA IACOZZILLI

TRASTEVERE
via Natale del Grande, 15/16
☎ *06/5812734*
• **Closed:** Tuesday afternoons; only on Sundays in summer

The old-fashioned Roman *salsamenterie* have now become rather rare but they can still be found with their 360° range of wares: sacks full of grain, bread, pasta, pre-soaked *baccalà* [dried salt cod] and chickpeas on Fridays, cheeses and cured meats - which in this case are produced by the Iacozzilli's themselves: pork or liver sausages, salami, and strong, salty *prosciutto di montagna*. Good fresh cuts of pork too, and reasonable prices.

VITTORIO LATELLA

CENTRO STORICO - GHETTO
via S. Maria del Pianto, 61
☎ *06/6864659*
• **Closed:** Thursday afternoons; Saturday afternoons in summer

In one of the streets that lead into the Jewish quarter, Vittorio Latella, from the heights of his marble counter, will sell you unimaginably wonderful *fiorentine* – the traditional Florentine thick premium steak, and first-class roast beef [made with rump steak or sirloin tip steak]. Also available: an excellent shoulder of veal, the flank and loin cuts of beef and veal, and sometimes liver and *rognoncini* [kidneys]. His dried meats are quite exceptional.

IL MANZO

TRIONFALE
via Cipro, 8
☎ *06/39720350*
• **Closed:** Thursday afternoons; Saturday afternons in summer

Il Manzo's speciality are the thick *fiorentina* steaks from cattle raised in the Pontino Marshes near Rome, personally selected by the owner and butchered at nearby Sezze. As well as the traditional cuts of fresh meat there's also a small selection of cured meats and ready-to-cook preparations.

NINO IL FIORENTINO

CENTRO STORICO - CAMPO DE' FIORI
Campo de' Fiori, 17/19
☎ *06/68801296*
• **Closed:** Sundays;
  and Saturday afternoons
  in summer

Nino has now retired and passed the business on to Claudio, but the shop has retained the old name and its vocation for ready-to-serve preparations: from bread-crumbed stuffed hamburgers to meat pies.

ENRICO PIERGENTILI

PRATI - COLA DI RIENZO
via Fabio Massimo, 29/31
☎ *06/3241837*
• **Closed:** Thursday
  afternoons

For years here in the Prati quarter the name Piergentili has been synonymous with reliability. All their cuts of meat, whether Danish beef, or Danish and Dutch veal, are first-class. Their speciality are *kosher* cured meats – beef, goose, turkey and chicken. Ready-to-cook preparations available on request.

PIETRANGELI

PRATI - COLA DI RIENZO
via dei Gracchi, 58/b
☎ *06/3212461*
• **Closed:** Thursday
  afternoons; Saturday
  afternoons in summer

A classic *Abbacchi e Polli* [spring lamb and poultry] shop almost opposite the markets in Piazza dell'Unità. Don't miss the truly exceptional spring lamb from Abruzzo; their free-range chickens, guinea fowl, turkeys, squab and rabbit are also well worth trying.

MACELLERIA RANIERI

TESTACCIO
via Luca della Robbia, 41
☎ *06/5742684*
• **Closed:** Thursday
  afternoons; Saturday
  afternoons in summer

A good local butcher's shop that sells excellent beef steaks.

RANUCCI

CENTRO STORICO - GHETTO
via S. Maria del Pianto, 60
☎ *06/68806675*
• **Closed:** Thursday
  afternoons; Saturday
  afternoons in summer

Elide Ranucci sells first-class spring lamb and free-range poultry, eggs and, on request, ready-to-cook chicken specialities.

SARANDREA

CENTRO STORICO - POPOLO
via di Ripetta, 30
☎ *06/3219448*
• **Closed:** Saturday afternoons

The Sarandrea butchery was already here on this very spot in beautiful Via di Ripetta in 1918. Over the years they've added a wide range of ready-to-cook and ready-to-serve preparations to the traditional array of cuts of meat: stuffed vegetables; crumbed cutlets; pockets of meat; *involtini* [roulades]; *saltimbocca* [veal, prosciutto and sage scallops]; roasts; chicken galantine; chicken salad; *vitello tonnato* [veal in a creamy tuna sauce]; chicken-liver pâté, and spreads for Tuscan *crostini* [in winter]. Sometimes prize *chianina* beef steaks are also available. Open from 7.30am onwards.

ANTICA NORCINERIA VIOLA

CENTRO STORICO - CAMPO DE' FIORI
Campo de' Fiori, 43/c
☎ *06/68806114*
• **Closed:** Thursday
  afternoons; July 15–Aug 31

This historic pork butchery has been on the same premises in this famous piazza since 1890. Their own production centres on typical Lazio specialities like *guanciale* [cured pork jowl], *coppa* [cured meat made from pig's head]; *lonza* [cured pork shoulder]; strong salty *prosciutto di montagna* and fresh sausages, as well as cured meats from other regions like pork *ciauscolo* from Le Marche; Tuscan *soppressata*; salami from Aquila and Hungary, cured sausages from Basilicata, and fresh cuts of pork, also available in ready-to-serve preparations.

OUTSIDE ROME

TAVOLONI

ALBANO LAZIALE [ROME]
p.zza Gramsci, 9
☎ *06/9323815*
• **Closed:** Thursday
  afternoons and Mondays

Tavoloni's fame has spread well beyond the confines of the Castelli Romani, so it's no surprise to find that some clients come all the way from Rome to this butcher's shop in Albano to buy its fabulous meat, selected from first-class producers all over the country: beef from Umbria and Le Marche; veal from Emilia Romagna; free-range poultry; pork; goat and spring lamb raised in the Roman countryside. On Fridays and Saturdays they also offer ready-to-cook preparations: *spiedini* [brochettes], roasts, crumbed chicken legs, and roulades. In season, and if you order in advance, they can supply geese, ducks and game.

EGIDIO CIOLI

ARICCIA [ROME]
p.zza della Repubblica, 3
☎ *06/9330596*
• **Closed:** Tuesdays

This classic *porchetta* [spicy roast pork] outlet opposite Palazzo Chigi is an institution in Arriccia, and the town itself has been famous for this Castelli Romani speciality since time immemorial. *Panini* made with homemade *casereccio* bread generously filled with thick slices of the delicious stuff can be bought here from 10am till 10pm [they close briefly at lunchtime].

FRESH FISH

ANTINORI

CENTRO STORICO - TRITONE
via della Panetteria, 4
☎ *06/6794701*
• **Closed:** Mondays
  and afternoons

Their fresh fish comes from both fish hatcheries and sea catches with the best, most varied displays on Tuesdays and Fridays - the traditional Catholic fasting days.

ITTICA ATTANASIO

CENTRO STORICO - CAMPO DE' FIORI
via del Biscione, 12
☎ *06/68801401*
• **Closed:** afternoons
  and Mondays

One of the best fish shops in the centre of Rome, run by a well-known name in fish importing and distributiion circles [the Attanasio family have a warehouse and wholesale outlet on the Isola Sacra at Fiumicino]. The fresh fish bought directly from the wharfs at Fiumicino, Anzio and other Mediterranean ports is displayed separately from the fish hatchery products and prices are clearly differentiated.

CESTRONI

PINCIANO
via Flavia, 30
☎ *06/4741930*
• **Closed:** afternoons
  and Mondays

Umberto Lumini has run this shop for several years now but it's still famous by the name of its founder, his grandfather, and is one of the most highly regarded and best patronised in the city, especially by restaurateurs.
You'll find all the most popular varieties laid out on thick beds of green leaves: *spigola* [seabass], *orata* [bream], cuttlefish and squid, shrimps, *sogliola* [sole], and so on. A word of advice: come early in the morning, otherwise you'll have to make do with what's left. The service is a trifle brusque.

FEDERMAR

PINCIANO
via Belisario, 2/a
☎ *06/4819398*
• **Closed:** afternoons

This minuscule fish shop in a little lane off Via Piave, run by Fabio and Maria Carosi, sells fish of every kind – both wholesale to restaurateurs and retail to private customers – frozen, smoked and fresh: *paranza* [straight off the boats] from the Mediterranean, from

hatcheries and even from international waters.

IL FORMIANO DI ENZO ROMANO

PINCIANO
via Ancona, 34
☎ *06/44249770*
• **Closed:** afternoons
  and Mondays

No entrancing displays here, only boxes scattered everywhere filled with excellent fresh fish from the fertile triangle of sea between Terracina, the Pontine Islands and Gaeta - a particularly fortunate fishing ground. Octopus, rock mullet, sea bass, mixed fresh fish for fries or soups, anchovies, piper, scorpion fish, as well as swordfish, shellfish and Northern European salmon. Local and imported lobster can be ordered in advance.

ANTICA PESCHERIA GALLUZZI 1894

VIMINALE
via Venezia, 26/28
☎ *06/4744444*
• **Closed:** afternoons
  and Mondays

The Galluzzi's, husband and wife, are hard workers who love their job. The best restaurants in the city buy from them and there are good reasons why.
This year we sampled every single type of fish on sale and never had the slightest problem with either freshness or quality - they could all have been quite happily eaten raw. The swordfish is exceptional and the scampi are splendid, but even the less noble varieties are honourably represented. Don't miss the home-preserved jars of anchovies - an authentic delicacy.

Marcello

TUSCOLANO
via Tuscolana, 1162
☎ *06/71543407*
• **Closed:** Wednesdays
and Saturdays; Monday
and Thursday mornings

This fish shop near the Lucio
Sesto metro station offers
one of the most spectacular
displays of seafood in the
city: king prawns, shrimps,
shellfish still palpitating,
tasty mackerel, sea bass,
bream, octopus, rock mullet,
etc. Here you'll find
freshness, variety, human
prices and a laudably clear
distinction made between
hatchery and trawler-
harvested fish, presented in
separate boxes at different
prices. There's another
Marcello outlet at the market
in Piazza del Tribuni-viale dei
Consoli.

Nitti di Renzo Taddei

CORSO FRANCIA
via F. S. Nitti, 58
☎ *06/36304683*
• **Closed:** afternoons
and Mondays

This shop offers good fresh
fish of the most popular
varieties: *sogliola* [sole],
merluzzo [cod], *orata*
[bream], *dentice* [sea
bream], *rombo* [turbot],
spigola [seabass], whole and
sliced salmon, swordfish,
crustaceans and other
shellfish.

Pescheria Messinese

NEMORENSE
via Lago di Lesina, 79
☎ *06/86213602*
• **Closed:** Mondays;
Wednesday, Thursday
and Saturday afternoons

This fish shop run by Nuccio
De Francesco offers the

standard repertoire of fish on
traditional fasting days
[Tuesdays and Fridays], in
particular *pesce azzurro*, a
generic term for fatty
Mediterranean fish, the
house speciality. Faithful to
his Messinese origins,
Nuccio displays anchovies,
sardines, and *maccarelli* all
year round, and from spring
to autumn, garfish, bonito,
tuna and swordfish. There
are also the more popular
varieties and, if you order in
advance, shellfish and wild
sea bass.

Orfeo Scafetti
La Stadera

CENTRO STORICO - SPAGNA
via della Croce, 71/a
☎ *06/6792683*
• **Closed:** Mondays;
Wednesday
and Saturday afternoons

Quality food shops in the
centro storico are a bit like
the panda – on the way to
extinction. Yet this minuscule
fish shop run by three
brothers, besieged as it is by
designer jeans shops and
modish boutiques, manages
to service and offer a
consistently good selection
of fresh quality fish.

FRESH PASTA

Giancarlo Franciosi

APPIO
via Licia, 4
☎ *06/77204340*
• **Closed:** Monday afternoons;
also Saturday afternoons
in summer

Homemade fresh pastas in
classic formats: *fettuccine,
quadrucci, pappardelle,
lombrichelli, trofie, tortellini,*
and *ravioli* filled with ricotta
and spinach.

Pasta all'uovo Gatti

TESTACCIO
via G. Branca, 13
☎ *06/5740595*
• **Closed:** every afternoon
except Friday and Saturday
[in winter], Friday afternoon
only in summer

Good fresh egg pasta: the
best are the simpler, non-
stuffed varieties like
*strozzapreti, tagliatelle,
tagliolini* and so on.

Gatti & Antonelli

NEMORENSE
via Nemorense, 211
☎ *06/86218044*
• **Closed:** Thursday
afternoons; Saturday
afternoons in summer

Anchored to tradition and the
traditional range of forms and
fillings, Gatti & Antonelli
prepare fresh classic pastas
of proven quality every single
day - *fettuccine, pappardelle,
tonnarelli; ravioli, agnolotti* or
cannelloni filled with ricotta
and spinach. The stuffed
pastas are particularly good,
with very tasty, well-balanced
fillings. The service is
courteous, competent and
fast, even when they're at
their busiest [which is quite
often].

Grand Gourmet

FLAMINIO
via C. Fracassini, 15/a
☎ *06/3201123*
• **Closed:** Mondays

 For a fresh pasta
shop this place has a
very unusual decor.
Wrought iron, mirrors and
designer tiles set off the
manicaretti prepared daily by
Pamela Marcantoni . You'll
also find *gnocchi, fettuccine,
lasagna,* classic *tortellini* [but
the smaller variety, better

known as *cappelletti*], ricotta and spinach-filled *ravioli, cannelloni*, meat-filled *tortelli*, pumpkin *tortelli* made according to the Mantuan recipe with *mostarda* [mustard-flavoured chutney] and *amaretti*. But creativity holds sway here and you'll also find *tortelli* filled with *radicchio* [red chicory] and *speck*, artichokes or truffles. The ravioli made from extra-thin sheets of pasta and filled with *pesto di mare* [classic Genoan pesto blended with fresh salmon, herb-scented vegetables and béchamel sauce] are excellent, and the pear and cheese-filled *tortelloni* are well worth trying. Best to order in advance, especially at weekends and holiday periods. Reasonable prices.

LA MADIA PRIMI PIATTI

TRIESTE
via Sebino, 10/12
☎ 06/8554943
• **Closed:** giovedì pomeriggio; sabato pomeriggio in estate

Here you'll find fresh pasta [from simple fettuccine to pastas stuffed with imaginative combinations like red chicory and smoked ham], ready-to-bake pasta dishes in their sealed aluminium trays like *lasagna*, stuffed pasta rolls and crêpes, *parmigiana*, potato gâteau, and rustic tortes with vegetables, cheese or cured meats, as well as *olive ascolane* [deep-fried stuffed olives] and dried vegetable-coloured pastas.

MARINI

TRIESTE
via Po, 47/a
☎ 06/8554134
• **Closed:** Thursday afternoons; Saturday afternoons in summer

Romans of a certain age know this historic fresh pasta shop well – it's been run by the Marini family since 1931. You go down a long stairway and find yourself in front of a counter displaying all the day's offerings: *quadrucci, fettuccine, tonnarelli, agnolotti, cappelletti, ravioli, rotoli, tortellini, lasagna* and *cannelloni*, as well as *olive ascolane* [deep-fried stuffed olives], potato *gnocchi* and traditionally Roman *gnocchi* made with semolina. Well-made products, reasonable prices and old world courtesy.

TADDEI

TRIONFALE
v.le delle Milizie, 9/g
☎ 06/3729853
• **Closed:** Thursday afternoons; every afternoon in summer

A tiny fresh pasta shop offering all the classic formats: *tagliatelle, quadrucci, stringozzi, ravioli* stuffed with ricotta and spinach, *tortellini* and potato or semolina *gnocchi* on Thursdays.

OUTSIDE ROME

LA BOTTEGA
DELLA PASTA ALL'UOVO

MARINO [ROME]
loc. S. Maria delle Mole
via N. Tommaseo, 14
☎ 06/93548419
• **Closed:** Thursday afternoons and Mondays; open Sunday mornings

Skilled pasta-roller Patrizia De Angelis continues to combine tradition and her own creative imagination. Next to various kinds of *fettuccine*, classic *ravioli, lasagna* and *cannelloni* you'll find minuscule stuffed *raviolini*, pasta roses filled with creamed spinach, porcini mushrooms, peas, shrimps, or scampi; *lasagna* with creamed pumpkin; the King's *bocconcini* [huge pasta rolls filled with cheese

and béchamel sauce], fish-filled *cannelloni*, shellfish *lasagna, rotolo alle melanzane* [eggplant-filled pasta rolls], and tasty croquettes.

FRUIT & VEGETABLES

ALBERTO AGOLINI

FLAMINIO
via Flaminia, 411
☎ 06/3233379
• **Closed:** Thursday afternoons; Saturday afternoons in summer

It ranks a good cut or two above the other fruit shops in the area, and Agolini's clientele keep increasing in number because of the laudable extras they offer: a number of rarities [wild *lampascione* onions, Chinese cabbage, wild asparagus, celery root, exotic fruits and berries]; several particularly tasty varieties of fruit and vegetables they grow themselves; ready-to-cook vegetable soup mixes; pre-washed and chopped salad greens and garden vegetables. Everything is fresh, excellent quality, and reasonably-priced. Courteous service.

AGRILANDIA

CENTRO STORICO - NAVONA
l.go del Teatro Valle, 5
☎ 06/68307875
• **Closed:** Saturday afternoons

About as central as you get, opposite the Church of Sant'Andrea della Valle in Corso Vittorio Emanuele, Agrilandia offers fruit and vegetables, seasonal specialities, out-of-season delicacies from warmer climes and exotic fruits.

AURELI

FLAMINIO
via Flaminia, 50/a
☎ *06/3203456*
• **Closed:** Thursday afternoons; Saturday afternoons in summer

Here in Via Flaminia for some years now, there've been a few modifications recently both to the range of products stocked and the prices [still pretty hefty]. You'll find seasonal fruit and vegetables, out-of-season specialities; a few exotic products; ready-to-cook vegetables and legumes; and several rarities like fresh aromatic herbs, wild *lampascione* onions, watercress, Tuscan black cabbage, *fico d'India* [prickly-pear fruit], citrons and wild asparagus.

CAPONE

MONTEVERDE VECCHIO
via G. Carini, 39/39a
☎ *06/5809166*
• **Closed:** Sundays

The Capone's have just celebrated their first forty years in business. Alfonso and Gino Capone were the first in Rome to sell out-of-season cherries at Christmas and grapes at Easter, rarities like wild asparagus, shallots, fresh rhubarb, citrons, prize mushrooms, aromatic herbs, root vegetables, squash of all kinds, and tropical fruit you couldn't find anywhere else. Since 1969 they've also sold wine, beer, first-press olive oil, a number of speciality preserved foodstuffs [from organic products to artisan-made dried pastas], ready-to-cook

vegetables and table-ready salad. Boutique prices.

CRESCENZI

PARIOLI
via Schiaparelli, 21
☎ *06/3216411*
• **Closed:** Saturday afternoons

Most of the popular varieties of fruit and vegetables are available here but Domenico and Cresimino Crescenzi specialise in rare products, especially the more unusual exotic fruits, like plantain bananas, cassava and passion fruit, and the friendly *fruttivendoli* will explain everything to do with their origins, characteristics and culinary uses. Other rarities include wild berries, out-of-season fruits and vegetables, fresh aromatic herbs; in season and if you order in advance they will also provide white Bassano asparagus. Open all day.

SILVIO FERRANTE

PRATI - MAZZINI
via Montello, 28
☎ *06/3721542*
• **Closed:** Tuesday afternoons; only Sundays in summer

You notice this shop straightaway because of the beautiful aromatic herb plants lined up at the entrance and along the footpath: rosemary, basil, parsley, chives, wall rue, chervil, lemonbalm, watercress, Roman mint, etc..

ORO FRUITS

APPIO
via Taranto, 166
☎ *no*
• **Closed:** Thursday afternoons

Very much one of a kind, Roberto Palma's fruit shop has two big entrances leading into a large space hung with paintings, mirrors and ornamental wall lamps. Inside

and out there are pyramids of various kinds of seasonal Mediterranean fruit at market prices. No exotic fruits or pre-washed vegetables, but good bargains if you buy large quantities.

RENZO PELLEGRINI

NEMORENSE
via Lucrino, 33
☎ *06/86324813*
• **Closed:** Sundays

This clean, no-frills fruit-and-veg shop is very professionally run by Renzo Pellegrini and offers quality products at affordable prices. He stocks mostly in-season Mediterranean varieties but you can also find strawberries from Nemi and Amalfi lemons, several exotic fruits and berries, and a few varieties of ready-to-cook vegetables. Flexible opening hours.

PRIMIZIE E VERDURA DI LUCA PERSIANI

PINCIANO
via Flavia, 36
☎ *06/4743726*
• **Closed:** Thursday afternoons; Saturday afternoons in summer

Luca Persiani deals in rather special fruit and vegetables[and has done for quite a while, unlike some of his competitors] attractively displayed at the entrance to his shop. Depending on the time of year you'll find a wide selection of root vegetables [horseradish, daikon, ginger, sweet potatoes]; fresh aromatic herbs; wild asparagus; Mantuan squash; porcini mushrooms; wild *lampascione* onions; red radicchio from Treviso; Tuscan cabbage; shallots; wild berries, and various exotic rarities from other climes. Pricey.

ADRIANO PRIORI

CENTRO STORICO - NAVONA
via delle Coppelle, 17
☎ *06/68802776*
• **Closed:** Thursday
afternoons; Saturday
afternoons in summer

This shop stocks mainly the
more popular varieties of
seasonal fruit and vegetables
and only a few are pre-
cleaned, but the quality is
high, the prices are fair, and
you'll sometimes find a few
out-of-season or exotic
specialities.

QUATTRO STAGIONI DI DANILO GROSSI

TRIESTE
via Sebino, 9
☎ *06/8416377*
• **Closed:** Sundays;
also Saturday afternoons
in summer

A little fruit-and-vegetable
boutique where among the
usual seasonal varieties
you'll also spy some more
inviting kinds: out-of-season
specialities, wild mushrooms
and asparagus, exotic fruit
and wild berries. Top quality,
high prices.

DAI SICILIANI

TRIESTE
via San Marino, 45
☎ *06/8540561*
• **Closed:** Thursday
afternoons; Saturday
afternoons throughout July

 You can't help but
stop entranced in front
of the scales heaped
with brilliantly-coloured exotic
fruit, the wicker baskets
bulging with apricots, and the
branches dripping flaming red
chilis that frame the doorway.
Husband and wife Paolo and
Paola Marino, Sicilians from
Marsala, are not only true

trade professionals but also
masters of the art of beautiful
presentation. The traditional
assortment of seasonal fruit
and vegetables is enriched by
typical specialities imported
directly from Sicily: wild
strawberries, blood oranges,
clementines, tangerines,
lemons, tomatoes, sweet
peppers and eggplant from
Pachino, stuffed olives, *fichi
d'India* [prickly-pear fruit],
cans of finest quality tuna
from Trapani. During the pre-
Christmas period they offer an
attractive selection of biscuits
and in summer-autumn
splendid porcini mushrooms
gathered in Sabina, the
source of a number of other
varieties of fruit and
vegetables, as well as the
extra vergine olive oil they
produce themselves. Food
baskets packed by Paolo
make original gifts. Typically
Sicilian courtesy.

HEALTH FOOD

L'ALBERO DEL PANE

CENTRO STORICO - GHETTO
*via S. Maria
del Pianto, 19/20*
☎ *06/6865016*
• **Closed:** Thursday afternoons

One of the historic Roman
health food shops where you
can find organic everything
except fruit and vegetables –
preserves, cheeses, bread,
legumes, savoury pies, cakes,
cosmetics, detergents, dietary
supplements, books and
ecologically sound stationery,
plus all imaginable aids and
accessories for healthy
eating. Open all day except in
July and August.

ALIMENTAZIONE

CENTRO STORICO - TRITONE
via della Panetteria, 8
☎ *06/6796259*
• **Closed:** Thursday
afternoons; Saturday
afternoons in summer

Another of the first natural
food shops to open in Rome,

Alimentazione was located
for many years in Piazza della
Maddalena. They stock
mostly dietary products and
supplements, plus
homemade wholemeal bread,
biscuits, cakes and sweets.
Open all day.

BIO DISPENSA

MONTI
via Santa Maria Maggiore, 118
☎ *06/4827958*
• **Closed:** Monday mornings

The compleat A to Z organic
food pantry, this *dispensa* has
everything from naturally
leavened wholemeal bread
made from a variety of cereals
to a small selection of fresh
fruit and vegetables, as well
as cheeses and yoghurt and
all the packaged standards.

IL CANESTRO

TESTACCIO
via Luca della Robbia, 12
☎ *06/5741031*
• **Closed:** Monday mornings
[never in summer]

One of the oldest and best
natural foods outlets – a one-
stop shop for all organic
products, from fresh fruit and
vegetables to cosmetics.
Hefty prices.

EMPORIUM NATURAE

TRIONFALE
v.le delle Milizie, 7/a
☎ *06/3725394*
• **Closed:** Monday mornings;
Sat afternoons
June 6-July 31

This shop offers the
complete repertoire of
organic foods, from
preserved products to fresh
fruit and vegetables. The
cheeses and dairy products
are particularly good: yoghurt;
caciotta; *pecorino*; plain and

HEALTH FOOD

aromatised goat's milk cheeses that arrive on Fridays, though not in summer.

AI MONASTERI

CENTRO STORICO - NAVONA
c.so Rinascimento, 72
☎ *06/68802783*
• **Closed:** Monday mornings

By the time this guidebook appears in the bookshops Ai Monasteri will have moved back to its original premises, at 72 Corso Rinascimento, less than ten metres from its temporary location. The phone number and the repertoire won't change: speciality foods and cosmetics made by monks from monasteries all over Italy, from the jams produced by the Trappist nuns of Vitorchiano to the liqueurs of the Cistercian monks from the Charterhouse of Trisulti.

SETTE SPIGHE

PRATI - COLA DI RIENZO
via Crescenzio, 89/d
☎ *06/68805566*
• **Closed:** Sundays

Except for fresh fruit and vegetables, every kind of organic foodstuff is on sale here: bread, pasta, sweet and savoury conserves, dietary supplements, detergents, cosmetics, and relevant texts. Flexible opening hours.

AL SOLE D'ORO

PRATI - CAVOUR
lungotevere dei Mellini, 44
☎ *06/3204977*
• **Closed:** Monday mornings; Sat afternoons in summer

A pleasant, tranquil shop selling organic products in the gallery that links Via

Visconti and Via Belli. Fresh fruit and vegetables, bread and other bakery products, packaged foods, excellent milk products and cheeses, cosmetics and detergents can all be bought here. Parking in a garage nearby, and home deliveries. Open all day.

ICE CREAM

PREMIATE GELATERIE FANTASIA DI BARCHIESI E FIGLI

MARCONI
via Oderisi da Gubbio, 230
☎ *06/5560239*
• **Closed:** Wednesdays; open 7 days a week in August
PRENESTINO
via Torpignattara, 46
☎ *06/2415642*
• **Closed:** Thursdays
APPIO
via La Spezia, 100/102
☎ *06/7012413*
• **Closed:** Wednesdays

Three *gelateria* that share a name and a philosophy: the one in Via Oderisi da Gubbio is the biggest, and also offers low-calorie diet gelati and night-time service; the San Giovanni shop has a bar as well as ice cream; while the Torpignattara parlour offers fewer flavours than the other two.

LE CAFÉ DU PARC

TESTACCIO
p.zza Porta San Paolo snc
☎ *06/5743363*
• **Closed:** Sundays; [never in summer]

This little kiosk on the edge of the park specialises in tiny tubs of typically Roman soft-serve *cremolati:* exquisite figs in whisky, melon in port, strawberries in

Maraschino liqueur, blackberries, mulberries and many others, plus all the classic flavours, including a particularly good coffee and chocolate. Delicious coffee granitas. Everything is rigorously homemade. Outdoor tables.

BAR CILE

PARIOLI
p.zza Santiago del Cile, 1
☎ *06/8070917*
• **Closed:** Sundays

A wide range of flavours - more than forty - ranging from classic creams and fruit sorbets to some more original creations. Lots of different kinds of chocolate: dark, milk and white; chocolate with orange, with coconut, with strawberries, with banana; the Mozart [like Viennese chocolate cake], the *cuneese* [with rum and toasted wafers] and vanilla cream-and-chocolate. Their own exclusive flavours are rum babà, Condorelli *torrone* [with toasted almonds and caramel], licorice and mint, peanut, Rossana candy, balsamic vinegar and vanilla, cappuccino, Grand Marnier cream and Rocher chocolate.

DE ANGELIS

NEMORENSE
via di Priscilla, 18/20
☎ *06/86200724*
• **Closed:** Tuesdays

Apart from the classic flavours [meaning *zabaglione,* chocolate, vanilla, hazelnut, coffee, Bacio Perugino, lemon, strawberry, and so on] the house specialities are their soft-serve *cremolati:* coffee all year round, and in season: melon, strawberry, blackberry, mulberry, blueberry and raspberry - all made from fresh fruit.

DUSE

PARIOLI
via Duse, 1/e
☎ 06/8079300
• **Closed:** Sundays

Classic ice creams with unusual fruit flavours [pawpaw, passion fruit, dates], *semifreddi* [chilled frozen mousse] and wonderful soft-serve fruit *cremolati,* the house speciality – blueberry, raspberry, tangerine and melon. Don't miss the *turbo:* a mixture of *zabaglione,* espresso coffee and whipped cream sprinkled with cocoa.

PALAZZO DEL FREDDO DI GIOVANNI FASSI

PRATI - COLA DI RIENZO
via Vespasiano, 56/a-b-c
☎ 06/39725164
• **Closed:** Mondays
ESQUILINO
via Principe Eugenio, 65/67
☎ 06/4464740
• **Closed:** Mondays

This famous gelateria, opened in 1924, makes no concession to passing trends and always offers the same traditional ice creams and classic sorbets in cones and *coppe* [cups], as well as *cassata, tartufi* [chocolate ice cream balls with hard chocolate centres], the *caterinetta* [whipped honey and vanilla], the *pezzo duro* with fruit or chocolate, *ninetto* and *frulletto* to enjoy at tables outside or inside in the courtyard and ice cream cakes like their *Torta Giuseppina* to take away. They do winter promotions, with half-price gelati on Thursdays and Fridays, and a 30% discount on Sundays and public holidays.

FEDELI

FLAMINIO
v.le Pinturicchio, 200
☎ 06/3208766
• **Closed:** open 7 days a week, but closed all January and February

Good, honest homemade gelato with particularly scrumptious classic cream varieties, especially the chocolate, zabaglione and hazelnut, and some seasonal fruit flavours, like melon.

FIOR DI LUNA

MONTEVERDE NUOVO
via P. Falconieri, 119
☎ 06/536084
• **Closed:** Thursdays

This anonymous-looking bar reserves unexpected delights - it offers good homemade gelati, guaranteed by the Mediterranean Certification Institute and [within the limits of the possible] made with only fresh, mostly organic, natural ingredients - no emulsifiers or artificial flavours. The classic flavours are 100% organic [including an excellent vanilla *crema* and hazelnut], while the fruit gelati are made with fresh fruit of the season. They also do lemon, mulberry, blackberry and watermelon granitas.

IL GELATO DI SAN CRISPINO

CENTRO STORICO - TRITONE
via della Panetteria, 42
☎ 06/6793924
• **Closed:** Tuesdays
APPIO
via Acaia, 56/56a
☎ 06/70450412
• **Closed:** Tuesdays

This gelateria run by the Alongi brothers and Paola Nesci has changed the face of Roman gelati-making. Following in its successful footsteps, a number of Roman gelati bars have changed or improved their product by abolishing [or at least limiting] the use of preservatives, additives and

artificial thickeners and using only fresh ingredients. San Crispino's keeps adding new flavours to its repertoire, so next to their legendary *zabaglione* with Vecchio Samperi De Bartoli Marsala wine, or lemon and Calvados sorbet and delicious fresh fruit flavours, you can now try the vanilla *crema* with strong sweet Passito di Pantelleria De Bartoli wine; ginger and cinnamon cream; or the Jamaican Blue Mountain coffee cream.

IL GELATO DI SAN PANCRAZIO

GIANICOLO
p.zza San Pancrazio, 18
☎ 06/58310338
• **Closed:** never

This gelateria continues to be a place where the trade is plied with passion and dedication and only first-rate fresh ingredients are used. Mini-cones to fill and take home in large numbers for dessert are one of their more recent innovations, but their *semifreddi* are well worth coming for, too. Among the flavours offered we recommend, as always, the *ciambellone,* the excellent pistacchio, and the walnut, pine nut, chocolate-streaked *stracciatella* and orange chocolate; while extra-good fruit tastes include fig, mandarin and strawberry. The coffee granita and the San Pancrazio coffee with a zabaglione float are also very good. Soymilk gelati are available for allergy-sufferers. Very reasonable prices and great service.

GIOLITTI

CENTRO STORICO - CAMPO MARZIO
via Uffici del Vicario, 40
☎ 06/6991243
• **Closed:** never

ICE CREAM

This famous gelateria just a stone's throw away from Parliament House at Palazzo Chigi offers a vast range of flavours - nearly 50 classic ice creams and sorbets. There's a big inside area with tables where you can sample their various sundaes including the sumptuous Coppa Giolitti with chocolate, vanilla, *torrone* and whipped cream. Open straight through from 7am till one in the morning.

GIOLITTI A TESTACCIO

TESTACCIO
via A. Vespucci, 35
☎ *06/5746006*
• **Closed:** Wednesdays

The most traditional gelateria imaginable, Giolitti a Testaccio does very good classic vanilla *crema*, hazelnut, coffee, chocolate and all the various fruit flavours made with real, fresh fruit. Courteous service and outdoor tables.

LA GRADISCA

PINCIANO
via Mantova, 18
☎ *06/8412747*
• **Closed:** Sundays

Extremely polite service and irreprehensibly high quality are the main ingredients of this excellent gelateria's success. The owners even do regular courses to keep abreast of trade developments [and live up to their clientele's expectations]. Among the various flavours: *zabaglione*, *crema al miele* [honey and vanilla cream], hazelnut, almond and many different fruit varieties, all smooth, creamy and delicious. They also offer frozen yoghurt. Mini-cones are still big this year - ideal for a quiet evening's indulgence at home with

friends. La Gradisca also has outlets at the Tennis Bar at Foro Italico and elsewhere in the city.

MARINARI

TRIESTE
c.so Trieste, 97/b
☎ *06/8555441*
• **Closed:** always open, except Mondays in winter

One of the various Marinari outlets and the name is its own guarantee in gelati-loving circles. Here you'll find gelati for all tastes, traditional or otherwise: yoghurt; silky *panna cotta*; the original *panna al cioccolato* with whipped cream and chocolate; soymilk and low-fat gelati and tiny *mignons* – all excellent. In summer they're open from 10.30am till one in the morning.

PELLACCHIA

PRATI - COLA DI RIENZO
via Cola di Rienzo, 103
☎ *06/3210807*
• **Closed:** Mondays

The doors of this historic *cremeria-latteria* have opened onto busy Via Cola di Rienzo for many years now, and its gelati have been famous forever. The choice of flavours ranges from sorbets to classic creams, including a heavenly chocolate and *zabaglione.* Try their hot chocolate in winter prepared with a special electric *cioccolatiera* machine and topped with fresh whipped cream. Courteous, helpful staff.

ALBERTO PICA

CENTRO STORICO - ARGENTINA
via della Seggiola, 12
☎ *06/68806153*
• **Closed:** Sunday mornings

Fifty or so offerings with both classic flavours and Alberto Pica's exclusive inventions: green apple, Amalfi lemon, *pastiera* [the traditional Neapolitan Easter pie – wheat berry, ricotta and

candied fruit], *zuppa inglese* [trifle], cinnamon or wild strawberry rice; *sinfonia azzurra* [pineapple, coconut, milk and Curaçao], *giantorrone* [gianduia and toasted nuts], Limoncello liqueur and fresh citrus [lemon, orange and grapefruit], biscuity *ciambella* etc. There's also a remarkable range of beers.

LE PROCOPE
IL GELATO DI PROCOPIO

APPIO
p.zza dei Re di Roma, 39
☎ *06/77200858*
• **Closed:** never

Always very busy with its mostly youthful clientele, this very good gelateria belongs to the Italian Gelati-makers' Association, which guarantees that only fresh natural ingredients are used. Classic flavours, mostly the creamy variety: *tiramisù*, *pinolato* [with pinenuts], *zabaglione*, coffee, cassata, vanilla swirled with Nutella or Rocher chocolate, but also coconut, pineapple, blackberry, strawberries and other fruit flavours. The unusual, excellent *panna al caffè* [coffee and whipped cream] deserves a special mention. There's a small corner devoted to yoghurt. Customer traffic is regulated by a numbers system, given to you with your receipt when you pay [before you order].

SAN FILIPPO

PARIOLI
via di Villa S. Filippo, 2/10
☎ *06/8079314*
• **Closed:** Mondays

The renovations are finished, and San Filippo's has reopened with nine doors on the corner of Via di Villa San Filippo-Piazza Bligny and Via

Salvini, not far from Piazzale delle Muse. The management hasn't changed and neither has the quality of their famous gelati, chief among them the classic creams and *semifreddi* [soft frozen mousse] - some of the best in Rome. Try the *zabaglione*, coffee, hazelnut and vanilla *crema*. Fruit flavours in season.

AL SETTIMO GELO

PRATI - MAZZINI
via Vodice, 21/a
☎ *06/3725567*
• **Closed:** never

 Mirella Fiumanò worked at a variety of different jobs before she decided to turn her hand to gelati-making and this very lack of standard trade training may be what enabled her to approach the field with fresh eyes. At any rate her naturally-made gelati are delicious: no preservatives, artificial flavours or colourings and only carob flour and guar gum are used as thickening agents. All the flavours are made with absolutely first-class ingredients – Lindt cocoa and van Houten chocolate chips; homemade meringues, fresh seasonal fruit [preferably organic], hazelnuts toasted in a wood-fired oven then grated, real homemade liqueur for the limoncello gelato, and real Malaga wine for the Malaga flavour. Even the sublime chestnut gelato is made from fresh chestnuts that have been boiled, peeled and blended. Mirella has invented a number of flavours of her own: Greek gelato - honey and yoghurt dusted with crushed walnuts; cardamom, and Sicilian *crema*. She also makes gluten-free gelati for allergy-sufferers.

Open straight through except for Saturdays and Sundays.

TRE SCALINI

CENTRO STORICO - NAVONA
p.zza Navona, 28
☎ *06/68801996*
• **Closed:** Wednesdays

Their speciality is the delicious chocolate *tartufo* – a chocolate ice cream ball with a hard chocolate centre – to enjoy at tables outside in the piazza. Hot chocolate in winter in the tearooms on the upstairs floor.

OUTSIDE ROME

BAR GELATERIA BELVEDERE

FRASCATI [ROME]
p.zza Roma, 1
☎ *06/9424986*
• **Closed:** Wednesdays

This prizewinning gelateria is located in Frascati's main piazza. In summer you can enjoy more than forty different varieties of excellent gelati at their outdoor tables, including classic creams, [the house speciality is the *zabaglione*], fruit flavours and frozen yoghurt.

LA TORRE DEL FREDDO

MARINO [ROME]
p.zza Matteotti, 11
☎ *06/93661307*
• **Closed:** Wednesdays

The classic *crema* are superb, especially the *nocciola* [hazelnut]. The fruit flavours offer a slightly wider choice – cherry, apricot, peach, pear, pineapple, coconut, mango, walnut, marron glacé. Don't miss their fabulous Sicilian *cassata*.

PREMIATA GELATERIA CREMERIA ALBALONGA

APPIO
via Albalonga, 9/11
☎ *06/7000418*
• **Closed:** Mondays

The supreme speciality of this bar and pastry shop, also known as Pompi's, is their *tiramisù*, both the traditional coffee and chocolate version and an exclusive strawberry variety.

CAVALLETTI

NEMORENSE
via Nemorense, 181
☎ *06/86324814*
• **Closed:** Tuesdays

Not just a good neighbourhood pastry shop doing classic cakes and pastries, *pasticcini* [micro-pastries] and feast-day goodies [*panettoni* at Christmas, *pastiera* at Easter, crunchy deep-fried *frappe* and *castagnole* at Carnival time] - the name Cavalletti is synonymous for Romans with *millefoglie* - weightless structures made of crisp pastry discs alternated with layers of pastry cream, zabaglione, strawberry or chocolate and delicately veiled with icing sugar – and theirs travel all over the world via the embassy staff who come here to buy them.

CECERE

TRASTEVERE
via B. Musolino, 45
☎ *06/5895014*
• **Closed:** Sundays afternoons

Fresh, high quality products both sweet and savoury, and very affordable prices are the reasons why there's always a football stadium-type crowd milling around this Trastevere pastry shop. You'll find savoury pies, gourmet *panettoni* [sweet leavened cakes], *tramezzini* [sandwiches], and *rustici* [savoury turnovers] side by side with pastries, *mignon* [tiny choux], cakes and biscuits. Their other outlet at 5, Via Marconi does pizzas and snacks – 06/5812228. [Opening hours: 7.30am – 2.30pm, closed Saturdays and Sundays].

CIPRIANI

ESQUILINO
via C. Botta, 19/23
☎ *06/70453930*
• **Closed:** Sundays

The specialities of the Prizewinning Cipriani Firm [as it's officially called], founded in 1906, are their sweet biscuits [chocolate-flavoured *tripolini, stelline, colombine, polentine,* wine or aniseed-flavoured *amaretti*] and their *fette biscottate* [dry breakfast biscuits] - traditional-style or with honey, sugar-free, wholemeal, or made with organic flour. They also make fancy biscuits and family-style cakes: chestnut *castagnaccio,* tarts, *torta della nonna* [granny's pie], strawberry *fragolona,* strudels and *pastiera* [Neapolitan ricotta, wheat berry and candied fruit pie].

DAGNINO

TERMINI
via Vittorio Emanuele Orlando, 75 [Galleria Esedra]
☎ *06/4818660*
• **Closed:** never

This huge place on two floors is in *centralissima* Galleria Esedra, just a few steps away from the piazza of the same name. The pastry and gelati section offers the classic repertoire of *cassata,* ricotta-filled *cannoli* pastry tubes, jellied fruit, typical Messinese *pignolate* with honey and pine nuts, granitas and marzipan.

LA DELIZIOSA

CENTRO STORICO - NAVONA
v.lo Savelli, 50
☎ *06/68803155*
• **Closed:** Mondays

Set a little way back from Corso Vittorio, this small firm sells one of the best ricotta tortes in the city. They also do very good custard and pine nut cakes, lemon tortes, savoury pies and traditional pastries in general. Very reasonable prices.

LA DOLCEROMA

CENTRO STORICO - GHETTO
via del Portico d'Ottavia, 20/b
☎ *06/6892196*
• **Closed:** Mondays and
  Sunday afternoons

One of the best Roman *pasticcerie,* specialising in Austrian and American cakes and pastries. Master pastry-chef, Stefano Ceccarelli, works only with first class ingredients: Bramley apples for the strudel and apple pie, fresh peanuts for the peanut butter cookies, pecans and Canadian maple syrup for the pecan pie. Internationally-minded gastronomes come here for the Sacher torte, strudel, Imperial Torte [thin crunchy pastry layers alternated with chocolate mousse and covered with marzipan and chocolate], Yoghurtorte [with wild berries on top], Maroniobersbombe [with marrons glacés], their Mozart, Nuss, Dobos and Linzer tortes, choc-chip cookies, cherry or lemon pie. Etcetera. High prices.

DURANTI

PIAZZA BOLOGNA
via Ugo Balzani, 61
☎ *06/8604429*
• **Closed:** Wednesdays

A small but very good pastry shop in a tranquil street near Piazza Bologna. Their specialities are soft-filled *bigné* and *granatine* choux pastries, delicious profiteroles, chocolate-coated *bombe* [with whipped cream and zabaglione inside], *millefoglie* [flaky pastry and custard slices], Saint-Honoré and Mimosa cakes, *pastiera* [Neapolitan ricotta, wheat berry and candied fruit pie] and Sicilian *cannoli* [rich flaky pastry tubes filled with ricotta and candied fruit].

FAGGIANI

PRATI - MAZZINI
via G. B. Ferrari, 23/25
☎ *06/39739742*
• **Closed:** Wednesdays

This historic pastry shop in the heart of the Prati quarter seems to have swung over to the Neapolitan tradition: *pastiera* [ricotta, wheat berry and candied fruit] pie or tarts; rum babàs; *sfogliatelle* [ricotta-filled puff pastry slices], now sit side by side with the national classics. Breakfast rites are gone through at their coffee bar with some of the best coffee in town: either an arabica and Robusta blend or Jamaican Blue Mountain with excellent *cornetti,* plain or filled with jam, chocolate or custard; deep-fried, sugar-coated *bombe* and *ciambelle;* Danish pastries, apple turnovers, *quaresimali, parigini, colombine, svizzeri, fazzoletti,* kipferl, and so on. Their lunchtime snacks are just as good: *focacce, tramezzini,* well-filled *panini* and fried *bocconcini* [mouthfuls] of various kinds. Outdoor tables.

IL FORNO DEL GHETTO

CENTRO STORICO - GHETTO
via del Portico d'Ottavia, 2
☎ *06/6878637*
• **Closed:** Saturdays

They've been making traditional Roman Jewish pastries here for a very long time, timeless classics in both name and substance: exquisite ricotta-and-chocolate, or ricotta-and-sour cherry tortes; delicious *mostaccioli* [also called *pizze*] with candied and dried fruit; almond cakes; tarts; *tozzetti* and honey-flavoured biscuits. In the morning, breakfast *cornetti*, *bombe* and *ciambelle* with the taste of bygone times; around 4 in the afternoon, hot freshly-made salted *bruscolini* [pumpkin seeds]. Only women – three generations of them - in the kitchen and behind the counter. Pricey.

INNOCENTI

TRASTEVERE
via della Luce, 21/a
☎ *06/5803926*
• **Closed:** Sunday afternoons; all day Sunday in summer

In the heart of the Trastevere quarter Enzo and Anna Innocenti – both authentic 7th generation Romans – make tea biscuits in a vast range of shapes and flavours as well as ricotta tortes, jam tarts, sponge-cakes and other traditional fare. *Tramezzini*, *rustici* and *pizzette* if you order in advance.

MALVINO MARINARI

TRIESTE
c.so Trieste, 95/b
☎ *06/8551045*
• **Closed:** Mondays

A rich array of cakes and assorted pastries, *mignon* [tiny choux pastries] and biscuits.

ORIANO MARINARI

QUARTIERE AFRICANO
p.zza S. Emerenziana, 20
☎ *06/86219332*
• **Closed:** Mondays

A wide range of tortes, *granatine* and *bighé* choux pastries, *mignon* [mini-choux] and jam tarts, tea biscuits and holiday season cakes and pastries.

MONDI

PONTE MILVIO
via Flaminia, 468
☎ *06/3336466*
• **Closed:** Mondays

Crazy about those tiny choux pastries Italians call *mignon*? This is the place for you then - you'll find every conceivable kind: sweet *bigné*, *granatine*, *diplomatici*, tartlets, mini-cassata, rum babàs, *savarin*, *sfogliatine*, *aragoste*, Sicilian *cannoli* and savoury *bottoncini*, *rustici*, *tramezzini*, *genovesi*, croissants, tiny toasted sandwiches, miniscule pies and pizzas – each one freshly-made, perfect and microscopic. They also do traditional cakes and pastries, gelati, pralines, chocolates and made-to-order cakes. Mondi's is also a great place to have breakfast, either at the indoor coffee bar or at the tables outside in the shade of big umbrellas. Their own brand of chocolates and pralines are on sale at their shop in the Prati quarter [Via Lucrezio Caro, 26 – phone 06/3212503, closed Sundays].

LA MOUSSE

TRIESTE
c.so Trieste, 163
☎ *06/86203425*
• **Closed:** Tuesdays

One of the best pastry shops in the Trieste and Africano quarters, run by the Brunetti's – he is Roman, she's from Messina. The *simpatica* pastry chef's southern origins explain the presence of so many wonderful Sicilian and Neapolitan specialities: big and small *cassata*, *cannoli*, rum babàs, *sfogliatelle*, *aragoste*. The fruit and cream mousses, *tortine* and savouries [*rustici*, *pizzette*, *salatini* and *pan brioche*] are also well worth trying. Open straight through from 7.30am till 9pm.

NATALIZI

PINCIANO
via Po, 124/126
☎ *06/85350736*
• **Closed:** Mondays

This traditional pastry shop has been a neighbourhood favourite since the Twenties – just the place to come for a trayful of pastries or a cake for a special occasion. Next to the timeless classics - *bigné*, *granatine*, biscuits, cakes and *semifreddo* [soft frozen mousse] and breakfast croissants and pastries to enjoy at their coffee bar, Natalizi offers good *rustici* [with anchovies, wurst or prosciutto] and one of the best catering services in the city providing high-quality homey fare.

PACI

SAN LORENZO
via dei Marsi, 35
☎ *06/4957804*
• **Closed:** Mondays

An artisanal *pasticceria* where skilled pastry chefs Luigi and Paola offer clients high quality pastries at reasonable prices. They make truly excellent *pasta frolla* pastry so consequently their tarts - ricotta, custard, classic jam or *occhi di bue* - are memorable. There's also a good breakfast section with *cornetti* and other breakfast buns and pastries and a Nutella cake for unrepentant sweet-tooths. Cakes for birthdays and other special occasions if you order in advance.

PANNOCCHI

PINCIANO
via Bergamo, 56/58/60
☎ 06/8552109
• **Closed:** Mondays

In business since 1927, Pannocchi's is an old acquaintance when it comes to cakes. They specialise in *Mitteleuropean* pastries, the legacy of a pastry chef from Trieste who worked here in the Forties and left them his recipes for *pinze, gubane,* Sacher torte and walnut cake. So for breakfast, next to the traditional plain or fancy *cornetti* you'll also find *krapfen* made according to the original Berlin recipe: two icing-topped leavened pastry discs joined together with sour-cherry jam. The house coffee blend [Robusta and arabica] is good and their *torta della nonna* is excellent. The lunchtime buffet offers well-filled savoury croissants made on the premises, *rustici, crostini, mozzarella in carrozza* [fried cheese sandwich], and *tramezzini.* Professional service.

ROMOLI

QUARTIERE AFRICANO
v.le Eritrea, 140/144
☎ 06/86325077
• **Closed:** Mondays

The day begins with an unbelievable assortment of breakfast buns and croissants to enjoy at the coffee bar counter, then around midday the gourmet ready-to-eat dishes start to appear. On the counter opposite there's a vast array of cakes, pastries and desserts: from Sicilian *cassata* to Austrian Krantz and Sacher tortes; *torta della nonna;* Neapolitan *sfogliatelle* and *pastiera; panna cotta;* bowls of wild strawberries; Bavarian cream; profiteroles; muffins; delicious chestnut and cream *Mont Blanc* cake and, if you order in advance, their giant *cornettone.* Gelati, *semifreddi,* granitas, and popsicles - the house speciality - in various flavours: *tripolino,* Nemi strawberry and *torrone,* or coffee and zabaglione. From late evening to the wee small hours fresh hot *cornetti* and *fagottini* for sweet-toothed nightbirds.

SAGGESE

PIAZZA BOLOGNA
via Michele di Lando, 13
☎ 06/44237950
• **Closed:** Mondays

Excellent breakfast *cornetti* [though unfortunately they don't have a coffee bar] and classics like jam tarts and delicious pastries with various fillings.
Their speciality are the traditional Neapolitan cakes and pastries: *pasticciotti, sfogliatelle, aragoste,* rum babà and *pastiera.* Their own exclusive inventions are the *sedani* - custard-filled choux pastries, and *sandrine* - custard-filled puff pastries.

SVIZZERA SICILIANA

AURELIO
p.zza Pio XI, 10/11
☎ 06/6374974
• **Closed:** Mondays

This excellent *pasticceria* has specialised for many years in an unusual combination of pastry-making traditions, as the name implies. Northern European treats include Sacher, Saint-Honoré and Cortina tortes, but the lion's share of their production is dedicated to Sicilian delicacies: *cassata* and *cassatine* ice creams coated with coloured icing and candied fruit; country-style gelati; *gelo di mellone* garnished with crushed pistacchio nuts; *sfinci, frutta Martorana, buccellati* and *cuccia* at Christmas time, marzipan lambs at Easter. The same skill evident in their cakes is also applied to their morning *lieviti* [plain and custard-filled *cornetti,* Danish pastries, *girelle*] to enjoy at the big semi-circular coffee bar counter. *Rustici,* croquettes and *anellini* timbales at lunchtime. Their still wines and dessert wines are also Sicilian.

TEFRAN 91

MONTEVERDE NUOVO
p.zza della Trasfigurazione, 4
☎ 06/536303
• **Closed:** Mondays

Pastries, cakes, Sicilian *cannoli,* tea biscuits and pastries, *zuppa inglese,* Sacher torte, and strudels but also *panini, rustici* and *tramezzini.* Don't miss their ricotta tart - the house speciality. In the coffee bar next door you can breakfast on their *cornetti.*

VALZANI

TRASTEVERE
via del Moro, 37/b
☎ 06/5803792
• **Closed:** Tuesdays;
  also Mondays in spring

Valzani's, one of the last traditional Roman pastry

shops, has been producing *mostaccioli, panpepati, pangialli, torrone* and *zuppa romana,* zabaglione and coffee gateaux for a very long time. In November you'll also find *fave dei morti* and on Saint Joseph's Day [March 19] the traditional *frittelle.* They also do an excellent Sacher torte.

OUTSIDE ROME

MILLETTI

FRASCATI [ROME]
via S. Francesco di Assisi, 42
☎ *06/9417373*
• **Closed:** Mondays
FRASCATI [ROME]
via Principe Amedeo, 54/56
☎ *06/9416555*
• **Closed:** Mondays

These pastry shops share a logo and the same consistently high quality products. The Via San Francesco d'Assisi shop specialises in gelati, *semifreddi* and tiny *mignon* choux pastries, while the *pasticceria* in Via Principe Amedeo is devoted to the preparation of classic cakes and pastries.

PURIFICATO

FRASCATI [ROME]
p.zza del Mercato, 4
☎ *06/9420282*
• **Closed:** Mondays

You'll find typical traditional Frascati cakes and pastries here: wine-flavoured *ciambelle* (ring-shaped biscuits), *tozzetti* biscuits spiced with black pepper and honey, hard and soft *torroncini,* and ricotta tart. You should also try their Sacher torte, apple strudel and the exclusive house speciality *torta di Chianciano,* a custard and ricotta filled

spongecake cased in pastry, and the *torta macedonia.*

LA PREFERITA

OSTIA [ROME]
via Sommi Picenardi, 12
☎ *06/5680864*
• **Closed:** Wednesdays

The specialities of this *pasticceria,* run by Domenico Amara since 1974, are the custard and fruit-filled *mignon;* Sicilian *cannoli* [flaky pastry tubes filled with ricotta and candied fruit]; *code di aragosta* and rich *sfogliatelle* pastries filled with ricotta and zabagalione cream. There's a coffee bar with outdoor tables, where you can also enjoy an aperitivo accompanied by a few nibbles.

WINE SHOPS

ALTOBELLI VINI PREGIATI

APPIO
v.le Furio Camillo, 10
☎ *06/7803591*

Even though it's small and quite a way from the centre, this wine shop in the Appio Tuscolano neighborhood remains the cherished haunt of a great many wine lovers. Apart from offering a wide choice, from the best national producers to the great wines of Burgundy and Bourdeaux and rare wines from California, at very affordable prices, Altobelli keeps an eye open for interesting new products. There's also a vast range of excellent liqueurs and exquisite confectionery as well as the graceful politeness and competence of the owner.

CENTROVINI ARCIONI

TRIONFALE
via della Giuliana, 11/13
☎ *06/39733205*
NEMORENSE
via Nemorense, 57/57a
☎ *06/86206616*

Old and famous wine shops: one in the Nemorense, the other in the Trionfale neighbourhood, where you can find one of the best selections of wines, champagnes and liqueurs around, including those distributed directly [and intelligently] by Claudio and Massimo Arcioni; and there's no lack of good beers, including a number of rarities. Quality and a wide choice in the specialty foodstuffs and gift sections, too.

BALDUINA

BALDUINA
via della Balduina, 204/206
☎ *06/35343486*

One of the best-stocked wine shops in north Rome, managed with great skill by Angelo and Piera Canitano, it offers a vast range of Italian wines from practically every region as well as champagnes, liqueurs, spirits, confectionery and speciality foodstuffs.

BERNABEI DAL 1933

TESTACCIO
via Luca della Robbia 24/28
☎ *06/57287464*
TRASTEVERE
v.le Trastevere, 93
☎ *06/5812818*

There's a wide choice of labels in the two Bernabei wine shops, the historic original in Viale Trastevere and its more recent offspring in Testaccio; you'll find both the best of Italian winemaking and foreign labels, from Californian through Chilean and including the great cru from Bordeaux, as well as spumanti, champagne, spirits and beers. Excellent prices for the quality for all products and a large assortment of wines under L.10,000.

BEVITORIA NAVONA

CENTRO STORICO - NAVONA
p.zza Navona, 72
☎ *06/68801022*

This *mescita* offering wine by the glass has a truly unique and extraordinary wine cellar: dug into the ancient foundations of Domitian's Stadium under present-day Piazza Navona. The Boccacci family offers a good selection of wines which you can sample at outdoor tables in the piazza in summer.

LA BOTTEGA DEL VINO DI ANACLETO BLEVE

CENTRO STORICO - GHETTO
via S. Maria
del Pianto, 9/a-11
☎ *06/6865970*

Anacleto has become a legend: his energy, *simpatia* and passion for his work have made this Ghetto wine bar deservedly famous. The choice of wines, whisky [among them the outstanding Samaroli selections], rum, spumanti and champagne is one of the finest in the city. An extraordinary buffet is set up at lunch time with ready-to-eat dishes prepared by his exceptionally talented wife, Tina: splendid cured meats, typical cheeses - some of them traditionally produced - and speciality foodstuffs, all accompanied by excellent wines, available by the glass. Great Italian and French

wines are ageing in the wine cellars below [you can hire space to age your own wine]. And to top it all off, Anacleto also organises discussions, wine-tasting evenings and courses about wine. Extremely courteous and efficient service.

BUCCONE

CENTRO STORICO - POPOLO
via di Ripetta, 19
☎ *06/3612154*

An attractive wine bar just a few steps away from Piazza del Popolo with a good selection of wines, champagne, spirits and culinary delights and a *mescita* counter where you can sample wine by the glass.
Maddalena Buccone and her sons Vincenzo and Francesco guide clients' choices from among the numerous bottles and serve glasses of white, red and bubbly at any hour of the day [or night – more or less]. There's also a coffee bar and a fine foods space with hot and cold dishes at lunch time and in the evenings.

BULZONI

PARIOLI
v.le Parioli, 36
☎ *06/8070494*

 Alessandro Bulzoni and family's wine shop has become without doubt one of the best in the city. Thanks to his grand passion he has arranged it so that one can find here not only the best of national wine production, but also a careful selection of Burgundies [including some practically impossible to find elsewhere like the Marc Colin], German and

Californian wines – fruits of his own careful personal research. The *mescita* counter offers a dozen different kinds. There's a choice of spirits, mainly pure malt whiskies, as well as a wide range of oils and a speciality foodstuffs corner. Particularly well-stocked just before Christmas.

GOFFREDO CHIRRA

CENTRO STORICO - TERMINI
via Torino, 133
☎ *06/485659*

This may well be the only wine shop in Rome where you can buy a bottle any time from 7am till 2 in the morning. The shelves lined with a wide selection of mostly excellent Italian wines and a few special treats from France are relegated to the back of what looks like a bar, which also serves hamburgers and hot dogs until closing time. "It's really a wine shop, though," says Goffredo, the owner. It opened in 1945, and he started work here as a *garzone* [errand boy] in 1953, gradually moving up the ladder until he took it over definitively in 1979. He met his wife when she worked here as a cashier, and their two sons work here today. They also offer a wide range of chocolates, speciality foods, artisan-made pasta, oil, spirits and champagne.

CIARLA

LAURENTINO
via della Canzone del Piave, 3
☎ *06/5010102*

A lot of very special labels here, mostly from Piedmont [Conterno, Sandrone, Altare, Gaja] and Campania, but the other regions are quite well represented too - they also stock some excellent prize Tuscan vintages at very good prices, good every-day table wines from L.8,000 a bottle upwards, and an excellent Colli Albani white by the litre. Giuseppe, expert sommelier, will offer suggestions as to what dishes the wines go best with. Spumanti, champagne and quality spirits, beautiful gift packs which they will deliver anywhere in the city and a *mescita* [wine by the glass] counter.

I COLONIALI

APPIO
via Appia Nuova, 277
☎ *06/7029620*

Apart from products like herbs, spices and tea, you'll also find a carefully-chosen selection of wines and spirits and a section devoted to coffee, which they'll grind for you then and there if you wish. Another speciality are the tasteful gift packs created by the owner, Gianclaudio Albergo.

COSTANTINI

PRATI - CAVOUR
p.zza Cavour, 16
☎ *06/3213210*

This is one of the best wine shops in the city, run with passionate dedication by Piero Costantini. In the big wine shop on the ground floor, you'll find the finest wines from all over the world, from local whites to the great French vintage reds, organised according to their region or country of origin. On the floor above there's an excellent selection of champagne, whisky and spirits. Courteous and efficient staff. The Simposio wine bar [see review] is on the same floor.

D'AGUANNO

CENTRO STORICO - TRITONE
via della Panetteria, 11
☎ *06/6790228*

Alessandro D'Aguanno took over this little *Vini e Oli* [wine and oil shop] a few months ago and is transforming it into a quality wine shop - the renovations now underway will be finished in 2000. He currently stocks good national [Tuscan, Piedmontese and Campanian, in particular] and international labels; grappas; Samoroli selection whiskies; first-press olive oil; balsamic vinegar and a few gourmet specialities, as well as mineral water which you can have home-delivered on request. Wine by the glass at lunchtime.

DEL FRATE

PRATI - COLA DI RIENZO
via degli Scipioni, 118/124
☎ *06/3211612*

A cosy place that has always specialised in whisky and spirits of all kinds. The wines offered include an excellent selection of Italian labels - Tuscan reds and Alto Adige and Friuli whites, in particular - and a small but very good choice of French wines. They also stock unusual formats and half-bottles, from Chiantis to Cervaro della Sala, and a small range of beers and speciality foods. Prices more than reasonable.

ENOTECA AL PARLAMENTO - ACHILLI

CENTRO STORICO - CAMPO MARZIO
via dei Prefetti, 15
☎ *06/6873446*

This famous, very old wine shop is only a few steps away from Palazzo Chigi - the Italian House of Parliament. It stocks a wide range of Italian and French products including an outstanding selection of exceptional bottles for enofiends and collectors, some in special formats. A good range of liqueurs and cognacs for all tastes, as well as gourmet delicacies, preserves, oils and confectionery. Wine by the glass is available at the *mescita* counter.

ENOTECA DEL CORSO

CENTRO STORICO - NAVONA
c.so Vittorio Emanuele II, 293
☎ *06/68801594*

A beautiful, spacious wine shop with a lot of little tables where in winter they serve various delicious snacks to go with the wines by the glass. There's a wide range of other products: quality sweets, both packaged and by the *etto* [100grams]; biscuits; speciality foodstuffs [jars of vegetables and mushrooms in oil, sauces, jams, preserves]; oils and vinegars; honey; artisan-made dried pastas; wild salmon; caviar and truffles. They also offer a substantial selection of spirits, special cognacs and vintage ports, prize champagne, a broad range of Italian wines, a display case devoted to the great French wines and, last but not least, wine-tasting glasses.

ORLANDO FERRAZZA

SAN LORENZO
via dei Volsci, 59
[ang. via dei Latini]
☎ *06/490506*

In what used to be the local supermarket, Orlando Ferrazza is throwing out the

WINE SHOPS

last remnants of the old mini-market stock, ripping off the fabric wallpaper and replacing it with wooden shelving he's building himself. He prefers to spend his money on widening the selection of wines and beers – already very impressive, including well-priced quality Italian wines, spumanti, liqueurs and spirits, and an interesting range of ports. The speciality foodstuffs, like artisan-made dried pastas and extra vergine olive oil, are mostly organic. Free wine-tasting on Saturdays after 6pm [open to the public]. All major credit cards accepted; home delivery service.

IL GOCCETTO

CENTRO STORICO - CAMPO DE' FIORI
via dei Banchi Vecchi, 14
☎ *06/6864268*

Sergetto's wine shop has become one of the city's most modish and as a result it's frequented by a varied and picturesque crowd. Experts and non come here to buy that little bottle by an as-yet-unknown winemaker, a great French cru, a vintage Barolo or a Supertuscan, but mainly to take the weight off their feet at one of the little tables and enjoy excellent cheeses and cured meats with their glasses of wine, expertly counselled by *simpatico* Sergetto.

LUCANTONI

VIGNA CLARA
l.go Vigna Stelluti, 33
☎ *06/3293743*

Quality and professionalism are the keynotes here in what continues to be one of the city's best wine shops. You'll find the finest Italian

wines, including some little-known labels personally selected by the owners, the Lucantoni brothers; foreign wines - French and Californian in particular; spumanti and champagne, liqueurs, spirits, beers and speciality foodstuffs [first-press olive oil, high quality vinegars, speciality sweets]. Wines and spumanti are also available by the glass.

ANTICA ENOTECA MANZONI

COLOMBO
p.le R. Ardigò, 27/29
☎ *06/5411535*

A solid and reliable port of call in a neighbourhood that is generally lacking in good wine shops, Manzoni's offer a vast selection of labels, ranging from low-priced everyday table wines to the great Italian and French cru, spirits, and exquisite speciality foodstuffs, especially during the Christmas and Easter periods.

MARCHETTI

PINCIANO
via Flavia, 28
☎ *06/4741745*

This wine shop in Via Flavia offers a wide range of wines - many of them Italian, but mostly French labels, Burgundies in particular, which the Marchetti's import directly from the region's most important producers. They also stock the great Bordeaux and Côte du Rhône wines, which they offer at very fair prices, as well as liqueurs, spirits [there's an excellent selection of whiskies and cognacs], spumanti, champagne, oil and gourmet specialities.

MARCO & GIANCARLO

CENTRO STORICO - CAMPO DE' FIORI
via di Monte della Farina, 38
☎ *06/68806989*

A small but well-stocked winery in one of the little streets close to Campo de' Fiori and Corso Vittorio Emanuele. The ambience is casual and characteristic: the bottles of wine and beer come directly out of a battered old fridge, quality wines are stacked next to cartons of mineral water, and the clients are mainly locals drinking wine by the glass. A good selection of Italian wines at reasonable prices.

PALOMBI

TESTACCIO
p.zza Testaccio, 38/42
☎ *06/5740039*

This famous store was transformed some time ago into an extremely well-stocked wine shop, and now there's been another quiet revolution - they've put in tables upstairs, making it the ideal extension of the pub below. Run with passionate commitment by the whole family, Palombi's also offers an incredible range of quality food products - *sottoli* [foods preserved in oil], exotic speciality foodstuffs, spices, jams, grappa and authentic German würstel. Their selection of more than 600 beers from Germany, Belgium, Great Britain, China, Mexico and elsewhere is legendary, and their excellent range of Italian wines at practically unbeatable prices is also very good. Cordial hospitality and great competence.

PELUSO

PINCIANO
via Sardegna, 36
☎ 06/42818995

Just a few short steps away from Via Veneto, Alfredo Peluso's beautiful wine shop offers an excellent selection of wines [including numerous outstanding foreign labels], some of which can only be found here. High quality Italian and foreign labels as well as prestigious spumanti, champagne, famous spirits and gourmet speciality foodstuffs.

ENNIO QUADROZZI

OSTIENSE
via Ostiense, 34
☎ 06/5746768

 This enormous, old-style *enoteca* offers a vast range of just about everything. On the upstairs floor there are speciality foodstuffs, confectionery, sweets and chocolates to buy by the *etto* [100 grams], biscuits, rice, artisan-made dried pastas and jams, vegetables preserved in oil, liqueurs, spirits, mineral water, extra vergine olive oil, wine glasses and all kinds of enological accessories. Downstairs there's a vast wine cellar, a source of justifiable pride to Signor Alberto Giansanti who runs it, with a range of mostly Italian wines including all the most famous national producers, organised according to their region of origin. There's also a section with several champagnes and a few other French wines. Reasonable prices.

VINERIA REGGIO

CENTRO STORICO - CAMPO DE' FIORI
p.zza Campo de' Fiori, 15
☎ 06/68803268

This Campo de' Fiori winery has been an institution for a long time now. Giorgio Reggio, its proprietor, offers takeaway bottles and wine by the glass at accessible prices. There are always plenty of habitués and passing tourists here sipping fruity whites or quaffing a good beer and munching on *panini* or one of the other snacks available.

ROMANI

PIAZZA BOLOGNA
via Livorno, 41/b
☎ 06/44244250

Opened in 1991, this wine shop is a solid reference point for neighbourhood wine lovers. It offers a great many good Italian bottles, in every price range; a selection of champagne; 60 varieties of whisky and a few interesting French labels, as well as a number of speciality foodstuffs, oils, artisan-made pastas, and wines to sample by the glass. Giusto Romani is assisted by his Piedmontese wife, Alda, who actually introduced him to the wine world in the first place. They make frequent business trips to her northern homeland and never come back empty-handed, especially as they hold exclusive Roman distribution rights for the wines of many small producers. Giustino, as his friends call him, has a great many clients who keep coming back for a vintage Barolo or one of his two principal passions: Barberas and magnums. Alda prepares gorgeous gift baskets at Christmas.

LE SOMMELIER DI MASSIMO CINTI

EUR - LAURENTINO
v.le Europa, 21
☎ 06/5923300

Massimo Cinti's wine shop offers a good selection of Italian labels with an emphasis on Tuscan wines, as well as a number of foreign bottles, excellent spirits, gourmet delicacies, wine glasses and other useful accessories. There's also an excellent choice of everyday table wines and some attractive gift packs.

IL TEMPIO DEL VINO

BOCCEA
via G. D. Paracciani, 26
☎ 06/6623391

In a neighbourhood afflicted by a grave shortage of decent wine merchants like the Aurelio-Boccea quarter, Alberto Taloni, his son Stefano and daughter-in-law Maria Gabriella Montani run this beautiful wine shop, where apart from carefully-selected, reasonably-priced wines you can also buy gourmet foodstuffs. There's a *mescita* counter offering wines by the glass with delicious snacks, and they also organise wine-tasting sessions and make home deliveries.

TRIMANI

TERMINI
via Goito, 20
☎ 06/4469661

With one of the biggest wine selections in the city, Trimani's is undoubtedly the most famous wine shop in Rome, offering the best of national and international production as well as gourmet specialities. There's a wide range of bottles to suit all tastes and pockets, with particular attention paid to new, as yet little-known producers, though not to the detriment of the famous labels. Next to the Italian

WINE SHOPS

wines you'll find good bottles from all over the word, as well as incomparable champagnes, liqueurs and spirits. On the upstairs floor there are wine accessories and all kinds of beverages to sample by the glass, from beer to Bordeaux. The Trimani family offer professional service and a courteous welcome. Their attractive wine bar is next door [see review].

VALENTINI

AURELIO
via Anastasio II, 38
☎ *06/633744*

Umberto Valentini's elegant wine shop offers well-priced wines from various regions of Italy; a good selection of foreign wines, Bordeaux in particular; a vast range of rare labels and prestigious vintages; champagnes, spirits and gourmet foodstuffs. Purchases can be made on-line by Internet but if you make a personal visit to the shop you can take advantage of the knowledgeable counsels of its *simpatico* owner.

OUTSIDE ROME

DEL GATTO

ANZIO [ROME]
via XX Settembre, 21
☎ *06/9846269*

More than three thousand selected labels from all over the world: Italy, France, California, New Zealand, Australia, South Africa … and mostly at very reasonable prices. Apart from the wines there's a wide range of excellent gourmet specialities and sweets made by the best Italian and foreign artisanal producers. Simonetta and Franco, the owners, have involved their children Cesare

and Daria, both sommeliers, in the enterprise. They've also recently doubled their floor space, and now organise wine-tasting evenings when wines by the most important Italian producers can be sampled.

CAMILLETTI

CIVITAVECCHIA [ROME]
via Bernini, 54
☎ *0766/20645*

One of the best wine shops in the northern part of the province of Rome, it offers a good range of Italian wines together with spumanti, liqueurs and spirits.

FAIOLA

FONDI [LT]
c.so Italia, 38
☎ *0771/513022*

An excellent selection of both Italian and foreign wines, including some outstanding labels available at very good prices. They also carry a range of quality gourmet foodstuffs, like Latini and Setaro pastas, magnificent French and Italian cheeses, and exceptional cured meats, almost impossible to find anywhere else, like Jamon Serrano and Pata Negra.

SAN MARCO

FRASCATI [ROME]
p.zza San Pietro, 8
☎ *06/9419519*

 The shop is quite small, but just a look in the window will convince you there's some pretty tempting stuff inside. The shelves are full of interesting bottles, starting with a broad, intelligently-selected range of Italian wines - from the prestigious Gaja, Sassicaia and Brunello labels to some excellent whites. There's also a small,

carefully-chosen selection of Alsatian and French wines and Sauternes, as well as a fine group of whiskies, Armagnacs and quality spirits together with a few special treats like the Americano made by Cocchi, for example, practically impossible to find elsewhere. There's also the complete range of wines produced by the San Marco firm itself, their extra vergine olive oil and even some grappas. Last but not least, a series of publications about wine and a few useful accessories for serving it. The reasonable prices and polite, attentive service make you want to keep on buying.

ENOTECA DEL LIDO

OSTIA [ROME]
via delle Gondole, 46
☎ *06/5673617*

Sara Adriani, the owner of this very attractive wine shop, has worked hard at seeking out quality products for her clients, and it shows. There's a good selection of wines including several prestigious labels. Gourmet speciality foods during the festive season.

SANGES

OSTIA [ROME]
p.zza Cesario Console, 9
☎ *06/5622357*

Youthful Fabio Canapini has set his seal on this well-stocked wine shop. The selection of wines has been very carefully made, and there's no shortage of finest quality liqueurs and spirits, together with a good choice of beers, sweets and gourmet delicacies. He periodically organises interesting wine-tasting events with the participation of the producers.

home & table

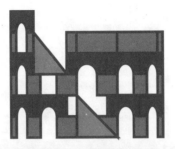

WINE ACCESSORIES

**HOME
& TABLE ACCESSORIES**

CURIOSITIES

WINE ACCESSORIES

CENTROVINI ARCIONI

NEMORENSE
via Nemorense, 57/57a
☎ 06/86206616

The Arcioni wine shop has a display window with a bit of everything in the way of wine-drinking accessories, from tasting glasses to professional bottle-openers, decanters and ice buckets for keeping the bottles cool.

LA BOTTEGA DEL VINO DA BLEVE

CENTRO STORICO - GHETTO
via Santa Maria del Pianto, 9a/12
☎ 06/6865970

Together with prize vintages and rare spirits Annibale Bleve's wine shop also sells wine-drinking accessories, from crystal wine glasses to professional bottle openers.

TRIMANI

TERMINI
via Goito, 20
☎ 06/4469661

The wide selection of wines offered at Trimani's is now flanked by a vast range of attractive accessories. Wine glasses of all kinds [Riedel and others], decanters, stoppers, ice-buckets, professional bottle-openers, both the wall-attached variety and country-style with plastic or metal arms. They also have the Bouquet Alphabet [*La Nez du Vin*] containing various types of aromas [from 12 to 54] designed to educate the nose, and specialist books and magazines.

HOME & TABLE ACCESSORIES

AZI

TRASTEVERE
via S. Francesco a Ripa, 170
☎ 06/5883303

A rich array of gorgeous items for the home, all made in Italy and based on Mediterranean-style 50's and 60's originals whose influence can also be seen in the ceramics bearing the AZI label. Only recycled materials are used, including glass and aluminium.

BADARACCO

CENTRO STORICO - POPOLO
via di Ripetta, 144
☎ 06/68803571

Knives, kitchen accessories and Swiss penknives in various formats. Open straight through.

BAGAGLI

CENTRO STORICO - CAMPO MARZIO
via Campo Marzio, 42
☎ 06/6871406

Originally a cork factory opened in the 1800's, Bagagli's has gradually been transformed into a shop specialising in objects for the kitchen and dining table, and over the last ten years has also changed its focus. They now stock mainly French and German dinner services and crystalware as well as batteries of saucepans, for a beautiful, practical and functional kitchen. Unusual knives and utensils.

FAUSTO BARBERINI

CENTRO STORICO - GHETTO
p.zza Margana, 40
☎ 06/6788802

A little unmarked door next to Tor Margana in one of Rome's most characteristic postcard *piazzette* leads to the workshop of Fausto Barberini - an absolute magician who specialises in glass restoration, in particular of opaline glass and crystal.

BARONE

PINCIANO
via Ancona, 40
☎ 06/44249741

Excellent brands of knives and scissors like Montana and Alexander for both professional and home use, as well as sporting knives like Opinel and the complete Victorinox series through to the SOS Set Survival Kit with 52 accessories. Knife-sharpening service.

IL BIANCO DI ELLEPI

CENTRO STORICO - SPAGNA
via della Croce, 4
☎ 06/6796835

Household and table linen in traditional, exclusive fabrics – they'll also make to measure.

BROGINI DAL 1888

CENTRO STORICO - SPAGNA
via Tomacelli, 128
☎ 06/6878373

Dedicated since 1888 to furnishing the beautiful, classically elegant dining table with timeless French Limoges and Sologne porcelain, fine German and Portuguese [Vista Alegre] china, supremely delicate Swiss and French crystalware and luxury cutlery - Christofle in particular.

HOME & TABLE

C.U.C.I.N.A.

CORSO FRANCIA
via Flaminia Vecchia, 679
☎ 06/3332202
CENTRO STORICO - POPOLO
via del Babuino, 118/a
☎ 06/6791275

Two shops dedicated to
kitchen utensils
and accessories with
a great many modern
objects, functional and
otherwise, from all over the
world - all gorgeous [and
they're definitely not giving
them away].
Lots of aluminium,
wood, shiny steel,
rustically elegant fabrics and
white porcelain for a kitchen
to delight the eye. High
prices.

CASIDEA

PARIOLI
via G. Antonelli, 22/24
☎ 06/8079277

A shop dedicated to the
table beautiful on a level with
the wealthy quarter it's
located in.
The most exclusive
brands of porcelain, French
and Italian crystal and
silverware.

CE.RI.EL.
CENTRO ASSISTENZA
TECNICA AUTORIZZATO

SAN LORENZO
p.zza Porta Maggiore, 9/10
☎ 06/7027222 - 7027284

A hospital for electrical
appliances of all makes
and models that does
everything from repairs to
replacing parts like
saucepan handles, rubber
rings and washers,
which they can make to
measure if necessary. Also
spare parts for food
processors, etc.

CESARI

CENTRO STORICO - SPAGNA
via del Babuino, 195
☎ 06/3613451 - 3207854

Finest quality household
linen: soft terry-towelling,
princely bed linen and refined
tablecloths, but also simple,
attractive tea-towels.

CHRISTOFLE

CENTRO STORICO - SPAGNA
via Bocca di Leone, 72
☎ 06/69940904

The renowmed Christofle
cutlery, but also silverware,
porcelain, and other
exquisite objects from the
famous French firm founded
in 1830.

COIN

PINCIANO
ex-fabbrica Peroni
via Mantova, 1
☎ 06/8415875 - 8415884
TUSCOLANO
Centro Commerciale
Cinecittà Due
via Tuscolana
☎ 06/7220931
APPIO
p.le Appio, 7
☎ 06/7080020
QUARTIERE AFRICANO
v.le Libia, 61
☎ 06/86219530

You can always while
away a pleasurable hour or
two in Coin's, especially the
store in the beautifully-
restored former
Peroni brewery,
among the porcelain,
kitchen utensils,
accessories and linen -
mostly made
in Asia but attuned to
Western tastes. Colours,
patterns and designs are
cheerful, attractive and
elegantly simple. Affordable
prices.

CINZIA DE SANTIS

TRIONFALE
via G. Scalia, 4/a
☎ 06/39720254

A vast display area with
kitchen equipment
[from small utensils for
everyday use to beautiful
expensive
Zani & Zani accessories],
porcelain from all over the
world [from costly French to
economical Eastern
European] and all sorts of
objects related to the dining
table, at lower than average
prices.

CUCCIOLLO

CENTRO STORICO - GHETTO
via del Tempio, 6
☎ 06/6868618

A huge display area
with electrical appliances of
every conceivable
brand, model, shape and
size. Excellent prices;
service not quite so good.

DOLCIMASCOLO

APPIO
via Gallia, 101/a
☎ 06/70475737
MONTI
via Cavour, 111
☎ 06/4883858

Knives of all kinds: for the
kitchen, including artisan-
made brands, for hunting
and for scuba-diving;
flick-knives, Swiss penknives
with up to 32 accessories,
and a chef's briefcase
containing nine blades and a
handle. They also
sharpen, restore and polish
both knives and scissors.
Wine-drinking
accessories. The Via Cavour
shop is better-stocked than
the one in Via Gallia, which
specialises in collectors'
items.

DURANTE

CENTRO STORICO - PANTHEON
p.zza della Rotonda, 64
☎ 06/6795221

This *centralissimo* and historic shop, opened in 1869, deals in sporting knives [Wenger], collectors' items and professional kitchen knives; also knife-sharpening and blade substitution for antique and modern cutlery. They have another outlet in Via Salaria.

DURASTANTE

CENTRO STORICO - CAMPO MARZIO
via della Fontanella Borghese, 70
☎ 06/6876548

This artisan's workshop specialises in expertly-done invisible mending and the restoration of clothing and fabric of all kinds. High prices, but the results justify the expense.

ENGLARO

TERMINI
via Manin, 18/20
☎ 06/4881574

A bit of everything in the way of household goods, from classic pepper pots and every-day dinnerware to the last word in kitchen utensils and ravishing porcelain. Courtesy, professionalism and lower-than-average prices.

FLAVONI

MARCONI
via D. Macaluso, 41/49
☎ 06/5566537-5593250

A good address to keep on hand for spare parts and technical assistence with kitchen utensils and electrical appliances. Polite, professional staff.

FRETTE

CENTRO STORICO - CORSO
via del Corso, 381
☎ 06/6786862
QUARTIERE AFRICANO
v.le Libia, 192
☎ 06/86203991
TERMINI
via Nazionale, 80
☎ 06/4882641
CENTRO STORICO - SPAGNA
p.zza di Spagna, 11
☎ 06/6790673

Traditional, high quality household and table linen.

GENEVIÈVE LETHU

PARIOLI
via Guidubaldo del Monte, 1/5
☎ 06/8079703

The French chain famous for its table and kitchenware has a dozen or more shops in Milan, Florence, Naples, Bari, Palermo and Rome, offering everything from accessories for everyday use to typically French curiosities: brightly coloured porcelain, classical glassware, soft baking moulds easy to pop cakes out of, and a thousand small kitchen utensils.

'GUSTO

CENTRO STORICO - CORSO
p.zza Augusto Imperatore, 9
☎ 06/3236363

As well as a restaurant, pizzeria and wine bar, 'Gusto now houses a wine shop complete with wine-drinking accessories, a delicatessen offering a wide selection of gourmet specialities and a culinary bookshop that also sells very tasteful cooking utensils.

ITALMERCURY

PINCIANO
via Nizza, 31
☎ 06/85354038

Sales, repairs and spare parts for small electrical appliances and an assortment of vacuum-cleaner bags. Reasonable prices and punctual service.

LEONE LIMENTANI

CENTRO STORICO - GHETTO
via Portico d'Ottavia, 47
☎ 06/68806949

A vast and varied range of household items and dining table accessories with all kinds of plates, saucepans, glasses and hundreds of affordable utensils piled high in dusty rooms and labyrinthine corridors. Next to the potato peelers you'll find the last word in Villeroy & Boch porcelain, crystalware and batteries of beautiful, functional saucepans. They sell single pieces as well as complete sets, prices are very reasonable and the hordes of customers are brought into line by a system of numbered palettes you'll find at the check-out desk near the entrance.

MAESANO

QUARTIERE AFRICANO
v.le Libia, 169
☎ 06/86204230
MONTESACRO
via U. Ojetti, 124
☎ 06/822281
PRATI - COLA DI RIENZO
p.zza Cola di Rienzo, 29
☎ 06/3215674

Traditional household and table linen, also available made to measure. Very professional.

HOME & TABLE

Mastro Raphael

CENTRO STORICO - CAMPO MARZIO
p.zza Montecitorio, 116
☎ 06/69200692

Inside beautiful Palazzo Macchi di Cellere, this Mastro Raphael showroom is the first to open in Rome. Splendid famed fabrics and magnificent tablecloths, also available made to measure, as well as a complete range of household linen.
High prices. Internet: www.mastroraphael.com

Non solo bianco

CENTRO STORICO - CAMPO MARZIO
via della Fontanella di Borghese, 38
☎ 06/6876657

Household and table linen in unusual fabrics, colours and designs.

Pepe Bianco

PINCIANO
via Tagliamento, 5/b
☎ 06/8549715

Apart from selling exquisite French and German porcelain, Pepe Bianco's will also personalise it for you with heraldic crests, monograms or any design you like, carried out by hand in exceptionally fine taste by Signora Paola Trevisan. A very useful address for anyone wanting to give an exclusive dinner service as a gift [or buy one for themselves], or replace a broken piece from an antique set by having the original pattern copied onto a modern substitute.
They also repair lamps and lampshades.

Vittorio Peroni

PRATI
p.zza dell'Unità, 29
☎ 06/3210852

Go through the door, down a few steps and you'll find yourself in one of the city's best-stocked household and kitchenware shops. It offers special treats for pastry-makers - baking moulds of every imaginable shape and size; as well as syphons, very cheap wine-drinking accessories, all kinds of saucepans and knives, and a number of odd, interesting items like special soap for getting kitchen smells off your hands, as well as electrical appliances and spare parts - a bazaar, in other words, full of practical useful things. Convenient opening hours - no siesta break.

Richard Ginori

CENTRO STORICO - SPAGNA
p.zza Trinità dei Monti, 18/b
☎ 06/6793836

The complete range of Italy's most famous porcelain maker as well as an assortment of other brands of crystal, silverware and cutlery. Single or second-choice pieces and complete dinner services from out-of-production lines can be bought at wholesale prices at La Botteguccia in 18, Via Rapagnano at Colle Salario on the way to Settebagni [phone: 06/8815558].

La Rinascente

PINCIANO
p.zza Fiume, 1
☎ 06/8841231

Rinascente occupies an entire modern *palazzina* with various departments, including men, women and children's clothing, perfumes and fashion accessories. But our favourite is the basement floor devoted to household goods where you can find a vast number of items, from expensive classics to more original pieces: articles for everyday use, fine china, futuristic batteries of saucepans, candles, cleaning products hard to come by elsewhere, linen, furnishings, fittings and beautiful decorative objects. They also do wedding gift lists. On the top floor there's a panoramic coffee bar and a *tavola calda* selling ready-to-eat lunchtime dishes.

Soleiado

CENTRO STORICO - POPOLO
via dell'Oca, 38/a
☎ 06/3610402

Typical Provençal designs on sheets, towels, tablecloths, place mats and cottons by-the-metre for curtains and wall hangings.

Spazio 7

CENTRO STORICO - ARGENTINA
via dei Barbieri, 7
☎ 06/6869708

This three-storey 16th century *palazzo* in the centre of the city is entirely devoted to the home, the kitchen and the dining table. For more than twenty years, Spazio 7 has gathered the most beautiful, avantgarde, curious and unusual products from all over the world under its vaulted and frescoed ceilings. Every object on sale here, whether it's a simple apron, a battery of professional saucepans, a butter-knife made of juniper wood, handwoven tablecloths or splendid designer

HOME & TABLE

furniture, is the outcome of constant research guided by exceptionally good taste.

STUDIO DUE PI

CENTRO STORICO - CAMPO MARZIO
p.zza Nicosia, 30/34
☎ *06/68307384*

Furniture and fittings for a beautiful, functional kitchen plus accessories for the culinary arts and the dining table, including Limoges porcelain, equally beautiful but rather more accessibly-priced fine Hungarian or Portuguese china, Italian cutlery and Swiss saucepans.

STUDIO PUNTO TRE

CENTRO STORICO - CAMPO DE' FIORI
via Giulia, 145
☎ *06/6864321*

In one of the most beautiful ancient *palazzi* in this very lovely street you'll find dining table accessories in exquisite taste, stunning furnishing fabrics and some gorgeous antiques and artisan-made objects.

T. A. D.

CENTRO STORICO - POPOLO
via di S. Giacomo, 5
☎ *06/36001679*

Modern furniture and fittings, plaster, paints and materials for the DIY maison, as well as German, English and Italian china for the kitchen, picnic baskets, candles, place mats, table and bed linen, fabrics by-the-metre including waterproof material, and gardening items. Pricey.

TEBRO

BALDUINA
p.le delle Medaglie d'Oro, 55
☎ *06/35420476*
PIAZZA BOLOGNA
via Ravenna, 50
☎ *06/44233229*
CENTRO STORICO - CAMPO MARZIO
via dei Prefetti, 46/54
☎ *06/6873441*

Classic household and table linen since 1867. Open all day Saturdays and Sundays.

TULIPANI BIANCHI

CENTRO STORICO - CAMPO MARZIO
via dei Bergamaschi, 59
☎ *06/6785449*

Not your typical florist, because its Swiss owners create their splendid compositions using very unusual flowers and materials with truly spectacular results. The flowers arrive directly [and exclusively] from San Remo so they're rather different from the ones you generally see around Rome - no long-stemmed roses, poinsettias or other commercial standards. Preference is given to Italian products used to their best advantage. Their creations reveal a *Mitteleuropean* taste and are customised for the client. Priced right for the quality.

VENIER COLOMBO

CENTRO STORICO - SPAGNA
via Frattina, 79
☎ *06/6792979*

Swiss muslin, Irish linen and other exquisite fabrics, but the principal material sold here is lace – for clothes or household linen. Very beautiful embroidered tablecloths and place mats and some remarkable Swiss print tablecloths.

OSCAR ZUCCHI

ESQUILINO
via S. Antonio all'Esquilino, 15
☎ *06/4465871*

Oscar Zucchi's sells cooking equipment and utensils to hotels, restaurants, bars, pastry-shops, canteens and anyone else who wants to fit out their kitchen with professional products. All the saucepans you can possibly imagine, in stainless steel or heavy aluminium, electrical appliances and food processors, vast numbers of accessories for pastry-making, from icing syringes, pastry bags and nozzles to baking moulds of every conceivable shape and size, and Zucchi's will custom-make any you can't find here. There's an anthological exposition in Via Cavour.

CURIOSITIES

IL MUSEO NAZIONALE DELLE PASTE ALIMENTARI

CENTRO STORICO - TRITONE
p.zza Scanderbeg, 117
☎ *06/6991119*

This museum in Palazzo Scanderbeg is the only one of its kind in the world. Its rooms enclose eight centuries of the history of Italy's most famous first course, from pasta-making machines to eyewitness acounts of memorable meals. The Rubino Scaglione Room devoted to the relationship between Pasta, Art and Theatre is very entertaining, while the Sala Napoli contains photos of various celebrities tackling their spaghetti, with much-loved Neapolitan comedian Totò well to the fore.

sleeping

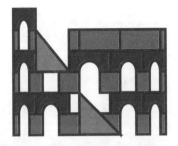

HOTELS
★★
★★★
★★★★
★★★★★

ABERDEEN
★★★
TERMINI
via Firenze, 48
☎ 06/4823920
fax 06/4821092
• **Closed:** never
• **Rooms:** 26
120/180,000
180/300,000
all ✳ sat. 🍷 ♦ 🚌 extra

Inside a beautiful and conveniently central *palazzo*, the Aberdeen offers cosy, attractive communal areas like the TV and reading rooms, a pretty breakfast room with a lavish buffet in the mornings, and quite spacious, tastefully-decorated guest rooms – all recently renovated. Bathrooms have showers and hairdryers. Air conditioning costs an extra L.20,000 per day. There's a pay garage.

ACCADEMIA
★★★
CENTRO STORICO - TRITONE
p.zza Accademia di San Luca, 74
☎ 06/69922607
fax 06/6785897
• **Closed:** never
• **Rooms:** 58
290/350,000
350/450,000
all ✳ sat. 🍷 ♦ & [1]

The hotel is located right in the city centre in a recently modernised *palazzo* just a few steps away from the Trevi Fountain. Guest rooms are quite large with well-equipped ensuite bathrooms and personal safes; some have double-glazing. A lavish buffet breakfast is served in the sunny dining room. Pay garage.

ADVENTURE
★★★
TERMINI
via Palestro, 88
☎ 06/4469026
fax 06/4460084
• **Closed:** never
• **Rooms:** 23
150/200,000
170/300,000
all ✳ 🗓 sat. 🍷 ♦ 🚌 extra

The hotel is located in a tastefully restored late-nineteenth century *palazzo* near Stazione Termini. There's a welcoming, family-style bar and breakfast area, reasonably comfortable rooms, each with a private safe, and functional bathrooms offering small courtesy sets and hairdryer. Complimentary newspapers in the mornings.

AFI HOTEL ROMA [FORMERLY FORTE AGIP]
★★★★
AURELIO
via Aurelia km 8, 400
☎ 06/66411200
fax 06/66414437
(800407407
• **Closed:** never
• **Rooms:** 213
250/350,000
265/460,000
all ✳ 🗓 sat. 🍷 ♦ 🅿 🏊 🍴

A modern, well-planned hotel ideal for receptions and conferences. Everything is organised to guarantee guests' comfort: large attractive communal areas, functionally furnished rooms with all the amenities including trouser presses, and adequate bathrooms, each with a courtesy set and hairdryer. There's also

a swimming pool with a buffet restaurant and barbeque, pool room, fitness centre, the Bell'Italia restaurant and a convenient shuttle bus service to the city centre.

ALDROVANDI PALACE
★★★★★ L
PARIOLI
via U. Aldrovandi, 15
☎ 06/3223993
fax 06/3221435
• **Closed:** never
• **Rooms:** 135
450/590,000
550/690,000
all ✳ 🗓 sat. 🍷 ♦ 🅿 🏊 🍴

This luxurious hotel with a view across the Villa Borghese gardens is inside an elegant late 19th century *palazzo*, formerly a boarding school, in the exclusive Parioli quarter. A refined, courteous atmosphere, elegantly quiet shared spaces, cocktail bar, piano bar, ten meeting rooms, a restaurant dining room with two verandas [one non-smoking] where a sumptuous breakfast buffet is arrayed, a wonderful garden filled with plants and flowers home to the La Ranocchia swimming pool, also open to the public. The Relais La Piscine restaurant with its beautiful outdoor dining area is just a short walk away. The rooms [some non-smoking] are very comfortable, with beautiful linen; ensuite bathrooms have special make-up mirrors, courtesy sets, hairdryers and telephones. There's also a gym for the health-conscious.

ALIMANDI
★★★
TRIONFALE
via Tunisi, 8
☎ 06/39723941
fax 06/39723943
• **Closed:** annual holiday varies
• **Rooms:** 35
160,000
240,000
extra 🗓 all ✳ 🗓 sat. ♦ 🚌 extra

Close to a metro stop and not far from the Vatican, this pleasant hotel run by the Alimandi family offers pristine, luminous communal areas – TV room, restaurant, bar and pool room – and a very attractive summer terrace. All the simply-furnished, cosy rooms have private safes and radios; the bathrooms have showers and hair-dryers. Buffet breakfast. Shuttle bus service to the airport.

ALPI
★★★
TERMINI
via Castelfidardo, 84/A
☎ 06/4441235
fax 06/4441257
• **Closed:** never
• **Rooms:** 47
140/220,000
160/280,000
all ✳ 🗓 sat. 🍷 ♦ 🚌 extra & [1]

In a beautiful late-19thcentury building, the Hotel Alpi has managed to preserve the charm of its complex weave of period atmospheres almost intact: marble pavements, console tables, late 18th century glazing and tapestries, Art

Nouveau lamps and wrought iron railings. The rooms are mostly spacious, tastefully decorated and each one has a private safe. The attractive bathrooms all have phones, hair-dryers and courtesy sets; some also have Jacuzzis. Lavish breakfast buffet. Special arrangement with a nearby restaurant.

AMALFI
★★★
ESQUILINO
via Merulana, 278
☎ 06/4744313
fax 06/4820575
• **Closed:** never
• **Rooms:** 22
◁ 150/250,000
◁ 200/350,000
▰ ▱ AE, CSi, Visa ✳
📷 sat. ▰ ♦ 🚗 extra

This small hotel in a Twenties' building between Santa Maria Maggiore and Termini Station offers good service and very reasonable prices, especially in the off-season. The modern bedrooms are simply and functionally furnished; bathrooms are large, comfortable and well-equipped. A continental breakfast is served in the coffee bar.

AMERICAN PALACE EUR
★★★
EUR
via Laurentina, 554
☎ 06/541971
fax 06/5911740
• **Closed:** never
• **Rooms:** 166
◁ 199,000
◁ 295,000
▰ ▱ all ✳ 📷 sat. ▰
♦ 🅿 ⚡ 🍽 🚗 ♿

One of the most reliable hotels in south Rome, conveniently close to a [B Line] metro stop, with large, pleasant, wheelchair-friendly communal areas. A buffet breakfast is served in the internal courtyard garden in summer. Comfortable, functional rooms; generous courtesy sets in the bathrooms. Minibars and hairdryers are provided only in the six suites. Free shuttle bus to airport on request. Also available: bar, sauna, gym, film hire and video-conferencing.

ANDREOTTI
★★★
TERMINI
via Castelfidardo, 55
☎ 06/4441006
fax 06/4453777
• **Closed:** never
• **Rooms:** 53
◁ 200/240,000
◁ 265/310,000
▰ ▱ all ✳ 📷 sat. ▰
🚗 ♦

A conveniently central location near Porta Pia, pleasant hospitality and attentive service make this hotel a very attractive place to stay. The rooms are spacious and comfortable, each with a private safe and trouser press. The bathrooms come in various sizes, each with phone, hair-dryer, courtesy set and, in some cases, computerised sauna and Jacuzzi. A very good buffet breakfast is served in a pleasant dining room. Professional service.

APPIA PARK
★★★
APPIO
via Appia Nuova, 932 [km 10, 300]
☎ 06/7180180
fax 06/7182457
• **Closed:** never
• **Rooms:** 21
◁ 80/250,000
◁ 100/350,000
▰ extra ▱ all ✳
📷 sat. ▰ 🅿 ♿ [1]

A small pretty villa surrounded by trees with a convenient carpark opposite, not far from the Ciampino airport [take Exit 23 off the Raccordo Anulare – Rome's ring road] and very close to the Castelli Romani and the archaeological sites along the ancient Via Appia. Next to the hotel building there's a separate conference and reception centre complete with catering service. Pleasant communal areas, particularly the various dayrooms and the bar. Bedrooms are fitted with private safes; well-equipped bathrooms.

ARCANGELO
★★★
PRATI - COLA DI RIENZO
via Boezio, 15
☎ 06/6874143
fax 06/6893050
• **Closed:** never
• **Rooms:** 33
◁ 180/225,000
◁ 220/310,000
▰ ▱ all ✳ 📷 ▰ 🚗 ♦
🅿 ♿

Conveniently located in the fairly central Prati quarter, this well-managed hotel inside an attractive late 19th century *palazzetto* combines elegant decor with functional comfort; some guest rooms have Art Nouveau windowpanes, coffered ceilings, *boiserie* panelling and huge mirrors. Comfortable bathrooms are

equipped with courtesy sets, hair-dryers and towel-warmers. Daily newspapers available on request. Complimentary parking; metro tickets on sale at the reception desk.

ARENULA
★★
CENTRO STORICO - GHETTO
via Santa Maria de' Calderari, 47
☎ 06/6879454
fax 06/6896188
• **Closed:** never
• **Rooms:** 50
◁ 110/170,000
◁ 140/220,000
▰ ▱ CSi, DC, Visa ✳
📷 sat. 🚗

Located in one of the most characteristic quarters of the *centro storico*, this is an attractive hotel with courteous staff. On the first floor there's the small lobby, TV room, breakfast room and ten bedrooms. Apart from four rooms on the third floor which only have showers, all the other quite comfortable rooms have well-equipped bathrooms. There's a L. 20,000 per day supplement for air-conditioning.

ARIS GARDEN
★★★★
AXA
loc. Axa
via Aristofane, 101
☎ 06/52362443
fax 06/52352968
(800840000
• **Closed:** never
• **Rooms:** 110
◁ 302,000
◁ 480,000
▰ ▱ all ✳ 📷 sat. ▰
🚗 ♦ 🅿 ⚡ ⚡ ♿ 🍽
🐕 ♿ [3]

This modern, well-organised hotel is located in a residential area 8 kilometres from the EUR quarter, and is linked to Fiumicino Airport by shuttle bus [available on request].
Rooms are comfortable and functional with private safes and ensuite bathrooms equipped with courtesy sets and hair-dryers.
There's a partly-covered Olympic swimming pool, a fitness centre with sauna and Turkish baths, beauty centre, tennis and squash courts. Efficient conference and reception facilities.

ARISTON
★★★★
TERMINI
via F. Turati, 16
☎ 06/4465399
fax 06/4465396
• **Closed:** never
• **Rooms:** 105
🛏 280,000
🛏 390,000
🍷 🖥 all ✳ 📺 sat. 🍸
🗝 ♦ 🅿 🚗 extra ♨
🐾 ♿ [5]

This rather tranquil, very comfortable hotel is close to Termini Station. Rooms are large and tastefully decorated with pay TV, air conditioning and minibars. Functional bathrooms offer small courtesy sets and hairdriers. Courteous, professional staff; safe deposit boxes available for clients; American style buffet breakfast.

ARTDECO
★★★★
TERMINI
via Palestro, 19
☎ 06/4457588
fax 06/4441483
(800820080
• **Closed:** never
• **Rooms:** 60
🛏 300,000
🛏 470,000
🍷 🖥 all ✳ 📺 sat. 🍸
🗝 ♦ 🚗 extra ♨ 🍽

A very comfortable hotel in a beautifully restored old *palazzo* near Termini station, it offers super-modern computerised amenities in guest rooms with Art Deco decor [some non-smoking], private safes, and comfortable ensuite bathrooms with hairdryers, Jacuzzi and saunas. There's a beautiful garden terrace with a piano bar, and the Il Pavone restaurant offers high quality food in elegant surroundings.

ARTEMIDE
★★★★
TERMINI
via Nazionale, 22
☎ 06/489911
fax 06/48991700
(800813013
• **Closed:** never
• **Rooms:** 80
🛏 350/380,000
🛏 490/540,000
🍷 🖥 all ✳ 📺 sat. 🍸
🗝 ♦ 🚗 extra ♨
🍽 ♿ [1]

Inside a beautiful, completely restored *palazzo* very close to Termini Station, the Artemide offers cosy, elegant communal areas, very well-equipped conference facilities, attractively-furnished, tranquil guest rooms with electronic passkeys and all the comforts, and pleasant, well-appointed bathrooms [eight have Jacuzzis]. Two bars, two restaurants.

ASTRID
★★★
FLAMINIO
l.go A. Sarti, 4
☎ 06/3236371
fax 06/3220806
• **Closed:** never
• **Rooms:** 32
🛏 170/260,000
🛏 260/360,000
🍷 🖥 all ✳ 📺 sat. 🍸
🗝 ♦ 🚗 extra
♿ [2]

This hotel is on the fifth floor of an elegant *palazzo* in a tranquil corner of Rome near the Tiber. Well-linked to the centre by ultra-modern trams, it has a beautiful hall, luminous day rooms and a pleasant little breakfast terrace. Rooms vary in size but are all quite spacious and attractively furnished with well-equipped bathrooms. Helpful, courteous staff.

AUGUSTEA
★★★
TERMINI
via Nazionale, 251
☎ 06/4883589
fax 06/4814872
• **Closed:** never
• **Rooms:** 20
🛏 90/240,000
🛏 120/320,000
🍷 🖥 all ✳ 📺 sat. 🍸
🗝 ♦ 🚗 extra 🐾

This hotel, on the second and third floors of an austere *palazzo* in *centralissima* Via Nazionale, is reasonably silent thanks to double glazing and the fact that numerous bedrooms don't face onto the street. Attractive classical decor, wall-to-wall carpets, private safes, well designed bathrooms with courtesy sets and hairdryers. Cosy day rooms, courteous staff; an ample continental breakfast buffet.

AVENTINO
★★
AVENTINO
via di San Domenico, 10
☎ 06/5743547
fax 06/5783604
• **Closed:** never
• **Rooms:** 23
🛏 150,000
🛏 230,000
🍷 🖥 all 📺 🍽 🅿

Owned by the same firm as the Sant'Anselmo, Villa San Pio and Villa San Lorenzo Maria hotels [see below], this is a pleasant, tranquil little hotel with a lovely garden where breakfast is served in summer. Check-in, check out and organisation of all the hotel services take place at the Sant'Anselmo. Simple, clean, comfortable bedrooms and bathrooms. Its central position and moderate prices make it a good address to remember.

BAROCCO
★★★★
CENTRO STORICO · TRITONE
p.zza Barberini, 9
☎ 06/4872001
fax 06/485994
• **Closed:** never
• **Rooms:** 28
🛏 199/380,000
🛏 299/630,000
🍷 🖥 all ✳ 📺 sat. 🍸
🗝 ♦ ♿ [1] 💙

In a beautiful early 19th century building in *centralissima* Piazza Barberini, this hotel has a pleasant lobby frescoed with views of Rome, a small bar and a terrace where a buffet breakfast is served in summer. There are various kinds of rooms available, some with small private terraces, all attractively furnished with music and electronic safes. The rather small marble bathrooms offer hairdryers, courtesy sets and towel-warmers. The restaurant is open only if you book. Special weekend rates.

BERNINI BRISTOL
★★★★★ L
CENTRO STORICO - TRITONE
p.zza Barberini, 23
☎ 06/4883051
fax 06/4824266
(800273126
• **Closed:** never
• **Rooms:** 125
⌁ 420,000
⌁ 590,000
☕ extra 🗐 all ✳
📺 sat. 🍷 📡 ♦
🍽 extra ⚡ ♿ 🍸 🐕

Located right near Via Veneto, the Bernini Bristol, founded in 1870, is an elegant hotel in the classical tradition. The beautifully- decorated foyer opens onto great salons and corridors hung with tapestries and old paintings, crystal chandeliers, antique furniture and beautiful flooring. The soundproof rooms are large, luminous and decorated in various styles with exquisite furniture and fabrics. Spacious bathrooms have baths, hairdryers and lavish courtesy sets. There's also a Presidential suite, a stunning roof garden, meeting rooms and the Il Corallo restaurant overlooking

Piazza Barberini. Laundry service, fitness centre [with sauna, Turkish baths, Jacuzzi and gym]. Safety deposit boxes are available at the reception desk.

BLED
★★★
ESQUILINO
via Santa Croce in Gerusalemme, 40
☎ 06/7027808
fax 06/7027935
• **Closed:** never
• **Rooms:** 48
⌁ 65/200,000
⌁ 105/300,000
☕ 🗐 all ✳ 📺 sat. 🍷
📡 ♦ 🅿 🍸 🐕

One of the best hotels in the area, the Bled is inside a rather charming Twenties' villa with decor that enhances its simple, essential lines. The guest rooms are comfortable and attractively furnished; many have private balconies. There's a L.10,000 per day extra charge for air-conditioning. Bathrooms are provided with hairdryers and courtesy sets. Parking at L.10,000 per day.

BOLIVAR
★★★
CENTRO STORICO
QUIRINALE
via della Cordonata, 6
☎ 06/6791614
fax 06/6791025
• **Closed:** never
• **Rooms:** 35
⌁ 130/300,000
⌁ 170/380,000
☕ 🗐 all ✳ 📺 sat. 🍷
📡 ♦ 🅿 🍽 🐕
♿ [4]

Very centrally located between Piazza Venezia and the Roman Forum, this hotel offers comfortable and pleasant surroundings. The modern guest rooms are spacious and welcoming with wall-to-wall carpets and

private safes; hairdryers, courtesy sets and sunlamps are provided in the practical, light-filled bathrooms. A buffet breakfast is served in the glass-walled roof garden on the top floor that offers panoramic views of the city. Cocktail bar; sauna with more sunlamps to relax under.

BORROMEO
★★★
ESQUILINO
via Cavour, 117
☎ 06/485856
   06/4884915
fax 06/4882541
• **Closed:** never
• **Rooms:** 30
⌁ 160/280,000
⌁ 180/380,000
☕ 🗐 all ✳ 📺 sat. 🍷
📡 ♦ 🅿 🐕 ♿

Inside a late 19th century building in central Via Cavour, this hotel has a small cosy lobby, attractive communal areas, and large, comfortable and attractively decorated guest rooms with electronic passkeys, private safes and cable tv. Well-equipped bathrooms come with phones, hairdryers, courtesy sets, towel-warmers and personalised linen. Roof garden, buffet breakfast, also available in bedrooms at no extra charge. Laundry service; bookings can be made for excursions. Pay parking.

BRITANNIA
★★★
VIMINALE
via Napoli, 64
☎ 06/4883153
fax 06/4882343
• **Closed:** never
• **Rooms:** 32
⌁ 250/350,000
⌁ 280/420,000
☕ 🗐 all ✳ 📺 sat. 🍷
📡 ♦ 🅿 🐕

Close to Piazza Santa Maria Maggiore and only a short distance away from Termini Station, the Britannia is a good, hospitable, welcoming hotel. There's a small dining room and bar off the lobby next door to the breakfast room. Guest rooms are modern and attractively decorated, with electronic passkeys, air-conditioning, sound-proof windows, radio, personal safes and beautiful bathrooms, some with double washbasins and Jacuzzis, all equipped with hairdryers, courtesy sets, phones and sunlamps. Italian and foreign newspapers are available for clients.

BUENOS AIRES
★★★
PINCIANO
via Clitunno, 9
☎ 06/8554854
fax 06/8415272
• **Closed:** never
• **Rooms:** 52
⌁ 199,000
⌁ 265,000
☕ 🗐 all ✳ 📺 sat. 🍷
📡 ♦ 🅿 🍽 🐕

A comfortable, tastefully-decorated hotel in the tranquil Salario quarter. Modern decor and modems in the bedrooms [many single rooms have smallish double beds]; rather small bathrooms with hairdryers. Special uncarpeted bedrooms for animal-lovers and their dogs. Laundry service; air and rail bookings can be made.

CAMPO DE' FIORI
★★

CENTRO STORICO
CAMPO DE' FIORI
via del Biscione, 6
☎ 06/68806865
   06/6874886
fax 06/6876003
• **Closed:** never
• **Rooms:** 29
🛏 150/180,000
🛏 220/250,000
☕ 🖬 CSi, Visa

🏨 A small, picturesque hotel with two delightful terraces overlooking one of Rome's most famous piazzas and romantic rooms with particularly attractive decor and atmosphere on the first floor. Nine rooms with ensuite bathrooms at the listed prices; the others [four have ensuite showers] are more economical. Mini-apartments, called *free houses* next to the hotel: two rooms, bathroom and tiny kitchen.

CANADA
★★★

TERMINI
via Vicenza, 58
☎ 06/4457770
fax 06/4450749
☎ 800820080
• **Closed:** never
• **Rooms:** 70
🛏 175/190,000
🛏 220/290,000
☕ 🖬 all ✱ 🖬 sat. 🖬
♦ 🚗 extra 🖬

🏨 This very tastefully decorated hotel offers professional, courteous hospitality and efficient service. The rooms [some non-smoking] with 17th century-style tiled floors and furnishings, are spacious [the singles have double beds] and fitted with private safes. The bathrooms offer phones, hairdryers, complete personalised courtesy sets and clothes-drying lines. Elegantly served breakfast; special hospitality for honeymooners. Various services: secretarial assistence, fax, transport to the airport, bar, and guided tours.

CARRIAGE
★★★

CENTRO STORICO - SPAGNA
via delle Carrozze, 36
☎ 06/6990124
fax 06/6788279
• **Closed:** never
• **Rooms:** 24
🛏 300,000
🛏 400,000
☕ 🖬 all ✱ 🖬 sat. 🍷
🖬 ♦

🏨 *Centralissimo* – just a stone's throw away from the Spanish Steps, in a pedestrians-only zone, this beautifully decorated, comfortable, welcoming hotel offers elegant surroundings, brass beds in the bedrooms and tasteful furnishings; well-equipped bathrooms with courtesy sets and hairdryers. The two rooms with balconies overlooking the rooftops of Rome need to be booked well in advance. There's also a beautiful terrace on the top floor with bar service, where continental breakfasts are served.

CASA VALDESE
★★

PRATI
via A. Farnese, 18
☎ 06/3215362
fax 06/3211843
• **Closed:** never
• **Rooms:** 33
🛏 125/139,000
🛏 172/192,000
☕ 🖬 AE, CSi, Visa ✱
🖬 ♦ 🖬 🍽 🖬 [2] ❤

🏨 This pleasant, well-run hotel is in a tranquil street in the Prati quarter, very close to the metro stop. There's a delightful panoramic terrace, a TV room and cosy communal areas.
The quiet guest rooms are simply furnished with attractive bathrooms.
Hairdryers and private TV are available on request. Book in advance.

CELIO
★★★

COLOSSEO
via dei Santi Quattro, 35/c
☎ 06/70495333
fax 06/7096377
• **Closed:** never
• **Rooms:** 16
🛏 180/290,000
🛏 220/340,000
☕ 🖬 all ✱ 🖬 sat. 🍷
🖬 🅿 🚗 extra 🖬
🖬 [1] ❤

🏨 This delightful cosy hotel, recently refurbished, is inside a tranquil 19th century *palazzo*. The comfortable rooms are named for the works of great artists reproduced as frescoes on the ceilings above the beds. Each one has trouser press, video, private safe and scales. The bathrooms, in marble with mosaic floors, are a bit on the small side, but come equipped with music, courtesy sets and hairdryers.
Splendid breakfasts are served in the rooms. Special prices for readers of this guide.

LA CISTERNA
★★★

TRASTEVERE
via della Cisterna, 7
☎ 06/5817212
   06/5881852
fax 06/5810091
• **Closed:** never
• **Rooms:** 18
🛏 150,000
🛏 180,000
☕ 🖬 all ✱ 🖬 sat.
🖬 ♦

Inside an ancient, historic 18th century *palazzo*, not far from the splendid church of Santa Maria in Trastevere, this hotel offers simply-furnished guest rooms.
There's only one single room, so solo travellers will almost certainly be put into doubles. There's a TV lounge and a dining room on the ground floor where continental breakfast is served, and a very pretty indoor courtyard where guests can relax outside in summer.
Hairdryers on request. Special rates at a nearby garage.

CITY
★★★

CENTRO STORICO
via Due Macelli, 97
☎ 06/6784037
fax 06/6797972
• **Closed:** never
• **Rooms:** 33
🛏 270,000
🛏 330,000
☕ 🖬 all ✱ 🖬 sat.
🖬 ♦

🏨 A hotel with a pleasant atmosphere inside a beautifully restored *palazzo* only 100 metres from the Spanish Steps, right in the heart of Rome's most elegant shopping district. The rooms are spacious, tastefully-furnished and cosy; comfortable bathrooms offer courtesy sets and hairdryers. A buffet breakfast is served in the dining room. Tiny bar; fax.

COLUMBUS
★★★★
VATICANO
via della Conciliazione, 33
☎ 06/6865435
fax 06/6864874
• **Closed:** never
• **Rooms:** 92
⚏ 370,000
⚏ 470,000
⚏ 🖻 all ✳ 🏛 sat. 🍷
🍽 ♦ 🄿 🕯 🍴 🐾

🛏 Only a few steps away from St. Peter's, the Colombus is inside a 15th century cardinal's palace with huge communal spaces where you breathe an atmosphere of austere elegance: coffered ceilings, aristocratic coats of arms, enormous oil paintings, tiled floors, a stone fireplace and splendid frescoes in the Veranda Room. There's a pleasant internal courtyard where guests can park their cars. Well-equipped, well-organised conference and reception facilities; a well-stocked bar; the La Veranda restaurant with garden; simply furnished rooms and functional bathrooms. Buffet breakfast.

CONCORDIA
★★★
CENTRO STORICO - SPAGNA
via Capo Le Case, 14
☎ 06/6791953
  06/6795693
fax 06/6795409
• **Closed:** never
• **Rooms:** 24
⚏ 140/280,000
⚏ 210/280,000
⚏ 🖻 all ✳ 🏛 sat. 🍷
🍽 ♦ 🚗 extra

🛏🛏 In the central but tranquil Monti quarter, this recently refurbished hotel offers spacious, simply furnished rooms with parquet floors and double-glazing, air-conditioning and cable TV. Bathrooms are small but attractive with showers, courtesy sets and hairdryers. There's a pretty terrace filled with plants and flowers for summer breakfasts with the dome of St. Peter's in the background. The basement floor contains a bar with a piano and a TV lounge. Breakfast can be served in the rooms at no extra charge.

CONTILIA
★★★
TERMINI
via Principe Amedeo, 81
☎ 06/4466942
fax 06/4466904
• **Closed:** never
• **Rooms:** 34
⚏ 100/170,000
⚏ 110/230,000
⚏ extra 🖻 all ✳ 🏛 🍽
♦ 🚗 extra

🛏 This hotel in a recently-restored ancient *palazzo* close to Termini Station is very conveniently located for visiting the city. It offers attractively-furnished, comfortable rooms with safes [extra charge for air-conditioning]; bathrooms with hairdryers; a bar; cosy communal areas, and

a breakfast room with a summer terrace. Special rates at a nearby garage.

COSMOPOLITA
★★★
CENTRO STORICO - TRITONE
via IV Novembre, 114
☎ 06/69941349
fax 06/69941360
• **Closed:** never
• **Rooms:** 55
⚏ 275,000
⚏ 350,000
⚏ 🖻 all ✳ 🏛 🍽 ♦
🚗 extra ♿

🛏 Just round the corner from *centralissima* Piazza Venezia, this hotel is on one of the upper floors of a 19th century palazzo with a view over the Colonna gardens, and you breathe the atmosphere of bygone times in the style of the rooms and the communal areas. The guest rooms are attractively furnished and fitted with safes; the bathrooms have hairdryers. Buffet breakfast. Special arrangements with a number of restaurants.

CROWNE PLAZA ROMA MINERVA
★★★★★ L
CENTRO STORICO - PANTHEON
p.zza della Minerva, 69
☎ 06/695201
fax 06/6794165
(800780360
• **Closed:** never
• **Rooms:** 134
⚏ 600,000
⚏ 750/900,000
⚏ 🖻 all ✳ 🏛 sat. 🍷
🍽 ♦ ⚡ 🕯 🍴 ♿ [1]

🛏🛏 In a splendid 17th century *palazzo* near the Pantheon, this hotel offers an extremely refined and elegant ambience and a beautiful roof garden with a marvellous panorama over the centre of the city. The

well-lit foyer is very beautifully furnished, the rooms are spacious and welcoming with reinforced doors, double-glazing, electronic safes and trouser presses. The marble bathrooms are equipped with hairdryers, scales, phones and lavish courtesy sets; some also have Jacuzzis. Elegant breakfast room; buffet business lunches, and a small fitness club.

D'INGHILTERRA
★★★★
CENTRO STORICO - SPAGNA
via Bocca di Leone, 14
☎ 06/699811
fax 06/69922243
(800010058
• **Closed:** never
• **Rooms:** 100
⚏ 370/400,000
⚏ 495/620,000
⚏ extra 🖻 all ✳
🏛 sat. 🍷 🍽 ♦ 🕯 🍴

🛏🛏 In the heart of the exclusive central shopping district, close to the Spanish Steps and Rome's most famous stores, this is a hotel in the grand tradition. Antique furniture, original paintings, old prints and crystal chandeliers create the atmosphere of the communal areas. The spacious guest rooms are tastefully fitted out with wall-to-wall carpets, double-glazing and classical music; those on the fifth floor have small terraces with views. The marble bathrooms offer complete courtesy sets and hairdryers. The roof garden is one of the most beautiful in the city; there's a bar and restaurant open to the public. Professional, courteous staff.

DANIELA
★★★
ESQUILINO
via L. Luzzatti, 31
☎ *06/7027817*
fax 06/7027922
• **Closed:** never
• **Rooms:** 47
⮠ 65/200,000
⮠ 105/300,000
☕ 🖥 all ✳ 📷 🏆 🛅 ◆
🅿 🍴 🐾 ✦

This conveniently-located, tranquil hotel is made up of two small buildings. It offers attractive rooms decorated in varying styles; only those in the main building have air-conditioning. Fairly standard bathrooms with courtesy sets and hairdryers. Bar service is provided in summer on the terrace and in their beautiful garden. Parking at L.10,000 per day.

DE LA VILLE INTERCONTINENTAL
★★★★
CENTRO STORICO - SPAGNA
via Sistina, 69
☎ *06/67331*
fax 06/6784213
(800872070
• **Closed:** never
• **Rooms:** 192
⮠ 710,000
⮠ 854,000
☕ 🖥 AE, CSi, Visa ✳
📷 sat. 🏆 🛅 ◆
🚗 extra 🔌 🍴

In a beautiful Art Nouveau *palazzo* in an enchanting position close to the Spanish Steps, this hotel offers an atmosphere of great style and refinement.

The Neo-Classical communal areas are elegant and welcoming; guest rooms are tastefully decorated and comfortable; the bathrooms all have baths, hairdryers and lavish courtesy sets. The single rooms are equally spacious, almost all have with smallish double beds, while the sixth floor rooms have small, beautiful, panoramic terraces. There's also a solarium on the same floor; a restaurant, La Piazzetta, a cocktail bar that turns into a piano bar in the evenings and a hairdresser's. Very professional staff. The prices quoted above are provisional and could change.

DE PETRIS
★★★
CENTRO STORICO
QUIRINALE
via Rasella, 142
☎ *06/4819626*
fax 06/4820733
• **Closed:** never
• **Rooms:** 45
⮠ 225/275,000
⮠ 270/370,000
☕ 🖥 all ✳ 📷 sat. 🏆
🛅 ◆ ✦

This cosy hotel offers well-organised, courteous management and tastefully-decorated, comfortable communal areas. Bathrooms are well-equipped with courtesy sets and hairdryers, and each of the very attractive guest rooms is different from the others. A lavish buffet breakfast is served in the dining room.

DEGLI ARANCI
★★★
PARIOLI
via B. Oriani, 11
☎ *06/8070202*
fax 06/8070704
• **Closed:** never
• **Rooms:** 54
⮠ 185/270,000
⮠ 270/375,000
☕ 🖥 all ✳ 📷 sat. 🏆
🛅 ◆ 🅿 🔌 🍴 ♿ [1]

This cosy, intimate hotel with its pleasantly recherché atmosphere is located in Parioli, one of Rome's most elegant residential quarters. The communal areas are comfortable and very carefully maintained: elegant conversation corners, a bar and a restaurant with a pleasant outdoor dining area in summer and a good business lunch menu. The guest rooms are comfortable and quiet; many have private terraces, and some of the well-equipped bathrooms have Jacuzzis. Laundry and secretarial service.

DEI CONGRESSI
★★★
EUR
v.le Shakespeare, 29
☎ *06/5926021*
06/5921264
fax 06/5911903
• **Closed:** never
• **Rooms:** 105
⮠ 200,000
⮠ 290,000
☕ 🖥 all ✳ 📷 🏆 🛅 ◆
🅿 🔌 🍴 🐾 ✦

The Hotel Dei Congressi with its garden café and La Glorietta restaurant [open to the public and closed on Sundays] is undoubtedly one of the best in the area. The foyer and communal areas are elegant and

welcoming, the spacious luminous rooms are comfortable, and the bathrooms offer all the necessary amenities. The hotel's convenient position close to the Eur Fermi metro stop on the city's B line offers easy access to the city centre. Laundry service.

DEI MELLINI
★★★★
PRATI - CAVOUR
via M. Clementi, 81
☎ *06/324771*
fax 06/32477801
(800813013
• **Closed:** never
• **Rooms:** 80
⮠ 370,000
⮠ 470,000
☕ 🖥 all ✳ 📷 sat.
🏆 🔌 ◆ 🚗 extra
🔌 ♿ [2]

This hotel in a carefully restored old building has a luminous elegant marble-paved foyer, cocktail bar, TV lounge, buffet breakfast room, a small pretty internal courtyard for summer use and a magnificent terrace. The rooms [some non-smoking] have electronic passkeys, English-style decor, outlets for modem, fax and mobile phones, radio, safe, trouser press [only in the suites] and marble bathrooms [some with double washbasins] with complete courtesy sets and hairdryers. Laundry service; professional, courteous staff. Special rates for companies and groups.

DEL SOLE AL PANTHEON
★★★★

CENTRO STORICO
PANTHEON
p.zza della Rotonda, 63
☎ 06/6780441
fax 06/69940689
• **Closed:** never
• **Rooms:** 25
🛏 380/400,000
🛏 550/570,000
🖥 📺 all ✳ 📱 sat. ♟
📶 ♦ 🚗 extra 🐕
♿ [1] ❤

This hotel with its romantic atmosphere and ancient traditions is located in one of Rome's most beautiful piazzas, now a pedestrian zone. Its logo is a stylized sun and you'll find it everywhere. The communal areas are decorated in restrained but excellent taste; the guest rooms are very attractive, and those overlooking the piazza have soundproof glazing. The bathrooms are luminous, comfortable and well-appointed. A buffet breakfast is served on the internal terrace in summer. Polite, attentive staff.

DELLA TORRE ARGENTINA
★★★

CENTRO STORICO
ARGENTINA
c.so Vittorio
Emanuele II, 102
☎ 06/6833886
fax 06/68801641
• **Closed:** never
• **Rooms:** 53
🛏 230,000
🛏 330,000
🖥 📺 all ✳ 📱 sat. ♟
📶 ♦ 🚗 extra

This conveniently central hotel is pleasant and attractive. The walls and arches in the dining room where a buffet breakfast is served date back to ancient Roman times. The guest rooms, of varying types, are simply and functionally decorated and all have pay TV; the bathrooms offer courtesy sets and hairdryers. Two rooms on the fifth floor open onto the communal terrace where clients can relax.

DELLE MUSE
★★★

PARIOLI
via T. Salvini, 18
☎ 06/8088333
fax 06/8085749
• **Closed:** never
• **Rooms:** 60
🛏 120/150,000
🛏 150/200,000
🖥 📺 all 📱 sat. 📶 ♦
🅿 🚗 extra 🛎 🐕

This comfortable, tranquil hotel in one of Rome's most elegant quarters is run with professionalism and courtesy, and is well linked to the centre by public transport. All the guest rooms are simply and tastefully decorated, with quite well-equipped bathrooms. There are meeting rooms, a bar, a restaurant [which moves to the beautiful private garden in summer] and safe deposit boxes at the reception desk. Attractively presented breakfasts. Readers of our Guide can take advantage of particularly favourable prices.

DIANA
★★★

TERMINI
via Principe Amedeo, 4
☎ 06/4827541
fax 06/486998
• **Closed:** never
• **Rooms:** 188
🛏 230,000
🛏 330,000
🖥 📺 all ✳ 📱 sat. ♟
📶 ♦ ♿ 🛎 🐕 🚗

Conveniently located near Termini Station, this hotel offers very comfortable communal spaces, a bar that never seems to close, the Uliveto roof garden with cocktail bar in summer, the Artemide Room, two meeting rooms, and a good restaurant. Bedrooms come in various sizes [including two junior suites with Jacuzzis] and offer quite a high standard of comfort with cable TV in each one; bathrooms have either bath or shower, courtesy sets and hairdryers. Attractive buffet breakfast. Because of the versatility of its facilities, the Diana often hosts cultural and social events.

DOMUS AVENTINA
★★★

AVENTINO
via di Santa
Prisca, 11/b
☎ 06/5746189
fax 06/57300044
• **Closed:** never
• **Rooms:** 26
🛏 250,000
🛏 380,000
🖥 📺 all ✳ 📱 sat.
♟ 📶

Situated in the green and tranquil Aventino quarter, this hotel is characterised by the simplicity and excellent taste displayed in the choice of colours and decor, whether it be the beautiful trompe l'oeil frescoes in the communal areas or the refined elegance of the large guest rooms equipped with all the necessary amenities. The bathrooms are comfortable, with either bath or shower, and offer courtesy sets and hairdryers. Attractive continental breakfasts.

DUCA D'ALBA
★★★

MONTI
via Leonina, 14
☎ 06/484471
fax 06/4884840
• **Closed:** never
• **Rooms:** 27
🛏 160/260,000
🛏 195/310,000
🖥 📺 all ✳ 📱 sat. ♟
📶 ♦ 🐕 ❤

This very attractive, classically styled hotel is located in a very central position in the characteristic Suburra quarter, only a few steps away from the Colosseum and the Roman Forum. The foyer is elegant and welcoming, and so is the spacious breakfast room with its adjacent bar decorated in marble. The beautifully furnished rooms are soundproof with electronic security locks, safes and satellite TV; the well-appointed bathrooms offer courtesy sets and hairdryers. The suite is extremely pleasant. Professional, courteous staff.

DUE TORRI
★★★
CENTRO STORICO
CAMPO MARZIO
v.lo del Leonetto, 23
☎ 06/6876983
06/6875765
fax 06/6865442
• **Closed:** never
• **Rooms:** 26
⚬ 170/190,000
⚬ 260/330,000
☕ 🖥 all ✳ 📺 sat. 🍷
📺 ♦ 🐾 ♥

In a very central but tranquil position inside a charming 19th century *palazzo* formerly the residence of illustrious cardinals and bishops, this delightful hotel offers its clients a high standard of hospitality and a very pleasant atmosphere. The communal spaces are welcoming and elegant, the guest rooms aren't huge but they're decorated in extremely good taste and are very comfortable; the irreprehensible bathrooms provide courtesy sets and hairdryers. We particularly recommend Room 503 and the fourth-floor rooms with balconies. Breakfast is served in a pretty dining room.

EDEN
★★★★★ L
PINCIANO
via Ludovisi, 49
☎ 06/478121
fax 06/4821584
(800820088
• **Closed:** never
• **Rooms:** 119
⚬ 650/770,000
⚬ 1,000/1,200,000
☕ extra 🖥 all ✳
📺 sat. 🍷 📺
♦ 🚗 extra 🐾 ♿
🍽 🐾 ♿

132

Inside a late 19th century *palazzo*, this elegant hotel has recently been refurbished. Communal spaces are embellished with tasteful furnishings, paintings and beautiful porcelain, while the guest rooms, many with magnificent views over the city, have antique furniture, VCR's, modems and impeccably-equipped bathrooms. The 500 sq.m. Ambassador's Suite, one the most costly suites in Europe, was recently inaugurated. The roof garden is one of the most beautiful in Rome and hosts a bar and the La Terrazza restaurant. A fitness centre with a well-equipped gym is available for clients.

EDERA
★★★
ESQUILINO
via A. Poliziano, 75
☎ 06/70454022
fax 06/70453769
• **Closed:** never
• **Rooms:** 52
⚬ 65/200,000
⚬ 105/300,000
☕ 🖥 all 📺 🍷 📺 ♦ 🅿
🐾 ♿ [1]

This welcoming, well-organised and tastefully-decorated hotel is situated in a tranquil position close to the Colosseum and the Roman Forum. The rooms are spacious and comfortable with TV, minibar and electric trouser press; tiled bathrooms are equipped with hairdryers and courtesy sets. A buffet breakfast is served in a small dining room, and there's also a very pleasant internal garden. Parking at L.10,000 per day.

ERDARELLI
★★
CENTRO STORICO - SPAGNA
via Due Macelli, 28
☎ 06/6791265
fax 06/6790705
• **Closed:** never
• **Rooms:** 28
⚬ 100/150,000
⚬ 140/200,000
☕ 🖥 all ✳ 📺 ♦

Strategically positioned in the heart of the city, just a few steps away from Piazza di Spagna, this hotel is characterised by cleanliness, essential comforts and efficient family management. TV lounge, breakfast room, basic single rooms with minuscule bathroms, functional doubles [with an extra charge of L.20,000 per day for air-conditioning]. Polite, professional staff.

EUROGARDEN
★★★
SALARIO
salita del Castel Giubileo, 197
[GRA uscita 7]
☎ 06/8852751
fax 06/88527577
• **Closed:** never
• **Rooms:** 48
⚬ 250,000
☕ 🖥 all ✳ 📺 sat. 🍷
📺 🅿 🏊

Immersed in a large private park, this hotel can be easily identified from the Grande Raccordo Anulare [Rome's ring road]. Welcoming, attractive communal areas and comfortable rooms [though unfortunately some are a bit noisy despite the double-glazing] with trouser presses and ensuite bathrooms complete with courtesy sets and hairdryer. There's an outdoor swimming pool, and newspapers are available in the foyer. Breakfast is buffet-style and charged for

separately. It can also be served in guest's rooms at no extra cost. Courteous staff.

EXCELSIOR ROMA
★★★★★ L
PINCIANO
via Vittorio Veneto, 125
☎ 06/47081
fax 06/4826205
(800790524
• **Closed:** never
• **Rooms:** 321
⚬ 473/550,000
⚬ 737/891,000
☕ extra 🖥 all ✳
📺 sat. 🍷 📺 ♦
🚗 extra ♿ 🍽 🐾

Just a few steps away from the Villa Borghese gardens inside a gorgeous *palazzo*, this hotel breathes luxury and refinement, starting with the exquisite antique furniture and gilded stucco-work in the communal areas and dining rooms. The Excelsior hosts cultural and social events of all kinds. The guest rooms are elegant and comfortable, and so are the well-appointed marble bathrooms. The suites are truly regal, especially the recently inaugurated one that occupies the entire sixth and seventh floors – 1,100 sq. metres, with its own wine cellar containing 200 wines, private fitness centre, cinema and swimming pool. There's also an interpreter service, a photographer, beauty salon, babysitting service, safety deposit boxes, bar and piano bar. Continental or American-style breakfasts. Very professional staff.

FARNESE
★★★★

PRATI - COLA DI RIENZO
via A. Farnese, 30
☎ 06/3212553
06/3212554
fax 06/3215129
• **Closed:** never
• **Rooms:** 23
🛏 300/340,000
🛏 400/500,000
🍽 🖥 all ✳ 📺 sat. 🍷
🛎 ♦ 🅿 ♥

🛎 This hotel in a
beautiful early
twentieth-century
building in the Prati
quarter is
characterised by great
good taste and
attention to detail.
The reception desk is
framed by a 17th
century altar canopy,
and the beautifully-
made furniture and
finishings create an
atmosphere of
elegant tranquility.
Situated in a quiet
position, but close to
a metro stop, it offers
comfortable,
noiseless rooms with
beautiful linen, cable
TV and bathrooms
with phones, pretty
courtesy sets,
hairdryers and make-
up mirrors.
There's also a very
pleasant little terrace
with bar service.
Excellent buffet
breakfast;
experienced,
courteous staff.

FIORI
★★

TERMINI
via Nazionale, 163
☎ 06/6797212
06/6795525
fax 06/6795433
• **Closed:** never
• **Rooms:** 19
🛏 130/160,000
🛏 170/220,000
🍽 🖥 all ✳ 📺 🍷 ♦

🛎 If you stay in this
hotel you'll have
all the city's most
important tourist
attractions within
walking distance, given
its magnificent
position only a few
steps away from the
Quirinale [the
Presidential Palace]
and the station.
Situated on the first
and third floors of an
elegant *palazzo*, the
Fiori is very
competently run by
youthful Danilo, and
offers comfortable
rooms with double-
glazing, ceiling fans,
TV and bathrooms with
showers. The first floor
rooms also have
minibars and air-
conditioning [L.10,000
per person per day].
Continental breakfasts
are served in the
dining room.

FLORA
★★★★

PINCIANO
via Vittorio
Veneto, 191
☎ 06/489929
fax 06/4820359
• **Closed:** never
• **Rooms:** 155
🛏 385/622,000
🛏 400/790,000
🍽 extra 🖥 all ✳
📺 sat. 🍷 🛎 ♦
🚗 extra ♿ 🍴 🐕 ♿

🛎 Close to the Villa
Borghese
gardens and recently
restored, this elegant
hotel inside a late
19th century *palazzo*
with its large, austere
communal areas, bar
and dining rooms has
a rather special
atmosphere. The
Empire Style rooms
are spacious and fitted
with private safes;
large, beautifully-
finished bathrooms
offer courtesy sets and
hairdryers. A lavish
buffet breakfast is
served in the dining
room to a very elastic
timetable. Restaurant,
fitness room and
business centre.

Special rates at a
nearby garage.

FONTANELLA BORGHESE
★★★

CENTRO STORICO
CAMPO MARZIO
l.go Fontanella
Borghese, 84
☎ 06/68809504
fax 06/6861295
• **Closed:** never
• **Rooms:** 24
🛏 190/250,000
🛏 300/400,000
🍽 🖥 all ✳ 📺 sat. 🍷
🛎 ♦ extra 🐕 ♥

🛎 Under the same
management as
the Due Torri [see
above] this delightful
hotel is on the second
and third floors of a
16th century *palazzo*
which once belonged
to the aristocratic
Borghese family. The
very agreeable
atmosphere combines
friendly hospitality with
discreet refinement.
Sunny, light-filled
communal areas, a
small TV lounge and a
dining room with a bar
where a buffet
breakfast is served.
The guest rooms are
tastefully decorated
using beautiful fabrics
[greens on the second
floor, blues on the
third] and where
possible the splendid
original tiles have been
kept, otherwise the
floors are parquet.
Comfortable, well-
equipped bathrooms.

GAMBRINUS
★★★

PINCIANO
via Piave, 29
☎ 06/4871250
fax 06/4742488
• **Closed:** never
• **Rooms:** 58
🛏 160/200,000
🛏 240/300,000
🍽 🖥 all ✳ 📺 sat. 🍷
🛎 ♦ 🚗 extra
🐕 ♿ [1]

🛎 This straightforward
hotel occupies the
second and third floors
of an early 20th century

building. Guest rooms
come in various sizes
with simple, classical
furnishings, and most
of them overlook the
gardens of the French
Ambassador to the
Holy See, so they're
rather quiet. The
bathrooms have
hairdryers. Bar and TV
lounge.

I GIGLI DELLA MONTAGNA

MONTESACRO
via Monte Senario, 83
☎ 06/8170232
fax 06/87193054
• **Closed:** never
• **Rooms:** 79
🛏 70/80,000
🛏 120/140,000
🍽 🖥 CSi, Visa ✳ 📺 ♦
🅿 ♿ 🍴 ♿ [1]

🛎 This hotel is run by
Ursuline nuns, the
same ones who
manage the Domus
Mariae Hotel in
Siracusa, Sicily.
Situated in a quiet
neighborhood with
lovely green outdoor
leisure areas, it offers
clients clean, simply
furnished rooms and
bathrooms with all the
essentials comforts.
There's a chapel for
religious services.
Pleasant communal
areas. Full or half
pension at attractive
prices.

GIGLIO DELL'OPERA
★★★

TERMINI
via Principe
Amedeo, 14
☎ 06/4880219
06/4871426
fax 06/4871425
• **Closed:** never
• **Rooms:** 61
🛏 100/280,000
🛏 150/400,000
🍽 🖥 all ✳ 📺 sat. 🍷
🛎 ♦ 🚗 extra ♿ 🐕

133

This traditional hotel inside a beautiful old building offers well-organised communal areas like the dining room where an attractive English breakfast is served. The guest rooms are clean and comfortable, with courtesy sets, hairdryers and original decor in the bathrooms. Italian and foreign newspapers are available for clients. Experienced, courteous staff.

GINEVRA
★★
ESQUILINO
via L. Pianciani, 17
☎ 06/70493766
fax 06/70476655
• **Closed:** never
• **Rooms:** 13
⬋ 130/160,000
⬋ 150/220,000
🛏 🖥 all ✳ 📺 📶
🅿 🐕

This minuscule hotel in a late 19th century *palazzo* near Termini Station has recently been restored. Particularly suited to younger clients, it offers welcoming, comfortable surroundings. The air-conditioned rooms are plainly furnished and not particularly spacious; the bathrooms are functional with little courtesy sets [hairdryers on request]. Breakfast is served in guests' rooms at no extra charge. Courteous staff. Discounts for families.

GIORGI
★★★
TERMINI
via Magenta, 11
☎ 06/4457555
fax 06/4441551
• **Closed:** never
• **Rooms:** 27
⬋ 155/210,000
⬋ 180/280,000
🛏 🖥 all ✳ 📺 📶 ◆
🐕 ♿ [1]

This well-run hotel is conveniently close to Termini Station and offers cosy, comfortable communal areas and attractive simply-furnished rooms [including two suites with Jacuzzis] fitted with personal safes; the very pleasant bathrooms offer either bath or shower, courtesy sets and hairdryers. Good breakfasts.

ST. REGIS GRAND [FORMERLY LE GRAND HOTEL
★★★★★ L
TERMINI
via V. E. Orlando, 3
☎ 06/47091
fax 06/4747307
• **Closed:** never
• **Rooms:** ✳
⬋ ✳
⬋ ✳
🛏 extra 🖥 all ✳
📺 sat. 📶 ◆ 🅿
🚗 extra 🍴

After a year of restoration, the work of 450 people at a cost of $35 million, the aristocratic Grand Hotel has re-opened as the St. Regis Grand. Each of its sumptuous 161 rooms and 25 suites is named for a Roman monument. The hotel offers a fitness center, a restaurant - Vivendo, open to the public, a wine bar- the Di vino, where tastings are held, and a cocktail bar open from 8:30am to 1:30am. Twenty-two butlers

are there to look after guests' needs.

GRAND HOTEL PALACE
★★★★
PINCIANO
via Vittorio Veneto, 70
☎ 06/478719
fax 06/47871800
📞 800253878
• **Closed:** never
• **Rooms:** 95
⬋ 630,000
⬋ 720,000
🛏 🖥 all ✳ 📺 sat. 🛏
📶 ◆ 🏊 🏋 🍴 🐕
♿ [3]

In a building designed by the famous architect Piacentini, this *centralissimo* hotel offers clients an atmosphere of sumptuous elegance beginning with the beautifully designed interiors of the communal areas. The rooms and suites are all soundproof, with beautiful furniture and all the comforts, including private safes; spacious bathrooms offer courtesy sets and hairdryers. Clients can also take advantage of modern facilities for conferences, meetings and social events, a good restaurant and a fitness centre with a swimming pool, massage [both cosmetic and therapeutic] and a solarium.

GREEN PARK DOVER
★★★
AURELIO
via della Pineta Sacchetti, 43
☎ 06/6622366
fax 06/6638835
• **Closed:** never
• **Rooms:** 59
⬋ 185/250,000
⬋ 280/350,000
🛏 🖥 all ✳ 📺 sat. 📶
◆ 🅿 🚗 extra 🍴 🐕

This hotel opposite the green Pinetta Sacchetti park offers modern, functional

facilities and attentive, courteous service with comfortable communal areas, a bar and spacious, attractive guest rooms with well-designed, well-equipped bathrooms. Though it's mostly patronised by groups, there are two floors reserved for individual clients. Abundant buffet breakfast, and a sports club open to the public very close by.

GREGORIANA
★★★
CENTRO STORICO - SPAGNA
via Gregoriana, 18
☎ 06/6794269
fax 06/6784258
• **Closed:** never
• **Rooms:** 20
⬋ 220,000
⬋ 380,000
🛏 🖥 no ✳ 📺 sat. 📶
◆ 🅿 🚗 🐕

Inside a 17th century ex-convent, the Gregoriana is a tranquil, well-run, comfortable little hotel very close to the Spanish Steps. Instead of numbers each guest room has a different letter of the alphabet designed by Ertè, the celebrated illustrator and exponent of Art Deco. Attractively furnished and equipped with air-conditioning and satellite TV, some also have small terraces. The few singles are quite spacious. Small courtesy sets in the bathrooms and hairdryer available on request. Breakfast is served in guests' rooms, except in summer when tables are laid on the terrace.

GRIFO
★★

MONTI
via del Boschetto, 144
☎ 06/4871395
06/4827596
fax 06/4742323
• **Closed:** never
• **Rooms:** 21
🛏 95/140,000
🛏 180/230,000
💺 📺 all 📺 🍷 📶 ♦ 🅿
📶 ♿

This little hotel is situated in the characteristic old Suburra quarter, between Via Nazionale and Via Cavour. The communal areas are simply decorated but welcoming, like the plainly furnished rooms and bathrooms. On the top floor there's a gorgeous little terrace with a view over the rooftops, where a very good breakfast is served in summer. Courteous hospitality.

HIBERIA
★★★

CENTRO STORICO
QUIRINALE
via XXIV Maggio, 8
☎ 06/6782662
06/6787560
fax 06/6794600
• **Closed:** never
• **Rooms:** 22
🛏 100/300,000
🛏 140/380,000
💺 📺 all ✳ 📺 sat. 🍷
📶 ♦ 🅿 🚗 extra 📶
📶 ♿ [2]

🛏🛏 The Hiberia is a small hotel in a convenient position close to the Quirinale [the Presidential Palace] that offers good service and cordial hospitality. The

communal areas and rooms are modern in design and each room is different; all are soundproof with satellite TV. The fourth-floor rooms are particularly in demand because of their wonderful panoramic views. Bar, laundry service and bookings for guided tours.

HOLIDAY INN ST. PETER'S
★★★★

AURELIO
via Aurelia Antica, 415
☎ 06/66420
fax 06/6637190
• **Closed:** never
• **Rooms:** 320
🛏 291/430,000
🛏 310/530,000
💺 📺 all ✳ 📺 sat. 📶
♦ 🅿 🏊 🎿 ⛱ 📶 📶 ♿
[3]

🛏🛏 This welcoming hotel with its well-lit, attractively furnished foyer is located in a tranquil leafy area. The rooms, each with its own small sitting room and balcony, are comfortable and fitted with electronic safes, voice mail and modems; bathrooms are well-equipped. There are special rooms for children, women travelling alone, non-smokers and fitness fanatics. The restaurant, open to the public as well as hotel guests, has very convenient opening hours – straight through from 6.30am till 11pm – and does Sunday brunch. Good facilities for conferences and other events. Shuttle bus service to the city centre and airport. Tennis courts, swimming pool, gym, sauna and massage for moments of pure relaxation.

HOMS
★★★

CENTRO STORICO · SPAGNA
via della Vite, 71/72
☎ 06/6792976
fax 06/6780482
• **Closed:** never
• **Rooms:** 48
🛏 120/230,000
🛏 220/350,000
💺 📺 all ✳ 📺 sat. 🍷
📶 ♦ 🚗 extra
📶 ♿ [1]

🛏 Located in the city's shopping and fashion heartland, the Homs offers an unpretentious, relaxing atmosphere and the benefits of experienced management. It has a small but welcoming foyer and guest rooms with double-glazing and tiny ensuite bathrooms equipped with showers, courtesy sets and hairdryers. In summer breakfast is served on a pleasant terrace with a view over the rooftops of Rome. Garage parking for clients. Laundry and ironing service. L.20,000 per day extra charge for air-conditioning.

IMPERO
★★★

VIMINALE
via del Viminale, 19
☎ 06/4820066
fax 06/483762
• **Closed:** never
• **Rooms:** 62
🛏 150/200,000
🛏 220/280,000
💺 📺 all ✳ 📺 🍷 📶 ♦
🅿 🚗 ⛱ 📶 ♿ [1]

🛏🛏 Very centrally located inside a beautiful *palazzo* close to the Opera House, this hotel has a very pleasant atmosphere. The communal areas are comfortable and well-designed, with a small bar, various lounges, a reading room, a veranda with a terrace and a small indoor breakfast room. The guest rooms are particularly charming,

with Twenties' furniture and doors decorated with painted scenes from daily life in ancient Rome; functional, well-equipped bathrooms. Pay parking facilities.

INTERNAZIONALE
★★★

CENTRO STORICO · SPAGNA
via Sistina, 79
☎ 06/69941823
fax 06/6784764
• **Closed:** never
• **Rooms:** 42
🛏 230,000
🛏 335,000
💺 📺 AE, CSi, Visa ✳
📺 sat. 🍷 📶 ♦
🚗 extra 📶

🛏🛏 Located in a re-designed 16th century convent building, this hotel has beautifully-decorated communal areas and panoramic terraces. Each guest room is different, some have a small sitting room, 13 on the fourth floor have a terrace, and others have baths with Jacuzzis; all have personal safes. The singles are spacious and almost all have European-size double beds. The bathrooms have piped music, generous courtesy sets and hairdryers. Lavish buffet breakfast. Children's needs are given special attention.

ISA
★★★

PRATI · CAVOUR
via Cicerone, 39
☎ 06/3212610
fax 06/3215882
• **Closed:** never
• **Rooms:** 40
🛏 200/270,000
🛏 250/330,000
💺 📺 all ✳ 📺 sat. 🍷
📶 ♦ 🅿 🚗 extra

Conveniently located in the Prati quarter with plentiful transport links to the centre and St. Peter's within walking distance, this hotel has a small, luminous reception area, a conversation lounge and a breakfast room where a buffet breakfast is served. The guest rooms are comfortable and tastefully decorated. Bathrooms come with either bath or shower and courtesy sets, hairdryers, towel-warmers and magnifying make-up mirrors; some also have double washbasins. Polite, courteous reception staff.

JOLLY HOTEL VITTORIO VENETO
★★★★
PINCIANO
c.so Italia, 1
☎ *06/8495*
fax 06/8841104
(800017703
• **Closed:** never
• **Rooms:** 203
⤙ 345/400,000
⤙ 400/505,000
🍷 🗂 all ✳ 🗂 sat. 🍷
🎤 ♦ 🚬 extra 🌿 🍽
🐕 ⅂ [4]

This modern hotel with beautiful views over the Villa Borghese gardens is just a short walk away from the centre. Much patronised by business people, it offers facilities for conferences and meetings of various kinds and soundproof guest rooms, including non-smoking rooms and rooms without carpets for allergy sufferers. The singles

have European-size double beds. Bathrooms have phones, towel-warmers, hair dryers and lavish courtesy sets. An American-style breakfast is served in the dining room. Newspapers to read in the spacious lounge, piano bar in the evenings.

JOLLY MIDAS
★★★★
AURELIO
via Aurelia, 800
☎ *06/66396*
fax 06/66418457
• **Closed:** never
• **Rooms:** 347
⤙ 250/300,000
⤙ 300/400,000
🍷 🗂 all ✳ 🗂 sat. 🍷
🎤 ♦ 🚬 ⅂ 🌿 🌿
🍽 🐕

Close to the Grande Raccordo Anulare, Rome's ring road, this modern hotel offers efficient facilities for conventions, receptions and other functions. Shops, bar, piano bar, three restaurants - all with a view across the garden and the Olympic swimming pool which together with two tennis courts keeps health-conscious clients happy. Comfortably-furnished rooms [including non-smoking rooms] with balconies. Bathrooms offer hairdryers and courtesy sets. Free shuttle bus.

JULIA
★★★
CENTRO STORICO - TRITONE
via Rasella, 29
☎ *06/4881637*
fax 06/4817044
• **Closed:** never
• **Rooms:** 33
⤙ 100/200,000
⤙ 120/300,000
🍷 🗂 all ✳ 🗂 sat. 🎤
♦ 🖸 🌿 🐕 ⅂ [2]

Located in the heart of the city near the Trevi Fountain, in a miraculously quiet, tranquil street, the Julia is a very comfortable hotel. A bar and breakfast room are located off the small lobby; the simply-furnished guest rooms have safes, and the bathrooms all have showers, hairdryers and courtesy sets. The singles are rather small, with European-size double beds.
Very courteous, helpful staff. Fax service at the reception desk.

KENT
★★★
PINCIANO
via Reggio Emilia, 71
☎ *06/8540797*
fax 06/8541040
• **Closed:** never
• **Rooms:** 17
⤙ 170/230,000
⤙ 230/280,000
🍷 🗂 all ✳ 🗂 sat. 🍷
♦ 🖸 🚬 extra

This hotel is inside a small *palazzetto* near Porta Pia. The communal areas are cosy and attractive; the guest rooms are comfortably furnished with European-size double beds in the singles, and bathrooms are equipped with hairdryers and towel-warmers.
Two rooms are on the top floor near the entrance to the terrace.
A very pleasant roof garden; lavish continental breakfast buffet; courteous, helpful staff. Special arrangement with a nearby garage. Private chauffeurs available.

LANCELOT
★★★
ESQUILINO
via Capo d'Africa, 47
☎ *06/70450615*
fax 06/70450640
• **Closed:** never
• **Rooms:** 6
⤙ 150,000
⤙ 250,000
🍷 🗂 all ✳ 🗂 sat. ♦
🖸 🍽 🐕 💗

More like a family home than a hotel, this very pleasant place is conveniently located close to the Colosseum and the Palatine Hill, as well as being not far from the metro and various other forms of public transport. As we go to press renovations which will make this agreeable little place even more comfortable are nearing completion. The rooms are spacious and sunny, each one different to the others but all attractively-decorated and cosy with adequate amenities. There's also a bar, sitting room, dining room and very pleasant outdoor area. Babysitting and bicycle rental are among the services available to clients. The owners are cordial and kindly.

LAURENTIA
★★★
SAN LORENZO
l.go degli Osci, 63
☎ *06/4450218*
fax 06/4453821
• **Closed:** never
• **Rooms:** 41
⤙ 160/210,000
⤙ 170/260,000
🍷 🗂 AE, CSi, Visa ✳
🗂 🍷 🎤 ♦ 🖸 🚬 extra
🌿 🐕 ⅂ [2]

In the heart of the characteristic San Lorenzo quarter, overlooking the piazza where the daily markets are held, the Laurentia offers attractive communal areas, including a reading room, breakfast room and conference room. The guest rooms are spacious, soundproof and simply-furnished. Rooms 402, 404 and 405 each have a little private terrace; but other guests can breakfast outside on the small communal terrace. Modern bathrooms come with hairdryers and lavish courtesy sets.

LEONARDO DA VINCI
★★★★
PRATI - COLA DI RIENZO
via dei Gracchi, 324
☎ *06/32499*
fax 06/361038
(800017703
• **Closed:** never
• **Rooms:** 257
280/325,000
325/425,000
all ✳ 📺 sat. 🍷
🛏 ♦ 🅿 🚗 extra
🍴 🐕

This hotel in the Prati quarter is well linked to the centre by public transport and offers elegant, attractive communal areas and functionally-furnished, well-equipped rooms. Bathrooms come with complete courtesy sets and hairdryers. American style buffet breakfast; hairdresser/barber and a souvenir shop. A good place for business people.

LOCARNO
★★★
CENTRO STORICO - POPOLO
via della Penna, 22
☎ *06/3610841*
fax 06/3215249
• **Closed:** never
• **Rooms:** 48
220,000
360,000
all ✳ 📺 sat. 🍷
🛏 ♦ 🚗 extra ♿
♿ [1] ❤

Art Nouveau decor and a very central position close to Piazza del Popolo: this hotel has a lovely facade covered by leafy vines and very attractive communal areas – a bar, the breakfast room where a lavish buffet is spread in the mornings and various conversation corners. The rooms are stylishly decorated and fitted with safes; some also have modems. Bathrooms have either bath or shower, music, hairdryers and towel warmers. There's a wonderful roof garden for summer use; free bicycles are available. Professionalism and courtesy from the entire staff.

LORD BYRON
★★★★★ L
PARIOLI
via G. De Notaris, 5
☎ *06/3220404*
fax 06/3220405
(800822005
• **Closed:** never
• **Rooms:** 37
352/440,000
440/682,000
all ✳ 📺 sat.
🍷 🛏 ♦ 🅿 🚗 extra ♿
🍴 🐕

Elegance, tranquility and extremely professional staff are the salient characteristics of this small, refined hotel in the Prati quarter. Single rooms have European-size double beds, while the

beautifully-decorated double rooms [Comfort, Superior and Deluxe] are all different, with pure linen sheets and bathtowels. Each bathroom has a phone, hairdryer and personalised courtesy set. Buffet breakfast is served in the dining room of their famous Relais Le Jardin restaurant; quick lunches can be had in the Salotto. Piano bar for evening relaxation.

LUXOR
★★★
VIMINALE
via A. Depretis, 104
☎ *06/485420*
fax 06/4815571
• **Closed:** never
• **Rooms:** 21
160/242,000
230/356,000
all ✳ 📺 sat. 🍷
🛏 ♦

This conveniently central hotel occupies three floors of a neo-Gothic *palazzetto*, and offers comfortable rooms of varying sizes – the ones overlooking the street are very spacious - with parquet floors, safe, double-glazing and antique furniture, and well-appointed ensuite bathrooms. There's a small roof garden and reading room. Courteous staff serve a cosmopolitan clientele.

LYDIA VENIER
★★
CENTRO STORICO - SPAGNA
via Sistina, 42
☎ *06/6793815*
06/6791744
fax 06/6797263
• **Closed:** never
• **Rooms:** 28
80/180,000
100/260,000
all 📺 🛏 ♦
🚗 extra 🐕

This very central and slightly spartan little

hotel has a family atmosphere. The guest rooms are simply furnished with ceiling fans, tiled floors and pale wood furniture; functional bathrooms offer small courtesy sets. The breakfast room is very pretty, with marble and wrought iron tables and frescoes on the ceiling. There's a bar for clients.

MAJESTIC
★★★★★ L
CENTRO STORICO - TRITONE
via Vittorio Veneto, 50
☎ *06/486841*
06/4828014
fax 06/4880984
• **Closed:** never
• **Rooms:** 97
500/580,000
690/790,000
all ✳ 📺 sat. 🍷
🛏 ♦ ♿ 🍴

Situated in one of the word's most famous streets, the Majestic occupies an entire elegant late-19th century *palazzo* with a lovely outdoor area, and offers elegant salons for conferences and private meetings. The guest rooms and eight suites are beautifully decorated with lavishly-equipped bathrooms. Breakfast is served in the excellent La Veranda restaurant, open to the public, whose windows give onto a lovely terrace overlooking Via Veneto. We can warmly recommend the Ninfa bar, perhaps the only one of its kind in the city, where you can have a snack or a meal until late at night.

MANFREDI
★★★

CENTRO STORICO - SPAGNA
via Margutta, 61
☎ *06/3207676*
   06/3207695
fax *06/3207736*
• **Closed:** never
• **Rooms:** 17
🛏 150/330,000
🛏 250/450,000
☕ 🖥 all ✳ 📺 sat. ☕
🔌 ◆

A small, tranquil, well-run hotel in one of the quietest and most characteristic streets in the centre of Rome, its guest rooms offer numerous amenities, including electronic safes and VCRS. There's a video-library with an extra charge for film rental. The single rooms are a fraction small but functional; bathrooms have hairdryers and mini courtesy sets. A buffet breakfast is served in a little dining room.

MARCELLA
★★★

PINCIANO
via Flavia, 106
☎ *06/4746451*
fax *06/4815832*
• **Closed:** never
• **Rooms:** 75
🛏 180/240,000
🛏 300/350,000
☕ 🖥 all ✳ 📺 sat. ☕
🔌 ◆ 🚌 extra 🐾

Fairly close to Porta Pia and well-linked to the centre by public transport, this hotel spreads over several floors. The communal areas are attractive and comfortable; the guest rooms are very attractively decorated with well-equipped functional bathrooms. A buffet breakfast is served on the pleasant roof garden on the seventh floor or on the veranda. There's also a coffee bar, a cocktail bar and a solarium. Special arrangements with nearby restaurants.

MARCUS
★★

CENTRO STORICO
CAMPO MARZIO
via del Clementino, 94
☎ *06/68300320*
   06/6873679
fax *06/68300312*
• **Closed:** never
• **Rooms:** 18
🛏 120/160,000
🛏 180/210,000
☕ 🖥 AE, CSi, Visa ✳
📺 sat. ☕ 🔌 ◆ ♿ [2]

This small hotel with its pleasant family atmosphere is very well run by Angela and Salvatore De Caro. The little breakfast room has incredibly high ceilings, original floors and a fireplace dating back to the 18th century. There's a small bar and reception area; very spacious guest rooms [some have antique fireplaces] with ceiling fans, air-conditioning [for an extra charge of L. 20,000 per day], personal safes, double-glazing and little bathrooms with showers and hairdryers.

MARGHERA
★★★

TERMINI
via Marghera, 29
☎ *06/4457184*
fax *06/4462539*
• **Closed:** never
• **Rooms:** 25
🛏 150/230,000
🛏 170/330,000
☕ 🖥 CSi, Visa ✳
📺 sat. ☕ ◆

Quite close to Termini Station, this excellent hotel with its pleasant English-style atmosphere has spacious comfortable guest rooms with beautiful linen, trouser presses, and modem outlets; the impeccable bathrooms are equipped with complete courtesy sets and hairdryers - some also have Jacuzzis. Lavish buffet breakfast. Special offers for our readers [enquire when you book].

MARGUTTA
★★

CENTRO STORICO - SPAGNA
via Laurina, 34
☎ *06/3223674*
fax *06/3200395*
• **Closed:** never
• **Rooms:** 21
🛏 170,000
🛏 190,000
☕ 🖥 all ◆

Very centrally located inside an 18th century *palazzo*, the Margutta is a small hotel with a pleasant atmosphere offering basic comforts. The guest rooms are simply decorated with dark wood furniture, wrought iron beds and minuscule, though quite well-equipped, bathrooms. The ones with baths are a fraction bigger than those with showers. Good quality for the price.

MASSIMO D'AZEGLIO
★★★★

MONTI
via Cavour, 18
☎ *06/4870270*
fax *06/4827386*
(800860004
• **Closed:** never
• **Rooms:** 203
🛏 330,000
🛏 450,000
☕ 🖥 all ✳ 📺 sat. ☕
🔌 ◆ 🚌 extra
♿ 🍴 🐾

Close to Termini Station, this traditional hotel in an austere *palazzo* with a late 19th century atmosphere offers a high standard of comfort and excellent amenities. Beautifully-furnished, pleasant sitting rooms open off the foyer, and great windows flood the breakfast room's *boiserie* woodwork, leather sofas and parquet floors with light. The guest rooms are spacious, with period furniture and safes. Buffet breakfast; a roof garden, bar and a restaurant open to the public.

MONDIAL
★★★★

VIMINALE
via Torino, 127
☎ *06/472861*
fax *06/4824822*
(800820080
• **Closed:** never
• **Rooms:** 84
🛏 327,000
🛏 465,000
☕ extra 🖥 all ✳
📺 sat. ☕ 🔌 ◆ 🅿
🚌 extra ♿

Opposite the Opera House and not far from Termini Station, this hotel offers rather attractively decorated rooms [some non-smoking] with piped-in music and well-equipped bathrooms. There are spacious communal areas available to clients, including a bar and two conference rooms. Buffet breakfast.

MONTECARLO
★★★
TERMINI
via Palestro, 17/A
☎ 06/4460000
fax 06/4460006
• **Closed:** never
• **Rooms:** 42
🛏 150/180,000
🛏 200/270,000
🖥 📺 all ✳ 📺 sat. 🍷
🛎 ♦ 🚌 extra
🐕 ♿ [1]

This hotel, close to Termini Station, has a rather attractive modern foyer and lounge, and simply-furnished rooms with minibars and satellite television. The bathrooms are clean and plain with hairdryers. There's a pleasant breakfast room. Bookings can be made for guided tours of Rome and environs. Special arrangements with a nearby restaurant and garage.

MORGANA
★★★
TERMINI
via F. Turati, 29/37
☎ 06/4467230
fax 06/4469142
• **Closed:** never
• **Rooms:** 96
🛏 160/420,000
🛏 185/500,000
🖥 📺 all ✳ 📺 🍷 🛎 ♦
🚌 extra

In a late 19th century *palazzo* next to Termini Station, this hotel offers modern amenities and hospitality characterised by careful attention to details. Pleasant communal areas and attractively-furnished guest rooms of varying sizes with satellite TV, minibars, safes and

double-glazing in the potentially noisier rooms. Well-equipped bathrooms. A buffet breakfast is served in a pleasant little breakfast room.

MOZART
★★★
CENTRO STORICO - CORSO
via dei Greci, 23
☎ 06/36001915
fax 06/36001735
• **Closed:** never
• **Rooms:** 53
🛏 200/260,000
🛏 280/340,000
🖥 📺 all ✳ 📺 sat. 🍷
🛎 ♦ 🚌 extra
♿ ♿ [3]

Pleasantly situated in a tranquil street in the pedestrians-only area between the Spanish Steps and Piazza del Popolo, this very attractively decorated hotel offers comfortable rooms with air-conditioning, cable TV, trouser press, electronic safe and rather small bathrooms with hairdryers and courtesy sets. Modern security systems. There's also a solarium, a very pleasant roof garden with bar service and a newly refurbished meeting room. Well-presented buffet breakfasts.

NERVA
★★★
COLOSSEO
via Tor de' Conti, 3
☎ 06/6781835
fax 06/69922204
• **Closed:** never
• **Rooms:** 19
🛏 140/250,000
🛏 180/360,000
🍷 extra 📺 all ✳
📺 sat. 🍷 🐕 ♦
🚌 extra 🐕

This hotel is in a unique position, practically inside the old Roman Forum, and offers cosy sitting rooms and comfortable, soundproof guest

rooms where care has been taken over every detail, with orthopedic mattresses and trouser presses. Adequately-equipped bathrooms provide bathrobes and hairdryers. There's a small bar, breakfast room and laundry service; bookings can be made for guided tours of Rome and environs.

OLY
★★★
COLOMBO
via Santuario Regina degli Apostoli, 36
☎ 06/594441
fax 06/5412027
• **Closed:** never
• **Rooms:** 104
🛏 260,000
🛏 380,000
🖥 📺 all ✳ 📺 sat. 🍷
🛎 ♦ 🅿 🚌 extra 🏊 🏃
♿ 🍴 ♿ [3]

Great changes have been made to this hotel near the San Paolo Metro station, situated halfway between the offices of Eur and the Garbatella quarter – a useful location for visiting business people. Now completely renovated, it offers spacious, attractive communal areas, a bar, a well-equipped convention centre, a restaurant open to the public and tastefully-furnished, soundproof rooms with electronic passkeys, personalised air-conditioning, modems, suitcase racks and bathrooms with hairdryers. There's also the "Body Touch" fitness centre with indoor swimming pool, gym, work-out equipment, sauna and Turkish baths. Special rates for companies.

OLYMPIC
★★★
PRATI - COLA DI RIENZO
via Properzio, 2/A
☎ 06/6896650
  06/6896652
fax 06/68308255
• **Closed:** never
• **Rooms:** 60
🛏 240,000
🛏 350,000
🖥 📺 all ✳ 📺 sat. 🍷
🛎 ♦ 🅿 🚌 extra 🐕

Only a few steps away from St. Peter's, this hotel is conveniently located in an area well-served by public transport. Communal spaces, like the two small ones that make up the breakfast room, are characterised by simple architectural lines and a welcoming atmosphere. Continental breakfasts are served either at the tables or in guests' rooms at no extra charge. Its spacious, tastefully-decorated rooms are toughtfully designed and many have double-glazing; comfortable bathrooms are equipped with courtesy sets and hairdryers. Grill service at the bar for quick snacks; laundry service, photo printing, fax and Internet access. Garage attendants take care of parking.

ORAZIA
★★★
ESQUILINO
via Buonarroti, 51
☎ 06/4467202
fax 06/4467226
• **Closed:** never
• **Rooms:** 28
🛏 100/250,000
🛏 150/300,000
🖥 📺 all ✳ 📺 sat. 🍷
🛎 ♦ 🍴

Well-linked to the rest of the city by metro and not far from Termini Station, this conveniently-located hotel focuses on the quality of its services. The breakfast room is spacious and welcoming; each guest room on the upper floor is decorated differently, while those on the fourth floor are standardised but cosy. Attractive bathrooms offer courtesy sets and hair dryers. Italian and foreign newspapers are available for clients. Centralised safe; and a snack bar. Efficient, courteous staff.

OXFORD
★★★
PINCIANO
via Boncompagni, 89
☎ *06/42828952*
fax 06/42815349
• **Closed:** never
• **Rooms:** 56
🛏 190/270,000
🛏 250/330,000
🍷 💾 all ✳ 📺 sat. 🍷
📶 ♦ 🅿 🚌 extra ✹ 🍴

This modern, comfortable hotel in a central position close to Via Veneto is well-linked to the rest of the city by public transport. The rooms are furnished so as to make maximum use of available space and offer every comfort. The spacious single rooms often communicate with the doubles so family suites can be created when required. Lavish buffet breakfast; laundry service, snack bar and a restaurant open in the evenings. Courteous, professional staff.

PAISIELLO PARIOLI
★★
PARIOLI
via G. Paisiello, 47
☎ *06/8554531*
fax 06/8542433
• **Closed:** never
• **Rooms:** 49
🛏 145,000
🛏 185,000
🍷 💾 all 📺 🏆 ♦ ✹
🍴 🐕

Very popular with groups and young people, situated in the heart of the Parioli quarter but only a short walk away from the Villa Borghese gardens, this hotel is an excellent place to stay at reasonable prices. The guest rooms and bathrooms are simply furnished; some rooms have small fridges. Plainly-furnished, attractive communal areas.

PARCO DEI PRINCIPI
★★★★★ L
PARIOLI
via G. Frescobaldi, 5
☎ *06/854421*
fax 06/8845104
• **Closed:** never
• **Rooms:** 175
🛏 430/550,000
🛏 700/800,000
🍷 💾 all ✳ 📺 sat. 🍷
📶 ♦ 🅿 🚌 extra 🏊 🏃
✹ 🍴 🅰 [4]

Immersed in greenery, in a magnificent position opposite the Villa Borghese gardens, this luxurious hotel has recently been completely renovated. It offers very comfortable, beautifully-furnished rooms and attractive, tranquil communal areas, the La Pomme bar, a very well-equipped convention centre, a fitness centre, laundry service, free shuttle bus to the city centre, and a magnificent

swimming pool among the trees where Sunday brunch is served in summer. There's also the "Villa Borghese Eventi" area for receptions and very stylish banquets, and a good restaurant open to the public. Professional, courteous service.

PENSIONE PARLAMENTO
★★
CENTRO STORICO - SPAGNA
via delle Convertite, 5
☎ *06/69921000*
fax 06/69921000
• **Closed:** never
• **Rooms:** 22
🛏 140/175,000
🛏 160/200,000
🍷 💾 all ✳ 📺 sat. ♦
🚗 extra 🐕

Right in the centre of Rome's political heartland, the Parlamento is a well-run hotel with a pleasant, welcoming atmosphere and simply-furnished, attractive rooms with double-glazing, satellite TV, personal safes and well-equipped bathrooms. There's a very pretty little panoramic terrace where breakfast is served in summer. Air-conditioning costs an extra L. 20,000 per day. Book in advance.

PATRIA
★★★
VIMINALE
via Torino, 36
☎ *06/4880756*
fax 06/4814872
📞 *800011531*
• **Closed:** never
• **Rooms:** 49
🛏 90/240,000
🛏 120/340,000
🍷 💾 all ✳ 📺 sat. 🍷
📶 ♦ 🐕

In a good central position close to Via Nazionale with attractive communal areas and a bar that never seems to close, this hotel is welcoming and well-conducted. Attractively-furnished, comfortable rooms with double-glazing and well-appointed bathrooms make for a pleasant stay. The owners' pride and joy is there EU-standard security system.

LA PERGOLA
★★★
MONTESACRO
via dei Prati Fiscali, 55
☎ *06/8107250*
fax 06/8124353
• **Closed:** never
• **Rooms:** 90
🛏 140/170,000
🛏 180/220,000
🍷 💾 all ✳ 📺 sat. 📶
♦ ✹ 🐕 ♿ [5]

This hotel in a modern neighbourhood is made up of two communicating buildings. The comfortable guest rooms each have a small terrace; bathrooms offer hairdryers and lavish courtesy sets. There's 24 hour-a-day room service, which more than makes up for the absence of minibars, and guests travelling alone can stay in a double room at the price of a single if there's one free. Newspapers are available in the lobby.There's also a garden where breakfast is served in summer. Special arrangement with a nearby garage; polite, attentive service.

SLEEPING

LE PETIT
★★

TERMINI
via Torino, 122
☎ 06/48907085
fax 06/4744645
• **Closed:** never
• **Rooms:** 11
🛏 140/210,000
🛏 210/240,000
🖵 💿 all ✳ 📺 sat. 🍷
♦ 🚗 extra

On the fourth floor of a beautiful late 19th century building [once home to Ernesto Nathan, Rome's first mayor] close to Termini Station and only a short distance from the centre and other areas of tourist interest, this little hotel has just been completely refurbished. It offers a few comfortable rooms with balconies, parquet floors, simple elegant furniture and brand-new bathrooms with showers and hairdryers. Room 3 is particularly spacious and picturesque with its semi-circular balcony framed by columns and furnished for relaxation. Cosy communal areas, including a bar corner in the reception area and a small dining room where breakfast is served. Special arrangement with a nearby garage.

PETRA RESIDENCE
★★★

LA ROMANINA
via S. Vandi, 124
☎ 06/7232444
fax 06/7234999
• **Closed:** never
• **Rooms:** 49
🛏 150/215,000
🛏 190/285,000
🖵 💿 all ✳ 📺 🍷 🍸 ♦
🅿 🚗 ⚓ ✄ ☂ 🍴 🐕 ⚓
⚓ [4]

This modern hotel complex with an entrance that reproduces the splendid Jordanian city of the same name is situated in the La Romanina quarter not far from Exit 20 off the Grande Raccordo Anulare [Rome's ring road] near the University of Tor Vergata. It offers functionally furnished rooms with small loggias and safes, attractive bathrooms with hairdryers, excellent conference facilities, spacious lounges, a cocktail bar, roof garden, and a swimming pool with poolside deckchairs. Small, very comfortable one or two-room apartments are available for longer stays.

PINCIO
★★★

CENTRO STORICO - SPAGNA
via Capo Le Case, 50
☎ 06/6790758
fax 06/6791233
• **Closed:** never
• **Rooms:** 16
🛏 110/190,000
🛏 150/275,000
🖵 💿 AE, CSi, Visa ✳
📺 sat. 🍷 🍸 ♦ 🅿
🚗 extra

This small, hospitable hotel is conveniently located in a characteristic little street not far from the Spanish Steps. Many of the communal areas have frescoed ceilings and marble floors. The decor is unostentatious but guest rooms offer every comfort, including electronic safes, and adequate bathrooms with courtesy sets and hairdryers. Breakfast is served in a very pleasant setting on a partly covered terrace. Pay parking and garage.

PONTE SISTO
★★★★★

CENTRO STORICO
CAMPO DE' FIORI
via dei Pettinari, 64
☎ 06/686311
fax 06/68631801
• **Closed:** never
• **Rooms:** 106
🛏 340/400,000
🛏 460/550,000
🖵 💿 all ✳ 📺 sat. 🍷
🍸 ♦ 🚗 extra ⚓
🍴 ⚓ [3] ❤

Inside a completely restored 18th century building, this recently-opened hotel is in an excellent central position.
On the ground floor there's the foyer, sitting rooms, bar area and two restaurants, one of which serves meals in the spacious, delightful indoor garden, and a picturesque glass staircase leading to the meeting rooms. Guest rooms have cherrywood furniture, comfortable beds, linen sheets, Internet access and safes. [The Belvedere room with two panoramic terraces is the most sought-after]. Well-equipped marble bathrooms.

PORTA MAGGIORE
★★★

ESQUILINO
p.zza di Porta Maggiore, 25
☎ 06/7027927
fax 06/7027025
• **Closed:** never
• **Rooms:** 210
🛏 230,000
🛏 300,000
🖵 💿 all ✳ 📺 🍷 ♦ ⚓
🍴 ✄ ⚓ [3]

Close to the ruins of the ancient Roman city gate of the same name, this hotel has lovely communal areas which recall Roman traditions in various ways. The sitting rooms and bar with their dark wooden beams are also very attractive. Guest rooms are quite comfortable and cosy with functional bathrooms, and there's a spacious roof garden with bar service, gazebo, wrought iron chairs and tables, deckchairs and masses of flowers.

PORTOGHESI
★★★

CENTRO STORICO
CAMPO MARZIO
via dei Portoghesi, 1
☎ 06/6864231
fax 06/6876976
• **Closed:** never
• **Rooms:** 31
🛏 190/210,000
🛏 250/290,000
🖵 💿 CSi, Visa ✳ 📺
🍸 ♦ 🐕 ✄

Inside an ancient *palazzo* that dates back to the end of the 1600's in the very central and characteristic Marzio quarter, the Portoghesi is a classical hotel with a wonderful atmosphere, very conveniently located for sightseeing.
The rooms are simply furnished, some with period furniture, and have personalised air-conditioning and well-equipped bathrooms. One suite has a terrace. There's also a very pleasant lounge with an adjoining terrace where breakfast is served in the summer.

PRESIDENT
★★★★

ESQUILINO
via E. Filiberto, 173
☎ 06/770121
fax 06/7008740
(800840000
- **Closed:** never
- **Rooms:** 193
🛏 332,000
🛏 480,000
🖳 🖵 all ✳ 📺 sat. 🎣
♦ 🚍 extra ♨ 🍽 🐾
♿ [5]

This comfortable well-equipped hotel is in the vicinity of the church of San Giovanni in Laterano and close to a metro station [the Manzoni stop]. Modern in style, the President offers pleasant communal areas, a cocktail bar, restaurant and well-equipped conference rooms. The guest rooms are quite attractively furnished and comfortable; functional bathrooms are provided with courtesy sets and hairdryers. Shuttle bus service on request.

REGINA BAGLIONI
★★★★★

PINCIANO
via Vittorio Veneto, 72
☎ 06/421111
fax 06/42012130
(800821057
- **Closed:** never
- **Rooms:** 130
🛏 460/550,000
🛏 640/740,000
🖳 🖵 all ✳ 📺 sat. 🎣
🎣 ♦ 🚍 extra ♨
🍽 ♿ [4]

This hotel is located inside one of the most beautiful *palazzi* in Via Veneto and combines modern comfort with marvellous elements of bygone times, like the magnicent column-lined entrance hall with its Art Nouveau staircase leading up to comfortable, inviting guest rooms furnished in early twentieth-century Italian style. Very rationally organised bathrooms are equipped with towel-warmers, magnifying makeup mirrors, hairdryers and generous courtesy sets. The seven suites [all with fax facilities] are glorious. A lavish breakfast is served in the Le Grazie restaurant.

REGNO
★★★

CENTRO STORICO
PANTHEON
via del Corso, 330
☎ 06/6792119
  06/6792162
fax 06/6789239
- **Closed:** never
- **Rooms:** 25
🛏 190/250,000
🛏 240/320,000
🖳 🖵 all ✳ 📺 sat. 🎣
🎣 ♦ 🚍 extra 🐾

This excellently-run, comfortable and *centalissimo* hotel in the heart of the city's shopping district is an ideal place to stay. The guest rooms are attractive and well-furnished; two on the sixth floor have beautiful terraces, four have balconies. The bathrooms are spacious, and almost all have baths as well as hair dryers and courtesy sets. Apart from the buffet breakfast room, communal areas include a TV lounge, snack bar and roof garden with deck-chairs for sunbathing in summer. Staff are extremely courteous and helpful. Special parking permits enable clients to park closeby. Reduced rates for companies.

RICHMOND
★★★

COLOSSEO
l.go C. Ricci, 36
☎ 06/69941256
fax 06/69941454
- **Closed:** never
- **Rooms:** 13
🛏 210,000
🛏 320,000
🖳 🖵 all ✳ 📺 sat. 🎣
🎣 ♦ 🚍 extra
♨ 🐾

This conveniently located hotel has a roof garden with a magnificent view over the Roman Forum where an American-style breakfast is served in summer, and comfortable, attractive rooms with soundproof windows, safes, minibars and trouser presses. Bathrooms offer courtesy sets, hairdryers, towel-warmers, scales, phones and slide-away elastic clothes-drying lines. The singles are slightly more spartan.

RIVOLI
★★★★

PARIOLI
via T. Taramelli, 7
☎ 06/3224042
fax 06/3227373
- **Closed:** never
- **Rooms:** 59
🛏 180/260,000
🛏 210/360,000
🖳 🖵 all ✳ 📺 sat. 🎣
🎣 ♦ 🅿 ♨ 🍽

In a tranquil area just a short walk away from the Villa Borghese gardens, this hotel offers reasonably comfortable, unostentatious but attractive guest rooms and well-equipped bathrooms; meeting rooms, an inviting bar area, grill room and garden. Laundry service; experienced, courteous staff.

ROME CAVALIERI HILTON
★★★★★ L

BALDUINA
via A. Cadlolo, 101
☎ 06/35091
fax 06/35092241
(800878346
- **Closed:** never
- **Rooms:** 376
🛏 525/700,000
🛏 700/875,000
🖳 extra 🖵 all ✳
📺 sat. 🎣 🎣 🅿
🚍 extra 🏊 🌳 ♨ 🍽
🐾 ♿

In a wonderfully panoramic position, this modern hotel complex boasts one of the biggest conference centres in the city. There's also space for two bars, two excellent restaurants [La Pergola and Il Giardino dell'Uliveto], a banqueting room, bank, travel agency, car rental services, and various shops. The guest rooms are all the same size except for the spacious Executive Floor suites which have their own concierges and secretarial services. The decor is quietly elegant, and marble bathrooms have baths, phones, hairdryers and small courtesy sets. Sporting facilities include tennis courts, jogging, a swimming pool, a garden with playground facilities and a fitness centre.

SLEEPING

LA ROVERE
★★★
VATICANO
v.lo Sant'Onofrio, 4/5
☎ 06/68806739
fax 06/68807062
• **Closed:** never
• **Rooms:** 18
🛏 160/240,000
🛏 200/300,000
💳 CSi, DC, Visa ✳
📺 sat. 🍷 ❄ ♦ ♥

🏨 Inside an ancient Roman *palazzetto* in a very central position on the edge of the Trastevere quarter but strategically close to both the Vatican and Piazza Navona, this little hotel has a pleasant atmosphere, attractive, cosy communal areas, a breakfast bar, tastefully-decorated guest rooms with personal safes and well-appointed bathrooms with courtesy sets, hairdryers and towel-warmers. The owners are friendly and courteous.

RUBINO
★★
TERMINI
via Milazzo, 3
☎ 06/4452323
06/4958232
fax 06/4454251
• **Closed:** never
• **Rooms:** 11
🛏 80/120,000
🛏 120/180,000
💳 all ✳ 📺 sat. ❄
🚌 extra 🐕

🏨 This hotel, on the second and third floors of a late 19th century building close to Termini Station, has a small lobby and very comfortable rooms. One has no bathroom, and three have only showers, but the others all have complete ensuite bathrooms. There's an extra charge of L. 20,000 per day for air-conditioning. The owners also manage the very similar Alvisini Hotel on the fifth floor of the same building which offers another ten rooms. Special arrangement with a nearby garage.

SAN GIUSTO
★★★
PIAZZA BOLOGNA
p.zza Bologna, 58
☎ 06/44244598
fax 06/44244583
• **Closed:** never
• **Rooms:** 73
🛏 65/200,000
🛏 105/300,000
💳 all 📺 sat. 🍷 ❄
♦ 🅿 🍴

Not far from Villa Torlonia and Tiburtina Station, and very close to the metro, this unassuming hotel has a small reception and TV lounge area, a breakfast room, restaurant and guest rooms with rather old-fashioned decor. The bathrooms offer either bath or shower, small courtesy sets and, in most cases, hairdryers [which can otherwise be had from reception]. There's also a bar, a small *taverna* and a terrace.

SANT'ANNA
★★★
VATICANO
borgo Pio, 133
☎ 06/68801602
fax 06/68308717
• **Closed:** never
• **Rooms:** 20
🛏 200/250,000
🛏 220/350,000
💳 all ✳ 📺 sat. 🍷
❄ 🅿 🚌 extra 🐕
🦽 [2] ♥

🏨 This small, picturesque hotel is close to the Vatican and well-linked to the rest of the city by public transport. All the communal areas are welcoming and decorated with careful attention to detail. The guest rooms are tranquil and comfortable, the doubles can often sleep three or four people, and the singles have European-size double beds. All are tastefully-furnished with personal safes; bathrooms are attractively finished with courtesy sets, hairdryers and makeup mirrors. There's a very pretty breakfast room and internal garden. Courteous professional staff.

SANT'ANSELMO
★★★
AVENTINO
p.zza di Sant'Anselmo, 2
☎ 06/5783214
fax 06/5783604
• **Closed:** never
• **Rooms:** 45
🛏 190,000
🛏 290,000
💳 extra 📺 all 📺 🅿 🦽

🏨 On the Aventine Hill, in one of Rome's most beautiful quarters, this hotel inside an early twentieth century *palazzetto* is immersed in tranquil, peaceful greenery. The pleasant guest rooms are all different in shape and size, and some offer panoramic views across the city; the bathrooms are not exactly huge, but equally comfortable. Breakfast is served under shady orange trees in the garden in summer.

SANTA CHIARA
★★★
CENTRO STORICO
PANTHEON
via di Santa Chiara, 21
☎ 06/6872979
fax 06/6873144
• **Closed:** never
• **Rooms:** 98
🛏 250/285,000
🛏 300/396,000
💳 all ✳ 📺 sat. 🍷
♦ 🦽 🦽 [1]

🏨 This elegant, *centralissimo* hotel has a very pleasant atmosphere and is decorated in excellent taste, whether it be the communal areas, the guest rooms or the seven spacious, luminous suites. Many of the rooms have kept their ancient ceiling beams, others have pretty sloping roofs, and bathrooms are comfortable with courtesy sets and hairdryers. The hotel also offers three small apartments with well-equipped kitchens and terraces. Lavish buffet breakfast.

SANTA COSTANZA
★★★
PIAZZA BOLOGNA
v.le XXI Aprile, 4
☎ 06/8600602
fax 06/8600786
• **Closed:** never
• **Rooms:** 50
🛏 170/300,000
🛏 240/450,000
💳 all ✳ 📺 sat. 🍷
♦ 🚌 🦽 🐕 🦽 [2]

🏨 One of the best hotels in the area, the Santa Costanza is well-run, well-linked to the centre and very attractively decorated. It offers facilities for conferences, meetings and receptions, a little multi-level garden and a cocktail bar. Breakfast is quite lavish. The guest rooms [six are non-smoking] are pleasantly furnished with well-equipped bathrooms. For leisure moments there's the Sant'Agnese sports club not far from the hotel.

SANTA PRASSEDE
★★

ESQUILINO
via di S. Prassede, 25
☎ *06/4814850*
fax 06/4746859
• **Closed:** never
• **Rooms:** 25
🛏 60/150,000
🛏 100/200,000
🍷 📷 all 📷 🍷 ⁉
🚗 extra 🐴

This pleasant, comfortable hotel is inside an ancient *palazzo* opposite the Church of Santa Maria Maggiore, only five minutes away from Termini Station. It offers its clientele tastefully-furnished, air-conditioned rooms with well-equipped ensuite bathrooms. Breakfast is served in a small dining room with a little bar; there's a TV lounge, laundry service and a centralised safe. Bookings can be made at reception for guided tours and excursions.

SELECT GARDEN
★★★

PIAZZA BOLOGNA
via V. Bachelet, 6
☎ *06/4456383*
fax 06/4441086
• **Closed:** never
• **Rooms:** 19
🛏 150/275,000
🛏 180/350,000
🍷 📷 all 📷 🍷 ⁉

Located halfway between the *Città Universitaria* [Rome's oldest university campus] and Termini Station and close to the principal government offices, this hotel is inside a small, tranquil early 20th-century villa with a garden. The building has been completely renovated in modern style; the rooms are all comfortable and very attractively decorated, with air-conditioning and personal safes; the bathrooms are adequate with courtesy sets and hairdryers provided. Special arrangements with restaurants and a garage. Very professional staff.

SHANGRI LÀ CORSETTI
★★★★

EUR
v.le Algeria, 141
☎ *06/5916441*
fax 06/5413813
• **Closed:** never
• **Rooms:** 52
🛏 232/270,000
🛏 316/371,000
🍷 📷 all 📷 🍷 ⁉
📷 📷 📷
📷 ⁉ [6]

In three elegant little buildings in the green, pine-dotted Eur quarter, this is one of the few appealing hotel complexes in the area, with a famous restaurant open to the public offering much better than average cuisine. The communal areas are attractively decorated, and the comfortable guest rooms have small terraces, safes, and ensuite bathrooms with hairdryers and courtesy sets. There are three swimming pools, one of them heated, conference and reception rooms, a bar, piano bar and discoteque.

SHERATON ROMA
★★★★

EUR
v.le del Pattinaggio, 100
☎ *06/54531*
fax 06/5940813
📞 800790524
• **Closed:** never
• **Rooms:** 637
🛏 383/480,000
🛏 487/582,000
🍷 📷 📷 📷 🍷 ⁉
📷 📷 📷 [1]

A modern hotel complex situated in a green tranquil area, the Sheraton is particularly well-organised for groups, congresses, banquets and receptions in general, with an open-air swimming pool, tennis and squash courts, jogging pathways and a gym available for guests. The functionally-furnished rooms vary in size; the bathrooms all offer hairdryers and courtesy sets. Special rates available for companies.

SIENA
★★★

CENTRO STORICO - SPAGNA
via di Sant'Andrea delle Fratte, 33
☎ *06/6796121*
fax 06/6787509
• **Closed:** variabili
• **Rooms:** 21
🛏 190/230,000
🛏 260/310,000
🍷 📷 all 📷 🍷 ⁉ ♦
🚗 🐴

This little hotel is in an extraordinarily good position, just a few metres away from the Spanish Steps but in a quiet street. The rooms, with parquet floors and pale wood furniture, offer every comfort; the bathrooms, though not very big, have hairdryers and courtesy sets. Continental buffet breakfast; laundry

service. Courteous, helpful staff.

SISTINA
★★★

CENTRO STORICO - SPAGNA
via Sistina, 136
☎ *06/4744176*
06/4818804
fax 06/4818867
• **Closed:** never
• **Rooms:** 26
🛏 100/260,000
🛏 145/380,000
🍷 📷 all 📷 sat. 🍷
⁉ ♦ 🚗

A pleasant hotel in a very central position with a large luminous foyer and a very pleasant terrace with bar service on the top floor. The soundproof guest rooms are decorated in muted colours with wall-to-wall carpets and spacious, well-equipped bathrooms. Polite, friendly staff.

SOFITEL ROMA
★★★★

PINCIANO
via Lombardia, 47
☎ *06/478021*
fax 06/4821019
• **Closed:** never
• **Rooms:** 113
🛏 410/520,000
🛏 700/900,000
🍷 📷 AE, CSi, Visa
📷 📷 sat. 🍷 ⁉
♦ 📷 🚗 extra ⁉ 📷
🐴 ⁉ [1]

Conveniently located close to Via Veneto and the Spanish Steps and not far from the metro, this beautiful hotel with its professional staff and facilities deserves its four-star listing. The guest rooms are soundproof and very attractively decorated with pay TV and well-equipped bathrooms. A beautiful panoramic terrace, a bar, meeting rooms and business facilities [fax, photocopies, etc.] are available for guests.

SOLE AL BISCIONE
★★
CENTRO STORICO
CAMPO DE' FIORI
via del Biscione, 76
☎ 06/68806873
fax 06/6893787
• **Closed:** never
• **Rooms:** 60
⚊ 105/130,000
⚊ 140/210,000
🛏 no 📱 ✦ 🅿 🚗

🛎 This *centralissimo* hotel has recently been further improved and offers hospitality and atmosphere reminiscent of times gone by: the sitting room is like an old-fashioned parlour with a sideboard, a sewing machine and a table in the centre. The highest of their three terraces looks out over ancient Roman rooftops, and the other two garden areas on the second and third floors are very pleasant. Ten guest rooms have cable TV and more than half have ensuite bathrooms [the prices quoted above refer to them].

SPRING HOUSE
★★★
TRIONFALE
via Mocenigo, 7
☎ 06/39720948
fax 06/39721047
• **Closed:** never
• **Rooms:** 51
⚊ 150/350,000
⚊ 170/400,000
🍽 📱 all ✳ 📱 sat. 🍷
🍴 ✦ 🅿
🚗 extra 🐕

🛎 Close to St. Peter's and the metro, this is a very attractive and well-run hotel with particularly courteous staff. The communal areas are pleasant and inviting and the guest rooms are continually being upgraded, with personal safes and attractively decorated bathrooms with hairdryers and courtesy sets. A buffet breakfast is served in an agreeable little dining room and the principal daily papers are available at the reception desk. There's also an airport shuttle bus, a bookings service for museums and bicycles.

STARHOTEL METROPOLE
★★★★
TERMINI
via Principe Amedeo, 3
☎ 06/4774
fax 06/4740413
📞 800860200
• **Closed:** never
• **Rooms:** 265
⚊ 295/370,000
⚊ 395/495,000
🍽 📱 all ✳ 📱 sat. 🍷
🍴 ✦ 🚗 🐾 🍴
🐕 ♿

🛎 This hotel is located close to Termini Station and offers spacious communal areas including a pleasant bar, a restaurant open to the public, conference and meeting rooms and a little boutique. The guest rooms are soundproof and very attractively decorated; the Executives are the best and the most expensive. Bathrooms offer courtesy sets and hairdryers. There's an Internet link, gift shop and laundry service available for guests.

TEATRO DI POMPEO
★★★
CENTRO STORICO
CAMPO DE' FIORI
l.go del Pallaro, 8
☎ 06/68300170
fax 06/68805531
• **Closed:** never
• **Rooms:** 13
⚊ 270,000
⚊ 350,000
🍽 extra 📱 all ✳
📱 sat. 🍷 🍴 ✦ ♿ [1]

🛎 In the heart of the *centro storico*, this little hotel offers professional, courteous hospitality in a friendly atmosphere. The semi-circular form of Pompey's ancient theatre can still be seen in the shape of the breakfast room and the small meeting room. Beautifully decorated guest rooms, some with coffered, others with sloping ceilings, and exemplary bathrooms equipped with hairdryers and courtesy sets. An excellent buffet breakfast is served between 7am and 10am.

TIRRENO
★★★
MONTI
via San Martino ai Monti, 17
☎ 06/4880778
fax 06/4884095
• **Closed:** never
• **Rooms:** 48
⚊ 60/290,000
⚊ 90/360,000
🍽 📱 all ✳ 📱 sat. 🍷
🍴 ✦ 🅿 🚗 extra

🛎 Conveniently situated in the heart of the old *centro storico*, between the church of Santa Maria Maggiore and the Colosseum in an ancient building which has just been completely renovated,

the Tirreno offers comfortable, simply-furnished rooms with safes [some also have a little terrace] and attractive, well-equipped bathrooms. There's a cocktail bar, a garden for sun-bathing, pleasant communal areas and a breakfast room.

TIZIANO
★★★
CENTRO STORICO
ARGENTINA
c.so V. Emanuele II, 110
☎ 06/6865019
fax 06/6865019
• **Closed:** never
• **Rooms:** 52
⚊ 150/280,000
⚊ 200/350,000
🍽 📱 all ✳ 📱 sat. 🍷
🍴 ✦ 🅿 🚗 🐾 🍴 🐕
♿ [2]

🛎 This is quite a comfortable hotel, just a few steps away from Largo Argentina. All guest rooms have double-glazing, a fire-alarm system and ensuite bathrooms with hairdryers, and on the third floor there's a tiny apartment with a little terrace. Lavish buffet breakfast; both the breakfast room and the restaurant are very pleasant. Extremely courteous staff.

TRE STELLE
★★★
TERMINI
via San Martino della Battaglia, 11
☎ 06/4463095
fax 06/4468229
• **Closed:** never
• **Rooms:** 42
⚊ 135/150,000
⚊ 160/180,000
🍽 📱 all ✳ 📱 sat. 🍷
🍴 ✦ 🅿 🐾 ♿ [4]

Inside an old building dating back to the nineteenth century, this hotel is conveniently located, just a few minutes away from Termini Station and well-linked to the centre by public transport. It offers pleasant, attractively-decorated communal areas, functionally-furnished rooms with safes, bathrooms with hairdryers, a bar and a laundry service.

TREVI
★★★
CENTRO STORICO - TRITONE
v.lo del Babuccio, 20/21
☎ 06/6789563
06/6785894
fax 06/69941407
• **Closed:** never
• **Rooms:** 19
🛏 180/260,000
🛏 220/340,000
🍽 🖥 all ✳ 📺 🍷 🍴 ♦ 🚐 extra

This hotel inside a beautiful ancient *palazzetto* just a couple of steps away from the *famosissima* piazza of the same name offers very attractive communal areas and tastefully-decorated guest rooms with safes and piped-in music. Four have coffered ceilings and independent entrances, and the bathrooms are very comfortable and well-equipped. Special arrangement with a nearby garage. A buffet breakfast is served among the flowers on the roof garden in summer.

TRITONE
★★★
CENTRO STORICO - TRITONE
via del Tritone, 210
☎ 06/69922575
fax 06/6782624
• **Closed:** never
• **Rooms:** 43
🛏 220/350,000
🛏 350/450,000
🍽 🖥 all ✳ 📺 sat. 🍴 ♦

In *centralissima* Via del Tritone, this hotel has a miniscule reception area at the top of a small flight of stairs. Daily papers and magazines are available in the adjacent hall. The rooms are pretty and offer all the necessary comforts; the bathrooms are a bit on the small side but comfortable, with courtesy sets and hairdryers. There's a very pleasant glassed-in breakfast room with a view across ancient Roman rooftops, and a summer roof garden.

TURNER
★★★
PINCIANO
via Nomentana, 29
☎ 06/44250077
fax 06/44250165
• **Closed:** never
• **Rooms:** 51
🛏 195/309,000
🛏 240/409,000
🍽 🖥 all ✳ 📺 sat. 🍷 🍴 ♦ 🚐 extra 🛗 ♿ [1] ❤

This delightful and extremely well-run hotel is located close to Porta Pia, inside a late 19th century *palazzo*. Its name is an act of homage to the illustrious English painter. The communal areas are elegant and welcoming, starting with the entrance hall; the breakfast room, with a small adjacent bar, offers an excellent morning buffet. The rooms are comfortable and beautifully

decorated, and all have double-glazing, satellite TV, a VCR and video library. Bathrooms offer complete courtesy sets and hairdryers. Their most recent innovation is a suite with a two-person Jacuzzi and antique furniture. Special arrangements with restaurants and shops. Discounts for regular clients and our readers.

UNIVERSO
★★★★
TERMINI
via Principe Amedeo, 5/B
☎ 06/476811
fax 06/4745125
📞 800840000
• **Closed:** never
• **Rooms:** 20
🛏 332,000
🛏 480,000
🍽 🖥 all ✳ 📺 sat. 🍴 ♦ 🚐 extra 🛗 🍴 🐾 ♿ [5]

In the vicinity of the Teatro dell'Opera and Termini Station, this modern, well-equipped hotel offers a high level of comfort: spacious, luminous communal areas, two restaurants, a cocktail bar, a congress centre, rather comfortable, functionally-furnished rooms and well-equipped bathrooms. There's a hotel bus service available on request.

VALADIER
★★★★
CENTRO STORICO - POPOLO
via della Fontanella, 15
☎ 06/3611998
fax 06/3201558
• **Closed:** never
• **Rooms:** 50
🛏 230/410,000
🛏 280/560,000
🍽 🖥 all ✳ 📺 sat. 🍷 🍴 ♦ 🚐 extra 🛗 🍴 🐾

In a historic old building in a very central position, the Valadier has a foyer and communal areas decorated in rather unusual taste, and very comfortable rooms and suites with electronic passkeys and safes; the marble bathrooms are rather small but have phones, hairdryers and courtesy sets. There are three conference rooms, a business centre, bar, piano bar, pizzeria and a restaurant - Il Valentino - open to the public. A continental breakfast is served in a delightful little dining room. They also have a panoramic roof garden which is extremely pleasant in summer. Special rates for weekends.

VALLE
★★★
ESQUILINO
via Cavour, 134
☎ 06/4815736
fax 06/4885837
• **Closed:** never
• **Rooms:** 33
🛏 240/260,000
🛏 325/345,000
🍽 🖥 all ✳ 📺 🍷 🍴 ♦ 🅿 🚐 extra 🛗 ♿ [2]

In the Esquilino quarter, in a conveniently central position, this hotel offers high level hospitality: an elegant, welcoming foyer, a breakfast room, a small meeting room with fax, photocopier and interpreter service, and attractively-decorated, comfortable guest rooms with complimentary newspapers on arrival, tasteful furniture, safes and trouser presses. Functional bathrooms are equipped with hairdryers and courtesy sets. We can recommend their nearby Residence Monti, with its six beautifully refurbished mini-appartments - ideal for longer stays. Room service for meals and snacks. Staff are always courteous and helpful.

VENETO
★★★
PINCIANO
via Piemonte, 63
☎ *06/487801*
fax 06/42814583
(800277470
• **Closed:** never
• **Rooms:** 97
⚏ 140/180,000
⚏ 200/240,000
⚌ 🗔 all ✳ 🗂 sat. ♟
🍽 ⅋ 🚗 ♦
🍴 ⅋ [1]

This welcoming hotel in a convenient central location well-served by public transport offers pleasant, functional communal areas and attractive guest rooms, mostly decorated with fabric wallpaper and wall-to-wall carpets [but they also have rooms with tiled floors and painted walls for allergy-sufferers]. Rational bathrooms with hairdryers and courtesy sets. Garage parking. A continental breakfast is served in a dining room that is part of the panoramic roof garden restaurant.

VENEZIA
★★★
TERMINI
via Varese, 18
☎ *06/4457101*
06/4463714
fax 06/4957687
• **Closed:** never
• **Rooms:** 60
⚏ 165/312,000
⚏ 219/345,000
⚌ 🗔 all ✳ 🗂 sat. ♟
🍽 ⅋

In a nineteenth-century building close to Termini Station, this welcoming hotel has a wonderful atmosphere. The communal areas are beautifully cared-for and mostly furnished with items from 17th-century churches. The spacious, tastefully-furnished rooms offer every comfort, including personal safes, piped-in music and impeccable, lavishly-equipped bathrooms. A very attractive buffet breakfast; coffee bar. Polite, friendly, efficient staff.

VILLA DEL PARCO
★★★
PINCIANO
via Nomentana, 110
☎ *06/44237773*
fax 06/44237572
• **Closed:** never
• **Rooms:** 30
⚏ 215,000
⚏ 300,000
⚌ 🗔 all ✳ 🗂 sat. ♟
🍽 ⅋ 🚗 extra
🐕 ♥

This pleasant late-nineteenth century villa has been run by the same family for decades. The relaxation and conversation areas are welcoming and decorated in English style; breakfast is served outside in the garden in summer. Small snacks are available at any time, also in guests' rooms, and this provides a very pleasant sense of being looked after. The rooms are spacious and very tastefully decorated; well-appointed bathrooms offer hairdryers and courtesy sets. Laundry service; an air and rail booking service. Experienced, courteous staff.

VILLA FLORENCE
★★★
PINCIANO
via Nomentana, 28
☎ *06/4403036*
fax 06/4402709
• **Closed:** never
• **Rooms:** 33
⚏ 200/250,000
⚏ 220/300,000
⚌ 🗔 all ✳ 🗂 ♟ 🍽 ♦
♿ [3]

This pretty, tranquil hotel in a beautiful Art Nouveau villa has a veranda, a garden and very attractive communal areas. Guest rooms are decorated with antique furniture and offer various amenities, including trouser presses, and each one is different. Bathrooms have either bath or shower, with hairdryers and courtesy sets provided. Continental breakfast. Discounts available for weekends and off-season.

VILLA GLORI
★★★
FLAMINIO
v.le del Vignola, 28
☎ *06/3227658*
fax 06/3219495
• **Closed:** never
• **Rooms:** 57
⚏ 260,000
⚏ 350,000
⚌ 🗔 all ✳ 🗂 sat. ♟
🍽 ⅋ 🚗 extra

Not far from the centre and well connected by public transport, Villa Glori is a beautifully-kept hotel in an unusual little street with a rather English atmosphere. It offers spacious communal areas and comfortable rooms with piped-in music, personal safes and modern furniture. Bathrooms are functional with courtesy sets. A continental buffet breakfast is served in the dining room and there's a small bar.

VILLA GRAZIOLI
★★★
PARIOLI
via Salaria, 241
☎ *06/8416587*
fax 06/8413385
• **Closed:** never
• **Rooms:** 30
⚏ 205,000
⚏ 270,000
⚌ 🗔 all ✳ 🗂 sat. ♟
🍽 ⅋ 🅿 ♥

A very pretty period villa has been adapted to create this pleasant hotel in a strategic position - situated in a green and tranquil area not far from the centre but easily reached by freeway. It offers its clientele well-furnished rooms fitted with personal safes and attractive bathrooms with hairdryers and towel-warmers, a bar, relaxed and cosy communal areas, and laundry service.

VILLA MANGILI
★★★

PARIOLI
via G. Mangili, 31
☎ *06/3217130*
fax 06/3224313
• **Closed:** never
• **Rooms:** 11
70/160,000
80/250,000
all ✳ 🛎 ♥ ⛲
🚗 extra 🐕

This hotel, in a tranquil street in the elegant Parioli quarter, is inside a small *palazzina* surrounded by greenery with a pleasantly discreet atmosphere. The double rooms are quite cosy, while some of the singles are rather spartan; the not very big bathrooms all have showers. Breakfast is served in the garden in summer.

VILLA PORPORA
★★

PINCIANO
via N. Porpora, 15
☎ *06/8554521*
fax 06/8542433
• **Closed:** never
• **Rooms:** 36
145,000
185,000
all 🛎 ♥ ♦ ⛲ 🐕

In a quiet street just a very short walk away from the Villa Borghese gardens, this hotel is an excellent place to stay at reasonable prices. The rooms and bathrooms are plain and unadorned; some have small fridges. The owners have another hotel in the same category a few hundred yards away, the Paisello [47,Via G. Paisello;

phone 06/8554531] more suited to groups and school trippers.

VILLA SAN LORENZO MARIA
★★★

SAN LORENZO
via dei Liguri, 7
☎ *06/4469988*
fax 06/4957378
• **Closed:** never
• **Rooms:** 40
130/170,000
180/260,000
AE, CSi, Visa ✳ 🛎 ♦ 🅿 🍴 🐕 ♿ [2]

In the heart of the characteristic San Lorenzo quarter close to the University, this hotel is in an agreeable *palazzetto* with well-designed spaces and a little garden that acts as a carpark in the evenings. There's a second garden in the internal courtyard. Guest rooms are modern and luminous, decorated in various styles with functional bathrooms equipped with hairdryers and towel-warmers. The restaurant is available to groups only, and you need to book in advance.

VILLA SAN PIO
★★★

AVENTINO
via di Sant'Anselmo, 19
☎ *06/5743547*
fax 06/5783604
• **Closed:** never
• **Rooms:** 54
190,000
90/290,000
all ✳ 🛎 sat. ♥ ♦ 🅿 ⛲ ♿ [2]

In the heart of one of the city's most tranquil, green and pleasant quarters, the Villa San Pio is a

pretty *palazzetto* surrounded by plants and flowers where you can thoroughly enjoy the peaceful, relaxing atmosphere of the Aventine Hill. Reception formalities and all guests' needs are handled by the Sant'Anselmo hotel [see above]. The Villa offers tasteful decor and comfortable bathrooms; it also has an elevator and a garden where you can eat outside in the morning on a very pleasant veranda extension off the breakfast room. Some of the rooms have independent entrances from the garden.

VILLA SPADA
★★★

NUOVO SALARIO
via M. E. Bettini, 20
☎ *06/8800723*
fax 06/8819638
• **Closed:** never
• **Rooms:** 24
120/160,000
160/190,000
AE, CSi, Visa ✳ 🛎 ⛲ 🅿 ⛲ 🍴 🐕 ♿ [3]

In a beautiful position on a little hill with a panoramic view, a little way out of the city, Villa Spada is a small, tranquil hotel, despite being close to the Grande Raccordo Anulare [Rome's ring road]. It's linked to the centre by a convenient train service [the *trenino*]. The rooms, decorated in various styles, are clean and spacious; all bathrooms have showers, hairdryers and courtesy sets. The Villa Spada restaurant adjoining has a vast banqueting room.

VILLA TORLONIA
★★★

PIAZZA BOLOGNA
via B. Eustachio, 3-5-7/A
☎ *06/4402630*
fax 06/4402637
• **Closed:** never
• **Rooms:** 81
280,000
350,000
all ✳ 🛎 sat. ♥ ⛲ ♦ 🚗 ⛲

This cosy hotel is located in a particularly pleasant, tranquil part of Rome, close to the historic Villa of the same name [former residence of Mussolini, now a public park]. It's composed of two adjacent buildings linked by a veranda. On the ground floor there's a bar, a conference room, two breakfast rooms and a meeting room. The guest rooms are of various kinds, sunny and attractively decorated with air-conditioning and every comfort; bathrooms have courtesy sets and hairdryers. Staff are efficient and courteous.

VILLAFRANCA
★★★

TERMINI
via Villafranca, 9
☎ *06/4440364*
fax 06/44700857
📞 800820080
• **Closed:** never
• **Rooms:** 70
150/200,000
200/300,000
all ✳ 🛎 sat. ♥ ⛲ ♦ 🚗 extra

Well connected to the centre by public transport, the Villafranca is a pleasant hotel with courteous, efficient staff. The communal areas, conversation lounges and tiny bar are attractive and very well-kept; the rooms [also non-smoking] are cosy and well-furnished; bathrooms have courtesy sets and hairdryers. Lavish breakfast buffet.

VIMINALE
★★★
ESQUILINO
via C. Balbo, 31
☎ 06/4881910
fax 06/4872018
• **Closed:** never
• **Rooms:** 53
310,000
420,000
all * 📺 sat.
🚗 extra

A tranquil hotel with a view across the rooftops of Santa Prudenziana, one of the city's most ancient churches. Completely renovated, it offers communal areas with lovely Art Nouveau decor and large, well-designed rooms - some have small balconies with a wonderful view over the church; bathrooms offer lavish courtesy sets. There's a bar, a panoramic terrace on the fourth floor and a solarium on the fifth. Excellent continental breakfast buffet.

VIRGILIO
★★★
VIMINALE
via Palermo, 30
☎ 06/4826512
fax 06/4884360
• **Closed:** never
• **Rooms:** 33
150/260,000
200/360,000
all * 📺
🚗

In a central position close to Via Nazionale, conveniently linked to Termini Station and the metro, the Virgilio is a little hotel on two floors. Guest rooms are of varying sizes: all have double-glazing, safes, minibars and modems. The bathrooms are a bit small, but comfortable; all have hairdryers and courtesy sets, and some have Jacuzzis.

WHITE
★★★★
CENTRO STORICO - TRITONE
via in Arcione, 77
☎ 06/6991242
fax 06/6788451
• **Closed:** never
• **Rooms:** 44
350/400,000
450/500,000
all * 📺 sat.
🚗 & [1]

This hotel, situated right in the city centre between Via del Tritone and the Trevi Fountain, is owned by the same proprietors as the Tritone and the Accademia [see reviews]. Completely soundproof, it offers functionally-decorated rooms of various sizes, with well-kept, well-equipped bathrooms. There's a cocktail bar, a meeting room, individual safety deposit boxes and a pay garage available for clients. Buffet breakfast.

OUTSIDE ROME

MIRALAGO
★★
ALBANO LAZIALE [ROME]
via dei Cappuccini, 12
☎ 06/9321018
fax 06/9325335
• **Closed:** never
• **Rooms:** 45
90,000
130,000
extra AE, CSi, Visa 📺 🚗
🍴

In a beautiful panoramic position overlooking Lake Albano, the Miralago is a simple, well-kept hotel with a restaurant equipped for receptions and a garden where guests can dine outside in summer. Rooms are plain with basic accessories and there are communal areas for relaxing. Their facilities include two meeting rooms, a bar and tobacconist's and a billiards room. Cordial, helpful staff.

I DUE LAGHI
★★★★
ANGUILLARA SABAZIA [ROME]
loc. Le Cerque
☎ 06/99607059
fax 06/99607068
• **Closed:** never
• **Rooms:** 32
150/180,000
200/250,000
AE, CSi, Visa *
📺 🚗 🍴 & [1]

This carefully-restored, characteristic old farmhouse on a beautiful rural estate deep in the green countryside between Lake Martignano and Lake Bracciano enjoys a splendid panoramic position. The Due Laghi is a welcoming country house offering ample space for relaxation and innumerable facilities: riding stables with qualified instructors and the opportunity to take courses or go for a leisurely ride; a swimming pool with a pool-side bar, a private lakeside beach, volleyball, tennis, football and basketball, and mountain bikes for hire. They also organise excursions.

There are various kinds of guest rooms, all very comfortable; bathrooms offer minimal courtesy sets and hairdryers. The delightful Junior suites are their most recent innovation. There's also a restaurant open to the public.

MACH 2
★★★
FIUMICINO [ROME]
via Portuense, 2465
☎ 06/6507149
fax 06/6505855
• **Closed:** never
• **Rooms:** 33
139,000
198,000
all * 📺 🚗 🅿
🍴 & [1]

This modern hotel complex in a tranquil position three kilometres away from the Leonardo da Vinci airport offers its clientele comfortable, functionally-decorated rooms with pay TV and personal safes, bathrooms with hairdryers, comfortable communal areas, and a bar. Full or half-pension available. Shuttle bus service for the airport or the centre of Rome.

COLONNA
★★★
FRASCATI [ROME]
p.zza del Gesù, 12
☎ 06/94018088
fax 06/9424900
• **Closed:** never
• **Rooms:** 20
100/120,000
150/180,000
all * 📺 sat.
🚗 extra & [1]

This comfortable, recently-opened hotel in a *palazzo* in the centre

of Frascati has been thoughtfully designed, with special attention paid to high-tech systems.
The rooms are soundproof and comfortable, with tasteful furniture, beautiful fabrics, wall-to-wall carpets and well-equipped bathrooms with either baths or showers.
The little breakfast room where a buffet breakfast is served has a delightful *trompe l'oeil* fresco depicting the ancient Roman villas of Tusculum. Panoramic solarium on the top floor.

EDEN TUSCOLANO
★★

FRASCATI [ROME]
via Tuscolana, 15 [km 18]
☎ 06/9408589
fax 06/9408591
• **Closed:** never
• **Rooms:** 32
🛏 70/95,000
🛏 100/130,000
☛ extra 🖻 all 🛢 🍷 ⫚
🄿 ⚘ ⫙
🐕 ♿ [6]

This cosy, family-run villa is set in an acre and a half of tranquil, green garden park, conveniently located between the Via Tuscolana and Via Anagnina. The rooms are quite comfortable, with small bathrooms equipped with hairdryers and courtesy sets. Continental breakfasts; the restaurant does wonderful banquets. Courteous service.

FLORA
★★★

FRASCATI [ROME]
via Vittorio Veneto, 8
☎ 06/9416110
fax 06/9416546
• **Closed:** never
• **Rooms:** 37
🛏 130/155,000
🛏 170/235,000
☛ extra 🖻 all ✳
🛢 sat. 🍷 ⫚ ⫙ 🄿
⚘ ♥

Inside an old aristocratic summer residence dating back to the end of the nineteenth century and immersed in greenery, this hotel has a charming atmosphere. It offers clients elegantly decorated rooms with closed circuit TV, personal safes and attractively finished bathrooms with towel-warmers, hairdryers and Jacuzzis. The communal areas are welcoming and attractive and there's also a congress centre, bar and laundry service. Well-presented breakfasts.

GIADRINA
★★★

FRASCATI [ROME]
via A. Diaz, 13/15
☎ 06/9419415
fax 06/9420440
• **Closed:** never
• **Rooms:** 29
🛏 100/120,000
🛏 130/150,000
☛ extra 🖻 all
🛢 sat. ⫙ 🄿 ⚘ ⫙
🐕 ♿ [2]

In a convenient central position with a panoramic view, this hotel in a pleasant building offers comfortable, functional rooms and adequately equipped bathrooms. A rather good breakfast is served in the dining room; the price of breakfast is included in the cost of a single room. Guests can also dine at the famous Cacciani restaurant,

one of the best in the area.

POGGIO REGILLO
★★

FRASCATI [ROME]
via di Pietra Porzia, 26 [ex Prataporci]
☎ 06/9417800
fax 06/9422182
• **Closed:** never
• **Rooms:** 25
🛏 50/70,000
🛏 90/120,000
☛ 🖻 AE, CSi, Visa
🛢 🄿

The Poggio Regillo is easy to get to on the Rome-Naples *autostrada* - just take the exit for Monteporzio Catone, follow the directions for Frascati for three kilometres then turn right and keep going for another 1.2 km. The hotel is in what was once a holiday home run by a religious institute in a pleasant, tranquil area surrounded by greenery, and offers simply-furnished, pristine guest rooms, adequate bathrooms, a TV lounge and breakfast room, and a panoramic terrace with deckchairs and umbrellas for sun-bathing. A hotel transport service is available on request.

VILLA TUSCOLANA
★★★★

FRASCATI [ROME]
via del Tuscolo km 1,500
☎ 06/942900
fax 06/9424747
• **Closed:** never
• **Rooms:** 110
🛏 175/280,000
🛏 250/400,000
☛ 🖻 all 🛢 sat. 🍷 ⫚
⫙ 🄿 ⚘ ⫙
🐕 ♿ [1]

In a tranquil position on top of a hill, this villa has a beautiful 18th-century facade designed by Vanvitelli and the lobby is in what were originally the old stables, with vaulted bare-brick ceilings. Well suited to group tours, it offers very attractive tranquil rooms with the original paving and well-equipped bathrooms. There are two restaurants, a gazebo, a games room with billiards and ping-pong tables, and modern conference facilities. Daily papers are on sale at the reception desk and there's a shuttle bus link to Frascati [only 2 km. away].

IL MIRAGGIO
★★

FREGENE [ROME]
v.le Sestri Ponente, 93
☎ 06/66560433
fax 06/66562284
• **Closed:** never
• **Rooms:** 26
🛏 70/90,000
🛏 100/120,000
☛ extra 🖻 all 🛢
🍷 ⫚ 🄿 ⫚ ⫙ ⚲ ⫙
🐕 ♿ [2]

The hotel is set in 500sq m of parkland 200 metres or so from the sea, where it maintains a private beach club with an outdoor swimming pool, restaurant, bar and *tavola calda* as well as facilities for sailing and other nautical sports and tennis. Tranquil, simply-furnished rooms. In summer they run a well-known [and very popular] discoteque.

Villa Fiorita
★★★

FREGENE [ROME]
via Castellammare, 86
☎ 06/66564590
fax 06/66560301
✆ 800220011
• **Closed:** never
• **Rooms:** 40
🛏 90/120,000
🛏 100/150,000
☕ 🖥 AE, CSi, Visa 📺
🍷 🛳 🅿 ♿ 🍽
🐾 ⓖ [2]

Situated right on the main road just a very short way from the beach, this pretty hotel immersed in the green shade of a Mediterranean pine wood has a delightful flower-filled garden set with umbrellas, tables and chairs, attractive welcoming communal areas and tastefully furnished rooms with adequate bathrooms. There's also a restaurant-pizzeria called Stuzzico, which offers economical fixed price menus.

Grand Hotel Villa Florio
★★★★

GROTTAFERRATA [ROME]
v.le Dusmet, 25
☎ 06/94548007
    06/94548008
fax 06/94548009
• **Closed:** never
• **Rooms:** 24
🛏 210,000
🛏 350,000
☕ extra 🖥 all ✱ 📺 🍷
🍷 🅿 🛳 ♿ 🍽
ⓖ [2] 💝

This hotel inside a beautiful, elegant Art Nouveau villa has an entrance area with several conversation corners, a fireplace, a piano bar and a wonderful atmosphere. The guest rooms are

attractively decorated with functional bathrooms complete with courtesy sets and hairdryers. There's a swimming pool immersed in the gaily-coloured vegetation of the English-style garden. Daily newpapers are available to clients in the reception area. The hotel facilities are well-suited to the organisation of receptions and conventions.

Park Villa Ferrata
★★★

GROTTAFERRATA [ROME]
via Tuscolana, 287
☎ 06/94548050
fax 06/94548049
• **Closed:** never
• **Rooms:** 74
🛏 80/130,000
🛏 100/190,000
☕ 🖥 all 📺 🍷 🍴 ♦ 🅿
🚗 🛳 ✂ ♿
🍽 ⓖ [2]

Immersed in the greenery of a large park with a swimming pool and a gazebo for outdoor lunches, this hotel complex has two modular conference rooms and four large restaurant dining rooms furnished in warm and inviting modern style. The guest rooms are cosy, especially those in the annexe, with balconies and personal safes. Lavish buffet breakfast; a shuttle bus service to Frascati and/or Rome, and medical assistence for clients from June to September.

Park Villa Grazioli
★★★★

GROTTAFERRATA [ROME]
via U. Pavoni, 19
☎ 06/945400
fax 06/9413506
• **Closed:** never
• **Rooms:** 58
🛏 280/370,000
🛏 330/420,000
☕ 🖥 all ✱ 📺 sat. 🍷
🍷 ♦ 🅿 ♿ 🍽 🐾
ⓖ [3] 💝

This splendid 16th-century villa has frescoes of such rare beauty they're protected by the Italian National Trust. Surrounded by exquisite Italian-style gardens, with 15,000 sq m of centuries-old parkland and a magnificent terrace with a view across Rome and the Castelli Romani, it offers elegant sitting rooms, congress facilities, well-furnished, comfortable guest rooms and bathrooms with towel-warmers, lavish courtesy sets and hairdryers. The adjoining Acquaviva restaurant also organises banquets. Buffet breakfast. Shuttle bus for Rome and Fiumicino Airport.

La Posta Vecchia
★★★★★ L

LADISPOLI [ROME]
loc. Palo Laziale
☎ 06/9949501
fax 06/9949507
• **Closed:** variabili
• **Rooms:** 17
🛏 775/2,380,000
☕ 🖥 all ✱ 📺 sat. 🍴
♦ 🅿 🛳 ✂ 🏊 ♿
🍽 💝

Built in 1640 to a design by the architect Vanvitelli, La

Posta Vecchia has been in the course of time a guest house, a way station for travellers, a *locanda,* and since 1965 the property of millionaire Paul Getty. The ruins of a Roman villa dating back to the fourth century BC which came to light during the restoration work deepen the spell of its charm. The stunningly elegant communal areas are decorated with antique furniture and valuable works of art, and the luxurious guest rooms each have something special that makes them quite unique. The bathrooms in pink or Carrara marble are impeccably equipped. There's also a swimming pool, private beach, restaurant, a private museum and a heliport.

Grand Hotel Helio Cabala
★★★★

MARINO [ROME]
via Spinabella, 13/15
☎ 06/93661235
fax 06/93661125
• **Closed:** never
• **Rooms:** 50
🛏 170/190,000
🛏 230/270,000
☕ 🖥 all ✱ 📺 sat. 🍷
🍴 ♦ 🅿 🛳 ♿ 🍽 🐾
ⓖ [1]

In a beautiful panoramic position, this hotel complex has a sunlit foyer that looks out onto a pretty belvedere decorated with fountains and garden tables. Large, comfortable guest rooms have beautful

bathrooms equipped with hairdryers and complete courtesy sets. Lavish, well-presented buffet breakfast.
There's a swimming pool for clients and in summer you can dine beside it by candlelight. Special arrangements with a local golf course and tennis courts; two conference rooms. The Il Platina restaurant specialises in banquets and receptions.

LA CHIOCCIOLA
AGRITURISMO
ORTE [VITERBO]
loc. Seripola
☎ *0761/402734*
fax 0761/402734
• **Closed:** 20-1/10-2
• **Rooms:** 8
🛏 105/115,000
🛏 150/160,000
🍽 🗎 CSi, POS, Visa
❄ 🅿 ⚒ 🕪 ❤

🛈 Take the Orte exit off the A1 Rome-Florence *autostrada*, then turn left in the direction of the city of Orte. After roughly three kilometres turn right for Amelia, keep going for another 300 metres, then turn left into the road that leads to Penne in Teverina.
Three more kilometres and you'll find the little road that leads to La Chiocciola on your left. This enchanting country house has guest rooms furnished in exquisite taste where attention has been paid to every last detail. There's a TV lounge, billiards, a swimming pool and

restaurant. Excellent breakfasts. They also organise trekking expeditions - on foot, by mountain bike or on horseback.

KURSAAL 2000
★★★
OSTIA [ROME]
via Isabella di Castiglia, 7
☎ *06/56470616*
fax 06/56470547
📞 *800652828*
• **Closed:** never
• **Rooms:** 39
🛏 100,000
🛏 125,000
🍽 extra 🗎 all
📺 sat. 🍽 🕪 ♦ 🅿 ⚒
🕪 ♿

A comfortable, economical hotel just a few metres from the sea, and well linked to Rome and the airport. There's a pleasant garden in front furnished for relaxation and well-equipped guest rooms of various kinds decorated in nautical style – they also have safes, and functional bathrooms with all the necessary comforts. Among the facilities at clients' disposal there's a restaurant, bar, terraces and a roof garden.

TIRRENIA
★★★
OSTIA [ROME]
Ostia Lido lungomare Paolo Toscanelli, 74
☎ *06/56304192*
fax 06/56324850
• **Closed:** never
• **Rooms:** 11
🛏 80/120,000
🛏 130/160,000
🍽 extra 🗎 all
📺 sat. 🕪 🅿

🛈 This traditional and rather austerely appointed hotel is in an ancient *palazzo* that has been modernised inside. It offers light-filled, panoramic guest rooms with simple furnishings and functional bathrooms with all the necessites. The communal areas are very attractive, especially the restaurant dining room.

EUROPA
★★★
ROCCA DI PAPA [ROME]
p.zza della Repubblica, 20/21
☎ *06/9498652*
fax 06/94749361
• **Closed:** 1-30/11
• **Rooms:** 38
🛏 80/130,000
🛏 90/150,000
🍽 🗎 CSi, Visa 🕪 ♦
🅿 ⚒ 🕪 🐴 🚗

🛈 This traditional and rather austerely appointed hotel is in an ancient *palazzo* that has been modernised inside. It offers light-filled, panoramic guest rooms with simple furnishings and functional bathrooms with all the necessites. The communal areas are very attractive, especially the restaurant dining room.

GRAND HOTEL DUCA D'ESTE
★★★★
TIVOLI [ROME]
loc. Bagni di Tivoli via Tiburtina Valeria, 330
☎ *0774/3883*
fax 0774/388101
📞 *800864119*
• **Closed:** never
• **Rooms:** 180
🛏 200/250,000
🛏 300/400,000
🍽 🗎 all ❄ 📺 sat. 🍽
🕪 ♦ 🅿 🚗 ⚒ ♪ ⚒
🕪 ♿

🛈 This comfortable hotel close to the thermal spa baths has efficient conference facilities and a grand room for special events like exhibitions, fashion shows, presentations, and conventions. Very attractively decorated guest rooms offer all modern comforts; bathrooms have complete courtesy sets and hairdryers; the suites have Jacuzzis. There are three restaurants ideal for banquets, one near the open-air swimming pool. There's also an indoor pool, tennis court, gym, sauna, Turkish baths and beauty salon.

SIRENE
★★★★
TIVOLI [ROME]
p.zza Massimo, 4
☎ *0774/330605*
fax 0774/330608
• **Closed:** never
• **Rooms:** 40
🛏 140/180,000
🛏 180/260,000
🍽 🗎 all ❄ 📺 sat. 🍽
🕪 ♦ 🅿 ⚒ 🕪 🐴 🚗

🛈 Conveniently located in a restored 19th-century villa just a short walk away from the Villa d'Este, this hotel is famous because it was the first one in the world to put in electric lighting. It has a bar, pleasant communal areas, a restaurant with panoramic terraces and cosy rooms with well-equipped ensuite bathrooms. Polite, helpful staff.

glossary

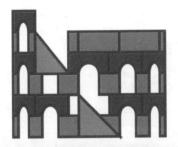

GLOSSARY

COOKING METHODS

affumicato
smoked
alla brace
charcoal-grilled
all'acqua pazza
poached in tomato-based
court bouillon
ai ferri
grilled
arrosto
roasted
brasato
braised
brodettato
in wine, lemon
and egg sauce
carpaccio
thinly sliced raw meat or
fish
in carpione
marinated
al cartoccio
baked in parchment
paper
in crosta
baked inside a pie
or bread crust
alla diavola
grilled, seasoned
with black pepper
farcito
stuffed
alla griglia
grilled
in guazzetto
simmered in tomato
sauce
mantecato
stirred with sauce, butter
and/or grated cheese
alla parmigiana
with grated
Parmigiano cheese

alla piastra
grilled
saltato
sautéed
a scottadito
grilled lamb chops
tartufato
with truffles
al tegame/tegamino
pan-cooked
tonnato
in tuna and mayonnaise
sauce
tortino
any small cake-
shaped preparation,
savoury or sweet
in umido
in sauce

ANTIPASTI

bruschetta
toasted garlic bread
caponata
vinegary Sicilian
vegetable antipasto
cianfotta
vegetable stew
crostini
toasted canapés
tartine
canapés

CURED MEATS

bresaola
cured lean beef
capocollo
cured lean pork,
generally made
from neck
and shoulder

ciauscolo
spreadable pork
sausage, speciality of
Marche
coppa
cooked sausage,
made from pig's head
cotechino
cooked pork
sausage, similar to
zampone, served sliced
culatello
premium cured
pork, similar
to prosciutto crudo,
speciality
of Parma
finocchiona
coarse-cut salami
flavored with fennel
seeds,
speciality of Tuscany
lardo
cured pork fat
mortadella
cured pork
salami, speciality of
Bologna
'nduja
peppery fresh
sausage,
speciality of Calabria
pancetta
similar to unsmoked
bacon
prosciutto cotto
cooked ham
prosciutto crudo
air-dried ham;
the best is from Parma or
San Daniele
**prosciutto
di montagna**
air-dried ham, saltier than
Parma

soppressata
various types
of pork salami,
sometimes smoked

speck
smoked cured pork,
speciality of Alto Adige

speck di anatra
smoked cured duck

zampone
stuffed pig's trotter

PASTA TYPES

agnolotti
fresh, similar
to ravioli,
generally meat-filled

bavette
long, narrow
[like linguine]

bombolotti
short, tubular

bucatini
long, tubular,
thicker than spaghetti

cannelloni
fresh, filled, rolled

cavatelli
small, curved,
ridged [like gnocchetti]

culurgione
large ravioli, from
Sardegna

farfalle
bowties
or butterflies

fettuccine
fresh, long, flat

garganelli
fresh, short, tubular

girelle
rolled oven-baked pasta,
similar to lasagna

gnocchi
bite-sized potato or
semolina dumplings

lasagna verde
fresh, large sheets,
spinach-flavored, baked

linguine
long, flat, narrow

lumachine
snail-shaped

malfatti
spinach and ricotta
dumplings

maltagliati
if dry, short
& tubular; if fresh,
irregular small
rhomboid shapes to add
to soup

maccheroncini
short, tubular

mezzemaniche
short, tubular, ridged [see
bombolotti]

orecchiette
"little ears"

pappardelle
fresh or dry, wide, flat

pasticcio
a mixture of ingredients
enclosed in a crust and
baked;
sometimes pasta strudel

pizzoccheri
long, flat, made with plain
and buckwheat flour

ravioli/ravioloni
fresh, filled

rigatoni
short, tubular, ridged

stringozzi
fresh, made without eggs,
flat, short

strozzapreti
gnocchi-shaped pasta

tagliatelle
fresh, long, flat, wider
than fettuccine

tagliolini
fresh, long, flat, very
narrow

tonnarelli
fresh, long, square in
cross-section

tortello
fresh, filled, generally
large

tortellini
small, meat-filled

trenette
long, flat, narrower than
linguine

trofie
fresh, made without eggs,
short, twisted

vermicelli
spaghetti

PASTA SAUCES

cacio e pepe
grated pecorino romano
cheese and black pepper

all'amatriciana
guanciale, tomato, chili
and pecorino romano
cheese

all'arrabbiata
spicy tomato

alla carbonara
egg, guanciale and black
pepper

alla gricia
guanciale, chili,
and pecorino romano
cheese

alla luciana
tomato, garlic,
chili

alla Norma
tomato, fried
eggplant,
salted ricotta
allo scarpariello
pan-crisped
pasta with
slow-cooked
meat, wine and
tomato sauce
ragù
meat sauce

SOUPS

minestra
soup
minestrone
vegetable
pasta e ceci
pasta and chickpeas
pasta e fagioli
pasta and beans
ribollita
beans, vegetables,
bread, Tuscan
cabbage
stracciatella
beaten egg cooked in
broth

MEAT

abbacchio
spring lamb
agnello
lamb
anatra
duck
arista
pork loin
bistecca
steak

bollito
boiled
[or combination
of boiled meats]
bue
beef
campanello
top round beef
chianina
Tuscan beef from
Val di Chiana
cicoli/ciccioli
cracklings
coniglio
rabbit
costoletta
cutlet
cotoletta
cutlet, generally
breaded and fried
[e.g. alla milanese]
faraona
guinea fowl
fegato grasso
foie gras
filetto
fillet
fiorentina
thick premium
rare Tuscan steak
galletto
small chicken
involtini
roulades
lombata
sirloin
maiale
pork
manzo
beef
oca
goose
ossobuco
braised
veal shank

piccione
squab
polpetta
meatball
polpettone
meat loaf
pollo [ruspante]
chicken [free range]
rollé
meat rolled around
a stuffing
salsiccia
sausage
saltimbocca
sautéed veal
scallops, prosciutto and
sage
scaloppa
thin slice of meat
or fish
selvaggina
game
spezzatino
stew
spiedo/ spiedino
cooked on a spit
spuntatura
spareribs
suino
pork
tacchino
turkey
tagliata
thickly sliced beef
vitello
veal
vitellino
milk-fed veal

INNARDS

animelle
sweetbreads and
pancreas

**coda
[alla vaccinara]**
oxtail [stew]
coratella/corata
lamb organ meats
guanciale
cured pork jowl
[similar
to pancetta]
fegatelli
chunks of pork liver
fegato
liver
frattaglie
organ meats
pajata/pagliata
milk-filled veal
intestines
rigaglie
giblets and crest
**rognone/
rognoncini**
kidneys
trippa
tripe

FISH

aguglia
gar-fish
anguilla
eel
arzilla
skate, thornback ray
baccalà
salt cod
branzino
sea bass
cernia
grouper
coccio
red gurnard
coda di rospo
monkfish, angler-fish

dentice
dentex, sea bream
gallinella
tub-gurnard
lattarini/latterini
sand-smelt
merluzzo
cod
muggine
mullet
nasello
hake
neonata
new-born anchovies
or sardines
orata
gilt-head bream
persico
perch
pesce spada
swordfish
pesce azzurro
small Mediterranean
fish such as
anchovies or
sardines
ricciola
amberjack
rombo
turbot
**sarda/sardella/
sardina**
sardine
salmone
salmon
scorfano
scorpion fish
sgombro
mackerel
sogliola
sole
spigola
sea bass
stoccafisso
dried cod

storione
sturgeon
tonno
tuna
triglia
red mullet
trota
trout
trota salmonata
pink-fleshed trout

SEAFOOD

aragosta
spiny lobster
astice
lobster
bottarga
salted dried mullet
or tuna roe
calamari
squid
**canocchia,
pannocchia,
cicala di mare**
mantis shrimp
cappesante
scallops
cozze
mussels
gamberi
shrimps, prawns
gamberoni
jumbo shrimp
mazzancolle
jumbo shrimp,
king prawns
moscardini
curled octopus
paranza
fishing boat, i.e.
the day's catch
polpo [verace]
octopus

GLOSSARY

riccio di mare
  sea-urchin
seppia
  cuttlefish
scampi
  shrimps, prawns
totano/totanetto
  flying squid
vongole [verace]
  clams

HERBS, SPICES, SEASONINGS

aceto
  vinegar
aceto balsamico
  balsamic vinegar
aglio
  garlic
alloro
  bay leaf
anice
  anise, aniseed
anice stellato
  star anise
cardamomo
  cardamom
cerfoglio
  chervil
finocchiella
  wild fennel
ginepro
  juniper
mentuccia
  mint
menta romana
  Roman mint
noce moscata
  nutmeg
origano
  oregano
prezzemolo
  parsley

rosmarino
  rosemary
salvia
  sage

PULSES, BEANS

ceci
  chickpeas
lenticchie
  lentils
cannellini
  white beans

SALADS

alla Catalana
  crustaceans with potato,
  tomato, onion and celery
cipollotti
  fresh onions
crescione
  watercress
finocchio
  fennel
lampascione
  bulb resembling
  onion, slightly bitter
lattuga
  lettuce
panzanella
  tomato and bread salad
pomodori
  tomatoes
pomodori pachino
  cherry tomatoes
pomodori secchi
  sun-dried tomatoes
puntarelle
  Roman variety
  of Catalogna chicory,
  always served with
  anchovy sauce

radicchio
  red-leaf chicory,
  somewhat bitter
**rughetta/ruchetta/
rucola**
  arugula, rocket
scarola
  escarole

VEGETABLES

bieta/bietola
  Swiss chard
carciofi
  artichokes
cicoria
  Catalogna chicory
fagioli
  beans
fagiolini
  string beans
fiori di zucca
  zucchini blossoms
friarelli
  young bitter greens found
  in Campania
friggitelli
  small mild green peppers
funghi
  mushrooms
melanzane
  eggplant
peperone
  bell pepper, capsicum
porro
  leek
primavera
  with spring vegetables
verza
  Savoy cabbage
zucca
  squash
zucchine
  zucchini, courgettes

DESSERTS

bavarese
cream, custard and
gelatin pudding
cassata
layers of sponge cake and
ricotta, chocolate and
candied fruit, often with
green icing; a layered
ice cream
charlotte
molded pudding,
whipped cream
and lady-fingers
crespelle
crêpes
millefoglie
light, layered, strudel-like
pastry
panna cotta
silky cream pudding
pastiera
Neapolitan ricotta,
wheat berry
and candied-fruit pie
seadas
honey-glazed Sardinian
cheese-
filled fried ravioli
semifreddo
soft frozen mousse
dessert
Saint Honoré
elaborate cake topped
with alternating
plain and chocolate
pastry cream
tarte tatin
upside down
apple tart
tiramisù
layers of coffee-soaked
ladyfingers and
mascarpone

torta caprese
chocolate cake
torta della nonna
cake with custard and
pine nuts
zabaione
custard flavored with
sweet wine

FRUIT

clementina
seedless citrus fruit,
a cross between a
tangerine and a
Seville orange
cedro
citron
cocomero
watermelon
fico d'India
prickly pear
fragola
strawberry
fragolina di bosco
wild strawberry
lampone
raspberry
mela
apple
mela cotogna
quince
melone
melon
pera
pear
ribes rosso/nero
red/black currants
uva
grape
uva passita
raisin
visciole
sour cherries

PIZZERIA

arancini
rice croquettes
calzoni
large pizza
turnovers
fiori di zucca ipieni
fried zucchini flowers
filled with mozzarella and
anchovies
granatina [Neapolitan]
small meatballs
mozzarella in carrozza
deep-fried mozzarella
sandwich
pagnottielli
pizza dough
filled with cheese, cured
meat and/or vegetables,
baked in wood-burning
oven
piadine
unleavened focaccia
pizza bianca romana
plain white pizza
pizza napoletana
thick crust with puffy
border
pizza a pala
baked in wood-
burning oven
pizza romana
thincrust and
crunchy
pizza al taglio
pizza sold by
the slice
pizzelle
small, fried pizza
topped with tomato and
Parmigiano
sartù
Neapolitan rice
and meat casserole

schiacciata
focaccia
supplì
deep-fried rice and
mozzarella croquettes
rustico
savoury turnover

AT THE COFFEE BAR

bomba
deep-fried jam or
custard-filled pastry
cannoli
fried crisp cylinders of
dough filled with
ricotta cream
ciambella
doughnut; cake
cornetto
sweet croissant
crema pasticciera
baker's custard
fagottino
croissant dough
filled with custard, jam, or
savoury filling
focaccia
general term
for pizza-like bread
frullato
fruit milk shake
granatina
sweet syrup to add to
mineral water or pour over
crushed ice
lieviti
leavened breakfast buns
[in general]
maritozzo
bun, often filled
with whipped cream
panino
bread roll; sandwich

tramezzino
crustless, triangular white
bread sandwich

COFFEE [FROM DARKEST TO LIGHTEST]

espresso
black
espresso macchiato
with a dash
of milk
cappuccino
more milk than
coffee, but well
-balanced
caffellatte
much more milk than
coffee
latte macchiato
milk with a dash of coffee

AT THE PASTRY SHOP

pasta frolla
shortcrust pastry
pasta brisé
flaky pastry
pasta sfoglia
puff pastry
pasta fillo
filo pastry

CAKES AND BISCUITS

amaretti
macaroons;
almond and egg-white
biscuits

castagnaccio
sweet, flat pie
made with
chestnut flour and pine
nuts
castagnole
sugary fried cake
spheres, Carnival
speciality
crostata
shortcrust tart, generally
jam-topped
frappe
fried strips of
sweetened dough,
sprinkled with
powdered sugar, Carnival
speciality
frutta Martorana
elaborate marzipan fruit
panettone
rich Christmas yeast
cake, usually with candied
fruit and raisins
savarin
yeast cake brushed
with orange and lemon
sauce and topped
with apricot glaze, served
with fruit
tarallucci
ring-shaped biscuits, to
accompany wine
torrone
honey almond
nougat
torroncino
vanilla ice cream
flavored with bits of
nougat
tozzetti
almond biscuits
generally served with
sweet Tuscan wine
[vin santo]

AT THE BAKERY

avena
  oats
farina di grano duro
  durum wheat flour
farro
  ancient cereal,
  ancestor to wheat
granoturco
  corn, maize
grano saraceno
  buckwheat
miglio
  millet
orzo
  barley
riso
  rice
grissini
  bread sticks
pane casereccio
  country-style bread
rosette
  puffy rolls, hollow inside

MISCELLANEOUS

fette biscottate
  crisp, golden, oven-dried
  white-bread slices
pinoli
  pine nuts
sott'olio
  preserved in oil
uovo
  egg
tartufo
  truffle
sformato
  timbale
olio di oliva
extravergine
  first-press olive oil
gianduia
  chocolate
  and hazelnut candy
Nutella
  popular chocolate and
  hazelnut spread

TRADITIONAL SHOPS/ EATERIES

alimentari
  general groceries
drogheria
  dried and packaged goods
enoteca
  wine shop/bar

forno
  bakery
gastronomia
  speciality foods;
  delicatessen
latteria
  milk, yoghurt, ice cream
macelleria
  butcher
pasticceria
  pastry shop
rosticceria
  roast chickens
  and other
  cooked food,
  generally for take away
salumeria,
salsamenteria
  cured meats,
  cheeses
tavola calda
  similar to
  rosticceria, more
  geared to food eaten
  on premises

index

EATING

INDEX BY AREA

INDEX

INDEX

OPEN ON MONDAYS

INDEX

INDEX

AT ALL HOURS

SHOPPING

INDEX

171

SLEEPING

INDEX

INDEX BY AREA

INDEX

175